Modern Compiler Implementation in Java

Modern Compiler Implementation in Java

Basic Techniques

ANDREW W. APPEL
Princeton University

Preliminary edition of *Modern Compiler Implementation in Java*

PUBLISHED BY THE PRESS SYNDICATE OF THE UNIVERSITY OF CAMBRIDGE
The Pitt Building, Trumpington Street, Cambridge CB2 1RP, United Kingdom

CAMBRIDGE UNIVERSITY PRESS
The Edinburgh Building, Cambridge CB2 2RU, United Kingdom
40 West 20th Street, New York, NY 10011-4211, USA
10 Stamford Road, Oakleigh, Melbourne 3166, Australia

First published 1997
Reprinted 1997

Printed in the United States of America

Typeset in Times, Courier, and Optima

Library of Congress Cataloguing-in-Publication data applied for

A catalog record for this book is available from the British Library

0-521-58275-X   Modern Compiler Implementation in ML: Basic Techniques (hardback)
0-521-58775-1   Modern Compiler Implementation in ML: Basic Techniques (paperback)
0-521-58387-X   Modern Compiler Implementation in Java: Basic Techniques (hardback)
0-521-58654-2   Modern Compiler Implementation in Java: Basic Techniques (paperback)
0-521-58389-6   Modern Compiler Implementation in C: Basic Techniques (hardback)
0-521-58653-4   Modern Compiler Implementation in C: Basic Techniques (paperback)

Contents

Preface

Over the past decade, there have been several shifts in the way compilers are built. New kinds of programming languages are being used: object-oriented languages with dynamic methods, functional languages with nested scope and first-class function closures; and many of these languages require garbage collection. New machines have large register sets and a high penalty for memory access, and can often run much faster with compiler assistance in scheduling instructions and managing instructions and data for cache locality.

This book is intended as a textbook for a one-semester or two-quarter course in compilers. Students will see the theory behind different components of a compiler, the programming techniques used to put the theory into practice, and the interfaces used to modularize the compiler. To make the interfaces and programming examples clear and concrete, I have written them in the Java programming language. Other editions of this book are available that use the C and ML languages.

The "student project compiler" that I have outlined is reasonably simple, but is organized to demonstrate some important techniques that are now in common use: Abstract syntax trees to avoid tangling syntax and semantics, separation of instruction selection from register allocation, sophisticated copy propagation to allow greater flexibility to earlier phases of the compiler, and careful containment of target-machine dependencies to one module.

This book, *Modern Compiler Implementation in Java: Basic Techniques,* is the preliminary edition of a more complete book to be published in 1998, entitled *Modern Compiler Implementation in Java.* That book will have a more comprehensive set of exercises in each chapter, a "further reading" discussion at the end of every chapter, and another dozen chapters on advanced material not in this edition, such as parser error recovery, code-generator generators, byte-code interpreters, static single-assignment form, instruction scheduling and software pipelining, parallelization techniques, and cache-locality optimizations such as prefetching, blocking, instruction-cache layout, and branch prediction.

Exercises. Each of the chapters in Part I has a programming exercise corresponding to one module of a compiler. Unlike many "student project compilers" found in textbooks, this one has a simple but sophisticated back end, allowing good register allocation to be done after instruction selection. Software useful for the programming exercises can be found at

```
http://www.cs.princeton.edu/~appel/modern/
```

There are also pencil and paper exercises in each chapter; those marked with a star * are a bit more challenging, two-star problems are difficult but solvable, and the occasional three-star exercises are not known to have a solution.

Acknowledgments. Several people have provided constructive criticism, course-tested the manuscript, or helped in other ways in the production of this book. I would like to thank Stephen Bailey, Maia Ginsburg, David Hanson, Elma Lee Noah, Todd Proebsting, Barbara Ryder, Amr Sabry, Zhong Shao, Mary Lou Soffa, Andrew Tolmach, and Kwangkeun Yi.

PART ONE

Fundamentals of Compilation

1
Introduction

A **compiler** was originally a program that "compiled" subroutines [a link-loader]. When in 1954 the combination "algebraic compiler" came into use, or rather into misuse, the meaning of the term had already shifted into the present one.

Bauer and Eickel [1975]

This book describes techniques, data structures, and algorithms for translating programming languages into executable code. A modern compiler is often organized into many phases, each operating on a different abstract "language." The chapters of this book follow the organization of a compiler, each covering a successive phase.

To illustrate the issues in compiling real programming languages, I show how to compile Tiger, a simple but nontrivial language of the Algol family, with nested scope and heap-allocated records. Programming exercises in each chapter call for the implementation of the corresponding phase; a student who implements all the phases described in Part I of the book will have a working compiler. Tiger is easily modified to be *functional* or *object-oriented* (or both), and exercises in Part II show how to do this. Other chapters in Part II cover advanced techniques in program optimization. Appendix A describes the Tiger language.

The interfaces between modules of the compiler are almost as important as the algorithms inside the modules. To describe the interfaces concretely, it is useful to write them down in a real programming language. This book uses Java – a simple object-oriented language. Java is *safe*, in that programs cannot circumvent the type system to violate abstractions; and it has garbage collection, which greatly simplifies the management of dynamic storage allocation.

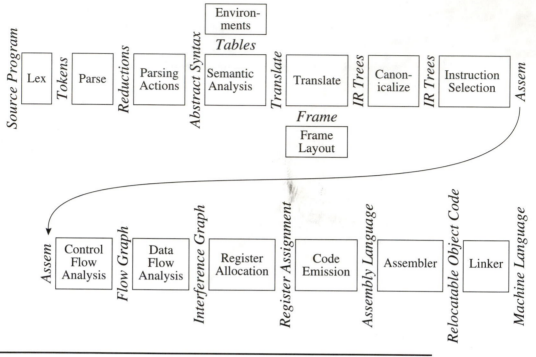

FIGURE 1.1.   Phases of a compiler, and interfaces between them.

Both of these properties are useful in writing compilers (and almost any kind of software).

This is not a textbook on Java programming. Students using this book who do not know Java already should pick it up as they go along, using a Java programming book as a reference. Java is a small enough language, with simple enough concepts, that this should not be difficult for students with good programming skills in other languages.

1.1   MODULES AND INTERFACES

Any large software system is much easier to understand and implement if the designer takes care with the fundamental abstractions and interfaces. Figure 1.1 shows the phases in a typical compiler. Each phase is implemented as one or more software modules.

Breaking the compiler into this many pieces allows for reuse of the components. For example, to change the target-machine for which the compiler produces machine language, it suffices to replace just the Frame Layout and Instruction Selection modules. To change the source language being compiled, only the modules up through Translate need to be changed. The compiler can be attached to a language-oriented syntax editor at the *Abstract Syntax* interface.

The learning experience of coming to the right abstraction by several iterations of *think–implement–redesign* is one that should not be missed. However, the student trying to finish a compiler project in one semester does not have this luxury. Therefore, I present in this book the outline of a project where the abstractions and interfaces are carefully thought out, and are as elegant and general as I am able to make them.

Some of the interfaces, such as *Abstract Syntax, IR Trees,* and *Assem,* take the form of data structures: for example, the Parsing Actions phase builds an *Abstract Syntax* data structure and passes it to the Semantic Analysis phase. Other interfaces are abstract data types; the *Translate* interface is a set of functions that the Semantic Analysis phase can call, and the *Tokens* interface takes the form of a function that the Parser calls to get the next token of the input program.

DESCRIPTION OF THE PHASES

Each chapter of Part I of this book describes one compiler phase, as shown in Table 1.2

This modularization is typical of many real compilers. But some compilers combine Parse, Semantic Analysis, Translate, and Canonicalize into one phase; others put Instruction Selection much later than I have done, and combine it with Code Emission. Simple compilers omit the Control Flow Analysis, Data Flow Analysis, and Register Allocation phases.

I have designed the compiler in this book to be as simple as possible, but no simpler. In particular, in those places where corners are cut to simplify the implementation, the structure of the compiler allows for the addition of more optimization or fancier semantics without violence to the existing interfaces.

1.2   TOOLS AND SOFTWARE

Two of the most useful abstractions used in modern compilers are *context-free grammars*, for parsing, and *regular expressions*, for lexical analysis. To make best use of these abstractions it is helpful to have special tools, such as *Yacc*

Chapter	Phase	Description
2	Lex	Break the source file into individual words, or *tokens*.
3	Parse	Analyze the phrase structure of the program.
4	Semantic Actions	Build a piece of *abstract syntax tree* corresponding to each phrase.
5	Semantic Analysis	Determine what each phrase means, relate uses of variables to their definitions, check types of expressions, request translation of each phrase.
6	Frame Layout	Place variables, function-parameters, etc. into activation records (stack frames) in a machine-dependent way.
7	Translate	Produce *intermediate representation trees* (IR trees), a notation that is not tied to any particular source language or target-machine architecture.
8	Canonicalize	Hoist side effects out of expressions, and clean up conditional branches, for the convenience of the next phases.
9	Instruction Selection	Group the IR-tree nodes into clumps that correspond to the actions of target-machine instructions.
10	Control Flow Analysis	Analyze the sequence of instructions into a *control flow graph* that shows all the possible flows of control the program might follow when it executes.
10	Dataflow Analysis	Gather information about the flow of information through variables of the program; for example, *liveness analysis* calculates the places where each program variable holds a still-needed value (is *live*).
11	Register Allocation	Choose a register to hold each of the variables and temporary values used by the program; variables not live at the same time can share the same register.
12	Code Emission	Replace the temporary names in each machine instruction with machine registers.

TABLE 1.2. Description of compiler phases.

(which converts a grammar into a parsing program) and *Lex* (which converts a declarative specification into a lexical analysis program). Fortunately, good versions of these tools are available for Java, and the project described in this book makes use of them.

The programming projects in this book can be compiled using Sun's Java

$$
\begin{array}{lr}
Stm \rightarrow Stm \ ; \ Stm & \text{(CompoundStm)} \\
Stm \rightarrow \texttt{id} := Exp & \text{(AssignStm)} \\
Stm \rightarrow \texttt{print} \ (\ ExpList\ ) & \text{(PrintStm)} \\
Exp \rightarrow \texttt{id} & \text{(IdExp)} \\
Exp \rightarrow \texttt{num} & \text{(NumExp)} \\
Exp \rightarrow Exp \ Binop \ Exp & \text{(OpExp)} \\
Exp \rightarrow (\ Stm\ ,\ Exp\ ) & \text{(EseqExp)}
\end{array}
$$

$$
\begin{array}{lr}
ExpList \rightarrow Exp\ ,\ ExpList & \text{(PairExpList)} \\
ExpList \rightarrow Exp & \text{(LastExpList)} \\
Binop \quad \rightarrow + & \text{(Plus)} \\
Binop \quad \rightarrow - & \text{(Minus)} \\
Binop \quad \rightarrow \times & \text{(Times)} \\
Binop \quad \rightarrow / & \text{(Div)}
\end{array}
$$

GRAMMAR 1.3.   A straight-line programming language.

Development Kit, or (in principle) any Java compiler. The lexical-analyzer generator *JavaLex* and the parser generator *CUP* are freely available on the Internet; for information see the Wide-World Web page

```
http://www.cs.princeton.edu/~appel/modern/
```

Source code for some modules of the Tiger compiler, support code for some of the programming exercises, example Tiger programs, and other useful files are also available from the same Web address.

Skeleton source code for the programming assignments is available from this Web page; the programming exercises in this book refer to this directory as `$TIGER/` when referring to specific subdirectories and files contained therein.

1.3   DATA STRUCTURES FOR TREE LANGUAGES

Many of the important data structures used in a compiler are *intermediate representations* of the program being compiled. Often these representations take the form of trees, with several node types, each of which has different attributes. Such trees can occur at many of the phase-interfaces shown in Figure 1.1.

Tree representations can be described with grammars, just like programming languages. To introduce the concepts, I will show a simple programming language with statements and expressions, but no loops or if-statements (this is called a language of *straight-line programs*).

The syntax for this language is given in Grammar 1.3.

The informal semantics of the language is as follows. Each *Stm* is a statement, each *Exp* is an expression. $s_1; s_2$ executes statement s_1, then statement

s_2. i:=e evaluates the expression e, then "stores" the result in variable i. $\text{print}(e_1, e_2, \ldots, e_n)$ displays the values of all the expressions, evaluated left to right, separated by spaces, terminated by a newline.

An *identifier expression*, such as i, yields the current contents of the variable i. A *number* evaluates to the named integer. An *operator expression* e_1 op e_2 evaluates e_1, then e_2, then applies the given binary operator. And an *expression sequence* s, e behaves like the C-language "comma" operator, evaluating the statement s for side effects before evaluating (and returning the result of) the expression e.

For example, executing this program

```
a := 5+3; b := (print(a, a-1), 10*a); print(b)
```

prints

```
8 7
80
```

How should this program be represented inside a compiler? One represen-tation is *source code*, the characters that the programmer writes. But that is not so easy to manipulate. More convenient is a tree data structure, with one node for each statement (Stm) and expression (Exp). Figure 1.4 shows a tree representation of the program; the nodes are labeled by the production labels of Grammar 1.3, and each node has as many children as the corresponding grammar production has right-hand-side symbols.

We can translate the grammar directly into data structure definitions, as shown in Figure 1.5. Each grammar symbol corresponds to an `abstract class` in the data structures:

Grammar	class
Stm	Stm
Exp	Exp
ExpList	ExpList
id	String
num	int

For each grammar rule, there is one *constructor* that belongs to the class for its left-hand-side symbol. We simply *extend* the abstract class with a "concrete" class for each grammar rule. The constructor (class) names are indicated on the right-hand side of Grammar 1.3.

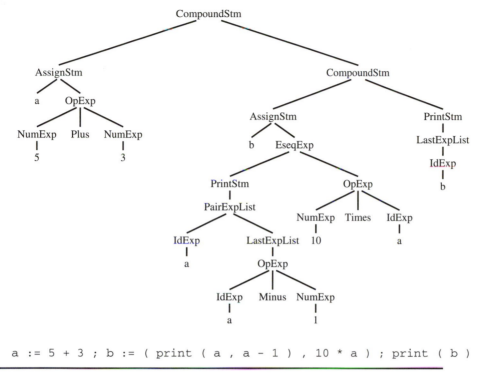

```
a := 5 + 3 ; b := ( print ( a , a - 1 ) , 10 * a ) ; print ( b )
```

FIGURE 1.4. Tree representation of a straight-line program.

Each grammar rule has right-hand-side components that must be represented in the data structures. The CompoundStm has two Stm's on the right-hand side; the AssignStm has an identifier and an expression; and so on. These become *fields* of the subclasses in the Java data structure. Thus, Compound-Stm has two fields (also called *instance variables*) called stm1 and stm2; AssignStm has fields id and exp.

For Binop we do something simpler. Although we could make a Binop class – with subclasses for Plus, Minus, Times, Div – this is overkill because none of the subclasses would need any fields. Instead we make an "enumeration" type (in Java, actually an integer) of constants (final int variables) local to the OpExp class.

Programming style. We will follow several conventions for representing tree data structures in Java:

1. Trees are described by a grammar.

```
public abstract class Stm {}

public class CompoundStm extends Stm {
   Stm stm1, stm2;
   public CompoundStm(Stm s1, Stm s2) {stm1=s1; stm2=s2;}}

public class AssignStm extends Stm {
   String id; Exp exp;
   public AssignStm(String i, Exp e) {id=i; exp=e;}}

public class PrintStm extends Stm {
   ExpList exps;
   public PrintStm(ExpList e) {exps=e;}}

public abstract class Exp {}

public class IdExp extends Exp {
   String id;
   public IdExp(String i) {id=i;}}

public class NumExp extends Exp {
   int num;
   public NumExp(int n) {num=n;}}

public class OpExp extends Exp {
   Exp left, right; int oper;
   final public static int Plus=1,Minus=2,Times=3,Div=4;
   public OpExp(Exp l, int o, Exp r) {left=l; oper=o; right=r;}}

public class EseqExp extends Exp {
   Stm stm; Exp exp;
   public EseqExp(Stm s, Exp e) {stm=s; exp=e;}}

public abstract class ExpList {}

public class PairExpList extends ExpList {
   Exp head; ExpList tail;
   public PairExpList(Exp h, ExpList t) {head=h; tail=t;}}

public class LastExpList extends ExpList {
   Exp head;
   public LastExpList(Exp h) {head=h;}}
```

PROGRAM 1.5.   Representation of straight-line programs.

2. A tree is described by one or more abstract classes, each corresponding to a symbol in the grammar.

3. Each abstract class is *extended* by one or more subclasses, one for each grammar rule.

4. For each nontrivial symbol in the right-hand side of a rule, there will be one field in the corresponding class. (A trivial symbol is a punctuation symbol such as the semicolon in CompoundStm.)

5. Every class will have a constructor function that initializes all the fields.

6. Data structures are initialized when they are created (by the constructor functions), and are never modified after that (until they are eventually discarded).

Modularity principles for Java programs. A compiler can be a big program; careful attention to modules and interfaces prevents chaos. We will use these principles in writing a compiler in Java:

1. Each phase or module of the compiler belongs in its own package.

2. "Import on demand" declarations will not be used. If a Java file begins with

```
import A.F.*; import A.G.*; import B.*; import C.*;
```

then the human reader *will have to look outside this file* to tell which package defines the X that is used in the expression X.put().

3. "Single-type import" declarations are a better solution. If the module begins,

```
import A.F.W; import A.G.X; import B.Y; import C.Z;
```

then you can tell *without looking outside this file* that X comes from A.G.

4. Java is naturally a multithreaded system. We would like to support multiple simultaneous compiler threads and compile two different programs simultaneously, one in each compiler thread. Therefore, static variables must be avoided unless they are `final` (constant). We never want two compiler threads to be updating the same (static) instance of a variable.

PROGRAM   STRAIGHT-LINE PROGRAM INTERPRETER

Implement a simple program analyzer and interpreter for the straight-line programming language. This exercise serves as an introduction to *environments* (symbol tables mapping variable-names to information about the variables); to *abstract syntax* (data structures representing the phrase structure of programs); to *recursion over tree data structures*, useful in many parts of a compiler; and to a *functional style* of programming without assignment statements.

It also serves as a "warm-up" exercise in Java programming. Programmers experienced in other languages but new to Java should be able to do this exercise, but will need supplementary material (such as textbooks) on Java.

Programs to be interpreted are already parsed into abstract syntax, as described by the data types in Program 1.5.

However, we do not wish to worry about parsing the language, so we write this program by applying data constructors:

```
Stm prog =
new CompoundStm(new AssignStm("a",
                    new OpExp(new NumExp(5),
                              OpExp.Plus, new NumExp(3))),
   new CompoundStm(new AssignStm("b",
      new EseqExp(new PrintStm(new PairExpList(new IdExp("a"),
               new LastExpList(new OpExp(new IdExp("a"),
                        OpExp.Minus,new NumExp(1))))),

            new OpExp(new NumExp(10), OpExp.Times,
                  new IdExp("a")))),
   new PrintStm(new LastExpList(new IdExp("b")))));
```

Files with the data type declarations for the trees, and this sample program, are available in the directory $TIGER/chap1.

Writing interpreters without side effects (that is, assignment statements that update variables and data structures) is a good introduction to *denotational semantics* and *attribute grammars*, which are methods for describing what programming languages do. It's often a useful technique in writing compilers, too; compilers are also in the business of saying what programming languages do.

Therefore, in implementing these programs, never assign a new value to any variable or object-field except when it is initialized. For local variables, use the initializing form of declaration (for example, int i=j+3;) and for each class, make a constructor function (like the CompoundStm constructor in Program 1.5).

1. Write a Java function int maxargs(Stm s) that tells the maximum number of arguments of any print statement within any subexpression of a given statement. For example, maxargs(prog) is 2.
2. Write a Java function void interp(Stm s) that "interprets" a program in this language. To write in a "functional programming" style – in which you never use an assignment statement – initialize each local variable as you declare it.

Your functions that examine each Exp will have to use instanceof to determine which subclass the expression belongs to and then cast to the proper subclass. Or you can add methods to the `Exp` and `Stm` classes to avoid the use of `instanceof`.

For part 1, remember that print statements can contain expressions that contain other print statements.

For part 2, make two mutually recursive functions `interpStm` and `interp-Exp`. Represent a "table," mapping identifiers to the integer values assigned to them, as a list of id × int pairs.

```
class Table {
    String id; int value; Table tail;
    Table(String i, int v, Table t) {id=i; value=v; tail=t;}
}
```

Then `interpStm` is declared as

```
Table_ interpStm(Stm s, Table_ t)
```

taking a table t_1 as argument and producing the new table t_2 that's just like t_1 except that some identifiers map to different integers as a result of the statement.

For example, the table t_1 that maps a to 3 and maps c to 4, which we write $\{a \mapsto 3, c \mapsto 4\}$ in mathematical notation, could be represented as the linked list $\boxed{a \mid 3 \mid} \longrightarrow \boxed{c \mid 4 \mid}$.

Now, let the table t_2 be just like t_1, except that it maps c to 7 instead of 4. Mathematically, we could write,

$$t_2 = \text{update}(t_1, c, 7)$$

where the update function returns a new table $\{a \mapsto 3, c \mapsto 7\}$.

On the computer, we could implement t_2 by putting a new cell at the head of the linked list: $\boxed{c \mid 7 \mid} \longrightarrow \boxed{a \mid 3 \mid} \longrightarrow \boxed{c \mid 4 \mid}$ as long as we assume that the *first* occurrence of c in the list takes precedence over any later occurrence.

Therefore, the `update` function is easy to implement; and the corresponding `lookup` function

```
int lookup(Table t, String key)
```

just searches down the linked list. Of course, in an object-oriented style, `lookup` should be a method of the `Table` class.

Interpreting expressions is more complicated than interpreting statements, because expressions return integer values *and* have side effects. We wish to simulate the straight-line programming language's assignment statements without doing any side effects in the interpreter itself. (The `print` statements will be accomplished by interpreter side effects, however.) The solution is to declare `interpExp` as

```
class IntAndTable {int i; Table t;
    IntAndTable(int ii, Table tt) {i=ii; t=tt;}
  }
IntAndTable interpExp(Exp e, Table t) ···
```

The result of interpreting an expression e_1 with table t_1 is an integer value i and a new table t_2. When interpreting an expression with two subexpressions (such as an `OpExp`), the table t_2 resulting from the first subexpression can be used in processing the second subexpression.

EXERCISES

1.1 This simple program implements *persistent* functional binary search trees, so that if `tree2=insert(x,tree1)`, then `tree1` is still available for lookups even while `tree2` can be used.

```
class Tree {Tree left; String key; right;
    Tree(Tree l, String k, Tree r) {left=l; key=k; right=r;}
}

Tree insert(String key, Tree t) {
  if (t==null) return new Tree(null, key, null)
  else if (key < t.key)
        return new Tree(insert(key,t.left),t.key,t.right);
  else if (key > t.key)
        return new Tree(t.left,t.key,insert(key,t.right));
  else return new Tree(t.left,key,t.right);
}
```

a. Implement a `member` function that returns `true` if the item is found, else `false`.

b. Extend the program to include not just membership, but the mapping of keys to bindings:

```
Tree insert(String key, Object binding, Tree t);
Object lookup(String key, Tree t);
```

c. These trees are not balanced; demonstrate the behavior on the following two sequences of insertions:

(a) t s p i p f b s t

(b) a b c d e f g h i

*d. Research balanced search trees in Sedgewick [1988] and recommend a balanced-tree data structure for functional symbol tables. (Hint: to preserve a functional style, the algorithm should be one that rebalances on insertion but not on lookup.)

e. Rewrite in an object-oriented style (but still "functional") style, so that insertion is now `t.insert(key)` instead of `insert(key,t)`. Hint: you'll need an `EmptyTree` subclass.

2

Lexical Analysis

lex-i-cal: of or relating to words or the vocabulary of a language as distinguished from its grammar and construction

Webster's Dictionary

To translate a program from one language into another, a compiler must first pull it apart and understand its structure and meaning, then put it together in a different way. The front end of the compiler performs analysis; the back end does synthesis.

The analysis is usually broken up into

Lexical analysis: breaking the input into individual words or "tokens";

Syntax analysis: parsing the phrase structure of the program; and

Semantic analysis: calculating the program's meaning.

The lexical analyzer takes a stream of characters and produces a stream of names, keywords, and punctuation marks; it discards white space and comments between the tokens. It would unduly complicate the parser to have to account for possible white space and comments at every possible point; this is the main reason for separating lexical analysis from parsing.

Lexical analysis is not very complicated, but we will attack it with high-powered formalisms and tools, because similar formalisms will be useful in the study of parsing and similar tools have many applications in areas other than compilation.

LEXICAL TOKENS

A lexical token is a sequence of characters that can be treated as a unit in the grammar of a programming languages. A programming language classifies lexical tokens into a finite set of token types. For example, some of the token types of a typical programming language are:

Type	Examples
ID	`foo  n14  last`
NUM	`73  0 00  515  082`
REAL	`66.1  .5  10.  1e67  5.5e-10`
IF	`if`
COMMA	`,`
NOTEQ	`!=`
LPAREN	`(`
RPAREN	`)`

Punctuation tokens such as IF, VOID, RETURN constructed from alphabetic characters are called *reserved words* and, in most languages, cannot be used as identifiers.

Examples of nontokens are

comment	`/* try again */`
preprocessor directive	`#include<stdio.h>`
preprocessor directive	`#define NUMS 5 , 6`
macro	`NUMS`
blanks, tabs, and newlines	

In languages weak enough to require a macro preprocessor, the preprocessor operates on the source character stream, producing another character stream that is then fed to the lexical analyzer. It is also possible to integrate macro processing with lexical analysis.

Given a program such as

```
void match0(char *s) /* find a zero */
{if (!strncmp(s, "0.0", 3))
  return 0.;
}
```

the lexical analyzer will return the stream

VOID	ID(match0)	LPAREN	CHAR	STAR	ID(s)	RPAREN
LBRACE	IF	LPAREN	BANG	ID(strncmp)	LPAREN	ID(s)

COMMA	STRING(0.0)	COMMA	NUM(3)	RPAREN	RPAREN
RETURN	REAL(0.0)	SEMI	RBRACE	EOF	

where the token type of each lexeme is reported; some of the tokens, such as identifiers and literals, have *semantic values* attached to them, giving auxiliary information in addition to the token type.

How should the lexical rules of a programming language be described? In what language should a lexical analyzer be written?

We can describe the lexical tokens of a language in English; here is a description of identifiers in C or Java:

> An identifier is a sequence of letters and digits; the first character must be a letter. The underscore _ counts as a letter. Upper- and lowercase letters are different. If the input stream has been parsed into tokens up to a given character, the next token is taken to include the longest string of characters that could possibly constitute a token. Blanks, tabs, newlines, and comments are ignored except as they serve to separate tokens. Some white space is required to separate otherwise adjacent identifiers, keywords, and constants.

And any reasonable programming language serves to implement an ad hoc lexer. But we will specify lexical tokens using the formal language of *regular expressions*, implement lexers using *deterministic finite automata*, and use mathematics to connect the two. This will lead to simpler and more readable lexical analyzers.

2.2   REGULAR EXPRESSIONS

Let us say that a *language* is a set of *strings*; a string is a finite sequence of *symbols*. The symbols themselves are taken from a finite *alphabet*.

The Pascal language is the set of all strings that constitute legal Pascal programs; the language of primes is the set of all decimal-digit strings that represent prime numbers; and the language of C reserved words is the set of all alphabetic strings that cannot be used as identifiers in the C programming language. The first two of these languages are infinite sets; the last is a finite set. In all of these cases, the alphabet is the ASCII character set.

When we speak of languages in this way, we will not assign any meaning to the strings; we will just be attempting to classify each string as in the language or not.

To specify some of these (possibly infinite) languages with finite descriptions, we will use the notation of *regular expressions*. Each regular expression stands for a set of strings.

> **Symbol:** For each symbol **a** in the alphabet of the language, the regular expression **a** denotes the language containing just the string a.
>
> **Alternation:** Given two regular expressions M and N, the alternation operator written as a vertical bar | makes a new regular expression $M \mid N$. A string is in the language of $M \mid N$ if it is in the language of M or in the language of N. Thus, the language of **a** | **b** contains the two strings a and b.
>
> **Concatenation:** Given two regular expressions M and N, the concatenation operator · makes a new regular expression $M \cdot N$. A string is in the language of $M \cdot N$ if it is the concatenation of any two strings α and β such that α is in the language of M and β is in the language of N. Thus, the regular expression $(\mathbf{a} \mid \mathbf{b}) \cdot \mathbf{a}$ defines the language containing the two strings aa and ba.
>
> **Epsilon:** The regular expression ϵ represents a language whose only string is the empty string. Thus, $(a \cdot b) \mid \epsilon$ represents the language { " ","ab" }.
>
> **Repetition:** Given a regular expression M, its Kleene closure is M^*. A string is in M^* if it is the concatenation of zero or more strings, all of which are in M. Thus, $((\mathbf{a} \mid \mathbf{b}) \cdot \mathbf{a})^*$ represents the infinite set { " ", "aa", "ba", "aaaa", "baaa", "aaba", "baba", "aaaaaa", ... }.

Using symbols, alternation, concatenation, epsilon, and Kleene closure we can specify the set of ASCII characters corresponding to the lexical tokens of a programming language. First, consider some examples:

$(\mathbf{0} \mid \mathbf{1}) \cdot (\mathbf{0} \mid \mathbf{1})^* \cdot \mathbf{0}$	Binary numbers that are multiples of two.
$(\mathbf{b}^*\mathbf{abb}^*)^*(\mathbf{a}\vert\epsilon)$	Strings of a's and b's with no consecutive a's.
$(\mathbf{a}\vert\mathbf{b})^*\mathbf{aa}(\mathbf{a}\vert\mathbf{b})^*$	Strings of a's and b's containing consecutive a's.

In writing regular expressions, we will sometimes omit the concatenation symbol or the epsilon, and we will assume that Kleene closure "binds tighter" than concatenation, and concatenation binds tighter than alternation; so that **ab** | **c** means $(\mathbf{a} \cdot \mathbf{b}) \mid \mathbf{c}$, and $(\mathbf{a} \mid)$ means $(\mathbf{a} \mid \epsilon)$.

Let us introduce some more abbreviations: [**abcd**] means $(\mathbf{a} \mid \mathbf{b} \mid \mathbf{c} \mid \mathbf{d})$, [**b-g**] means [**bcdefg**], [**b-gM-Qkr**] means [**bcdefgMNOPQkr**], M? means $(M \mid \epsilon)$, and M^+ means $(M \cdot M^*)$. These extensions are convenient, but none extend the descriptive power of regular expressions: Any set of strings that can be described with these abbreviations could also be described by just the basic set of operators. All the operators are summarized in Figure 2.1.

Using this language, we can specify the lexical tokens of a programming language (Figure 2.2). For each token, we supply a fragment of Java code that reports which token type has been recognized.

a	An ordinary character stands for itself.
ϵ	The empty string.
	Another way to write the empty string.
$M \mid N$	Alternation, choosing from M or N.
$M \cdot N$	Concatenation, an M followed by an N.
MN	Another way to write concatenation.
M^*	Repetition (zero or more times).
M^+	Repetition, one or more times.
$M?$	Optional, zero or one occurrence of M.
$[\mathbf{a - zA - Z}]$	Character set alternation.
.	A period stands for any single character except newline.
`"a.+*"`	Quotation, a string in quotes stands for itself literally.

FIGURE 2.1. Regular expression notation.

```
if                                      {return IF;}
[a-z][a-z0-9]*                          {return ID;}
[0-9]+                                  {return NUM;}
([0-9]+"."[0-9]*)|([0-9]*"."[0-9]+)     {return REAL;}
("--"[a-z]*"\n")|(" "|"\n"|"\t")+       {  /* do nothing */ }
.                                       {error();}
```

FIGURE 2.2. Regular expressions for some tokens.

The fifth line of the description recognizes comments or white space, but does not report back to the parser. Instead, the white space is discarded and the lexer resumed. The comments for this lexer begin with two dashes, contain only alphabetic characters, and end with newline.

Finally, a lexical specification should be *complete*, always matching some initial substring of the input; we can always achieve this by having a rule that matches any single character (and in this case, prints an "illegal character" error message and continues).

These rules are a bit ambiguous. For example, does `if8` match as a single identifier or as the two tokens `if` and `8`? Does the string `if 89` begin with an identifier or a reserved word? There are two important disambiguation rules used by Lex, JavaLex, and other similar lexical-analyzer generators:

Longest match: The longest initial substring of the input that can match any regular expression is taken as the next token.

Rule priority: For a *particular* longest initial substring, the first regular expres-

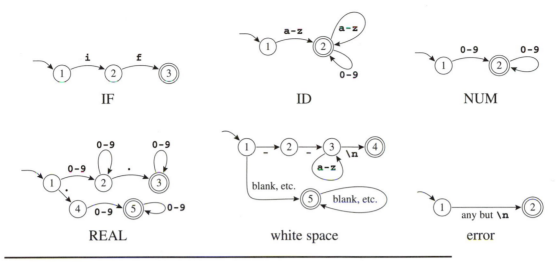

FIGURE 2.3. Finite automata for lexical tokens. The states are indicated by circles; final states are indicated by double circles. The start state has an arrow coming in from nowhere. An edge labeled with several characters is shorthand for many parallel edges.

sion that can match determines its token type. This means that the order of writing down the regular-expression rules has significance.

Thus, if8 matches as an identifier by the longest-match rule, and if matches as a reserved word by rule-priority.

2.3   FINITE AUTOMATA

Regular expressions are convenient for specifying lexical tokens, but we need a formalism that can be implemented as a computer program. For this we can use finite automata (N.B. the singular of automata is automaton). A finite automaton has a finite set of *states*; *edges* lead from one state to another, and each edge is labeled with a *symbol*. One state is the *start* state, and certain of the states are distinguished as *final* states.

Figure 2.3 shows some finite automata. We number the states just for convenience in discussion. The start state is numbered 1 in each case. An edge labeled with several characters is shorthand for many parallel edges; so in the ID machine there are really twenty-six edges each leading from state 1 to 2, each labeled by a different letter.

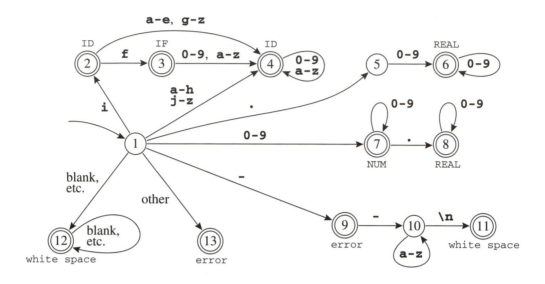

FIGURE 2.4.   Combined finite automaton.

In a *deterministic* finite automaton (DFA), no two edges leading from the same state are labeled with the same symbol. A DFA *accepts* or *rejects* a string as follows. Starting in the start state, for each character in the input string the automaton follows exactly one edge to get to the next state. The edge must be labeled with the input character. After making n transitions for an n-character string, if the automaton is in a final state, then it accepts the string. If it is not in a final state, or if at some point there was no appropriately labeled edge to follow, it rejects. The *language* recognized by an automaton is the set of strings that it accepts.

For example, it is clear that any string in the language recognized by automaton ID must begin with a letter. Any single letter leads to state 2, which is final; so a single-letter string is accepted. From state 2, any letter or digit leads back to state 2, so a letter followed by any number of letters and digits is also accepted.

In fact, the machines shown in Figure 2.3 accept the same languages as the first four regular expressions of Figure 2.2.

These are four separate automata; how can they be combined into a single machine that can serve as a lexical analyzer? We will study formal ways of doing this in the next section, but here we will just do it ad hoc: Figure 2.4 shows such a machine. Each final state must be labeled with the token-type that it accepts. State 2 in this machine has aspects of state 2 of the IF machine and state 2 of the ID machine; since the latter is final, then the combined state must be final. State 3 is like state 3 of the IF machine and state 3 of the ID machine; because these are both final we use *rule priority* to disambiguate – we label state 3 with IF because we want this token to be recognized as a reserved word, not an identifier.

We can encode this machine as a transition matrix: a two-dimensional array (a vector of vectors), subscripted by state number and input character. There will be a "dead" state (state 0) that loops to itself on all characters; we use this to encode the absence of an edge.

```
int edges[][] = {   /* ···0 1 2···-···e f g h i j··· */
/* state 0 */      {0,0,···0,0,0···0···0,0,0,0,0,0···},
/* state 1 */      {0,0,···7,7,7···9···4,4,4,4,2,4···},
/* state 2 */      {0,0,···4,4,4···0···4,3,4,4,4,4···},
/* state 3 */      {0,0,···4,4,4···0···4,4,4,4,4,4···},
/* state 4 */      {0,0,···4,4,4···0···4,4,4,4,4,4···},
/* state 5 */      {0,0,···6,6,6···0···0,0,0,0,0,0···},
/* state 6 */      {0,0,···6,6,6···0···0,0,0,0,0,0···},
/* state 7 */      {0,0,···7,7,7···0···0,0,0,0,0,0···},
/* state 8 */      {0,0,···8,8,8···0···0,0,0,0,0,0···},
   et cetera
}
```

There must also be a "finality" array, mapping state numbers to actions – final state 2 maps to action ID, and so on.

RECOGNIZING THE LONGEST MATCH

It is easy to see how to use this table to recognize whether to accept or reject a string, but the job of a lexical analyzer is to find the longest match, the longest initial substring of the input that is a valid token. While interpreting transitions, the lexer must keep track of the longest match seen so far, and the position of that match.

Keeping track of the longest match just means remembering the last time the automaton was in a final state with two variables, Last-Final (the state number of the most recent final state encountered) and Input-Position-at-Last-Final. Every time a final state is entered, the lexer updates these variables; when a *dead* state (a nonfinal state with no output transitions) is reached, tell what token was matched, and where it ended.

Figure 2.5 shows the operation of a lexical analyzer that recognizes longest matches; note that the current input position may be far beyond the most recent position at which the recognizer was in a final state.

Last Final	Current State	Current Input	Accept Action
0	1	⊤if --not-a-com	
2	2	|i⊥f --not-a-com	
3	3	|if⊤ --not-a-com	
3	0	|if⊤ --not-a-com	*return* IF
0	1	if⊤ --not-a-com	
12	12	if|⊤--not-a-com	
12	0	if|⊤--not-a-com	*found white space; resume*
0	1	if ⊤--not-a-com	
9	9	if |⊤not-a-com	
9	10	if |⊤not-a-com	
9	10	if |⊤n⊥ot-a-com	
9	10	if |⊤no⊥t-a-com	
9	10	if |⊤not⊥-a-com	
9	0	if |⊤not-⊥a-com	*error, illegal token '-'; resume*
0	1	if ⊤-not-a-com	
9	9	if -|⊤not-a-com	
9	0	if -|⊤n⊥ot-a-com	*error, illegal token '-'; resume*

FIGURE 2.5.   The automaton of Figure 2.4 recognizes several tokens. The symbol | indicates the input position at each successive call to the lexical analyzer, the symbol ⊥ indicates the current position of the automaton, and ⊤ indicates the most recent position in which the recognizer was in a final state.

2.4   NONDETERMINISTIC FINITE AUTOMATA

A nondeterministic finite automaton (NFA) is one that has a choice of edges – labeled with the same symbol – to follow out of a state. Or it may have special edges labeled with ϵ (the Greek letter epsilon), that can be followed without eating any symbol from the input.

Here is an example of an NFA:

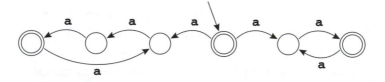

In the start state, on input character a, the automaton can move either right or left. If left is chosen, then strings of a's whose length is a multiple of three will be accepted. If right is chosen, then even-length strings will be accepted. Thus, the language recognized by this NFA is the set of all strings of a's whose length is a multiple of two or three.

On the first transition, this machine must choose which way to go. It is required to accept the string if there is *any* choice of paths that will lead to acceptance. Thus, it must "guess," and must always guess correctly.

Edges labeled with ϵ may be taken without using up a symbol from the input. Here is another NFA that accepts the same language:

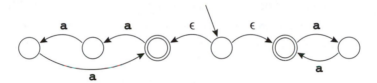

Again, the machine must choose which ϵ-edge to take. If there is a state with some ϵ-edges and some edges labeled by symbols, the machine can choose to eat an input symbol (and follow the corresponding symbol-labeled edge), or to follow an ϵ-edge instead.

CONVERTING A REGULAR EXPRESSIONS TO AN NFA

Nondeterministic automata are a useful notion because it is easy to convert a (static, declarative) regular expression to a (simulatable, quasi-executable) NFA.

The conversion algorithm turns each regular expression into an NFA with a *tail* (start edge) and a *head* (ending state). For example, the single-symbol regular expression **a** converts to the NFA

The regular expression **ab**, made by combining **a** with **b** using concatenation is made by combining the two NFAs, hooking the head of **a** to the tail of **b**. The resulting machine has a tail labeled by **a** and a head into which the **b** edge

flows.

In general, any regular expression M will have some NFA with a tail and head:

We can define the translation of regular expressions to NFAs by induction. Either an expression is primitive (a single symbol or ϵ) or it is made from smaller expressions. Similarly, the NFA will be primitive or made from smaller NFAs.

Figure 2.6 shows the rules for translating regular expressions to nondeterministic automata. We illustrate the algorithm on some of the expressions in Figure 2.2 – for the tokens IF, ID, NUM, and **error**. Each expression is translated to an NFA, the "head" state of each NFA is marked final with a different token type, and the tails of all the expressions are joined to a new start node. The result is shown in Figure 2.7.

CONVERTING AN NFA TO A DFA

As we saw in Section 2.3, implementing deterministic finite automata (DFAs) as computer programs is easy. But implementing NFAs is a bit harder, since most computers don't have good "guessing" hardware.

We can avoid the need to guess by trying every possibility at once. Let us simulate the NFA of Figure 2.7 on the string in. We start in state 1. Now, instead of guessing which ϵ-transition to take, we just say that at this point the NFA might take any of them, so it is in one of the states $\{1, 4, 8, 12\}$; that is, we compute the ϵ-*closure* of $\{1\}$. Clearly, there are no other states reachable without eating the first character of the input.

Now, we make the transition on the character i. From state 1 we can reach 2, from 4 we reach 5, from 8 we go nowhere, and from 12 we reach 13. So we have the set $\{2, 5, 13\}$. But again we must compute ϵ-closure: from 5 there is an ϵ transition to 7, and from 7 to 6. So the NFA must be in one of the states $\{2, 5, 6, 7, 13\}$.

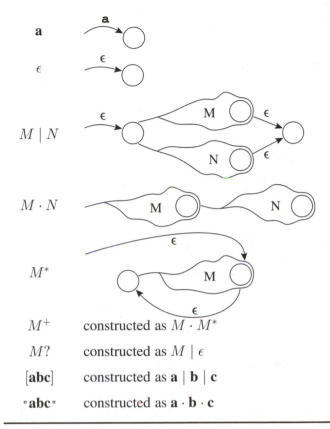

a

ϵ

$M \mid N$

$M \cdot N$

M^*

M^+ constructed as $M \cdot M^*$

$M?$ constructed as $M \mid \epsilon$

[**abc**]   constructed as **a** $\mid$ **b** $\mid$ **c**

"**abc**"   constructed as **a** $\cdot$ **b** $\cdot$ **c**

FIGURE 2.6.   Translation of regular expressions to NFAs.

On the character n, we get from state 6 to 7, from 2 to nowhere, from 5 to nowhere, from 13 to nowhere, and from 7 to nowhere. So we have the set $\{7\}$; its ϵ-closure is $\{6, 7\}$.

Now we are at the end of the string in; is the NFA in a final state? One of the sets in our possible-states set is 7, which is final. Thus, in is an ID token.

We formally define ϵ-closure as follows. Let **edge**(s, c) be the set of all NFA states reachable by following a single edge with label c from state s. For a set of states S, **closure**(S) is the set of states that can be reached from a state in S without consuming any of the input, that is, by going only through ϵ edges. Mathematically, we can express the idea of going through ϵ edges by saying that **closure**(S) is smallest set T such that

$$T = S \cup \left(\bigcup_{s \in T} \mathbf{edge}(s, \epsilon) \right).$$

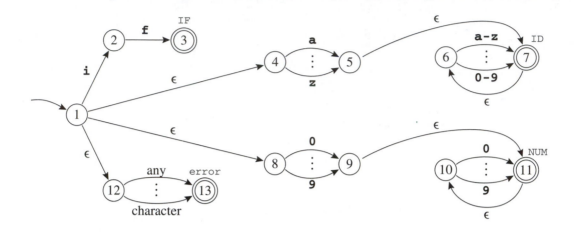

FIGURE 2.7.   Four regular expressions translated to an NFA.

We can calculate T by iteration:

$$T \leftarrow S$$
$$\textbf{repeat } T' \leftarrow T$$
$$T \leftarrow T' \cup \left(\bigcup_{s \in T'} \textbf{edge}(s, \epsilon)\right)$$
$$\textbf{until } T = T'$$

Why does this algorithm work? T can only grow in each iteration, so the final T must include S. If $T = T'$ after an iteration step, then T must also include $\bigcup_{s \in T'} \textbf{edge}(s, \epsilon)$. Finally, the algorithm must terminate, because there are only a finite number of distinct states in the NFA.

Now, when simulating an NFA as described above, suppose we are in a set $d = \{s_i, s_k, s_l\}$ of NFA states s_i, s_k, s_l. By starting in d and eating the input symbol c, we reach a new set of NFA states; we'll call this set **DFAedge**(d, c):

$$\textbf{DFAedge}(d, c) = \textbf{closure}\left(\bigcup_{s \in d} \textbf{edge}(s, c)\right)$$

Using **DFAedge**, we can write the NFA simulation algorithm more formally. If the start state of the NFA is s_1, and the input string is $c_1, \ldots, c_k$, then the algorithm is:

$$d \leftarrow \textbf{closure}(\{s_1\})$$
$$\textbf{for } i \leftarrow 1 \textbf{ to } k$$
$$d \leftarrow \textbf{DFAedge}(d, c_i)$$

Manipulating sets of states is expensive – too costly to want to do on every character in the source program that is being lexically analyzed. But it is possible to do all the sets-of-states calculations in advance. We make a DFA from the NFA, such that each set of NFA states corresponds to one DFA state. Since the NFA has a finite number n of states, the DFA will also have a finite number (at most 2^n) of states.

DFA construction is easy once we have **closure** and **DFAedge** algorithms. The DFA start state d_1 is just **closure**(s_1), as in the NFA simulation algorithm. Abstractly, there is an edge from d_i to d_j labeled with c if $d_j = $ **DFAedge**(d_i, c). We let Σ be the alphabet.

```
states[0] ← {};     states[1] ← closure({s_1})
p ← 1;     j ← 0
while j ≤ p
  foreach c ∈ Σ
    e ← DFAedge(states[j], c)
    if e = states[i] for some i ≤ p
      then trans[j, c] ← i
      else p ← p + 1
           states[p] ← e
           trans[j, c] ← p
    j ← j + 1
```

The algorithm does not visit unreachable states of the DFA. This is extremely important, because in principle the DFA has 2^n states, but in practice we usually find that only about n of them are reachable from the start state. It is important to avoid an exponential blowup in the size of the DFA interpreter's transition tables, which will form part of the working compiler.

A state d is *final* in the DFA if any NFA-state in states$[d]$ is final in the NFA. Labeling a state *final* is not enough; we must also say what token is recognized; and perhaps several members of states$[d]$ are final in the NFA. In this case we label d with the token-type that occurred first in the list of regular expressions that constitute the lexical specification. This is how *rule priority* is implemented.

After the DFA is constructed, the "states" array may be discarded, and the "trans" array is used for lexical analysis.

Applying the DFA construction algorithm to the NFA of Figure 2.7 gives the automaton in Figure 2.8.

This automaton is suboptimal. That is, it is not the smallest one that recognizes the same language. In general, we say that two states s_1 and s_2 are equivalent when the machine starting in s_1 accepts a string σ if and only if

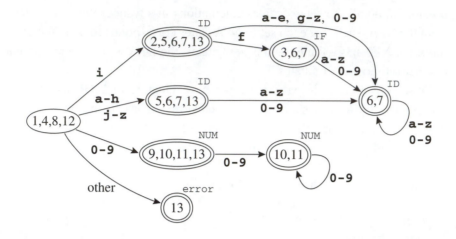

FIGURE 2.8. NFA converted to DFA.

starting in s_2 it accepts σ. This is certainly true of the states labeled $\boxed{5,6,7,13}$ and $\boxed{6,7}$ in Figure 2.8; and of the states labeled $\boxed{9,10,11,13}$ and $\boxed{10,11}$. In an automaton with two equivalent states s_1 and s_2, we can make all of s_2's incoming edges point to s_1 instead and delete s_2.

How can we find equivalent states? Certainly, s_1 and s_2 are equivalent if, for any symbol c, $\text{trans}[s_1, c] = \text{trans}[s_2, c]$; $\boxed{9,10,11,13}$ and $\boxed{10,11}$ satisfy this criterion. But this condition is not sufficiently general; consider the automaton

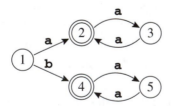

Here, states 2 and 4 are equivalent, but $\text{trans}[2, a] \neq \text{trans}[4, a]$.

After constructing a DFA it is useful to apply an algorithm to minimize it by finding equivalent states; see Exercise 2.6.

JavaLex: A LEXICAL ANALYZER GENERATOR

DFA construction is a mechanical task easily performed by computer, so it makes sense to have an automatic *lexical analyzer generator* to translate regular expressions into a DFA.

JavaLex is a lexical analyzer generator that produces a Java program from a *lexical specification*. For each token type in the programming language to be lexically analyzed, the specification contains a regular expression and an *action*. The action communicates the token type (perhaps along with other information) to the next phase of the compiler.

The output of JavaLex is a program in Java – a lexical analyzer that interprets a DFA using the algorithm described in Section 2.3 and executes the action fragments on each match. The action fragments are just Java statements that return token values.

The tokens described in Figure 2.2 are specified in JavaLex as shown in Program 2.9.

The first part of the specification, above the `%%` mark, contains package declarations, import declarations, and classes that may be used by the Java code in the remainder of the file.

The second part of the specification contains regular-expression abbreviations and state declarations. For example, the declaration `digits=[0-9]+` in this section allows the name `{digits}` to stand for a nonempty sequence of digits within regular expressions.

The third part contains regular expressions and actions. The actions are fragments of ordinary Java code. Each action must return a value of the "lexical token" class declared by the `%type` declaration. If the action does not return, then the current token will be discarded and the lexer will re-invoke itself to match the next token.

In the action fragments, several special variables and methods are available. The string matched by the regular expression is `yytext()`. The file position of the beginning of the matched string is `yychar`.

In this particular example, each token is a member of the `Symbol` class, which lives in the `java_cup.runtime` package exported by the CUP parser generator (to be described in Chapter 3). For reporting error messages, this class has integer values denoting the positions of the beginning and end of the token in the input file. These are generally set to `yychar` and `yychar+yylength()`. `Symbol` also has an integer denoting what kind of token was matched (`Syms.IF`, `Syms.ID`, etc.). Finally, there is a field of class

Java preamble:
```
package Parse;
import ErrorMsg.ErrorMsg;

%%
private java_cup.runtime.Symbol tok(int k, Object value) {
     return new java_cup.runtime.Symbol(k, yychar, yy-
char+yylength(), value);
}
%%
```
/ JavaLex Definitions: */*
```
%function nextToken
%type java_cup.runtime.Symbol
%char
%eofval{
          {return tok(Syms.EOF,NULL); }
%eofval}

digits=[0-9]+

%%
```
/ Regular Expressions and Actions: */*
```
if                {return tok(sym.IF, NULL);}
[a-z][a-z0-9]*    {return tok(sym.ID, yytext());}
{digits}          {return tok(Syms.NUM, new Int(Int.parseInt(yytext())))}
({digits}"."[0-9]*)|([0-9]*"."{digits})
                  {return tok(sym.REAL, new Dou-
ble(Double.valueOf(yytext())));}
("--"[a-z]*"\n")|(" "|"\n"|"\t")+     {}
.                 {errorMsg.error(yychar,"illegal character");}
```

PROGRAM 2.9. JavaLex specification of the tokens from Figure 2.2.

Object to carry the semantic value (of those tokens that have them).

```
class Symbol {
  int sym;              /* which token type */
  int left, right;      /* position in source file */
  Object value;         /* semantic value */
  Symbol(int s, int l, int r, int v) {
    sym=s; left=l; right=r; value=v;
  }
}
```

The class sym lists all the token types:

```
class sym {
  final static int EOF=0, IF=1, ID=2, NUM=3, REAL=4, ···
}
```

The semantic values can be computed from `yytext()`, which always returns the actual characters matched.

START STATES

Regular expressions are *static* and *declarative*; automata are *dynamic* and *imperative*. That is, you can see the components and structure of a regular expression without having to simulate an algorithm, but to understand an automaton it is often necessary to "execute" it in your mind. Thus, regular expressions are usually more convenient to specify the lexical structure of programming-language tokens.

But sometimes the step-by-step, state-transition model of automata is appropriate. JavaLex has a mechanism to mix states with regular expressions. One can declare a set of *start states*; each regular expression can be prefixed by the set of start states in which it is valid. The action fragments can explicitly change the start state. In effect, we have a finite automaton whose edges are labeled, not by single symbols, but by regular expressions. This example shows a language with simple identifiers, `if` tokens, and comments delimited by `(*` and `*)` brackets:

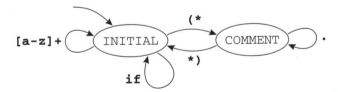

Though it is possible to write a single regular expression that matches an entire comment, as comments get more complicated it becomes more difficult, or even impossible if nested comments are allowed.

The JavaLex specification corresponding to this machine is

```
    ⋮      the usual preamble ...
%{ private java_cup.runtime.Symbol tok(int kind, Object v) {
      return new java_cup.runtime.Symbol(
                 kind, yychar, yychar+yylength(), v);
    }
    private java_cup.runtime.Symbol tok(int kind) {
      return tok(kind, null);
    }
%}
%start COMMENT
%%
<YYINITIAL>if          {return tok(sym.IF);}
<YYINITIAL>[a-z]+      {return tok(sym.ID, yytext());}
<YYINITIAL>"(*"         {yybegin(COMMENT);}
<COMMENT>"*)"          {yybegin(INITIAL);}
<COMMENT>.             {}
```

where YYINITIAL is the start state, provided by default in all specifications. Any regular expression not prefixed by a <STATE> operates in all states; this feature is rarely useful.

This example can be easily augmented to handle nested comments, via a global variable that is incremented and decremented in the semantic actions.

PROGRAM LEXICAL ANALYSIS

Use JavaLex to implement a lexical analyzer for the Tiger language. Appendix A describes, among other things, the lexical tokens of Tiger.

This chapter has left out some of the specifics of how the lexical analyzer should be initialized and how it should communicate with the rest of the compiler. You can learn this from the JavaLex manual, but the "skeleton" files in the $TIGER/chap2 directory will also help get you started.

Along with the tiger.lex file you should turn in documentation for the following points:

- how you handle comments;
- how you handle strings;
- error handling;
- end-of-file handling;
- other interesting features of your lexer.

Supporting files are available in $TIGER/chap2 as follows:

Parse/sym.java Class sym with definitions of the token-kind constants.

`java_cup/runtime/Symbol.java` This class is provided in the `runtime` directory of the CUP parser generator and is used by the lexical analyzer to report tokens (with associated semantic values) to the parser.

`Parse/Lexer.java` The `Lexer` interface, to be supported by the lexical analyzer.

`ErrorMsg/ErrorMsg.java` The `ErrorMsg` package, useful for producing error messages with file names and line numbers.

`Main.java` A test scaffold to run your lexer on an input file.

`Parse/Tiger.lex` The beginnings of a lexical analyzer specification.

`makefile` A "makefile" to compile everything.

When reading the *Tiger Language Reference Manual* (Appendix A), pay particular attention to the paragraphs with the headings **Identifiers, Comments, Integer literal,** and **String literal**.

The reserved words of the language are: `while`, `for`, `to`, `break`, `let`, `in`, `end`, `function`, `var`, `type`, `array`, `if`, `then`, `else`, `do`, `of`, `nil`.

The punctuation symbols used in the language are:

`, : ; ( ) [ ] { } . + - * / = <> < <= > >= & | :=`

The string value that you return for a string literal should have all the escape sequences translated into their meanings.

There are no negative integer literals; return two separate tokens for `-32`.

Detect unclosed comments (at end of file) and unclosed strings.

The directory `$TIGER/testcases` contains a few sample Tiger programs.

To get started: Make a directory and copy the contents of `$TIGER/chap2` into it. Make a file `test.tig` containing a short program in the Tiger language. Then type `make`; JavaLex will run on `Tiger.lex`, producing `Yylex.java`, and then the appropriate Java files will be compiled.

Finally, `java Parse.Main test.tig` will lexically analyze the file using a test scaffold.

Now edit `Toy.lex`, and try again.

FURTHER READING

Lex was the first lexical-analyzer generator based on regular expressions [Lesk 1975]; it is still widely used.

Computing ϵ-closure can be done more efficiently by keeping a queue or stack of states whose edges have not yet been checked for ϵ-transitions [Aho et al. 1986]. Regular expressions can be converted directly to DFAs without going through NFAs [McNaughton and Yamada 1960; Aho et al. 1986].

DFA transition tables can be very large and sparse. If represented as a simple two-dimensional matrix ($states \times symbols$) they take far too much memory. In practice, tables are compressed; this reduces the amount of memory required, but increases the time required to look up the next state [Aho et al. 1986].

Lexical analyzers, whether automatically generated or handwritten, must manage their input efficiently. Of course, input is buffered, so that a large batch of characters is obtained at once; then the lexer can process one character at a time in the buffer. The lexer must check, for each character, whether the end of the buffer is reached. By putting a *sentinel* – a character that cannot be part of any token – at the end of the buffer, it is possible for the lexer to check for end-of-buffer only once per token, instead of once per character [Aho et al. 1986]. Gray [1988] uses a scheme that requires only one check per line, rather than one per token, but cannot cope with tokens that contain end-of-line characters. Bumbulis and Cowan [1993] check only once around each cycle in the DFA; this reduces the number of checks (from once per character) when there are long paths in the DFA.

Automatically generated lexical analyzers are often criticized for being slow. In principle, the operation of a finite automaton is very simple and should be efficient, but interpreting from transition tables adds overhead. Gray [1988] shows that DFAs translated directly into executable code (implementing states as case statements) can run as fast as hand-coded lexers. The Flex "fast lexical analyzer generator" [Paxson 1995] is significantly faster than Lex.

EXERCISES

2.1 Write regular expressions for each of the following.

a. Strings over the alphabet $\{a, b, c\}$ where the first a precedes the first b.

b. Strings over the alphabet $\{a, b, c\}$ with an even number of a's.

c. Binary numbers that are multiples of four.

d. Binary numbers that are greater than 101001.

e. Strings over the alphabet $\{a, b, c\}$ that don't contain the contiguous substring baa.

f. The language of nonnegative integer constants in C, where numbers beginning with 0 are *octal* constants and other numbers are *decimal* constants.

g. Binary numbers n such that there exists an integer solution of $a^n + b^n = c^n$.

2.2 For each of the following, explain why you're not surprised that there is no regular expression defining it.

a. Strings of a's and b's where there are more a's than b's.

b. Strings of a's and b's that are palindromes (the same forward as backward).

c. Syntactically correct ML programs.

2.3 Explain in informal English what each of these finite state automata recognizes.

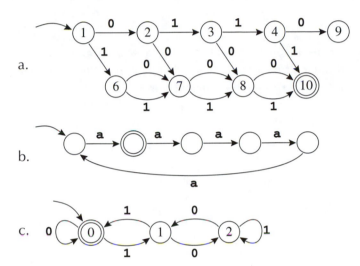

a.

b.

c.

2.4 Convert these regular expressions to nondeterministic finite automata.

a. $(\mathbf{if}|\mathbf{then}|\mathbf{else})$

b. $\mathbf{a}((\mathbf{b}|\mathbf{a}^*\mathbf{c})\mathbf{x})^*|\mathbf{x}^*\mathbf{a}$

2.5 Convert these NFAs to deterministic finite automata.

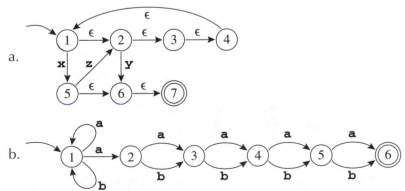

a.

b.

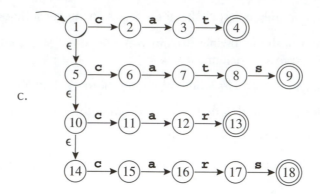

C.

2.6 Find two equivalent states in the following automaton, and merge them to produce a smaller automaton that recognizes the same language. Repeat until there are no longer equivalent states.

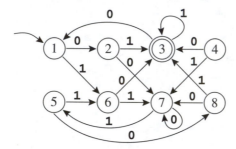

Actually, the general algorithm for minimizing finite automata works in reverse. First, find all pairs of inequivalent states. States X, Y are inequivalent if X is final and Y is not or (by iteration) if $X \xrightarrow{a} X'$ and $Y \xrightarrow{a} Y'$ and X', Y' are inequivalent. After this iteration ceases to find new pairs of inequivalent states, then X, Y are equivalent if they are not inequivalent. See Hopcroft and Ullman [1979], Theorem 3.10.

2.7 Any DFA can be converted to a regular expression. Convert the DFA of Exercise 2.3c to a regular expression. Hint: first, pretend state 1 is the start state. Then write a regular expression for excursions to state 2 and back, and a similar one for excursions to state 0 and back. Or look in Hopcroft and Ullman [1979], Theorem 2.4, for the algorithm.

2.8 Suppose this DFA were used by Lex to find tokens in an input file.

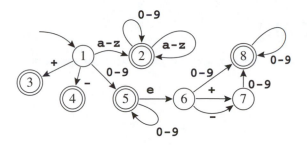

a. How many characters past the end of a token might Lex have to examine before matching the token?

b. Given your answer k to part (a), show an input file containing at least two tokens such that *the first call* to Lex will examine k characters *past the end of the first token* before returning the first token. If the answer to part (a) is zero, then show an input file containing at least two tokens, and indicate the endpoint of each token.

2.9 An interpreted DFA-based lexical analyzer uses two tables,

edges indexed by state and input symbol, yielding a state number, and
final indexed by state, returning 0 or an action-number.

Starting with this lexical specification,

```
(aba)+      (action 1);
(a(b*)a)    (action 2);
(a|b)       (action 3);
```

generate the edges and final tables for a lexical analyzer.

Then show each step of the lexer on the string abaabbaba. Be sure to show the values of the important internal variables of the recognizer. There will be repeated calls to the lexer to get successive tokens.

**2.10 Lex has a *lookahead* operator / so that the regular expression abc/def matches abc only when followed by def (but def is not part of the matched string, and will be part of the next token(s). Aho et al. [1986] describe, and Lex [Lesk 1975] uses, an incorrect algorithm for implementing lookahead (it fails on (a|ab)/ba with input aba, matching ab where it should match a). Flex [Paxson 1995] uses a better mechanism that works correctly for (a|ab)/ba but fails (with a warning message) on zx*/xy*.

Design a better lookahead mechanism.

3

Parsing

---

syn-tax: the way in which words are put together to form phrases, clauses, or sentences.

Webster's Dictionary

The abbreviation mechanism in JavaLex, whereby a symbol stands for some regular expression, is convenient enough that it is tempting to use it in interesting ways:

digits = [0 − 9]+
sum = (*digits* "+")* *digits*

These regular expressions define sums of the form 28+301+9.

But now consider

digits = [0 − 9]+
sum = *expr* "+" *expr*
expr = " (" *sum* ") " | *digits*

This is meant to define expressions of the form:

```
(109+23)
61
(1+(250+3))
```

in which all the parentheses are balanced. But it is impossible for a finite automaton to recognize balanced parentheses (because a machine with N states cannot remember a parenthesis-nesting depth greater than N), so clearly *sum* and *expr* cannot be regular expressions.

So how does JavaLex manage to implement regular-expression abbreviations such as `digits`? The answer is that the right-hand-side (`[0-9]+`) is simply substituted for digits wherever it appears in regular expressions, *before* translation to a finite automaton.

This is not possible for the *sum*-and-*expr* language; we can first substitute *sum* into *expr*, yielding

$$expr = \text{“}(\text{”} \; expr \; \text{“}+\text{”} \; expr \; \text{“})\text{”} \mid digits$$

but now an attempt to substitute expr into itself leads to

$$expr = \text{“}(\text{”} \; (\; \text{“}(\text{”} \; expr \; \text{“}+\text{”} \; expr \; \text{“})\text{”} \mid digits \;) \; \text{“}+\text{”} \; expr \; \text{“})\text{”} \mid digits$$

and the right-hand side now has just as many occurrences of *expr* as it did before – in fact, it has more!

Thus, the notion of abbreviation does not add expressive power to the language of regular expressions – there are no additional languages that can be defined – unless the abbreviations are recursive (or mutually recursive, as are sum and expr).

The additional expressive power gained by recursion is just what we need for parsing. Also, once we have abbreviations with recursion, we do not need alternation except at the top level of expressions, because the definition

$$expr = ab(c \mid d)e$$

can always be rewritten using an auxiliary definition as

$$aux \; = c \mid d$$
$$expr = a \; b \; aux \; e$$

In fact, instead of using the alternation mark at all, we can just write several allowable expansions for the same symbol:

$$aux \; = c$$
$$aux \; = d$$
$$expr = a \; b \; aux \; e$$

The Kleene closure is not necessary, since we can rewrite it so that

$$expr = (a \; b \; c)*$$

becomes

$$expr = (a \; b \; c) \; expr$$
$$expr = \epsilon$$

$_1 \quad S \rightarrow S\,;\,S$
$_2 \quad S \rightarrow \text{id} := E$
$_3 \quad S \rightarrow \text{print}\,(\,L\,)$

$_4 \quad E \rightarrow \text{id}$
$_5 \quad E \rightarrow \text{num}$
$_6 \quad E \rightarrow E + E$
$_7 \quad E \rightarrow (\,S\,,\,E\,)$

$_8 \quad L \rightarrow E$
$_9 \quad L \rightarrow L\,,\,E$

GRAMMAR 3.1. A syntax for straight line programs.

What we have left is a very simple notation, called *context-free grammars*. Just as regular expressions can be used to define lexical structure in a static, declarative way, grammars define syntactic structure declaratively. But we will need something more powerful than finite automata to parse languages described by grammars.

In fact, grammars can also be used to describe the structure of lexical tokens, although regular expressions are adequate – and more concise – for that purpose.

3.1 CONTEXT-FREE GRAMMARS

As before, we say that a *language* is a set of *strings*; each string is a finite sequence of *symbols* taken from a finite *alphabet*. For parsing, the strings are source programs, the symbols are lexical tokens, and the alphabet is the set of token types returned by the lexical analyzer.

A context-free grammar describes a language. A grammar has a set of *productions* of the form

$$symbol \;\rightarrow\; symbol \; symbol \;\cdots\; symbol$$

where there are zero or more symbols on the right-hand side. Each symbol is either *terminal*, meaning that it is a token from the alphabet of strings in the language, or *nonterminal*, meaning that it appears on the left-hand side of some production. No token can ever appear on the left-hand side of a production. Finally, one of the nonterminals is distinguished as the *start symbol* of the grammar.

Grammar 3.1 is an example of a grammar for straight-line programs. The start symbol is S (when the start symbol is not written explicitly it is conventional to assume that the left-hand nonterminal in the first production is the start symbol). The terminal symbols are

id print num , + ( ) := ;

$\underline{S}$
$S\,;\,\underline{S}$
$\underline{S}\,;\,\text{id}\,:=E$
$\text{id}\,:=\underline{E}\,;\,\text{id}\,:=E$
$\text{id}\,:=\text{num}\,;\,\text{id}\,:=\underline{E}$
$\text{id}\,:=\text{num}\,;\,\text{id}\,:=E\,+\,\underline{E}$
$\text{id}\,:=\text{num}\,;\,\text{id}\,:=\underline{E}\,+\,(S\,,\,E\,)$
$\text{id}\,:=\text{num}\,;\,\text{id}\,:=\text{id}\,+\,(\underline{S}\,,\,E\,)$
$\text{id}\,:=\text{num}\,;\,\text{id}\,:=\text{id}\,+\,(\text{id}\,:=\underline{E}\,,\,E\,)$
$\text{id}\,:=\text{num}\,;\,\text{id}\,:=\text{id}\,+\,(\text{id}\,:=E\,+\,E\,,\,\underline{E}\,)$
$\text{id}\,:=\text{num}\,;\,\text{id}\,:=\text{id}\,+\,(\text{id}\,:=\underline{E}\,+\,E\,,\,\text{id}\,)$
$\text{id}\,:=\text{num}\,;\,\text{id}\,:=\text{id}\,+\,(\text{id}\,:=\text{num}\,+\,\underline{E}\,,\,\text{id}\,)$
$\text{id}\,:=\text{num}\,;\,\text{id}\,:=\text{id}\,+\,(\text{id}\,:=\text{num}\,+\,\text{num}\,,\,\text{id}\,)$

DERIVATION 3.2.

and the nonterminals are S, E, and L. One sentence in the language of this grammar is

```
id := num; id := id + (id := num + num, id)
```

where the source text (before lexical analysis) might have been

```
a := 7;
b := c + (d := 5 + 6, d)
```

The token-types (terminal symbols) are id, num, :=, and so on; the names (a,b,c,d) and numbers (7,5,6) are *semantic values* associated with some of the tokens.

DERIVATIONS

To show that this sentence is in the language of the grammar, we can perform a *derivation*: start with the start symbol, then repeatedly replace any nonterminal by one of its right-hand sides, as shown in Derivation 3.2.

There are many different derivations of the same sentence. A *leftmost* derivation is one in which the leftmost nonterminal symbol is always the one expanded; in a *rightmost* derivation, the rightmost nonterminal is always next to be expanded.

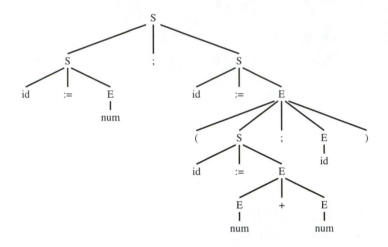

FIGURE 3.3. Parse tree.

Derivation 3.2 is neither leftmost nor rightmost; a leftmost derivation for this sentence would begin,

$$\underline{S}$$
$$\underline{S} \; ; \; S$$
$$\text{id} := \underline{E} \; ; \; S$$
$$\text{id} := \text{num} \; ; \; \underline{S}$$
$$\text{id} := \text{num} \; ; \; \text{id} := \underline{E}$$
$$\text{id} := \text{num} \; ; \; \text{id} := \underline{E} + E$$
$$\vdots$$

PARSE TREES

A *parse tree* is made by connecting each symbol in a derivation to the one from which it was derived, as shown in Figure 3.3. Two different derivations can have the same parse tree.

AMBIGUOUS GRAMMARS

A grammar is *ambiguous* if it can derive a sentence with two different parse trees. Grammar 3.1 is ambiguous, since the sentence id := id+id+id has two parse trees (Figure 3.4).

Grammar 3.5 is also ambiguous; Figure 3.6 shows two parse trees for the sentence 1-2-3, and Figure 3.7 shows two trees for 1+2*3. Clearly, if we

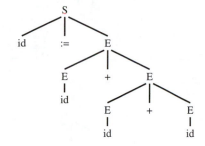

FIGURE 3.4. Two parse trees for the same sentence using Grammar 3.1.

$E \rightarrow \mathrm{id}$
$E \rightarrow \mathrm{num}$
$E \rightarrow E * E$
$E \rightarrow E \; / \; E$
$E \rightarrow E + E$
$E \rightarrow E - E$
$E \rightarrow (\, E \,)$

GRAMMAR 3.5.

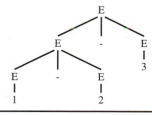
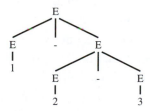

FIGURE 3.6. Two parse trees for the sentence 1–2–3 in Grammar 3.5.

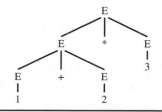
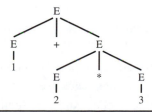

FIGURE 3.7. Two parse trees for the sentence 1+2*3 in Grammar 3.5.

$$E \to E + T \qquad T \to T * F \qquad F \to \text{id}$$
$$E \to E - T \qquad T \to T / F \qquad F \to \text{num}$$
$$E \to T \qquad T \to F \qquad F \to (E)$$

GRAMMAR 3.8.

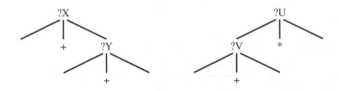

FIGURE 3.9.   Parse trees that Grammar 3.8 will never produce.

use parse trees to interpret the meaning of the expressions, the two parse trees for 1-2-3 mean different things: $(1 - 2) - 3 = -4$ versus $1 - (2 - 3) = 2$. Similarly, $(1 + 2) \times 3$ is not the same as $1 + (2 \times 3)$. And indeed, compilers do use parse trees to derive meaning.

Therefore, ambiguous grammars are problematic for compiling: in general we would prefer to have unambiguous grammars. Fortunately, we can often transform ambiguous grammars to unambiguous grammars.

Let us find an unambigous grammar that accepts the same language as Grammar 3.5. First, we would like to say that * *binds tighter* than +, or has *higher precedence*. Second, we want to say that each operator *associates to the left*, so that we get $(1 - 2) - 3$ instead of $1 - (2 - 3)$. We do this by introducing new nonterminal symbols to get Grammar 3.8.

The symbols E, T, and F stand for *expression*, *term*, and *factor*; conventionally, factors are things you multiply and terms are things you add.

This grammar accepts the same set of sentences as the ambiguous grammar, but now each sentence has exactly one parse tree. Grammar 3.8 can never produce parse trees of the form shown in Figure 3.9 (see Exercise 3.14).

Had we wanted to make * associate to the right, we could have written its production as $T \to F * T$.

We can usually eliminate ambiguity by transforming the grammar. Though there are some languages (sets of strings) that have ambiguous grammars but no unambiguous grammar, such languages may be problematic as *programming* languages because the syntactic ambiguity may lead to problems in writing and understanding programs.

$S \rightarrow E \, \$$

$E \rightarrow E + T$

$E \rightarrow E - T$

$E \rightarrow T$

$T \rightarrow T * F$

$T \rightarrow T \, / \, F$

$T \rightarrow F$

$F \rightarrow \text{id}$

$F \rightarrow \text{num}$

$F \rightarrow (\, E \,)$

GRAMMAR 3.10.

$S \rightarrow \text{if } E \text{ then } S \text{ else } S$

$S \rightarrow \text{begin } S \, L$

$S \rightarrow \text{print } E$

$L \rightarrow \text{end}$

$L \rightarrow \, ; \, S \, L$

$E \rightarrow \text{num} \, = \, \text{num}$

GRAMMAR 3.11.

END-OF-FILE MARKER

Parsers must read not only terminal symbols such as +, –, num, and so on, but also the end-of-file marker. We will use $ to represent end of file.

Suppose S is the start symbol of a grammar. To indicate that $ must come after a complete S-phrase, we augment the grammar with a new start symbol S' and a new production $S' \rightarrow S\$$.

In Grammar 3.8, E is the start symbol, so an augmented grammar is Grammar 3.10.

3.2   PREDICTIVE PARSING

Some grammars are easy to parse using a simple algorithm known as *recursive descent*. In essence, each grammar production turns into one clause of a recursive function. We illustrate this by writing a recursive-descent parser for Grammar 3.11.

A recursive-descent parser for this language has one function for each nonterminal and one clause for each production.

```
final int IF=1, THEN=2, ELSE=3, BEGIN=4, END=5, PRINT=6,
          SEMI=7, NUM=8, EQ=9;

int tok = getToken();

void advance() {tok=getToken();}
void eat(int t) {if (tok==t) advance(); else error();}

void S() {switch(tok) {
     case IF:    eat(IF); E(); eat(THEN); S();
                    eat(ELSE); S(); break;
     case BEGIN: eat(BEGIN); S(); L(); break;
     case PRINT: eat(PRINT); E(); break;
     default:    error();
     }}
void L() {switch(tok) {
     case END:   eat(END); break;
     case SEMI:  eat(SEMI); S(); L(); break;
     default:    error();
     }}
void E() {  eat(NUM); eat(EQ); eat(NUM); }
```

With suitable definitions of `error` and `getToken`, this program will parse very nicely.

Emboldened by success with this simple method, let us try it with Grammar 3.10:

```
void S() {  E(); eat(EOF); }
void E() {switch (tok) {
        case ?: E(); eat(PLUS); T(); break;
        case ?: E(); eat(MINUS); T(); break;
        case ?: T(); break;
        default: error();
        }}
void T() {switch (tok) {
        case ?: T(); eat(TIMES); F(); break;
        case ?: T(); eat(DIV); F(); break;
        case ?: F(); break;
        default: error();
        }}
```

There is a *conflict* here: the E function has no way to know which clause to use. Consider the strings `(1*2-3)+4` and `(1*2-3)`. In the former case, the initial call to E should use the $E \rightarrow E + T$ production, but the latter case should use $E \rightarrow T$.

$Z \rightarrow d$	$Y \rightarrow$	$X \rightarrow Y$
$Z \rightarrow X\,Y\,Z$	$Y \rightarrow c$	$X \rightarrow a$

GRAMMAR 3.12.

Recursive-descent, or *predictive*, parsing works only on grammars where the *first terminal symbol* of each subexpression provides enough information to choose which production to use. To understand this better, we will formalize the notion of FIRST sets, and then derive conflict-free recursive-descent parsers using a simple algorithm.

Just as lexical analyzers can be constructed from regular expressions, there are parser-generator tools that build predictive parsers. But if we are going to use a tool, then we might as well use one based on the more powerful LR(1) parsing algorithm, which will be described in Section 3.3.

Sometimes it's inconvenient or impossible to use a parser-generator tool. The advantage of predictive parsing is that the algorithm is simple enough that we can use it to construct parsers by hand – we don't need automatic tools.

FIRST AND FOLLOW SETS

Given a string γ of terminal and nonterminal symbols, $\mathrm{FIRST}(\gamma)$ is the set of all terminal symbols that can begin any string derived from γ. For example, let $\gamma = T * F$. Any string of terminal symbols derived from γ must start with id, num, or (. Thus,

$\mathrm{FIRST}(T * F) = \{\mathrm{id}, \mathrm{num}, (\}$.

If two different productions $X \rightarrow \gamma_1$ and $X \rightarrow \gamma_2$ have the same left-hand-side symbol (X) and their right-hand sides have overlapping FIRST sets, then the grammar cannot be parsed using predictive parsing. If some terminal symbol I is in $\mathrm{FIRST}(\gamma_1)$ and also in $\mathrm{FIRST}(\gamma_2)$, then the X function in a recursive-descent parser will not know what to do if the input token is I.

The computation of FIRST sets looks very simple: if $\gamma = X\,Y\,Z$, it seems as if Y and Z can be ignored, and $\mathrm{FIRST}(X)$ is the only thing that matters. But consider Grammar 3.12. Because Y can produce the empty string – and therefore X can produce the empty string – we find that $\mathrm{FIRST}(X\,Y\,Z)$ must include $\mathrm{FIRST}(Z)$. Therefore, in computing FIRST sets, we must keep track of which symbols can produce the empty string; we say such symbols are *nullable*. And we must keep track of what might follow a nullable symbol.

With respect to a particular grammar, given a string γ of terminals and nonterminals,

- nullable(X) is true if X can derive the empty string.
- FIRST(γ) is the set of terminals that can begin strings derived from γ.
- FOLLOW(X) is the set of terminals that can immediately follow X. That is, $t \in$ FOLLOW(X) if there is any derivation containing Xt. This can occur if the derivation contains $XYZt$ where Y and Z both derive ϵ.

A precise definition of FIRST, FOLLOW, and nullable is that they are the smallest sets for which these properties hold:

For each terminal symbol Z, FIRST[Z] = $\{Z\}$.

for each production $X \rightarrow Y_1 Y_2 \cdots Y_k$

    for each i from 1 to k, each j from $i + 1$ to k,

        if all the Y_i are nullable

          then nullable[X] = true

        if $Y_1 \cdots Y_{i-1}$ are all nullable

          then FIRST[X] = FIRST[X] $\cup$ FIRST[Y_i]

        if $Y_{i+1} \cdots Y_k$ are all nullable

          then FOLLOW[Y_i] = FOLLOW[Y_i] $\cup$ FOLLOW[X]

        if $Y_{i+1} \cdots Y_{j-1}$ are all nullable

          then FOLLOW[Y_i] = FOLLOW[Y_i] $\cup$ FIRST[Y_j]

The algorithm for computing FIRST, FOLLOW, and nullable just follows from these facts; we simply replace each equation with an assignment statement, and iterate:

Algorithm to compute FIRST, FOLLOW, *and* nullable.

Initialize FIRST and FOLLOW to all empty sets, and nullable to all false.

for each terminal symbol Z

    FIRST[Z] $\leftarrow \{Z\}$

repeat

    for each production $X \rightarrow Y_1 Y_2 \cdots Y_k$

      for each i from 1 to k, each j from $i + 1$ to k,

        if all the Y_i are nullable

          then nullable[X] $\leftarrow$ true

        if $Y_1 \cdots Y_{i-1}$ are all nullable

          then FIRST[X] $\leftarrow$ FIRST[X] $\cup$ FIRST[Y_i]

        if $Y_{i+1} \cdots Y_k$ are all nullable

          then FOLLOW[Y_i] $\leftarrow$ FOLLOW[Y_i] $\cup$ FOLLOW[X]

      if $Y_{i+1} \cdots Y_{j-1}$ are all nullable

          then FOLLOW[Y_i] $\leftarrow$ FOLLOW[Y_i] $\cup$ FIRST[Y_j]

until FIRST, FOLLOW, and nullable did not change in this iteration.

Of course, to make this algorithm efficient it helps to examine the productions in the right order; see Section 16.4. Also, the three relations need not be computed simultaneously; nullable can be computed by itself, then FIRST, then FOLLOW.

This is not the first time that a group of equations on sets has become the algorithm for calculating those sets; recall the algorithm on page 28 for computing ϵ-closure. Nor will it be the last time; the technique of iteration to a fixed point is applicable in dataflow analysis for optimization, in the back end of a compiler.

We can apply this algorithm to Grammar 3.12. Initially, we have:

	nullable	FIRST	FOLLOW
X	no		
Y	no		
Z	no		

In the first iteration, we find that $a \in$ FIRST$[X]$, Y is nullable, $c \in$ FIRST$[Y]$, $d \in$ FIRST$[Z]$, $d \in$ FOLLOW$[X]$, $c \in$ FOLLOW$[X]$, $d \in$ FOLLOW$[Y]$. Thus:

	nullable	FIRST	FOLLOW
X	no	a	c d
Y	yes	c	d
Z	no	d	

In the second iteration, we find that X is nullable, $c \in$ FIRST$[X]$, $\{a, c\} \subseteq$ FIRST$[Z]$, $\{a, c, d\} \subseteq$ FOLLOW$[X]$, $\{a, c, d\} \subseteq$ FOLLOW$[Y]$. Thus:

	nullable	FIRST	FOLLOW
X	yes	a c	a c d
Y	yes	c	a c d
Z	no	a c d	

The third iteration finds no new information, and the algorithm terminates.

It is useful to generalize the FIRST relation to strings of symbols:

$$\text{FIRST}(X\gamma) = \text{FIRST}[X] \qquad \text{if not nullable}[X]$$
$$\text{FIRST}(X\gamma) = \text{FIRST}[X] \cup \text{FIRST}(\gamma) \quad \text{if nullable}[X]$$

and similarly, we say that a string γ is nullable if each symbol in γ is nullable.

	a	c	d
X	$X \to a$ $X \to Y$	$X \to Y$	$X \to Y$
Y	$Y \to$	$Y \to$ $Y \to c$	$Y \to$
Z	$Z \to XYZ$	$Z \to XYZ$	$Z \to d$ $Z \to XYZ$

FIGURE 3.13.   Predictive parsing table for Grammar 3.12.

CONSTRUCTING A PREDICTIVE PARSER

Consider a recursive-descent parser. The parsing function for some nonterminal X has a clause for each X-production; it must choose one of these clauses based on the next token T of the input. If we can choose the right production for each (X, T), then we can write the recursive-descent parser. All the information we need can be encoded as a two-dimensional table of productions, indexed by nonterminals X and terminals T. This is called a *predictive parsing* table.

To construct this table, enter production $X \to \gamma$ in row X, column T of the table for each $T \in \text{FIRST}(\gamma)$. Also, if γ is nullable, enter the production in row X, column T for each $T \in \text{FOLLOW}[X]$.

Figure 3.13 shows the predictive parser for Grammar 3.12. But some of the entries contain more than one entry! The presence of duplicate entries means that predictive parsing will not work on Grammar 3.12.

If we examine the grammar more closely, we find that it is ambiguous. The sentence d has many parse trees, including:

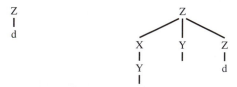

An ambiguous grammar will always lead to duplicate entries in a predictive parsing table. If we need to use the language of Grammar 3.12 as a programming language, we will need to find an unambiguous grammar.

Grammars whose predictive parsing tables contain no duplicate entries are called LL(1). This stands for *Left-to-right parse, Leftmost-derivation, 1-symbol lookahead*. Clearly a recursive-descent (predictive) parser examines the input left-to-right in one pass (some parsing algorithms do not, but these are generally not useful for compilers). The order in which a predictive parser expands nonterminals into right-hand sides (that is, the recursive-descent parser calls functions corresponding to nonterminals) is just the order in which a leftmost derivation expands nonterminals. And a recursive-descent parser does its job just by looking at the next token of the input, never looking more than one token ahead.

We can generalize the notion of FIRST sets to describe the first k tokens of a string, and to make an LL(k) parsing table whose rows are the nonterminals and columns are every sequence of k terminals. This is rarely done (because the tables are so large), but sometimes when you write a recursive-descent parser by hand you a need to look more than one token ahead.

Grammars parsable with LL(2) parsing tables are called LL(2) grammars, and similarly for LL(3), etc. Every LL(1) grammar is an LL(2) grammar, and so on. No ambiguous grammar is LL(k) for any k.

ELIMINATING LEFT RECURSION

Suppose we want to build a predictive parser for Grammar 3.10. The two productions

$$E \rightarrow E + T$$
$$E \rightarrow T$$

are certain to cause duplicate entries in the LL(1) parsing table, since any token in $\mathrm{FIRST}(T)$ will also be in $\mathrm{FIRST}(E + T)$. The problem is that E appears as the first right-hand-side symbol in an E-production; this is called *left recursion*. Grammars with left recursion cannot be LL(1).

To eliminate left recursion, we will rewrite using right recursion. We introduce a new nonterminal E', and write

$$E \rightarrow T\ E'$$

$$E' \rightarrow +\ T\ E'$$
$$E' \rightarrow$$

This derives the same set of strings (on T and +) as the original two productions, but now there is no left recursion.

In general, whenever we have productions $X \rightarrow X\gamma$ and $X \rightarrow \alpha$, where α does not start with X, we know that this derives strings of the form $\alpha\gamma*$, an

$$S \rightarrow E\ \$$$

$$E \rightarrow T\ E'$$

$$E' \rightarrow +\ T\ E'$$
$$E' \rightarrow -\ T\ E'$$
$$E' \rightarrow$$

$$T \rightarrow F\ T'$$

$$T' \rightarrow *\ F\ F'$$
$$T' \rightarrow /\ F\ F'$$
$$T' \rightarrow$$

$$F \rightarrow \text{id}$$
$$F \rightarrow \text{num}$$
$$F \rightarrow (\ E\ )$$

GRAMMAR 3.14.

	nullable	FIRST	FOLLOW
S	no	(id num	
E	no	(id num	) $
E'	yes	+ -	) $
T	no	(id num	) + - $
T'	yes	* /	) + - $
F	no	(id num	) * / + - $

TABLE 3.15.

α followed by zero or more γ. So we can rewrite the regular expression using right recursion:

$$\begin{pmatrix} X \rightarrow X\ \gamma_1 \\ X \rightarrow X\ \gamma_2 \\ X \rightarrow \alpha_1 \\ X \rightarrow \alpha_2 \end{pmatrix} \implies \begin{pmatrix} X \rightarrow \alpha_1\ X' \\ X \rightarrow \alpha_2\ X' \\ X' \rightarrow \gamma_1\ X' \\ X' \rightarrow \gamma_2\ X' \\ X' \rightarrow \end{pmatrix}$$

Applying this transformation to Grammar 3.10, we obtain Grammar 3.14.

To build a predictive parser, first we compute nullable, FIRST, and FOL-LOW (Table 3.15). The predictive parser for Grammar 3.14 is shown in Table 3.16.

LEFT FACTORING

We have seen that left recursion interferes with predictive parsing, and that it can be eliminated. A similar problem occurs when two productions for the

	+	*	id	(	)	$
S			$S \to E\$$	$S \to E\$$		
E			$E \to TE'\$$	$E \to TE'\$$		
E'	$E' \to +TE'$				$E' \to$	$E' \to$
T			$T \to FT'\$$	$T \to FT'\$$		
T'	$T' \to$	$T' \to *FT'$			$T' \to$	$T' \to$
F			$F \to$ id	$F \to ($		

TABLE 3.16.   Predictive parsing table for Grammar 3.14. We omit the columns for num, /, and -, as they are similar to others in the table.

same nonterminal X start with the same symbols. For example:

$S \to$ if E then S *else* S
$S \to$ if E then S

In such a case, we can *left factor* the grammar – that is, take the sequence if E then S and make a new nonterminal I to stand for it:

$S \ \to$ if E then S X
$X \to$
$X \to$ else S

The resulting productions will not pose a problem for a predictive parser.

ERROR RECOVERY

Armed with a predictive parsing table, it is easy to write a recursive-descent parser. Here is a representative fragment of a parser for Grammar 3.14:

```
void T(void) {switch (tok) {
     case ID:
     case NUM:
     case LPAREN:  F(); Tprime(); break;
     default:    error!
   }}

void Tprime(void) {switch (tok) {
     case PLUS:     break;
     case TIMES:    eat(TIMES); F(); Tprime(); break;
     case EOF:      break;
     case RPAREN:   break;
     default:    error!
   }}
```

A blank entry in row T, column x of the LL(1) parsing table indicates that the parsing function T() does not expect to see token x – this will be a syntax error. How should *error* be handled? It is safe just to raise an exception and quit parsing, but this is not very friendly to the user. It is better to print an error message and recover from the error, so that other syntax errors can be found in the same compilation.

A syntax error occurs when the string of input tokens is not a sentence in the language. Error recovery is a way of finding some sentence similar to that string of tokens. This can proceed by deleting, replacing, or inserting tokens.

For example, error recovery for T could proceed by inserting a num token. It's not necessary to adjust the actual input; it suffices to pretend that the num was there, print a message, and return normally.

```
void T() {switch (tok) {
    case ID:
    case NUM:
    case LPAREN: F(); Tprime(); break;
    default:  print("expected id, num, or left-paren");
  }}
```

It's a bit dangerous to do error recovery by insertion, because if the error cascades to produce another error, the process might loop infinitely. Error recovery by deletion is safer, because the loop must eventually terminate when end-of-file is reached.

Simple recovery by deletion works by skipping tokens until a token in the FOLLOW set is reached. For example, error recovery for T' could work like this:

```
int Tprime_follow [] = {PLUS, TIMES, RPAREN, EOF};

void Tprime() { switch (tok) {
    case PLUS:   break;
    case TIMES:  eat(TIMES); F(); Tprime(); break;
    case RPAREN: break;
    case EOF:    break;
    default:   print("expected +, *, right-paren,
                      or end-of-file");
             skipto(Tprime_follow);
  }}
```

A recursive-descent parser's error-recovery mechanisms must be adjusted (sometimes by trial and error) to avoid a long cascade of error-repair messages resulting from a single token out of place.

3.3   LR PARSING

The weakness of LL(k) parsing techniques is that they must *predict* which production to use, having seen only the first k tokens of the right-hand side. A more powerful technique, LR(k) parsing, is able to postpone the decision until it has seen input tokens corresponding to the entire right-hand side of the production in question (and k more input tokens beyond).

LR(k) stands for *Left-to-right parse, Rightmost-derivation, k-token lookahead.* The use of a rightmost derivation seems odd; how is that compatible with a left-to-right parse? Figure 3.17 illustrates an LR parse of the program

```
a := 7;
b := c + (d := 5 + 6, d)
```

using Grammar 3.1, augmented with a new start production $S' \rightarrow S\$$.

The parser has a *stack* and an *input*. The first k tokens of the input are the *lookahead*. Based on the contents of the stack and the lookahead, the parser performs two kinds of actions:

Shift: move the first input token to the top of the stack.
Reduce: Choose a grammar rule $X \rightarrow A\ B\ C$; pop C, B, A from the top of the stack; push X onto the stack.

Initially, the stack is empty and the parser is at the beginning of the input. The action of shifting the end-of-file marker $\$$ is called *accepting* and causes the parser to stop successfully.

In Figure 3.17, the stack and input are shown after every step, along with an indication of which action has just been performed. The concatenation of stack and input is always one line of a rightmost derivation; in fact, Figure 3.17 shows the rightmost derivation of the input string, upside-down.

LR PARSING ENGINE

How does the LR parser know when to shift and when to reduce? By using a deterministic finite automaton! The DFA is not applied to the input – finite automata are too weak to parse context-free grammars – but to the stack. The edges of the DFA are labeled by the symbols (terminals and nonterminals) that can appear on the stack. Table 3.18 is the transition table for Grammar 3.1.

The elements in the transition table are labeled with four kinds of actions:

Stack	Input	Action
$_1$	a := 7 ; b := c + (d := 5 + 6 , d) \$	*shift*
$_1$ id$_4$	:= 7 ; b := c + (d := 5 + 6 , d) \$	*shift*
$_1$ id$_4$:=$_6$	7 ; b := c + (d := 5 + 6 , d) \$	*shift*
$_1$ id$_4$:=$_6$ num$_{10}$	; b := c + (d := 5 + 6 , d) \$	*reduce* $E \to$ num
$_1$ id$_4$:=$_6$ E	; b := c + (d := 5 + 6 , d) \$	*reduce* $S \to$ id:=E
$_1$ S_2	; b := c + (d := 5 + 6 , d) \$	*shift*
$_1$ S_2 ;$_3$	b := c + (d := 5 + 6 , d) \$	*shift*
$_1$ S_2 ;$_3$ id$_4$	:= c + (d := 5 + 6 , d) \$	*shift*
$_1$ S_2 ;$_3$ id$_4$:=$_6$	c + (d := 5 + 6 , d) \$	*shift*
$_1$ S_2 ;$_3$ id$_4$:=$_6$ id$_{20}$	+ (d := 5 + 6 , d) \$	*reduce* $E \to$ id
$_1$ S_2 ;$_3$ id$_4$:=$_6$ E_{11}	+ (d := 5 + 6 , d) \$	*shift*
$_1$ S_2 ;$_3$ id$_4$:=$_6$ E_{11} +$_{16}$	(d := 5 + 6 , d) \$	*shift*
$_1$ S_2 ;$_3$ id$_4$:=$_6$ E_{11} +$_{16}$ ($_8$	d := 5 + 6 , d) \$	*shift*
$_1$ S_2 ;$_3$ id$_4$:=$_6$ E_{11} +$_{16}$ ($_8$ id$_4$	:= 5 + 6 , d) \$	*shift*
$_1$ S_2 ;$_3$ id$_4$:=$_6$ E_{11} +$_{16}$ ($_8$ id$_4$:=$_6$	5 + 6 , d) \$	*shift*
$_1$ S_2 ;$_3$ id$_4$:=$_6$ E_{11} +$_{16}$ ($_8$ id$_4$:=$_6$ num$_{10}$	+ 6 , d) \$	*reduce* $E \to$ num
$_1$ S_2 ;$_3$ id$_4$:=$_6$ E_{11} +$_{16}$ ($_8$ id$_4$:=$_6$ E_{11}	+ 6 , d) \$	*shift*
$_1$ S_2 ;$_3$ id$_4$:=$_6$ E_{11} +$_{16}$ ($_8$ id$_4$:=$_6$ E_{11} +$_{16}$	6 , d) \$	*shift*
$_1$ S_2 ;$_3$ id$_4$:=$_6$ E_{11} +$_{16}$ ($_8$ id$_4$:=$_6$ E_{11} +$_{16}$ num$_{10}$	, d) \$	*reduce* $E \to$ num
$_1$ S_2 ;$_3$ id$_4$:=$_6$ E_{11} +$_{16}$ ($_8$ id$_4$:=$_6$ E_{11} +$_{16}$ E_{17}	, d) \$	*reduce* $E \to E + E$
$_1$ S_2 ;$_3$ id$_4$:=$_6$ E_{11} +$_{16}$ ($_8$ id$_4$:=$_6$ E_{11}	, d) \$	*reduce* $S \to$ id:=E
$_1$ S_2 ;$_3$ id$_4$:=$_6$ E_{11} +$_{16}$ ($_8$ S_{12}	, d) \$	*shift*
$_1$ S_2 ;$_3$ id$_4$:=$_6$ E_{11} +$_{16}$ ($_8$ S_{12} ,$_{18}$	d) \$	*shift*
$_1$ S_2 ;$_3$ id$_4$:=$_6$ E_{11} +$_{16}$ ($_8$ S_{12} ,$_{18}$ id$_4$	) \$	*reduce* $E \to$ id
$_1$ S_2 ;$_3$ id$_4$:=$_6$ E_{11} +$_{16}$ ($_8$ S_{12} ,$_{18}$ E_{21}	) \$	*shift*
$_1$ S_2 ;$_3$ id$_4$:=$_6$ E_{11} +$_{16}$ ($_8$ S_{12} ,$_{18}$ E_{21})$_{22}$	\$	*reduce* $E \to (S; E)$
$_1$ S_2 ;$_3$ id$_4$:=$_6$ E_{11} +$_{16}$ E_{17}	\$	*reduce* $E \to E + E$
$_1$ S_2 ;$_3$ id$_4$:=$_6$ E_{11}	\$	*reduce* $S \to$ id:=E
$_1$ S_2 ;$_3$ S_5	\$	*reduce* $S \to S; S$
$_1$ S_2	\$	*accept*

FIGURE 3.17. Shift-reduce parse of a sentence. Numeric subscripts in the *Stack* are DFA state numbers; see Table 3.18.

sn	Shift into state n;
gn	Goto state n;
rk	Reduce by rule k;
a	Accept;
	Error (denoted by a blank entry in the table).

To use this table in parsing, treat the shift and goto actions as edges of a DFA, and scan the stack. For example, if the stack is id := E, then the DFA goes from state 1 to 4 to 6 to 11. If the next input token is a semicolon, then the ";" column in state 11 says to reduce by rule 2. The second rule of the grammar is $S \to$ id:=E, so the top three tokens are popped from the stack

	id	num	print	;	,	+	:=	(	)	$	S	E	L
1	s4		s7								g2		
2				s3						a			
3	s4		s7								g5		
4							s6						
5				r1	r1					r1			
6	s20	s10						s8				g11	
7								s9					
8	s4		s7								g12		
9												g15	g14
10				r5	r5	r5			r5	r5			
11				r2	r2	s16				r2			
12				s3	s18								
13				r3	r3					r3			
14					s19				s13				
15					r8				r8				
16	s20	s10						s8				g17	
17				r6	r6	s16			r6	r6			
18	s20	s10						s8				g21	
19	s20	s10						s8				g23	
20				r4	r4	r4			r4	r4			
21									s22				
22				r7	r7	r7			r7	r7			
23					r9	s16			r9				

TABLE 3.18.   LR parsing table for Grammar 3.1.

and S is pushed.

The action for "+" in state 11 is to shift; so if the next token had been + instead, it would have been eaten from the input and pushed on the stack.

Rather than rescan the stack for each token, the parser can remember instead the state reached for each stack element. Then the parsing algorithm is:

Look up top stack state, and input symbol, to get action;

If action is

Shift(n):   Advance input one token; push n on stack.

Reduce(k): Pop stack as many times as the number of symbols on the right-hand side of rule k;
Let X be the left-hand-side symbol of rule k;
In the state now on top of stack, look up X to get "goto n";
Push n on top of stack.

Accept: Stop parsing, report success.

Error: Stop parsing, report failure.

$_0$ $S' \rightarrow S\$$

$_3$ $L \rightarrow S$

$_1$ $S \rightarrow (L)$

$_4$ $L \rightarrow L , S$

$_2$ $S \rightarrow x$

GRAMMAR 3.19.

LR(0) PARSER GENERATION

An LR(k) parser uses the contents of its stack and the next k tokens of the input to decide which action to take. Table 3.18 shows the use of one symbol of lookahead. For $k = 2$, the table has columns for every two-token sequence and so on; in practice, $k > 1$ is not used for compilation. This is partly because the tables would be huge, but more because most reasonable programming languages can be described by $LR(1)$ grammars.

LR(0) grammars are those that can be parsed looking only at the stack, making shift/reduce decisions without any lookahead. Though this class of grammars is too weak to be very useful, the algorithm for constructing LR(0) parsing tables is a good introduction to the LR(1) parser construction algorithm.

We will use Grammar 3.19 to illustrate LR(0) parser generation. Consider what the parser for this grammar will be doing. Initially, it will have an empty stack, and the input will be a complete S-sentence followed by $\$$; that is, the right-hand side of the S' rule will be on the input. We indicate this as $S' \rightarrow .S\$$ where the dot indicates the current position of the parser.

In this state, where the input begins with S, that means that it begins with any possible right-hand side of an S-production; we indicate that by

$$
\boxed{
\begin{array}{l}
S' \rightarrow .S\$ \\
S \rightarrow .x \\
S \rightarrow .(L)
\end{array}
}
\quad 1
$$

Call this state 1. A grammar rule, combined with the dot that indicates a position in its right-hand side, is called an *item* (specifically, an *LR(0) item*). A state is just a set of items.

Shift actions. In state 1, consider what happens if we shift an x. We then know that the end of the stack has an x; we indicate that by shifting the dot past the x in the $S \rightarrow x$ production. The rules $S' \rightarrow .S\$$ and $S \rightarrow .(L)$ are irrelevant to this action, so we ignore them; we end up in state 2:

$$\boxed{S \rightarrow x.}^{\,2}$$

Or in state 1 consider shifting a left parenthesis. Moving the dot past the parenthesis in the third item yields $S \rightarrow (.L)$, where we know that there must be a left parenthesis on top of the stack, and the input begins with some string derived by L, followed by a right parenthesis. What tokens can begin the input now? We find out by including all L-productions in the set of items. But now, in one of those L-items, the dot is just before an S, so we need to include all the S-productions:

$$\boxed{\begin{array}{l} L \rightarrow (.L) \\ L \rightarrow .L, S \\ L \rightarrow .S \\ S \rightarrow .(L) \\ S \rightarrow .x \end{array}}^{\,3}$$

Goto actions. In state 1, consider the effect of parsing past some string of tokens derived by the S nonterminal. This will happen when an x or left-parenthesis is shifted, followed (eventually) by a reduction of an S-production. All the right-hand-side symbols of that production will be popped, and the parser will execute the *goto* action for S in state 1. The effect of this can be simulated by moving the dot past the S in the first item of state 1, yielding state 4:

$$\boxed{S' \rightarrow S.\$}^{\,4}$$

Reduce actions. In state 2 we find the dot at the end of an item. This means that on top of the stack there must be a complete right-hand side of the corresponding production $(S \rightarrow x)$, ready to reduce. In such a state the parser could perform a reduce action.

The basic operations we have been performing on states are **closure**(I), and **goto**(I, X), where I is a set of items and X is a grammar symbol (terminal or nonterminal). **Closure** adds more items to a set of items when there is a dot to the left of a nonterminal; **goto** moves the dot past the symbol X in all items.

Closure(I) =
    repeat
        for any item $A \rightarrow \alpha.X\beta$ in I
            for any production $X \rightarrow \gamma$
                $I \leftarrow I \cup \{X \rightarrow .\gamma\}$
    until I does not change.
    return I

Goto(I, X) =
    set J to the empty set
    for any item $A \rightarrow \alpha.X\beta$ in I
        add $A \rightarrow \alpha X.\beta$ to J
    return Closure(J)

Now here is the algorithm for LR(0) parser construction. First, augment the grammar with an auxiliary start production $S' \rightarrow S\$$. Let T be the set of states seen so far, and E the set of (shift or goto) edges found so far.

Initialize T to $\{\mathbf{Closure}(\{S' \rightarrow .S\$\})\}$

Initialize E to empty.

repeat
        for each state I in T
            for each item $A \rightarrow \alpha.X\beta$ in I
                let J be **goto**(I, X)
                $T \leftarrow T \cup \{J\}$
                $E \leftarrow E \cup \{I \xrightarrow{X} J\}$
    until E and T did not change in this iteration

However, for the symbol $\$$ we do not compute **goto**($I, \$$); instead we will make an **accept** action.

For Grammar 3.19 this is illustrated in Figure 3.20.

Now we can compute set R of LR(0) reduce actions:

$R \leftarrow \{\}$
for each state I in T
    for each item $A \rightarrow \alpha.$ in I
        $R \leftarrow R \cup \{(I, A \rightarrow \alpha)\}$

We can now construct a parsing table for this grammar (Table 3.21). For each edge $I \xrightarrow{X} J$ where X is a terminal, we put the action *shift* J at position (I, X) of the table; if X is a nonterminal we put *goto* J at position (I, X). For each state I containing an item $S' \rightarrow S.\$$ we put an *accept* action at $(I, \$)$. Finally, for a state containing an item $A \rightarrow \gamma.$ (production n with the dot at the end), we put a *reduce* n action at (I, Y) for every token Y.

In principle, since LR(0) needs no lookahead, we just need a single action for each state: a state will shift or reduce, but not both. In practice, since we

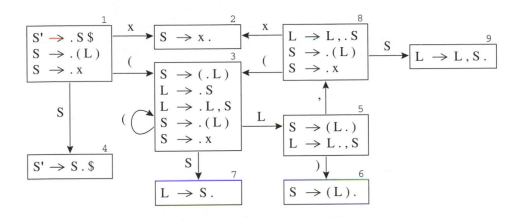

FIGURE 3.20.   LR(0) states for Grammar 3.19.

	(	)	x	,	$	S	L
1	s3		s2			g4	
2	r2	r2	r2	r2	r2		
3	s3		s2			g7	g5
4					a		
5		s6		s8			
6	r1	r1	r1	r1	r1		
7	r3	r3	r3	r3	r3		
8	s3		s2				g9
9	r4	r4	r4	r4	r4		

TABLE 3.21.   LR(0) parsing table for Grammar 3.19.

$_0$ $S \rightarrow E \, \$$ $_2$ $T \rightarrow (\, E \,)$

$_1$ $E \rightarrow E + T$ $_3$ $T \rightarrow x$

GRAMMAR 3.22.

need to know what state to shift into, we have rows headed by state numbers and columns headed by grammar symbols.

SLR PARSER GENERATION

Let us attempt to build an LR(0) parsing table for Grammar 3.22. The LR(0) states and parsing table are shown in Figure 3.23.

In state 3, on symbol +, there is a duplicate entry: the parser must shift into state 4 and also reduce by production 2. This is a conflict and indicates that

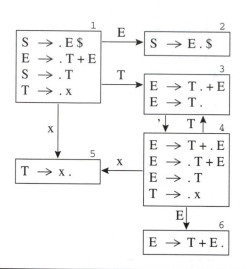

	x	+	$	E	T
1	s5			g2	g3
2			a		
3	r2	s4,r2	r2		
4	s5			g6	g3
5	r3	r3	r3		
6	r1	r1	r1		

FIGURE 3.23.   LR(0) states and parsing table for Grammar 3.22.

the grammar is not LR(0) – it cannot be parsed by an LR(0) parser. We will need a more powerful parsing algorithm.

A simple way of constructing better-than-LR(0) parsers is called SLR, which stands for Simple LR. Parser construction for SLR is almost identical to that for LR(0), except that we put reduce actions into the table only where indicated by the FOLLOW set.

Here is the algorithm for putting reduce actions into an SLR table:

$$R \leftarrow \{\}$$
for each state I in T
    for each item $A \rightarrow \alpha.$ in I
        for each token X in $\text{FOLLOW}(A)$
            $R \leftarrow R \cup \{(I, X, A \rightarrow \alpha)\}$

The action $(I, z, A \rightarrow \alpha)$ indicates that in state I, on lookahead symbol z, the parser will reduce by rule $A \rightarrow \alpha$.

Thus, for Grammar 3.22 we use the same LR(0) state diagram (Figure 3.23), but we put fewer reduce actions into the SLR table, as shown in Figure 3.24.

The SLR class of grammars is precisely those grammars whose SLR parsing table contains no conflicts (duplicate entries). Grammar 3.22 belongs to this class, as do many useful programming-language grammars.

	x	+	$	E	T
1	s5			g2	g3
2			a		
3		s4	r2		
4	s5			g6	g3
5		r3	r3		
6			r1		

FIGURE 3.24.   SLR parsing table for Grammar 3.22.

LR(1) ITEMS; LR(1) PARSING TABLE

Even more powerful than SLR is the LR(1) parsing algorithm. Most programming languages whose syntax is describable by a context-free grammar have an LR(1) grammar.

The algorithm for constructing an LR(1) parsing table is similar to that for LR(0), but the notion of an *item* is more sophisticated. An LR(1) item consists of a *grammar production*, a *right-hand-side position* (represented by the dot), and a *lookahead symbol*. The idea is that an item $(A \rightarrow \alpha.\beta, \ x)$ indicates that the sequence α is on top of the stack, and at the head of the input is a string derivable from βx.

An LR(1) state is a set of LR(1) items, and there are **closure** and **goto** operations for LR(1) that incorporate the lookahead:

Closure$(I) =$
  repeat
    for any item $(A \rightarrow \alpha.X\beta, z)$ in I
      for any production $X \rightarrow \gamma$
        for any $w \in \text{FIRST}(\beta z)$
          $I \leftarrow I \cup \{(X \rightarrow .\gamma, \ w)\}$
  until I does not change
  return I

Goto$(I, X) =$
  set J to the empty set
  for any item $(A \rightarrow \alpha.X\beta, \ z)$ in I
    add $(A \rightarrow \alpha X.\beta, \ z)$ to J
  return Closure(J).

The start state is the closure of the item $(S' \rightarrow .S \$, \ ?)$, where the lookahead symbol ? will not matter, because the end-of-file marker will never be shifted. The reduce actions are chosen by this algorithm:

$R \leftarrow \{\}$
for each state I in T
  for each item $(A \rightarrow \alpha. \ , \ z)$ in I
    $R \leftarrow R \cup \{(I, z, A \rightarrow \alpha)\}$

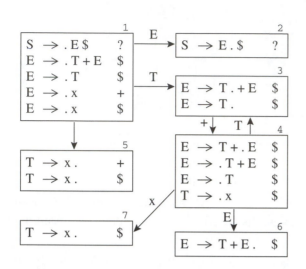

	x	+	$	E	T
1	s5			g2	g3
2			a		
3		s4	r2		
4	s7			g6	g3
5		r3	r3		
6			r1		
7			r3		

FIGURE 3.25.   LR(1) states and parsing table for Grammar 3.22.

The action $(I, z, A \rightarrow \alpha)$ indicates that in state I, on lookahead symbol z, the parser will reduce by rule $A \rightarrow \alpha$.

Figure 3.25 illustrates the LR(1) state diagram for Grammar 3.22.

LALR(1) PARSING TABLES

LR(1) parsing tables can be very large, with many states. A smaller table can be made by merging any two states whose items are identical except for lookahead sets. For example, the items in states 5 and 7 of the LR(1) parser for Grammar 3.22 (Figure 3.25) are identical if the lookahead sets are ignored. The result parser is called an LALR(1) parser, for *Look-Ahead LR(1)*.

Merging states 5 and 7 gives the parsing table shown in Figure 3.24. For Grammar 3.22, the LALR(1) parsing table is the same as the SLR table, but this is not always the case.

HIERARCHY OF GRAMMAR CLASSES

A grammar is said to be LALR(1) if its LALR(1) parsing table contains no conflicts. All SLR grammars are LALR(1), but not vice versa. Figure 3.26 shows the relationship between several classes of grammars.

Any reasonable programming language has a LALR(1) grammar, and there are many parser-generator tools available for LALR(1) grammars. For this

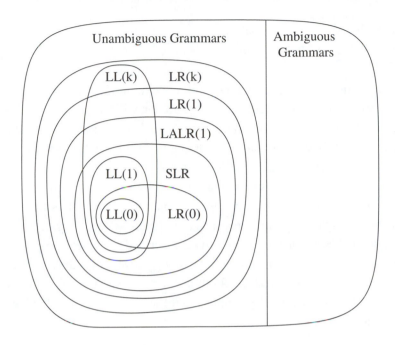

FIGURE 3.26.   A hierarchy of grammar classes.

reason, LALR(1) has become a standard for programming languages and for automatic parser generators.

LR PARSING OF AMBIGUOUS GRAMMARS

Many programming languages have grammar rules such as

$S \rightarrow$ if E then S else S
$S \rightarrow$ if E then S

which allow programs such as

```
if a then if b then s1 else s2
```

Such a program could be understood in two ways:

```
(1)        if a then { if b then s1 else s2 }
(2)        if a then { if b then s1 } else s2
```

In most programming languages, an `else` must match the most recent possible `then`, so interpretation *(1)* is correct. In the LR parsing table there will be a shift-reduce conflict:

$$\begin{array}{|ll|}
\hline
S \rightarrow \text{if } E \text{ then } S \text{ .} & \text{else} \\
S \rightarrow \text{if } E \text{ then } S \text{ . else } S & (any) \\
\hline
\end{array}$$

Shifting corresponds to interpretation *(1)* and reducing to interpretation *(2)*.

As explained on page 54, factoring the grammar will eliminate the ambiguity. But instead, we can leave the grammar unchanged and tolerate the shift-reduce conflict. In constructing the parsing table this conflict should be resolved by shifting, since we prefer interpretation *(1)*.

It is often possible to use ambiguous grammars by resolving shift-reduce conflicts in favor of shifting or reducing, as appropriate. But it is best to use this technique sparingly, and only in cases (such as the *dangling-else* described here, and operator-precedence to be described on page 72) that are well understood. Most shift-reduce conflicts, and probably all reduce-reduce conflicts, should not be resolved by fiddling with the parsing table. They are symptoms of an ill-specified grammar, and they should be resolved by eliminating ambiguities.

3.4 USING PARSER GENERATORS

The task of constructing LR(1) or LALR(1) parsing tables is simple enough to be automated. And it is so tedious to do by hand that LR parsing for realistic grammars is rarely done except using parser-generator tools. *CUP* ("Construction of Useful Parsers") is one such tool, modeled on the classic *Yacc* ("Yet another compiler-compiler") parser generator.

A CUP specification has a *preamble*, which declares lists of terminal symbols, nonterminals, and so on, followed by *grammar rules*. The preamble also specifies how the parser is to be attached to a lexical analyzer and other such details.

The *grammar rules* are productions of the form

```
exp ::=    exp PLUS exp    { : semantic action : }
```

where `exp` is a nonterminal producing a right-hand side of `exp+exp`, and `PLUS` is a terminal symbol (token). The *semantic action* is written in ordinary Java and will be executed whenever the parser reduces using this rule.

Consider Grammar 3.27. It can be encoded in CUP as shown in Grammar 3.28. The CUP manual gives a complete explanation of the directives

$$1 \quad P \rightarrow L$$

$$2 \quad S \rightarrow \text{id} := \text{id}$$
$$3 \quad S \rightarrow \text{while id do } S$$
$$4 \quad S \rightarrow \text{begin } S \text{ end}$$
$$5 \quad S \rightarrow \text{if id then } S$$
$$6 \quad S \rightarrow \text{if id then } S \text{ else } S$$

$$7 \quad L \rightarrow S$$
$$8 \quad L \rightarrow L \, ; \, S$$

GRAMMAR 3.27.

```
terminal ID, WHILE, BEGIN, END, DO, IF, THEN, ELSE, SEMI, ASSIGN;

non terminal  prog, stm, stmlist;

start with   prog;

prog ::=  stmlist;

stm ::= ID ASSIGN ID
      |    WHILE ID DO stm
      |    BEGIN stmlist END
      |    IF ID THEN stm
      |    IF ID THEN stm ELSE stm;

stmlist ::= stm
          |    stmlist SEMI stm;
```

GRAMMAR 3.28. CUP version of Grammar 3.27. Semantic actions are omitted and will be discussed in Chapter 4.

in a grammar specification; in this grammar, the terminal symbols are ID, WHILE, etc.; the nonterminals are prog, stm, stmlist; and the grammar's start symbol is prog.

CONFLICTS

CUP reports shift-reduce and reduce-reduce conflicts. A shift-reduce conflict is a choice between shifting and reducing; a reduce-reduce conflict is a choice of reducing by two different rules. By default, CUP resolves shift-reduce conflicts by shifting, and reduce-reduce conflicts by using the rule that appears earlier in the grammar.

CUP will report that this Grammar 3.27 has a shift-reduce conflict. Any conflict is cause for concern, because it may indicate that the parse will not be

state 0:
  prog ::= . stmlist

  ID   shift 6
  WHILE shift 5
  BEGIN shift 4
  IF   shift 3
  prog   goto 21
  stm   goto 2
  stmlist goto 1
  .   error

state 1:
  prog ::= stmlist .
  stmlist ::= stmlist . SEMI stm

  SEMI   shift 7
  .   reduce by rule 0

state 2:
  stmlist ::= stm .

  .   reduce by rule 6

state 3:
  stm ::= IF . ID THEN stm
  stm ::= IF . ID THEN stm ELSE stm

  ID   shift 8
  .   error

state 4:
  stm ::= BEGIN . stmlist END

  ID   shift 6
  WHILE shift 5
  BEGIN shift 4
  IF   shift 3
  stm   goto 2
  stmlist goto 9
  .   error

state 5:
  stm ::= WHILE . ID DO stm

  ID   shift 10
  .   error

state 6:
  stm ::= ID . ASSIGN ID

  ASSIGN shift 11
  .   error

state 7:
  stmlist ::= stmlist SEMI . stm

  ID   shift 6
  WHILE shift 5
  BEGIN shift 4
  IF   shift 3
  stm   goto 12
  .   error

state 8:
  stm ::= IF ID . THEN stm
  stm ::= IF ID . THEN stm ELSE stm

  THEN   shift 13
  .   error

state 9:
  stm ::= BEGIN stmlist . END
  stmlist ::= stmlist . SEMI stm

  END   shift 14
  SEMI   shift 7
  .   error

state 10:
  stm ::= WHILE ID . DO stm

  DO   shift 15
  .   error

state 11:
  stm ::= ID ASSIGN . ID

  ID   shift 16
  .   error

state 12:
  stmlist ::= stmlist SEMI stm .
  .   reduce by rule 7

state 13:
  stm ::= IF ID THEN . stm
  stm ::= IF ID THEN . stm ELSE stm

  ID   shift 6
  WHILE shift 5
  BEGIN shift 4
  IF   shift 3
  stm   goto 17
  .   error

state 14:
  stm ::= BEGIN stmlist END .

  .   reduce by rule 3

state 15:
  stm ::= WHILE ID DO . stm

  ID   shift 6
  WHILE shift 5
  BEGIN shift 4
  IF   shift 3
  stm   goto 18
  .   error

state 16:
  stm ::= ID ASSIGN ID .

  .   reduce by rule 1

state 17: **shift/reduce conflict**
                      (shift ELSE, reduce 4)
  stm ::= IF ID THEN stm .
  stm ::= IF ID THEN stm . ELSE stm

  ELSE   shift 19
  .   reduce by rule 4

state 18:
  stm ::= WHILE ID DO stm .

  .   reduce by rule 2

state 19:
  stm ::= IF ID THEN stm ELSE . stm

  ID   shift 6
  WHILE shift 5
  BEGIN shift 4
  IF   shift 3
  stm   goto 20
  .   error

state 20:
  stm ::= IF ID THEN stm ELSE stm .

  .   reduce by rule 5

state 21:

  EOF   accept
  .   error

FIGURE 3.29.   LR states for Grammar 3.27.

	id	num	+	-	*	/	(	)	$	E
1	s2	s3					s4			g7
2			r1	r1	r1	r1		r1	r1	
3			r2	r2	r2	r2		r2	r2	
4	s2	s3					s4			g5
5								s6		
6			r7	r7	r7	r7		r7	r7	
7			s8	s10	s12	s14			a	
8	s2	s3					s4			g9
9			s8,r5	s10,r5	s12,r5	s14,r5		r5	r5	
10	s2	s3					s4			g11
11			s8,r6	s10,r6	s12,r6	s14,r6		r6	r6	
12	s2	s3					s4			g13
13			s8,r3	s10,r3	s12,r3	s14,r3		r3	r3	
14	s2	s3					s4			g15
15			s8,r4	s10,r4	s12,r4	s14,r4		r4	r4	

TABLE 3.30.   LR parsing table for Grammar 3.5.

as the grammar-designer expected. The conflict can be examined by reading the verbose description file that CUP produces. Figure 3.29 shows this file.

A brief examination of state 17 reveals that the conflict is caused by the familiar dangling `else`. Since CUP's default resolution of shift-reduce conflicts is to shift, and shifting gives the desired result of binding an `else` to the nearest `then`, this conflict is not harmful.

Shift-reduce conflicts are acceptable in a grammar if they correspond to well understood cases, as in this example. But most shift-reduce conflicts, and all reduce-reduce conflicts, are serious problems and should be eliminated by rewriting the grammar.

PRECEDENCE DIRECTIVES

No ambiguous grammar is LR(k) for any k; the LR(k) parsing table of an ambiguous grammar will always have conflicts. However, ambiguous grammars can still be useful if we can find ways to resolve the conflicts.

For example, Grammar 3.5 is highly ambiguous. In using this grammar to describe a programming language, we intend it to be parsed so that $*$ and $/$ bind more tightly than $+$ and $-$, and that each operator associates to the left. We can express this by rewriting the unambiguous Grammar 3.8.

But we can avoid introducing the T and F symbols and their associated "trivial" reductions $E \rightarrow T$ and $T \rightarrow F$. Instead, let us start by building the LR(1) parsing table for Grammar 3.5, as shown in Table 3.30. We find many conflicts. For example, in state 13 with lookahead $+$ we find a conflict between *shift into state 8* and *reduce by rule 3*. Two of the items in state 13 are:

$$E \rightarrow E * E \,. \qquad +$$
$$E \rightarrow E \,.\, + E \qquad (any)$$

In this state the top of the stack is $\cdots E * E$. Shifting will lead to a stack $\cdots E * E+$ and eventually $\cdots E * E + E$ with a reduction of $E + E$ to E. Reducing now will lead to the stack $\cdots E$ and then the $+$ will be shifted. The parse trees obtained by shifting and reducing are:

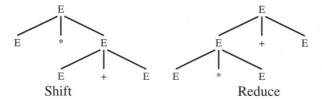

Shift   Reduce

If we wish $*$ to bind tighter than $+$, we should reduce instead of shift. So we fill the $(13, +)$ entry in the table with r3 and discard the s8 action.

Conversely, in state 9 on lookahead $*$, we should shift instead of reduce, so we resolve the conflict by filling the $(9, *)$ entry with s12.

The case for state 9, lookahead $+$ is

$$E \rightarrow E + E \,. \qquad +$$
$$E \rightarrow E \,.\, + E \qquad (any)$$

Shifting will make the operator right-associative; reducing will make it left-associative. Since we want left associativity, we fill $(9, +)$ with r5.

Consider the expression $a - b - c$. In most programming languages, this associates to the left, as if written $(a - b) - c$. But suppose we believe that this expression is inherently confusing, and we want to force the programmer to put in explicit parentheses, either $(a - b) - c$ or $a - (b - c)$. Then we say that the minus operator is *nonassociative*, and we would fill the $(11, -)$ entry with an error entry.

The result of all these decisions is a parsing table with all conflicts resolved (Table 3.31).

CUP has *precedence directives* to indicate the resolution of this class of shift-reduce conflicts. A series of declarations such as

	+	-	*	/
		$\vdots$		
9	r5	r5	s12	s14
11			s12	s14
13	r3	r3	r3	r3
15	r4	r4		
		$\vdots$		

(Row 9 and 11 flanked by $\cdots$ on both sides)

TABLE 3.31. Conflicts of Table 3.30 resolved.

```
precedence nonassoc EQ, NEQ;
precedence left PLUS, MINUS;
precedence left TIMES, DIV;
precedence right EXP;
```

indicates that + and – are left-associative and bind equally tightly; that * and / are left-associative and bind more tightly than +; that ˆ is right-associative and binds most tightly; and that = and $\neq$ are nonassociative, and bind more weakly than +.

In examining a shift-reduce conflict such as

$$
\begin{array}{ll}
E \rightarrow E * E . & + \\
E \rightarrow E . + E & (any)
\end{array}
$$

there is the choice of shifting by a *token* and reducing by a *rule*. Should the rule or the token be given higher priority? The precedence declarations (precedence left, etc.) give priorities to the tokens; the priority of a rule is given by the last token occurring on the right-hand side of that rule. Thus the choice here is between a rule with priority * and a token with priority +; the rule has higher priority, so the conflict is resolved in favor of reducing.

When the rule and token have equal priority, then a left precedence favors reducing, right favors shifting, and nonassoc yields an error action.

Instead of using the default "rule has precedence of its last token," we can assign a specific precedence to a rule using the %prec directive. This is commonly used to solve the "unary minus" problem. In most programming languages a unary minus binds tighter than any binary operator, so $-6 * 8$ is parsed as $(-6) * 8$, not $-(6 * 8)$. Grammar 3.32 shows an example.

The token UMINUS is never returned by the lexer; it is merely a placeholder in the chain of precedence declarations. The directive %prec UMINUS gives

```
terminal    INT, PLUS, MINUS, TIMES, UMINUS;
non terminal    exp;
start with    exp;

precedence left PLUS, MINUS;
precedence left TIMES;
precedence left UMINUS;

exp  ::=  INT
      |    exp PLUS exp
      |    exp MINUS exp
      |    exp TIMES exp
      |    MINUS exp %prec UMINUS;
```

GRAMMAR 3.32.

the rule `exp::= MINUS exp` the highest precedence, so reducing by this rule takes precedence over shifting any operator, even a minus sign.

Precedence rules are helpful in resolving conflicts, but they should not be abused. If you have trouble explaining the effect of a clever use of precedence rules, perhaps instead you should rewrite the grammar to be unambiguous.

SYNTAX VERSUS SEMANTICS

Consider a programming language with *arithmetic expressions* such as $x + y$ and *boolean expressons* such as $x+y = z$ or $a\&(b = c)$. Arithmetic operators bind tighter than the boolean operators; there are arithmetic variables and boolean variables; and a boolean expression cannot be added to an arithmetic expression. Grammar 3.33 gives a syntax for this language.

The grammar has a reduce-reduce conflict, as shown in Figure 3.34. How should we rewrite the grammar to eliminate this conflict?

Here the problem is that when the parser sees an identifier such as a, it has no way of knowing whether this is an arithmetic variable or a boolean variable – syntactically they look identical. The solution is to defer this analysis until the "semantic" phase of the compiler; it's not a problem that can be handled naturally with context-free grammars. A more appropriate grammar is:

$$S \to \text{id} := \text{id}$$

$$E \to \text{id}$$
$$E \to E \& E$$
$$E \to E = E$$
$$E \to E + E$$

```
terminal ID, ASSIGN, PLUS, MINUS, AND, EQUAL;
non terminal  stm, be, ae;
start with stm;
precedence left OR;
precedence left AND;
precedence left PLUS;

stm ::= ID ASSIGN ae
     |   ID ASSIGN be;

be  ::= be OR be
     |    be AND be
     |    ae EQUAL ae
     |    ID;

ae  ::= ae PLUS ae
     |    ID
```

GRAMMAR 3.33.

Now the expression $a + 5\&b$ is syntactically legal, and a later phase of the compiler will have to reject it and print a semantic error message.

PROGRAM   PARSING

Use CUP to implement a parser for the Tiger language. Appendix A describes, among other things, the syntax of Tiger.

You should turn in the file tiger.grm and a README.

Supporting files available in $TIGER/chap3 include:

makefile The "makefile."

ErrorMsg/ErrorMsg.java The ErrorMsg class, useful for producing error messages with file names and line numbers.

Parse/Yylex.class The lexical analyzer. I haven't provided the source file, but I've compiled it so you will be able to use the .class file if your lexer isn't working.

Parsetest.java A driver to run your parser on an input file.

java_cup/runtime/* Support files for CUP parser.

java_cup/Main.java The CUP parser generator.

Grm.cup The skeleton of a Tiger parser specification you must fill in.

The sym.java file will be automatically produced by CUP from the token specification of your grammar.

Your grammar should have as few shift-reduce conflicts as possible, and

state 0:
  stm ::= . ID ASSIGN ae
  stm ::= . ID ASSIGN be

ID   shift 1
stm   goto 14
.   error

state 1:
  stm ::= ID . ASSIGN ae
  stm ::= ID . ASSIGN be

ASSIGN shift 2
.   error

state 2:
  stm ::= ID ASSIGN . ae
  stm ::= ID ASSIGN . be

ID   shift 5
be   goto 4
ae   goto 3
.   error

state 3:
  stm ::= ID ASSIGN ae .
  be ::= ae . EQUAL ae
  ae ::= ae . PLUS ae

PLUS   shift 7
EQUAL shift 6
.   reduce by rule 0

state 4:
  stm ::= ID ASSIGN be .
  be ::= be . AND be

AND   shift 8
.   reduce by rule 1

state 5: reduce/reduce conflict
      between rule 6 and
      rule 4 on EOF
  be ::= ID .
  ae ::= ID .

PLUS   reduce by rule 6
AND   reduce by rule 4
EQUAL reduce by rule 6
EOF   reduce by rule 4
.   error

state 6:
  be ::= ae EQUAL . ae

ID   shift 10
ae   goto 9
.   error

state 7:
  ae ::= ae PLUS . ae

ID   shift 10
ae   goto 11
.   error

state 8:
  be ::= be AND . be

ID   shift 5
be   goto 13
ae   goto 12
.   error

state 9:
  be ::= ae EQUAL ae .
  ae ::= ae . PLUS ae

PLUS   shift 7
.   reduce by rule 3

state 10:
  ae ::= ID .

.   reduce by rule 6

state 11:
  ae ::= ae . PLUS ae
  ae ::= ae PLUS ae .

.   reduce by rule 5

state 12:
  be ::= ae . EQUAL ae
  ae ::= ae . PLUS ae

PLUS   shift 7
EQUAL shift 6
.   error

state 13:
  be ::= be . AND be
  be ::= be AND be .

.   reduce by rule 2

state 14:

EOF   accept
.   error

FIGURE 3.34.   LR states for Grammar 3.33.

no reduce-reduce conflicts. Furthermore, your accompanying documentation should list each shift-reduce conflict (if any) and explain why it is not harmful.

My grammar has one shift-reduce conflict, by the way. It is related to the confusion between

    variable [expression]
    type-id [expression] **of** expression

In fact, I had to add a seemingly redundant grammar rule to handle this confusion. Perhaps there is a way to do this that does not produce a shift-reduce conflict.

Use the `precedence` directives (`left`, `nonassoc`, `right`) *when it is straightforward to do so.*

Do not attach any semantic actions to your grammar rules for this exercise.

EXERCISES

3.1 Translate each of these regular expressions into a context-free grammar.

a. $((xy^*x)|(yx^*y))$?

b. $((0|1)^+\text{"}.\text{"}(0|1)^*)|((0|1)^*\text{"}.\text{"}(0|1)^+)$

3.2 Write a grammar for English sentences using the words `time`, `arrow`, `banana`, `flies`, `like`, `a`, `an`, `the`, `fruit` and the semicolon. Be sure to include all the senses (noun, verb, etc.) of each word. Then show that this grammar is ambiguous by exhibiting more than one parse tree for "time flies like an arrow; fruit flies like a banana."

3.3 Write an unambigous grammar for each of the following languages. Hint: One way of verifying that a grammar is unambiguous is to run it through Yacc and get no conflicts.

a. Palindromes over the alphabet $\{a, b\}$ (strings that are the same backward and forward).

b. Strings that match the regular expression $a * b*$ and have more a's than b's.

c. Balanced parentheses and square brackets. Example: `([] (()[()][]))`.

*d. Balanced parentheses and square brackets, where a closing square bracket also closes any outstanding open parentheses (up to the previous open square bracket). Example: `[([] (() [(][])]`. Hint: First, make the language of balanced parentheses and square brackets, where extra open parentheses are allowed; then make sure this nonterminal must appear within square brackets.

e. All subsets and permutations of the keywords `public final static synchronized transient`. (Then comment on how best to handle this situation in a real compiler.)

f. Statement blocks in Pascal or ML where the semicolons *separate* the statements:

    `( statement ; ( statement ; statement ) ; statement )`

g. Statement blocks in C where the semicolons *terminate* the statements:

    `{ expression; { expression; expression; } expression; }`

3.4 Write a grammar that accepts the same language as Grammar 3.1, but that is suitable for LL(1) parsing. That is, eliminate the ambiguity, eliminate the left-recursion, and (if necessary) left-factor.

3.5 Find nullable, FIRST, and FOLLOW sets for this grammar; then construct the LL(1) parsing table.

0 $S' \rightarrow S \,\$$

1 $S \rightarrow$
2 $S \rightarrow X \, S$

3 $B \rightarrow \backslash \, \texttt{begin} \, \{ \, \texttt{WORD} \, \}$
4 $B \rightarrow \backslash \, \texttt{end} \, \{ \, \texttt{WORD} \, \}$

5 $X \rightarrow B \, S \, E$
6 $X \rightarrow \{ \, S \, \}$
7 $X \rightarrow \texttt{WORD}$
8 $X \rightarrow \texttt{begin}$
9 $X \rightarrow \texttt{end}$
10 $X \rightarrow \backslash \, \texttt{WORD}$

3.6 a. Left-factor this grammar.

0 $S \rightarrow G \,\$$
1 $G \rightarrow P$
2 $G \rightarrow P \, G$

3 $P \rightarrow \texttt{id} : R$
4 $R \rightarrow$
5 $R \rightarrow \texttt{id} \, R$

b. Show that the resulting grammar is LL(2). You can do this by constructing FIRST sets (etc.) containing two-symbol strings; but it is simpler to construct an LL(1) parsing table and then argue convincingly that any conflicts can be resolved by looking ahead one more symbol.

c. Show how the `tok` variable and `advance` function should be altered for recursive-descent parsing with two-symbol lookahead.

d. Use the grammar class hierarchy (Figure 3.26) to show that the (left-factored) grammar is LR(2).

e. Prove that no string has two parse trees according to this (left-factored) grammar.

3.7 Make up a tiny grammar containing left-recursion, and use it to demonstrate that left-recursion is not a problem for LR parsing. Then show a small example comparing growth of the LR parse stack with left-recursion versus right-recursion.

3.8 Diagram the LR(1) states for the grammar of Exercise 3.6 (without left-factoring), and construct the LR(1) parsing table. Indicate clearly any conflicts.

3.9 Construct the LR(0) states for this grammar, and then determine whether it is an SLR grammar.

0 $S' \rightarrow B \,\$$

1 $B \rightarrow \texttt{id} \, P$
2 $B \rightarrow \texttt{id} \, (\, E \,]$

3 $P \rightarrow$
4 $P \rightarrow (\, E \,)$

5 $E \rightarrow B$
6 $E \rightarrow B , E$

3.10 a. Build the LR(0) DFA for this grammar:

    0 $S \rightarrow E \; \$$

    1 $E \rightarrow \text{id}$
    2 $E \rightarrow \text{id} \; (\; E \;)$
    3 $E \rightarrow E \; + \; \text{id}$

    b. Is this an LR(0) grammar? Give evidence.

    c. Is this an SLR grammar? Give evidence.

    d. Is this an LR(1) grammar? Give evidence.

3.11 Show that this grammar is LALR(1) but not SLR:

    0 $S \rightarrow X \; \$$ 3 $X \rightarrow d \, c$
    1 $X \rightarrow M \, a$ 4 $X \rightarrow b \, d \, a$
    2 $X \rightarrow b \, M \, c$ 5 $M \rightarrow d$

3.12 Feed this grammar to Yacc; from the output description file, construct the LALR(1) parsing table for this grammar, with duplicate entries where there are conflicts. For each conflict, show whether shifting or reducing should be chosen so that the different kinds of expressions have "conventional" precedence. Then show the Yacc-style precedence directives that resolve the conflicts this way.

    0 $S \rightarrow E \; \$$

    1 $E \rightarrow \text{while } E \text{ do } E$
    2 $E \rightarrow \text{id} := E$
    3 $E \rightarrow E \; + \; E$
    4 $E \rightarrow \text{id}$

3.13 Explain how to resolve the conflicts in this grammar, using precedence directives, or grammar transformations, or both. Use CUP as a tool in your investigations, if you like.

                                  3 $B \rightarrow +$
    1 $E \rightarrow \text{id}$ 4 $B \rightarrow -$
    2 $E \rightarrow E \, B \, E$ 5 $B \rightarrow \times$
                                    6 $B \rightarrow /$

3.14 Prove that Grammar 3.8 cannot generate parse trees of the form shown in Figure 3.9. Hint: What nonterminals could possibly be where the $?X$ is shown? What does that tell us about what could be where the $?Y$ is shown?

4

Abstract Syntax

ab-stract: disassociated from any specific instance

Webster's Dictionary

A compiler must do more than recognize whether a sentence belongs to the language of a grammar – it must do something useful with that sentence. The *semantic actions* of a parser can do useful things with the phrases that are parsed.

In a recursive-descent parser, semantic action code is interspersed with the control flow of the parsing actions. In a parser specified in CUP, semantic actions are fragments of Java program code attached to grammar productions.

4.1 SEMANTIC ACTIONS

Each terminal and nonterminal may be associated with its own type of semantic value. For example, in a simple calculator using Grammar 3.32, the type associated with exp and INT might be int; the other tokens would not need to carry a value. The type associated with a token must, of course, match the type that the lexer returns with that token.

For a rule $A \to B\ C\ D$, the semantic action must return a value whose type is the one associated with the nonterminal A. But it can build this value from the values associated with the matched terminals and nonterminals B, C, D.

RECURSIVE DESCENT

In a recursive-descent parser, the semantic actions are the values returned by parsing functions, or the side effects of those functions, or both. For each terminal and nonterminal symbol, we associate a *type* (from the implementation

```
class Token {int kind; Object val;
             Token(int k, Object v) {kind=k; val=v;}
            }
final int EOF=0, ID=1, NUM=2, PLUS=3, MINUS=4,  ···

int lookup(String id) {  ···  }

int F_follow[] = { PLUS, TIMES, RPAREN, EOF };

int F() {switch (tok.kind) {
        case ID:    advance(); return lookup((String)(tok.val));
        case NUM:   advance(); return (((Integer)(tok.val)).intValue());
        case LPAREN:  eat(LPAREN);
                      int i = E();
                      eatOrSkipTo(RPAREN, F_follow);
                      return i;
        case EOF:   print("expected factor"); return 0;
        default:    print("expected +, *, left-paren, or EOF");
                    skipto(F_follow);
                    return 0;
        }}

int T_first[] = { ID, NUM, LPAREN };

int T() {switch (tok.kind) {
        case ID:
        case NUM:
        case LPAREN: return Tprime(F());
        default: print("expected ID, NUM, or left-paren");
                 skipto(T_first);
                 return 0;
        }}

int Tprime(int a) = {switch (tok.kind) {
        case TIMES: eat(TIMES); return Tprime(a*F());
        case PLUS:
        case RPAREN:
        case EOF:   return a;
        default:  ···
        }}

void eatOrSkipTo(int expected, int[] stop) {
   if (tok.kind==expected)
        eat(expected);
   else {print(···); skipto(stop);}
}
```

PROGRAM 4.1.   Recursive-descent interpreter for Grammar 3.14.

```
terminal PLUS, MINUS, TIMES, UMINUS;
terminal Integer  INT;
non terminal Exp  exp;
start with  exp;

precedence left PLUS, MINUS;
precedence left TIMES;
precedence left UMINUS;

exp  ::=  INT:i
               {: RETURN = i; :}
      |   exp:e1 PLUS exp:e2
               {: RETURN = new Integer(e1.intValue()+e2.intValue()); :}
      |   exp:e1 MINUS exp:e2
               {: RETURN = new Integer(e1.intValue()-e2.intValue()); :}
      |   exp:e1 TIMES exp:e2
               {: RETURN = new Integer(e1.intValue()*e2.intValue()); :}
      |   MINUS exp:e %prec UMINUS
               {: RETURN = new Integer(-e.intValue()); :};
```

GRAMMAR 4.2.

language of the compiler) of *semantic values* representing phrases derived from that symbol.

Program 4.1 is a recursive-descent interpreter for Grammar 3.14. The tokens ID and NUM must now carry values of type `string` and `int`, respectively. We will assume there is a lookup table mapping identifiers to integers. The type associated with E, T, F, etc. is `int`, and the semantic actions are easy to implement.

The semantic action for an artificial symbol such as T' (introduced in the elimination of left recursion) is a bit tricky. Had the production been $T \rightarrow T * F$ then the semantic action would have been

```
int a = T(); eat(TIMES); int b=F(); return a*b;
```

With the rearrangement of the grammar, the production $T' \rightarrow *FT'$ is missing the left operand of the $*$. One solution is for T to pass the left operand as an argument to T', as shown in Program 4.1.

CUP-GENERATED PARSERS

A parser specification for CUP consists of a set of grammar rules, each annotated with a semantic action that is a Java statement. Whenever the

Stack	Input	Action
	1 + 2 * 3 $	shift
[1 / INT]	+ 2 * 3 $	reduce
[1 / exp]	+ 2 * 3 $	shift
[1 / exp] [+]	2 * 3 $	shift
[1 / exp] [+] [2 / INT]	* 3 $	reduce
[1 / exp] [+] [2 / exp]	* 3 $	shift
[1 / exp] [+] [2 / exp] [*]	3 $	shift
[1 / exp] [+] [2 / exp] [*] [3 / INT]	$	reduce
[1 / exp] [+] [2 / exp] [*] [3 / exp]	$	reduce
[1 / exp] [+] [6 / exp]	$	reduce
[7 / exp]	$	accept

FIGURE 4.3.   Parsing with a semantic stack.

generated parser reduces by a rule, it will execute the corresponding semantic action fragment.

Grammar 4.2 shows how this works for Grammar 3.32. Every INT terminal carries an Integer value, and every exp nonterminal carries an Exp value. To access this value, give the terminal or nonterminal a "name" in the grammar rule (such as i or e1 in Grammar 4.2), and access this name as a variable in the semantic action. The variable RETURN is the "name" of the left-hand-side nonterminal of the grammar rule.

In a more realistic example, there might be several nonterminals each carrying a different type.

A CUP-generated parser implements semantic values by keeping a stack of them parallel to the state stack. Where each symbol would be on a simple parsing stack, now there is a semantic value. When the parser performs a reduction, it must execute a Java-language semantic action; it satisfies each reference to a right-hand-side semantic value by a reference to one of the top k elements of the stack (for a rule with k right-hand-side symbols). When the parser pops the top k elements from the symbol stack and pushes a nonterminal symbol, it also pops k from the semantic value stack and pushes the value obtained by executing the Java semantic action code.

Figure 4.3 shows an LR parse of a string using Grammar 4.2. The stack holds states and semantic values (in this case, the semantic values are all integers). When a rule such as $E \rightarrow E + E$ is reduced (with a semantic action such as `exp1+exp2`), the top three elements of the semantic stack are `exp1`, empty (a place-holder for the trivial semantic value carried by $+$), and `exp2`, respectively.

A MINI-INTERPRETER IN SEMANTIC ACTIONS

To illustrate the power of semantic actions, let us write an interpreter for the language whose abstract syntax is given in Program 1.5. In Chapter 1 we interpreted the abstract syntax trees; with Yacc we can interpret the real thing, the concrete syntax of the language.

Program 4.4 is a CUP grammar with semantic actions that build expression-objects of classes `PlusExp`, `MinusExp`, `IdExp` (and so on) and statement-objects of classes `CompoundStm`, `AssignStm`, `PrintStm` (and so on).

Figure 4.5 implements the `Table` class. A `Table` has just one method, `lookup`, that maps an identifier to a number. There are two implementations of `Table`:

`EmptyTable` whose `lookup` method always throws an error, and
`Update` which makes a table just like `base`, except that the identifier `id` maps to `val`.

Chapter 5 discusses more efficient versions of such tables.

Program 4.6 shows the implementation of the `Exp` class. The method `eval` is a function from `Table` to integer; roughly, "you give me a table to look up identifiers, and I'll give you back an integer." Thus, `eval` for a simple identifier `IdExp(x)` is, "give me a table, and I'll look up x and give you what I find." The `eval` method for `NumExp(5)` is even simpler: "give me a table, and I'll ignore it and give you the integer 5." Finally, `eval` for $e_1 + e_2$ is, "give me a table t, and first I'll apply e_1 to t, then do $e_2(t)$, then add the resulting integers."

Program 4.7 shows the `Stm` class. The method `eval` is a function from `Table` to `Table`; roughly, "you tell me what the state of the world looked like

```
terminal Integer INT;
terminal String ID;
terminal token PLUS, MINUS, TIMES, DIV, ASSIGN, PRINT,
              LPAREN, RPAREN, COMMA, SEMICOLON;
non terminal Exp exp;
non terminal Stm stm;
non terminal ExpList exps;
non terminal Table prog;

precedence left SEMICOLON, COMMA;
precedence left PLUS, MINUS;
precedence left TIMES, DIV;

start with prog;

prog ::= stm:s                      {:RETURN=s.eval(new EmptyTable());:}

stm  ::= stm:a SEMICOLON stm:b      {:RETURN=new CompoundStm(a,b);:}
stm  ::= ID:i ASSIGN exp:e          {:RETURN=new AssignStm(i,e);:}
stm  ::= PRINT LPAREN exps:e RPAREN {:RETURN=new PrintStm(e);:}

exps ::= exp:e                      {:RETURN=new ExpList(e,null);:}
exps ::= exp:e COMMA exps:es        {:RETURN=new ExpList(e,es);:}

exp  ::= INT:i                      {:RETURN=new NumExp(i.intValue());:}
exp  ::= ID:id                      {:RETURN=new IdExp(id);:}
exp  ::= exp:a PLUS exp:b           {:RETURN=new PlusExp(a,b);:}
exp  ::= exp:a MINUS exp:b          {:RETURN=new MinusExp(a,b);:}
exp  ::= exp:a TIMES exp:b          {:RETURN=new TimesExp(a,b);:}
exp  ::= exp:a DIV exp:b            {:RETURN=new DivExp(a,b);:}
exp  ::= stm:s COMMA exp:e          {:RETURN=new EseqExp(a,b);:}
exp  ::= LPAREN exp:e RPAREN        {:RETURN=e;:}
```

PROGRAM 4.4.   An interpreter for straight-line programs.

before this statement executed, I'll show you the 'after' state." The statement $b:=6$, applied to a table t, returns a new table t' that is just like t except that t'.lookup(b) $= 6$. And to implement the compound statement $s_1; s_2$ applied to a table t, we first get a table t' by s_1.eval(t), then calculate s_2.eval(t').

This interpreter contains a major error: an assignment statement inside an expression has no permanent effect (see Exercise 4.2).

AN IMPERATIVE INTERPRETER IN SEMANTIC ACTIONS

Grammar 4.2 and Program 4.4 show how semantic values for nonterminals can be calculated from the semantic values of the right-hand side of the

```
abstract class Table {abstract int lookup(String id);}
class EmptyTable extends Table {
    int lookup(String id) {throw new Error("Empty Table");}
}
class Update extends Table {
    private Table base; String id; int val;
    Update(Table b, String i, int v) {base=b; id=i; val=v;}
    int lookup(String i) {
        if (i==id) return val;
        else return base.lookup(i);
    }
}
```

PROGRAM 4.5.   Table class for Program 4.4.

```
abstract class Exp {abstract int eval(Table env);}

class Num extends Exp {private int i;
        Num(int ii) {i=ii;}
        int eval(Table env) {return i;}
}
class Id extends Exp {private String id;
        Id(String i) {id=i;}
        int eval(Table env) {return env.lookup(id);}
}
class Plus extends Exp {private Exp a,b;
        Plus(Exp aa, bb) {a=aa; b=bb;}
        int eval(Table env) {return aa.eval(env) + bb.eval(env);}
}
class Minus extends Exp {private Exp a,b;
        Minus(Exp aa, bb) {a=aa; b=bb;}
        int eval(Table env) {return aa.eval(env) + bb.eval(env);}
}
class Times extends Exp {private Exp a,b;
        Times(Exp aa, bb) {a=aa; b=bb;}
        int eval(Table env) {return aa.eval(env) + bb.eval(env);}
}
class Div extends Exp {private Exp a,b;
        Div(Exp aa, bb) {a=aa; b=bb;}
        int eval(Table env) {return aa.eval(env) + bb.eval(env);}
}
class Eseq extends Exp {private Stm stm, Exp exp;
        Eseq(Stm s, Exp e) {stm=s; exp=e;}
        int eval(Table env) {return exp.eval(stm.eval(env));}
}
```

PROGRAM 4.6.   Exp class for Program 4.4.

```
abstract class Stm {abstract Table eval(Table env);}

class CompoundStm extends Stm {private Stm stm1, stm2;
        CompoundStm(Stm s1, Stm s2) {stm1=s1; stm2=s2;}
        Table eval(Table env) {return stm2.eval(stm1.eval(env));}
}
class AssignStm extends Stm {private String id; Exp exp;
        AssignStm(String i, Exp e) {id=e; exp=e;}
        Table eval(Table env) {return new Update(env,id,exp.eval(env));}
}
class PrintStm extends Stm {private ExpList exps;
        PrintStm(ExpList e) {exps=e;}
        Table eval(Table env) {exps.eval(env); return env;}
}

class ExpList {private Exp head, ExpList tail;
        ExpList(Exp h, ExpList t) {head=h; tail=t;}
        void eval(Table env) {System.out.print(head.eval(env));
                              if (tail!=null) tail.eval(env);}
}
```

PROGRAM 4.7.   Stm and ExpList classes for Program 4.4.

productions. The semantic actions in these examples do not have *side effects* that change any global state, so the order of evaluation of the right-hand-side symbols does not matter.

However, an LR parser does perform reductions, and associated semantic actions, in a deterministic and predictable order: a bottom-up, left-to-right traversal of the parse tree. In other words, the (virtual) parse tree is traversed in *postorder*. Thus, one can write *imperative* semantic actions with global side effects, and be able to predict the order of their occurrence.

Program 4.8 shows an imperative version of the interpreter.

4.2   ABSTRACT PARSE TREES

It is possible to write an entire compiler that fits within the semantic action phrases of a CUP parser. However, such a compiler is difficult to read and maintain. And this approach constrains the compiler to analyze the program in exactly the order it is parsed.

To improve modularity, it is better to separate issues of syntax (parsing) from issues of semantics (type-checking and translation to machine code).

```
action code {: java.util.Dictionary dict = new java.util.Hashtable();
              int get(String id) {
                    return ((Integer)dict.get(id.intern())).intValue();
              }
              void put(String id, int v) {
                    dict.put(id.intern(), new Integer(v));
              }
            :}

terminal int INT;
terminal String ID;
terminal token PLUS, MINUS, TIMES, DIV, ASSIGN, PRINT,
              LPAREN, RPAREN, COMMA, SEMICOLON;
non terminal int exp;
non terminal void stm, exps, prog;

precedence left SEMICOLON, COMMA;
precedence left PLUS, MINUS;
precedence left TIMES, DIV;

start with prog;

prog ::= stm:s

stm  ::= stm:a SEMICOLON stm:b
stm  ::= ID:id ASSIGN exp:e            {: put(id,e); :}
stm  ::= PRINT LPAREN exps:e RPAREN {: System.out.println() :}

exps ::= exp:e                         {: System.out.print(e); :}
exps ::= exps COMMA exp

exp  ::= INT:i                         {:RETURN=i;:}
exp  ::= ID:id                         {:RETURN=get(id);:}
exp  ::= exp:a PLUS exp:b              {:RETURN=a+b;:}
exp  ::= exp:a MINUS exp:b             {:RETURN=a-b;:}
exp  ::= exp:a TIMES exp:b             {:RETURN=a*b;:}
exp  ::= exp:a DIV exp:b               {:RETURN=a/b;:}
exp  ::= stm:s COMMA exp:e             {:RETURN=b;:}
exp  ::= LPAREN exp:e RPAREN           {:RETURN=e;:}
```

PROGRAM 4.8.   An interpreter in imperative style.

$$S \rightarrow S \; ; \; S \qquad\qquad L \rightarrow$$
$$S \rightarrow \text{id} := E \qquad\quad L \rightarrow L \, E$$
$$S \rightarrow \text{print} \, L$$
$$E \rightarrow \text{id} \qquad\qquad\qquad B \rightarrow +$$
$$E \rightarrow \text{num} \qquad\qquad\; B \rightarrow -$$
$$E \rightarrow E \, B \, E \qquad\qquad B \rightarrow \times$$
$$E \rightarrow S \, , \, E \qquad\qquad B \rightarrow /$$

GRAMMAR 4.9. Abstract syntax of straight-line programs.

One way to do this is for the parser to produce a *parse tree* – a data structure that later phases of the compiler can traverse. Technically, a parse tree has exactly one leaf for each token of the input and one internal node for each grammar rule reduced during the parse.

Such a parse tree, which we will call a *concrete parse tree* representing the *concrete syntax* of the source language, is inconvenient to use directly. Many of the punctuation tokens are redundant and convey no information – they are useful in the input string, but once the parse tree is built, the structure of the tree conveys the structuring information more conveniently.

Furthermore, the structure of the parse tree depends too much on the grammar! The grammar transformations shown in Chapter 3 – factoring, elimination of left-recursion, elimination of ambiguity – involve the introduction of extra nonterminal symbols and extra grammar productions for technical purposes. These details should be confined to the parsing phase and should not clutter the semantic analysis.

An *abstract syntax* makes a clean interface between the parser and the later phases of a compiler (or, in fact, for the later phases of other kinds of program-analysis tools such as dependency analyzers). The abstract syntax tree conveys the phrase structure of the source program, with all parsing issues resolved but without any semantic interpretation.

Many early compilers did not use an abstract syntax data structure because early computers did not have enough memory to represent an entire compilation unit's syntax tree. Modern computers rarely have this problem. And many modern programming languages (ML, Modula-3, Java) allow forward reference to identifiers defined later in the same module; using an abstract syntax tree makes compilation easier for these languages. It may be that Pascal and C require clumsy *forward* declarations because their designers wanted to avoid an extra compiler pass on the machines of the 1970s.

Grammar 4.9 shows the abstract syntax of a straight-line-program language. This grammar is completely impractical for parsing: the grammar is quite ambiguous, since precedence of the operators is not specified, and many of the punctuation keywords are missing.

However, Grammar 4.9 is not meant for parsing. The parser uses the *concrete syntax* (Program 4.4) to build a parse tree for the *abstract syntax*. The semantic analysis phase takes this *abstract syntax tree*; it is not bothered by the ambiguity of the grammar, since it already has the parse tree!

The compiler will need to represent and manipulate abstract syntax trees as data structures. In Java, these data structures are organized according to the principles outlined in Section 1.3: an abstract class for each nonterminal, a subclass for each production, and so on. In fact, the classes of Programs 4.7 and 4.6 are abstract syntax classes for Grammar 4.9. An alternate arrangement, with all the different binary operators grouped into an OpExp class, is shown in Program 1.5.

IS IT OBJECT-ORIENTED?

The abstract syntax classes of Program 1.5 have no methods. The constructors build a syntax-tree data structure, which can then be examined by using instanceof and fetching public class variables that represent subtrees. This is a *syntax separate from interpretations* style of programming.

In contrast, the classes of Programs 4.6 and 4.7 have no public class variables. Any use of these objects must be through their eval method. This is an *object-oriented* style of programming.

The choice of style affects the modularity of the compiler. In a situation such as this, we have several *kinds* of objects: compound statements, assignment statements, print statements, and so on. And we also may have several different *interpretations* of these objects: type-check, translate to Pentium code, translate to Sparc code, optimize, interpret, and so on.

Each *interpretation* must be applied to each *kind*; if we add a new kind we must implement each interpretation for it, and if we add a new interpretation we must implement it for each kind. Figure 4.10 illustrates the orthogonality of kinds and interpretations – for compilers, and for graphic user interfaces, where the *kinds* are different widgets and gadgets, and the *interpretations* are move, hide, and redisplay commands.

If the *syntax separate from interpretations* style is used, then it is easy and modular to add a new *interpretation:* one new function is written, with clauses

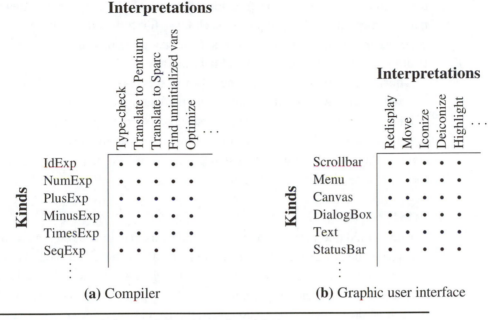

(a) Compiler   **(b)** Graphic user interface

FIGURE 4.10.   Orthogonal directions of modularity.

for the different kinds all grouped logically together. On the other hand, it will not be modular to add a new *kind*, since a new clause must be added to every interpretation function.

With the *object-oriented* style, each interpretation is just a *method* in all the classes. It is easy and modular to add a new *kind:* all the interpretations of that kind are grouped together as methods of the new class. But it is not modular to add a new *interpretation:* a new method must be added to every class.

For graphic user interfaces, each application will want to make its own kinds of widgets; it is impossible to predetermine one set of widgets for everyone to use. On the other hand, the set of common operations (interpretations) is fixed: the window manager demands that each widget support only a certain interface. Thus, the *object-oriented* style works well, and the *syntax separate from interpretations* style would not be as modular.

For programming languages, on the other hand, it works very well to fix a syntax and then provide many interpretations of that syntax. If we have a compiler where one interpretation is *translate to Pentium* and we wish to port that compiler to the Sparc, then not only must we add operations for generating Sparc code but we might also want to remove (in this configuration) the Pentium code generation functions. This would be very inconvenient in the object-oriented style, requiring each class file to be edited. In the *syntax separate from interpretations* style, such a change is modular: we remove a Pentium-related module and add a Sparc module.

Thus, in this book we will generally use a non-object-oriented style for abstract syntax, and for other similar intermediate representations.

The CUP (or recursive-descent) parser, parsing the *concrete syntax*, constructs the *abstract* syntax tree. In fact, whether the syntax/interpretations style or the object-oriented style is used, the semantic actions of the parser look the same, as shown in Program 4.4.

POSITIONS

In a traditional one-pass compiler, lexical analysis, parsing, and semantic analysis (type-checking) are all done simultaneously. If there is a type-checking error that must be reported to the user, the *current* position of the lexical analyzer is a reasonable approximation of the position of the error within the source program. In such a compiler, the lexical analyzer keeps a "current position" global variable, and the error-message routine just prints the value of that variable with each message.

A compiler that uses abstract-syntax-tree data structures need not do all the parsing and semantic analysis in one pass. This makes life easier in many ways, but slightly complicates the production of semantic error messages. The lexer reaches the end of file before semantic analysis even begins; so if a semantic error is detected in traversing the abstract syntax tree, the *current* position of the lexer (at end of file) will not be useful in generating a line-number for the error message. Thus, the source-file position of each node of the abstract syntax tree must be remembered, in case that node turns out to contain a semantic error.

To remember positions accurately, the abstract-syntax data structures must be sprinkled with pos fields. These indicate the position, within the original source file, of the characters from which these abstract syntax structures were derived. Then the type-checker can produce useful error messages.

The lexer must pass the source-file positions of the beginning and end of each token to the parser. We can augment the (abstract) classes Exp and Stm with a position field; then each constructor for all the subclasses of Exp and Stm must take a pos argument to initialize this field. The positions of leaf nodes of the syntax tree can be obtained from the tokens returned by the lexical analyzer; internal-node positions can be derived from the positions of their subtrees. This is tedious but straightforward.

ABSTRACT SYNTAX FOR Tiger

Figure 4.11 shows classes for the abstract syntax of Tiger. The meaning of each constructor in the abstract syntax should be clear after a careful study of Appendix A, but there are a few points that merit explanation.

In Java, definition of `Exp` and its subclass `StringExp` would actually be written as

```
/* Absyn/Absyn.java */
package Absyn;
abstract public class Absyn {public int pos;}

/* Absyn/Exp.java */
package Absyn;
abstract public class Exp extends Absyn {}

/* Absyn/StringExp.java */
package Absyn;
public class StringExp extends Exp {
   public String value;
   public StringExp(int p, String v) {pos=p; value=v;}
}
```

The Tiger program

```
(a := 5; a+1)
```

translates into abstract syntax as

SeqExp(1,**ExpList**(
          AssignExp(4,**SimpleVar**(2,symbol("a")),
                IntExp(7,5)),
      ExpList(
      OpExp(11,**VarExp**(10,**SimpleVar**(10,symbol("a"))),
      PLUS,
      IntExp(12,1)),
    null)))

This is a *sequence expression* containing two expressions separated by a semicolon: an *assignment expression* and an *operator expression*. Within these are a *variable expression* and two *integer constant expressions*.

The positions (1,4,2,7,11,10,10,12) sprinkled throughout are source-code character count. The position I have chosen to associate with an `AssignExp`

```
package Absyn;

abstract class Var
```
SimpleVar(int pos, Symbol name)
FieldVar(int pos, Var var, Symbol field)
SubscriptVar(int pos, Var var, Exp index)

```
abstract class Exp
```
VarExp(int pos, Var var)
NilExp(int pos)
IntExp(int pos, int value)
StringExp(int pos, String value)
CallExp(int pos, Symbol func, ExpList args)
OpExp(int pos, Exp left, int oper, Exp right)
RecordExp(int pos, Symbol typ, FieldExpList fields)
SeqExp(int pos, ExpList list)
AssignExp(int pos, Var var, Exp exp)
IfExp(int pos, Exp test, Exp thenclause)   *// elseclause is null*
IfExp(int pos, Exp test, Exp thenclause, Exp elseclause)
WhileExp(int pos, Exp test, Exp body)
ForExp(int pos, VarDec var, Exp hi, Exp body)
BreakExp(int pos)
LetExp(int pos, DecList decs, Exp body)
ArrayExp(int pos, Symbol typ, Exp size, Exp init)

```
abstract class Dec
```
FunctionDec(int pos, Symbol name, FieldList params, NameTy result,
                   Exp body, FunctionDec next)   *// result may be null*
VarDec(int pos, Symbol name, NameTy typ, Exp init) *// typ may be null*
TypeDec(int pos, Symbol name, Ty ty, TypeDec next)

```
abstract class Ty
```
NameTy(int pos, Symbol name)
RecordTy(int pos, FieldList fields)
ArrayTy(int pos, Symbol typ)

miscellaneous classes
DecList(Dec head, DecList tail)
ExpList(Exp head, ExpList tail)
FieldExpList(int pos, Symbol name, Exp init, FieldExpList tail)
FieldList(int pos, Symbol name, Symbol typ, FieldList tail)

constants for oper field of **OpExp**
```
final static int OpExp.PLUS, OpExp.MINUS, OpExp.MUL, OpExp.DIV,
    OpExp.EQ, OpExp.NE, OpExp.LT, OpExp.LE, OpExp.GT, OpExp.GE;
```

FIGURE 4.11.   Abstract syntax for the Tiger language. Only the constructors
are shown; the object field variables correspond exactly to the
names of the constructor arguments.

is that of the : = operator, for an `OpExp` that of the + operator, and so on. *These decisions are a matter of taste;* they represent my guesses about how they will look when included in semantic error messages.

Now consider

```
let var a := 5
    function f() : int = g(a)
    function g(i: int) = f()
  in f()
end
```

The Tiger language treats *adjacent* function declarations as (possibly) mutually recursive. The `FunctionDec` constructor of the abstract syntax takes a *list* of function declarations, not just a single function. The intent is that this list is a maximal consecutive sequence of function declarations. Thus, functions declared by the same `FunctionDec` can be mutually recursive. Therefore, this program translates into the abstract syntax,

new **LetExp**(
  new **DecList**(new **VarDec**(symbol("a"),
                null,new **IntExp**(5)),
    new **DecList**(new **FunctionDec**(symbol("f"),null,symbol("int"),
                new **CallExp**(symbol("g"), ···),
              new **FunctionDec**(symbol("g"),
                new **FieldList**(symbol("i"),symbol("int"),null),
                null,
                new **CallExp**(symbol("f"), ···),
              null)),
        null)),
    new **CallExp**(symbol("f"), null))

where the positions are omitted for clarity.

The `TypeDec` constructor also takes a list of type declarations, for the same reason; consider the declarations

```
type tree = {key: int, children: treelist}
type treelist = {head: tree, tail: treelist}
```

which translate to *one* `DecList` element containing a two-`TypeDec` sequence:

new **DecList**(
  new **TypeDec**((symbol("tree"),

```
        new RecordTy(
            new FieldList(symbol("key"),symbol("int"),
            new FieldList(symbol("children"),symbol("treelist"),
            null))),
    new TypeDec(symbol("treelist"),
        new RecordTy(
            new FieldList(symbol("head"),symbol("tree"),
            new FieldList(symbol("tail"),symbol("treelist"),
            null))),
        null))),
    null)
```

There is no abstract syntax for "&" and "|" expressions; instead, $e_1 \& e_2$ is translated as if e_1 then e_2 else 0, and $e_1 | e_2$ is translated as though it had been written if e_1 then 1 else e_2.

Similarly, unary negation $(-i)$ should be represented as subtraction $(0 - i)$ in the abstract syntax. [1]

By using these representations for &, |, and unary negation, we keep the abstract syntax data type smaller and make fewer cases for the semantic analysis phase to process. On the other hand, it becomes harder for the type-checker to give meaningful error messages that relate to the source code.

The lexer returns ID tokens with string values. The abstract syntax requires identifiers to have symbol values. Function Symbol.Symbol.symbol (package Symbol, class Symbol, method symbol) converts strings to symbols, and the method toString() converts back. The representation of symbols is discussed in Chapter 5.

The semantic analysis phase of the compiler will need to keep track of which local variables are used from within nested functions. The escape component of a VarDec or FieldList is used to keep track of this. This escape field is not mentioned in the class constructor parameters, but is always initialized to true, which is a conservative approximation. the field type is used for both formal parameters and record fields; escape has meaning for formal parameters, but for record fields it can be ignored.

Having the escape fields in the abstract syntax is a "hack," since escaping is a global, non-syntactic property. But leaving escape out of the Absyn would require another data structure for describing escapes.

---

[1] This might not be adequate in an industrial-strength compiler. The most negative two's complement integer of a given size cannot be represented as $0 - i$ for any i of the same size. In floating point numbers, $0 - x$ is not the same as x if $x = 0$. We will neglect these issues in the Tiger compiler.

PROGRAM ABSTRACT SYNTAX

Add semantic actions to your parser to produce abstract syntax for the Tiger language.

You should turn in the file `Grm.cup`.

For modularity, all the abstract syntax classes reside in the package `Absyn`. This means that all uses of the constructors must be prefixed by "`Absyn.`" which is tedious but straightforward.

Supporting files available in `$TIGER/chap4` include:

`Absyn/*` The abstract syntax classes for Tiger.

`Absyn/Print.java` A pretty-printer for abstract syntax trees, so you can see your results.

`ErrorMsg/*` As before.

`Parse/Yylex.class` Use this only if your own lexical analyzer still isn't working.

`Symbol/*` A module to turn strings into `symbols`.

`makefile` As usual.

`Parse/Parse.java` A driver to run your parser on an input file.

`Grm.cup` The skeleton of a grammar specification.

EXERCISES

4.1 Write a package of Java classes to express the abstract syntax of regular expressions.

4.2 When Program 4.4 interprets straight-line programs, statements embedded inside expressions have no permanent effect – any assignments made within those statements "disappear" at the closing parenthesis. Thus, the program

```
a := 6; (a := a+1, a+4) + a; print(a)
```

prints 17 instead of 18. To fix this problem, change the type of semantic values for exp so that it can produce a value *and* a new table; that is:

```
class ValAndTable {int val; Table table;
                   ValAndTable(···){···}}
abstract class Exp {ValAndTable eval(Table env);}
```

Then change the semantic actions of Program 4.4 accordingly.

4.3 Program 4.4 is not a purely functional program; the semantic action for PRINT contains a Java print statement, which is a side effect. You can make the interpreter purely functional by having each statement return, not only a table, but also a list of values that would have been printed. Thus,

```
class IntList {int head; IntList tail;
                 IntList(cdots) {···} }
class TableAndIntList {Table table;  IntList list;
                     TableAndIntList(···){···}  }
abstract class Stm {TableAndIntList eval(Table env);}
```

Adjust the Exp class accordingly, and rewrite Program 4.4.

4.4 Combine the ideas of Exercises 4.2 and 4.3 to write a purely functional version of the interpreter that handles printing and statements-within-expressions correctly.

4.5 Implement Program 4.4 as a recursive-descent parser, with the semantic actions embedded in the parsing functions.

5

Semantic Analysis

se·man·tic: of or relating to meaning in language

Webster's Dictionary

The *semantic analysis* phase of a compiler connects variable definitions to their uses, checks that each expression has a correct type, and translates the abstract syntax into a simpler representation suitable for generating machine code.

5.1

SYMBOL TABLES

This phase is characterized by the maintenance of *symbol tables* (also called *environments*) mapping identifiers to their types and locations. As the declarations of types, variables, and functions are processed, these identifiers are bound to "meanings" in the symbol tables. When *uses* (non-defining occurrences) of identifiers are found, they are looked up in the symbol tables.

Each local variable in a program has a *scope* in which it is visible. For example, in a Tiger expression let D in E end all the variables, types, and functions declared in D are visible only until the end of E. As the semantic analysis reaches the end of each scope, the identifier bindings local to that scope are discarded.

An environment is a set of *bindings* denoted by the $\mapsto$ arrow. For example, we could say that the environment σ_0 contains the bindings $\{g \mapsto string, a \mapsto int\}$; meaning that the identifier a is an integer variable and g is a string variable.

Consider a simple example in the Tiger language:

```
1            function f(a:int, b:int, c:int) =
2                (print_int(a+c);
3                 let var j := a+b
4                     var a := "hello"
5                  in print(a); print_int(j);
6                 end;
7                 print_int(b)
8                )
```

Suppose we compile this program in the environment σ_0. The formal parameter declarations on line 1 give us the table σ_1 equal to $\sigma_0 + \{a \mapsto int, b \mapsto int, c \mapsto int\}$, that is, σ_0 extended with new bindings for a, b, and c. The identifiers in line 2 can be looked up in σ_1. At line 3, the table $\sigma_2 = \sigma_1 + \{j \mapsto int\}$ is created; and at line 4, $\sigma_3 = \sigma_2 + \{a \mapsto string\}$ is created.

How does the $+$ operator for tables work when the two environments being "added" contain different bindings for the same symbol? When σ_2 and $\{a \mapsto string\}$ map a to int and string, respectively? To make the scoping rules work the way we expect them to in real programming languages, we want $\{a \mapsto string\}$ to take precedence. So we say that $X + Y$ for tables is not the same as $Y + X$; bindings in the right-hand table override those in the left.

Finally, in line 6 we discard σ_3 and go back to σ_1 for looking up the identifier b in line 7. And at line 8, we discard σ_1 and go back to σ_0.

How should this be implemented? There are really two choices. In a *functional* style, we make sure to keep σ_1 in pristine condition while we create σ_2 and σ_3. Then when we need σ_1 again, it's rested and ready.

In an *imperative* style, we modify σ_1 until it becomes σ_2. This *destructive update* "destroys" σ_1; while σ_2 exists, we cannot look things up in σ_1. But when we are done with σ_2, we can *undo* the modification to get σ_1 back again. Thus, there is a single global environment σ which becomes $\sigma_0, \sigma_1, \sigma_2, \sigma_3, \sigma_1, \sigma_0$ at different times and an "undo stack" with enough information to remove the destructive updates. When a symbol is added to the environment, it is also added to the undo stack; at the end of scope (e.g., at line 6 or 8), symbols popped from the undo stack have their latest binding removed from σ (and their previous binding restored).

Either the functional or imperative style of environment management can be used regardless of whether the language being compiled, or the implementation language of the compiler, is a "functional" or "imperative" or "object-oriented" language.

```
structure M = struct                package M;
   structure E = struct             class E {
      val a = 5;                        static int a = 5;
   end                              }
   structure N = struct             class N {
      val b = 10                       static int b = 10;
      val a = E.a + b                  static int a = E.a + b;
   end                              }
   structure D = struct             class D {
      val d = E.a + N.a                static int d = E.a + N.a;
   end                              }
end
```

(a) An example in ML   (b) An example in Java

FIGURE 5.1.   Several active environments at once.

MULTIPLE SYMBOL TABLES

In some languages there can be several active environments at once: each module, or class, or record, in the program has a symbol table σ of its own.

In analyzing Figure 5.1, let σ_0 be the base environment containing predefined functions, and let

$$\sigma_1 = \{a \mapsto int\}$$
$$\sigma_2 = \{E \mapsto \sigma_1\}$$
$$\sigma_3 = \{b \mapsto int, a \mapsto int\}$$
$$\sigma_4 = \{N \mapsto \sigma_3\}$$
$$\sigma_5 = \{d \mapsto int\}$$
$$\sigma_6 = \{D \mapsto \sigma_5\}$$
$$\sigma_7 = \sigma_2 + \sigma_4 + \sigma_6$$

In ML, the N is compiled using environment $\sigma_0 + \sigma_2$ to look up identifiers; D is compiled using $\sigma_0 + \sigma_1 + \sigma_2$, and the result of the analysis is $\{M \mapsto \sigma_7\}$.

In Java, forward reference is allowed (so inside N the expression $D.d$ would be legal), so N and D are both compiled in the environment σ_7; for this program the result is still $\{M \mapsto \sigma_7\}$.

EFFICIENT IMPERATIVE SYMBOL TABLES

Because a large program may contain thousands of distinct identifiers, symbol tables must permit efficient lookup.

```
class Bucket {String key; Object binding; Bucket next;
      Bucket(String k, Object b, Bucket n) {key=k; binding=b; next=n;}
}

class HashT {
   final int SIZE = 256;
   Bucket table[] = new Bucket[SIZE];

   int hash(String s) {
       int h=0;
       for(int i=0; i<s.length(); i++)
          h=h*65599+s.charAt(i);
       return h;
   }

   void insert(String s, Binding b) {
       int index=hash(s)%SIZE
       table[index]=new Bucket(s,b,table[index]);
   }

   Object lookup(String s) {
       int index=hash(s)%SIZE
       for (Binding b = table[index]; b!=null; b=b.next)
         if (s.equals(b.key)) return b.binding;
       return null;
   }

   void pop(String s) {
       int index=hash(s)%SIZE
       table[index]=table[index].next;
   }
}
```

PROGRAM 5.2.   Hash table with external chaining.

Imperative-style environments are usually implemented using hash tables, which are very efficient. The operation $\sigma' = \sigma + \{a \mapsto \tau\}$ is implemented by inserting τ in the hash table with key a. A simple *hash table with external chaining* works well and supports deletion easily (we will need to delete $\{a \mapsto \tau\}$ to recover σ at the end of the scope of a).

Program 5.2 implements a simple hash table. The ith bucket is a linked list of all the elements whose keys hash to $i \bmod$ SIZE.

Consider $\sigma + \{a \mapsto \tau_2\}$ when σ contains $a \mapsto \tau_1$ already. The insert function leaves $a \mapsto \tau_1$ in the bucket and puts $a \mapsto \tau_2$ earlier in the list. Then, when pop(a) is done at the end of a's scope, σ is restored. Of course, pop

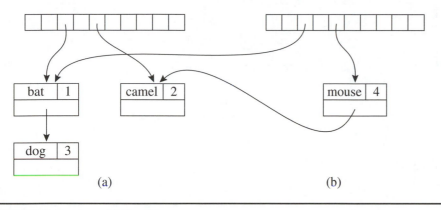

(a)   (b)

FIGURE 5.3.   Hash tables.

works only if bindings are inserted and popped in a stacklike fashion.

An industrial-strength implementation would improve on this in several ways; see Exercise 5.1.

EFFICIENT FUNCTIONAL SYMBOL TABLES

In the functional style, we wish to compute $\sigma' = \sigma + \{a \mapsto \tau\}$ in such a way that we still have σ available to look up identifiers. Thus, instead of "altering" a table by adding a binding to it we create a new table by computing the "sum" of an existing table and a new binding. Similarly, when we add $7 + 8$ we don't alter the 7 by adding 8 to it; we create a new value 15 – and the 7 is still available for other computations.

However, nondestructive update is not efficient for hash tables. Figure 5.3a shows a hash table implementing mapping m_1. It is fast and efficient to add *mouse* to the fifth slot; just make the *mouse* record point at the (old) head of the fifth linked list, and make the fifth slot point to the *mouse* record. But then we no longer have the mapping m_1: we have destroyed it to make m_2. The other alternative is to copy the array, but still share all the old buckets, as shown in Figure 5.3b. But this is not efficient: the array in a hash table should be quite large, proportional in size to the number of elements, and we cannot afford to copy it for each new entry in the table.

By using binary search trees we can perform such "functional" additions to search trees efficiently. Consider, for example, the search tree in Figure 5.4, which represents the mapping

$$m_1 = \{bat \mapsto 1, \ camel \mapsto 2, \ dog \mapsto 3\}.$$

103

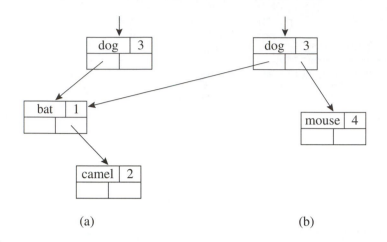

(a)   (b)

FIGURE 5.4.   Binary search trees.

We can add the binding $mouse \mapsto 4$, creating the mapping m_2 without destroying the mapping m_1, as shown in Figure 5.4b. If we add a new node at depth d of the tree, we must create d new nodes – but we don't need to copy the whole tree. So creating a new tree (that shares some structure with the old one) can be done as efficiently as looking up an element: in $\log(n)$ time for a balanced tree of n nodes. This is an example of a *persistent data structure;* a persistent *red-black* tree can be kept balanced to guarantee $\log(n)$ access time (see Exercise 1.1c, and also page 276).

SYMBOLS IN THE Tiger COMPILER

The hash table of Program 5.2 must examine every character of the string s for the hash operation, and then again each time it compares s against a string in the ith bucket. To avoid unnecessary string comparisons, we can convert each string to a symbol, so that all the different occurrences of any given string convert to the same symbol object.

The Symbol module implements symbols and has these important properties:

- Comparing two symbols for equality is very fast (just pointer or integer comparison).
- Extracting an integer hash-key is very fast (in case we want to make hash table mapping symbols to something else).
- Comparing two symbols for "greater-than" (in some arbitrary ordering) is very fast (in case we want to make binary search trees).

```
package Symbol;

public class Symbol {
  public String toString();
  public static Symbol symbol(String s);
}

public class Table {
  public Table();
  public void put(Symbol key, Object value);
  public Object get(Symbol key);
  public void beginScope();
  public void endScope();
  public java.util.Enumeration keys();
}
```

PROGRAM 5.5.   The interface of package `Symbol`.

Even if we intend to make functional-style environments mapping symbols to bindings, we can use a destructive-update hash table to map strings to symbols: we need this to make sure the second occurrence of "abc" maps to the same symbol as the first occurrence. Program 5.5 shows the interface of the `Symbol` module.

Environments are implemented in the `Symbol.Table` class as `Tables` mapping `Symbols` to bindings. We want different notions of `binding` for different purposes in the compiler – type bindings for types, value bindings for variables and functions – so we let the bindings be `Object`, though in any given table every binding should be a type binding, or every binding should be a value binding, and so on.

To implement the `Symbol` class (Program 5.6), we rely on the `intern()` method of the `java.lang.String` class to give us a unique object for any given character sequence; we can map from `Symbol` to `String` by having each symbol contain a string variable, but the reverse mapping must be done using a hash table (we use `java.util.Hashtable`).

For the Tiger compiler in Java we choose to use destructive-update environments. The `Table` constructor of the `Symbol` package makes a new table.

To handle the "undo" requirements of destructive update, the interface function `beginScope` remembers the current state of the table, and `endScope` restores the table to where it was at the most recent `beginScope` that has not already been ended.

```
package Symbol;
public class Symbol {
  private String name;
  private Symbol(String n) {name=n; }
  private static java.util.Dictionary dict = new java.util.Hashtable();

  public String toString() {return name;}

  public static Symbol symbol(String n) {
        String u = n.intern();
        Symbol s = (Symbol)dict.get(u);
        if (s==null) {s = new Symbol(u); dict.put(u,s); }
        return s;
  }
}
```

PROGRAM 5.6.   Symbol table implementation.

An imperative table is implemented using a hash table. When the binding $x \mapsto b$ is entered (table.put(x,b)), x is hashed into an index i, and a Binder object $x \mapsto b$ is placed at the head of the linked list for the ith bucket. If the table had already contained a binding $x \mapsto b'$, that will still be in the bucket, hidden by $x \mapsto b$. This is important because it will support the implementation of *undo* (beginScope and endScope).

The key x is not a character string, but is the Symbol object itself.

There must also be an auxiliary stack, showing in what order the symbols were "pushed" into the symbol table. When $x \mapsto b$ is entered, then x is pushed onto this stack. A beginScope operation pushes a special marker onto the stack. Then, to implement endScope, symbols are popped off the stack down to and including the topmost marker. As each symbol is popped, the head binding in its bucket is removed.

The auxiliary stack can be integrated into the Binder by having a global variable top showing the most recent Symbol bound in the table. Then "pushing" is accomplished by copying top into the prevtop field of the Binder. Thus, the "stack" is threaded through the binders.

FUNCTIONAL-STYLE SYMBOL TABLES

If we wanted to use functional-style symbol tables in the Tiger compiler, the Table interface might look like this:

```
package Types;

public abstract class Type {
        public Type actual() {return this;}
}
```

subclasses of Type:
```
public INT();
public STRING();
public RECORD(Symbol.Symbol fieldName, Type fieldType, RECORD tail);
public ARRAY(Type element);
public NIL();
public VOID();
public NAME(Symbol.Symbol name);
```

PROGRAM 5.7.   Package Types.

```
public class Table {
  public Table();
  public Table put(Symbol key, Object value);
  public Object get(Symbol key);
  public java.util.Enumeration keys();
}
```

The put function would return a new table without modifying the old one. We wouldn't need beginScope and endScope, because we could keep an old version of the table even as we use the new version.

5.2   BINDINGS FOR THE Tiger COMPILER

With what should a symbol table be filled – that is, what is a binding? Tiger has two separate name spaces, one for types and the other for functions and variables. A type identifier will be associated with a Types.Type. The Types module describes the structure of types, as shown in Figure 5.7.

The primitive types in Tiger are int and string; all types are either primitive types or constructed using records and arrays from other (primitive, record, or array) types.

Record types carry additional information: the names and types of the fields.

Arrays work just like records: the ARRAY constructor carries the type of the array elements.

For array and record types, there is another implicit piece of information carried by the ARRAY or RECORD object: the address of the object itself. That is, every Tiger-language "record type expression" creates a new (and different) record type, even if the fields are similar. We can encode this in our compiler by using == to compare record types to see if they are the same.

If we were compiling some other language, we might have the following as a legal program:

```
let type a = {x: int, y: int}
    type b = {x: int, y: int}
    var i : a := ···
    var j : b := ···
in i := j
end
```

This is illegal in Tiger, but would be legal in a language where structurally equivalent types are interchangeable. To test type equality in a compiler for such a language, we would need to examine record types field by field, recursively.

However, the following Tiger program is legal, since type c is the same as type a:

```
let type a = {x: int, y: int}
    type c = a
    var i : a := ···
    var j : c := ···
in i := j
end
```

It is not the type *declaration* that causes a new and distinct type to be made, but the type *expression* {x:int,y:int}.

In Tiger, the expression nil belongs to any record type. We handle this exceptional case by inventing a special "nil" type. There are also expressions that return "no value," so we invent a type VOID.

When processing mutually recursive types, we will need a place-holder for types whose name we know but whose definition we have not yet seen. The NAME class has a bind method to fill in the place-holder when the definition is known. Then the actual() method (which for an ordinary type t simply returns t) for NAME types returns the filled-in binding:

```
package Types;

public class NAME extends Type {
   public Symbol.Symbol name;
   private Type binding;
   public NAME(Symbol.Symbol n) {name=n;}
   public Type actual() {return binding.actual();}
   public void bind(Type t) {binding = t;}
}
```

ENVIRONMENTS

The `table` type of the `Symbol` module provides mappings from symbols to bindings. Thus, we will have a *type environment* and a *value environment*. The following Tiger program demonstrates that one environment will not suffice:

```
let type a = int
    var a : a = 5
    var b : a = a
 in b+a
end
```

The symbol a denotes the type "a" in syntactic contexts where type-identifiers are expected, and the variable "a" in syntactic contexts where variables are expected.

For a type identifier, we need to remember only the type that it stands for. Thus a type environment is a mapping from symbol to `Types.Type` – that is, a `Symbol.Table` whose `get` function always returns `Types.Type` objects. As shown in Figure 5.8, the `Env` class contains the table `tenv`, which is initialized to the "base" or "predefined" type environment. This maps the symbol `int` to `Types.INT` and `string` to `Types.STRING`.

We need to know, for each value identifier, whether it is a variable or a function; if a variable, what is its type; if a function, what are its parameter and result types, and so on. The type `enventry` holds all this information, as shown in Figure 5.8; and a value environment is a mapping from symbol to environment-entry.

A variable will map to a `VarEntry` telling its type. When we look up a function we will obtain a `FunEntry` containing:

formals The types of the formal parameters.
result The type of result returned by the function (or `UNIT`).

For type-checking, only `formals` and `result` are needed; we will add other fields later for translation into intermediate representation.

```
package Semant;

class Env {
    Table venv;    // value environment
    Table tenv;    // type environment
    ErrorMsg.ErrorMsg errorMsg;
    Env(ErrorMsg.ErrorMsg err) {
        errorMsg=err;
        initialize venv and tenv with predefined identifiers
    }
}


abstract class Entry {}
class VarEntry extends Entry {
    Types.Type ty;
    VarEntry(Types.Type t) {ty=t;}
}
class FunEntry extends Entry {
    Types.RECORD formals;
    Types.Type result;
    public FunEntry(Types.RECORD f, Types.Type r) {formals=f; result=r;}
}
```

FIGURE 5.8.   Environments for type-checking.

The `Env` class constructor initializes the `venv` environment by putting bindings for predefined functions `flush`, `ord`, `chr`, `size`, and so on, described in Appendix A.

Environments are used during the type-checking phase.

As types, variables, and functions are declared, the type-checker augments the environments; they are consulted for each identifier that is found during processing of expressions (type-checking, intermediate code generation).

5.3   TYPE-CHECKING EXPRESSIONS

The class `Semant.Semant` performs semantic analysis – including type-checking – of abstract syntax. It contains a class variable `env` for accessing environments and printing error messages:

package Semant contains classes for type-checking
    class Semant the only public class in this package; the main type-checking module.
    abstract class Entry for bindings in value environments.
        class VarEntry for variable bindings.
        class FunEntry for function bindings.
    class OneFunc helps in processing function declarations.
    class OneType helps in processing type declarations.
    class ExpTy holds the result of translating and type-checking an expression.
    class Env holds a value-environment, type-environment, and error-message printer; and
       is responsible for initializing the environments with predefined identifiers.
package Types describes Tiger-language types.
package Symbol handles symbols and environment-tables.
    class Symbol makes strings into unique Symbol objects.
    class Table does environments with Scopes.

TABLE 5.9.   Organization of packages for semantic analysis.

```
public class Semant {
 Env env;
 public Semant(ErrorMsg.ErrorMsg err) {this(new Env(err));}
 Semant(Env e) {env=e;}

 ExpTy transVar(Absyn.Var e) { ··· }
 ExpTy transExp(Absyn.Exp e) { ··· }
 Exp   transDec(Absyn.Exp e) { ··· }
 Ty    transTy (Absyn.Ty  e) { ··· }
}
```

The type-checker is a recursive function of the abstract syntax tree. I will call it `transExp` because we will later augment this function not only to type-check but also to translate the expressions into intermediate code. The arguments of `transExp` are a value environment `venv`, a type environment `tenv`, and an expression. The result will be an `ExpTy`, containing a translated expression and its Tiger-language type:

```
import Translate.Exp;
class ExpTy { Exp exp; Type ty;
   ExpTy(Exp e, Type t) {exp=e; ty=t;}
}
```

where `Translate.Exp` is the translation of the expression into intermediate code, and `ty` is the type of the expression.

To avoid a discussion of intermediate code at this point, let us define a dummy `Translate` module:

```
package Translate;
abstract class Exp
```

and use `null` for every `Exp` value. We will flesh out the `Translate.Exp` type in Chapter 7.

Let's take a very simple case: an addition expression $e_1 + e_2$. In Tiger, both operands must be integers (the type-checker must check this) and the result will be an integer (the type-checker will return this type).

In most languages, addition is *overloaded*: the + operator stands for either integer addition or real addition. If the operands are both integers, the result is integer; if the operands are both real, the result is real. And in many languages if one operand is an integer and the other is real, the integer is implicitly converted into a real, and the result is real. Of course, the compiler will have to make this conversion explicit in the machine code it generates.

Tiger's nonoverloaded type-checking is easy to implement:

```
ExpTy transExp(Absyn.OpExp e) {
   ExpTy left = transExp(e.left);
   ExpTy right = transExp(e.right);
   if (e.oper == Absyn.OpExp.PLUS) {
       if (! (left.ty instanceof Types.INT))
           error(e.left.pos, "integer required");
       if (! (right.ty instanceof Types.INT))
           error(e.right.pos, "integer required");
       return new ExpTy(null, new Types.INT());
   }
}
```

This works well enough, although we have not yet written the cases for other kinds of expressions (and operators other than +), so when the recursive calls on `left` and `right` are executed, it won't work. You can fill in the other cases yourself (see page 118).

It's also a bit clumsy. The case of checking for an integer type is common enough to warrant a function definition, `checkInt`. A cleaned-up version of `transExp` looks like:

```
Exp checkInt(ExpTy et, int pos) { ... ;   return et.exp; }

Types.Type INT = new Types.INT();

ExpTy transExp(Absyn.OpExp e) {
   switch (e.oper) {
       case Absyn.OpExp.PLUS:
            checkInt(transExp(e.left,e.left.pos));
            checkInt(transExp(e.right,e.left.pos));
            return new ExpTy(null, INT);
   }
}


ExpTy transExp(Absyn.Exp e) {
   if (e instanceof Absyn.VarExp)
            return transExp((Absyn.VarExp)e);
   if (e instanceof Absyn.IntExp)
            return transExp((Absyn.IntExp)e);
   if (e instanceof Absyn.CallExp)
            return transExp((Absyn.CallExp)e);
            ⋮
   if (e instanceof Absyn.ArrayExp)
            return transExp((Absyn.ArrayExp)e);
   throw new Error("transExp");
}
```

TYPE-CHECKING VARIABLES, SUBSCRIPTS, AND FIELDS

Each (overloaded) version of `transExp` operates on a different subclass of `Absyn.Exp`. Then a "dispatch" function `transExp(Absyn.Exp e)`, admittedly rather tedious to write, chooses from among the various overloaded versions of `transExp`. Similar dispatch functions will be necessary for `transVar` and `transDec` as well.

```
ExpTy transVar(Absyn.SimpleVar v) {
   Entry x = (Entry)env.venv.get(v.name);
   if (x instanceof VarEntry) {
     VarEntry ent = (VarEntry)x;
     return new ExpTy(null, ent.ty);
   }
   else {
     error(v.pos, "undefined variable");
     return new ExpTy(null, INT);   // anything will do!
   }
}
```

The clause of `transVar` that type-checks a `SimpleVar` illustrates the use of environments to look up a variable binding. If the identifer is present in the environment *and* is bound to a `VarEntry` (not a `FunEntry`), then its type is the one given in the `VarEntry` (Figure 5.8).

The type in the `VarEntry` will really be a "NAME type" (Program 5.7), and all the types returned from `transExp` should be "actual" types (with the names traced through to their underlying definitions). It is therefore useful to have a new method in the `Types.Type` class, perhaps called `actual()`, to skip past all the NAMEs. The result will be a `Types.ty` that is not a NAME, though if it is a record or array type it might contain NAME types to describe its components.

For function calls, it is necessary to look up the function identifier in the environment, yielding a `FunEntry` containing a list of parameter types. These types must then be matched against the arguments in the function-call expression. The `FunEntry` also gives the result type of the function, which becomes the type of the function call as a whole.

Every kind of expression has its own type-checking rules, but in all the cases I have not already described the rules can be derived by reference to the *Tiger Language Reference Manual* (Appendix A).

5.4   TYPE-CHECKING DECLARATIONS

Environments are constructed and augmented by declarations. In Tiger, declarations appear only in a `let` expression. Type-checking a `let` is easy enough, using `transDec` to translate declarations:

```
ExpTy transExp(Absyn.LetExp e) {
    env.venv.beginScope();
    env.tenv.beginScope();
    for (Absyn.DecList p=e.decs; p!=null; p=p.tail)
        transDec(p.head);
    ExpTy et = transExp(e.body);
     env.venv.endScope();
     env.tenv.endScope();
    return new ExpTy(null, et.ty);
}
```

Here `transExp` marks the current "state" of the environments using `beginScope()`; calls `transDec` to augment the environments (venv, tenv) with new declarations; translates the body expression; then reverts to the original state of the environments using `endScope()`.

VARIABLE DECLARATIONS

In principle, processing a declaration is quite simple: a declaration augments an environment by a new binding, and the augmented environment is used in the processing of subsequent declarations and expressions.

The only problem is with (mutually) recursive type and function declarations. So we will begin with the special case of nonrecursive declarations.

For example, it is quite simple to process a variable declaration without a type constraint, such as `var x :=` *exp*.

```
Exp transDec(Absyn.VarDec d) {
    env.venv.put(d.name, new VarEntry(null,e.ty));
    return null;
}
```

What could be simpler? In practice, if `d.typ` is present, as in

```
var x : type-id := exp
```

it will be necessary to check that the constraint and the initializing expression are compatible. Also, initializing expressions of type `NIL` must be constrained by a `RECORD` type.

TYPE DECLARATIONS

Nonrecursive type declarations are not too hard:

```
Exp transDec(Absyn.TypeDec d) {
  env.tenv.put(d.name, transTy(d.ty));
}
```

The `transTy` function translates type expressions as found in the abstract syntax (`Absyn.Ty`) to the digested type descriptions that we will put into environments (`Types.Type`). This translation is done by recurring over the structure of an `Absyn.Type`, turning `Absyn.RecordTy` into `Types.RECORD`, etc. While translating, `transTy` just looks up any symbols it finds in the type environment `tenv`.

The program fragment shown is not very general, since it handles only a type-declaration list of length 1, that is, a singleton list of mutually recursive type declarations. The reader is invited to generalize this to lists of arbitrary length.

FUNCTION DECLARATIONS

Function declarations are a bit more tedious:

```
Exp transDec(Absyn.FunctionDec d) {
        Types.Type result = transTy(d.result);
        Types.RECORD formals=transTypeFields(d.params);
        env.venv.put(d.name, new FunEntry(formals,result));
        env.venv.beginScope();
        for(p=dec.params; p!=null; p=p.tail)
           env.venv.put(p.name,
              new VarEntry(null,
                          (Types.Type)env.tenv.get(p.typ)));
        transExp(d.body);
        env.venv.endScope();
}
```

This is a very stripped-down implementation: it handles only the case of a single function; it does not handle recursive functions; it handles only a function with a result (a function, not a procedure); it doesn't handle program errors such as undeclared type identifiers, etc; and it doesn't check that the type of the body expression matches the declared result type.

So what does it do? Consider the Tiger declaration

```
function f(a: ta, b: tb) : rt = body.
```

First, `transDec` looks up the result-type identifier `rt` in the type environment. Then it calls the local function `transTypeFields` on each formal parameter; this yields a "record type," $(a, t_a), (b, t_b)$ where t_a is the NAME type found by looking up `ta` in the type environment. Now `transDec` has enough information to construct the `FunEntry` for this function and enter it in the value environment.

Next, the formal parameters are entered (as `VarEntry`s) into the value environment; this environment is used to process the *body* (with the `transExp` function). Finally, `endScope()` discards the formal-parameters (but not the `FunEntry`) from the environment; the resulting environment is used for processing expressions that are allowed to call the function `f`.

RECURSIVE DECLARATIONS

The implementations above will not work on recursive type or function declarations, because they will encounter undefined type or function identifiers (in `transTy` for recursive record types or `transExp(body)` for recursive functions).

The solution for a set of mutually recursive things (types or functions) $t_1, ..., t_n$ is to put all the "headers" in the environment first, resulting in an environment e_1. Then process all the "bodies" in the environment e_1. During processing of the bodies it will be necessary to look up some of the newly defined names, but they will in fact be there – though some of them may be empty headers without bodies.

What is a header? For a type declaration such as

```
type list = {first: int, rest: list}
```

the header is approximately `type list =`.

To enter this header into an environment `tenv` we can use a `NAME` type with an empty binding :

```
env.tenv.put(name, new Types.NAME(name));
```

Now, we can call `transTy` on the "body" of the type declaration, that is, on the record expression `{first: int, rest: list}`.

It's important that `transTy` stop as soon as it gets to any `NAME` type. If, for example, `transTy` behaved like `Types.Type.actual()` and tried to look "through" the `NAME` type bound to the identifier `list`, all it would find (in this case) would be `null` – which it is certainly not prepared for. This `null` can be replaced only by a valid type after the entire `{first:int, rest:list}` is translated.

The type that `transTy` returns can then be assigned into a private field within the `NAME` object, using the `bind()` method. Now we have a fully complete type environment, on which `actual()` will not have a problem.

Every cycle in a set of mutually recursive type declarations must pass through a record or array declaration; the declaration

```
type a = b
type b = d
type c = a
type d = a
```

contains an illegal cycle $a \rightarrow b \rightarrow d \rightarrow a$. Illegal cycles should be detected by the type-checker.

Mutually recursive functions are handled similarly. The first pass gathers information about the *header* of each function (function name, formal parameter list, return type) but leaves the bodies of the functions untouched. In this pass, the *types* of the formal parameters are needed, but not their names (which cannot be seen from outside the function).

The second pass processes the bodies of all functions in the mutually recursive declaration, taking advantage of the environment augmented with all the function headers. For each body, the formal parameter list is processed again, this time entering the parameters as `VarEntrys` in the value environment.

PROGRAM

TYPE-CHECKING

Write a type-checking phase for your compiler, a class with the following interface:

```
package Semant;

public class Semant {
  public Semant(ErrorMsg.ErrorMsg err);
  public void transProg(Absyn.Exp exp);
}
```

that type-checks an abstract syntax tree and produces any appropriate error messages about mismatching types or undeclared identifiers.

Also provide the implementation of the `Env` class described in this chapter. Make a module `Main` that calls the parser, yielding an `Absyn.Exp`, and then calls `transProg` on this expression.

You must use precisely the `Absyn` interface described in Figure 4.11, but you are free to follow or ignore any advice given in this chapter about the internal organization of the `Semant` module.

You'll need your parser that produces abstract syntax trees. In addition, supporting files available in `$TIGER/chap5` include:

`Types/` Describes data types of the Tiger language.

and other files as before. Modify the makefile from the previous exercise as necessary.

Part a. Implement a simple type-checker and declaration processor that does not handle recursive functions or recursive data types (forward references to functions or types need not be handled). Also don't bother to check that each **break** statement is within a **for** or **while** statement.

Part b. Augment your simple type-checker to handle recursive (and mutually recursive) functions; (mutually) recursive type declarations; and correct nesting of **break** statements.

EXERCISES

5.1 Improve the hash table implementation of Figure 5.2:

a. Double the size of the array when the average bucket length grows larger than 2 (so `table` is now a pointer to a dynamically allocated array). To double an array, allocate a bigger one and rehash the contents of the old array; then discard the old array.

b. Allow for more than one table to be in use by making the table a parameter to `insert` and `lookup`.

c. Hide the representation of the `table` type inside an abstraction module, so that clients are not tempted to manipulate the data structure directly (only through the `insert`, `lookup`, and `pop` operations).

***5.2 In many applications, we want a $+$ operator for environments that does more than add one new binding; instead of $\sigma' = \sigma + \{a \mapsto \tau\}$, we want $\sigma' = \sigma_1 + \sigma_2$, where σ_1 and σ_2 are arbitrary environments (perhaps overlapping, in which case bindings in σ_2 take precedence).

Balanced trees can implement $\sigma + \{a \mapsto \tau\}$ efficiently (in $\log(N)$ time, where N is the size of σ), but take $O(N)$ to compute $\sigma_1 + \sigma_2$, if σ_1 and σ_2 are both about size N.

Find an efficient algorithm and data structure for environment "adding." To abstract the problem, solve the general nondisjoint integer-set union problem.

The input is a set of commands of the form,

$$s_1 = \{4\} \quad (\textit{define singleton set})$$
$$s_2 = \{7\}$$
$$s_3 = s_1 \cup s_2 \; (\textit{nondestructive union})$$
$$6 \stackrel{?}{\in} s_3 \quad (\textit{membership test})$$
$$s_4 = s_1 \cup s_4$$
$$s_5 = \{9\}$$
$$s_6 = s_4 \cup s_5$$
$$7 \stackrel{?}{\in} s_2$$

An efficient algorithm is one that can process an input of N commands, answering all membership queries, in less then $o(N^2)$ time.

Design an efficient algorithm for this problem. Then collect your PhD.

5.3 The Tiger language definition states that every cycle of type definitions must go through a record or array. But if the compiler forgets to check for this error, nothing terrible will happen. Explain why.

6

Activation Records

stack: an orderly pile or heap

Webster's Dictionary

In almost any modern programming language, a function may have *local* variables that are created upon entry to the function. Several invocations of the function may exist at the same time, and each invocation has its own *instantiations* of local variables.

In the Tiger function,

```
function f(x: int) : int =
  let var y := x+x
   in if y < 10
          then f(y)
          else y-1
  end
```

a new instantiation of x is created (and initialized by f's caller) each time that f is called. Because there are recursive calls, many of these x's exist simultaneously. Similarly, a new instantiation of y is created each time the body of f is entered.

In many languages (including C, Pascal, and Tiger), local variables are destroyed when a function returns. Since a function returns only after all the functions it has called have returned, we say that function calls behave in last-in-first-out (LIFO) fashion. If local variables are created on function entry and destroyed on function exit, then we can use a LIFO data structure – a stack – to hold them.

```
fun f(x) =                          int (*)() f(int x) {
   let fun g(y) = x+y                   int g(int y) {return x+y}
   in g                                 return g;
   end                              }

val h = f(3)                        int (*h)() = f(3);
val j = f(4)                        int (*j)() = f(4);

val z = h(5)                        int z = h(5);
val w = j(7)                        int w = j(7);
```

(a) Written in ML   (b) Written in pseudo-C

PROGRAM 6.1.   An example of higher-order functions.

HIGHER-ORDER FUNCTIONS

But in languages supporting both nested functions *and* function-valued variables, it may be necessary to keep local variables after a function has returned! Consider Program 6.1: This is legal in ML, but of course in C one cannot really nest the function g inside the function f.

When $f(3)$ is executed, a new local variable x is created for the activation of function f. Then g is returned as the result of $f(x)$; but g has not yet been called, so y is not yet created.

At this point f has returned, but it is too early to destroy x, because when $h(5)$ is eventually executed it will need the value $x = 3$. Meanwhile, $f(4)$ is entered, creating a *different* instance of x, and it returns a *different* instance of g in which $x = 4$.

It is the combination of *nested functions* (where inner functions may use variables defined in the outer functions) and *functions returned as results* (or stored into variables) that causes local variables to need lifetimes longer than their enclosing function invocations.

Pascal (and Tiger) have nested functions, but they do not have functions as returnable values. C has functions as returnable values, but not nested functions. So these languages can use stacks to hold local variables.

ML, Scheme, and several other languages, have both nested functions and functions as returnable values (this combination is called *higher-order functions*). So they cannot use stacks to hold all local variables. This complicates the implementation of ML and Scheme – but the added expressive power of higher-order functions justifies the extra implementation effort.

For the remainder of this chapter we will consider languages with stackable local variables and postpone discussion of higher-order functions to Chapter 15.

6.1 STACK FRAMES

The simplest notion of a *stack* is a data structure that supports two operations, *push* and *pop*. However, it turns out that local variables are pushed in large batches (on entry to functions) and popped in large batches (on exit). Furthermore, when local variables are created they are not always initialized right away. Finally, after many variables have been pushed, we want to continue accessing variables deep within the stack. So the abstract *push* and *pop* model is just not suitable.

Instead, we treat the stack as a big array, with a special register – the *stack pointer* – that points at some location. All locations beyond the stack pointer are considered to be garbage, and all locations before the stack pointer are considered to be allocated. The stack usually grows only at the entry to a function, by an increment large enough to hold all the local variables for that function, and, just before the exit from the function, shrinks by the same amount. The area on the stack devoted to the local variables, parameters, return address, and other temporaries for a function is called the function's *activation record* or *stack frame*. For historical reasons, run-time stacks usually start at a high memory address and grow toward smaller addresses. This can be rather confusing: stacks grow downward and shrink upward, like icicles.

The design of a frame layout takes into account the particular features of an instruction set architecture and the programming language being compiled. However, the manufacturer of a computer often prescribes a "standard" frame layout to be used on that architecture, where possible, by all compilers for all programming languages. Sometimes this layout is not the most convenient one for a particular programming language or compiler. But by using the "standard" layout, we gain the considerable benefit that functions written in one language can call functions written in another language.

Figure 6.2 shows a typical stack frame layout. The frame has a set of *incoming arguments* (technically these are part of the previous frame but they are at a known offset from the frame pointer) passed by the caller. The *return address* is created by the CALL instruction and tells where (within the calling function) control should return upon completion of the current function. Some *local variables* are in this frame; other local variables are kept

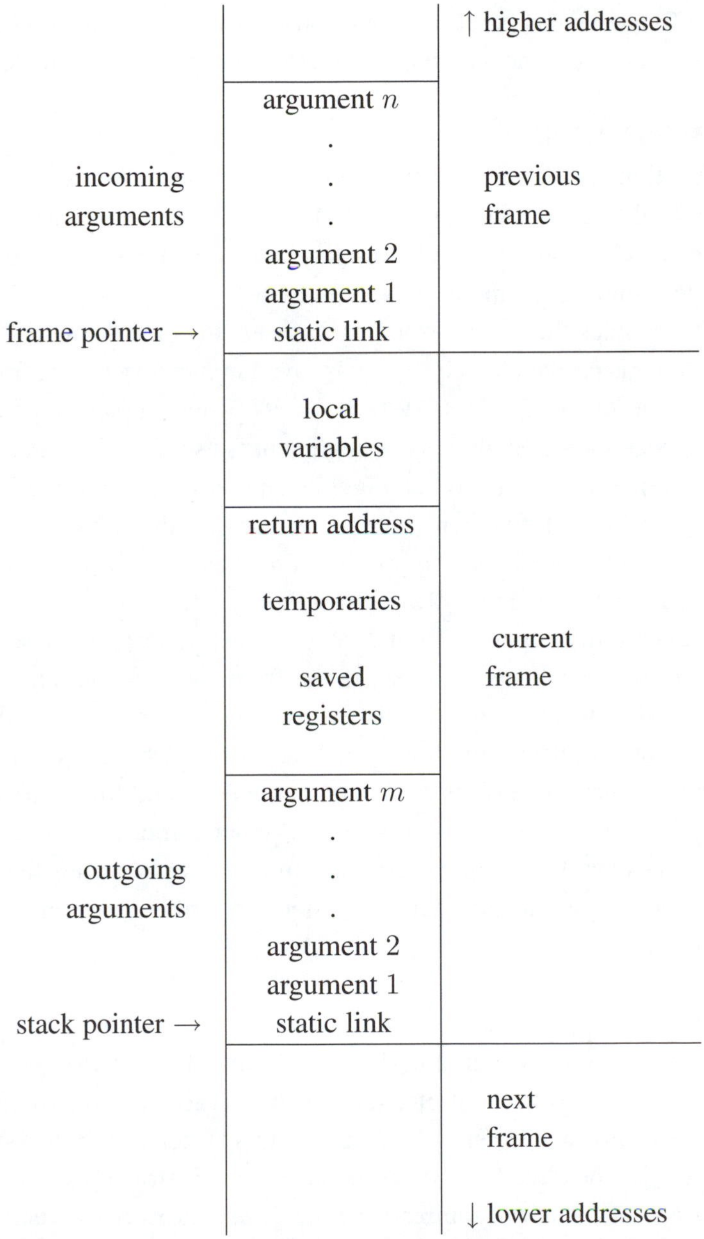

FIGURE 6.2. A stack frame.

in machine registers. Sometimes a local variable kept in a register needs to be *saved* into the frame to make room for other uses of the register; there is an area in the frame for this purpose. Finally, when the current function calls other functions, it can use the *outgoing argument* space to pass parameters.

THE FRAME POINTER

Suppose a function $g(\ldots)$ calls the function $f(a_1, \ldots, a_n)$. We say g is the *caller* and f is the *callee*. On entry to f, the stack pointer points to the first argument that g passes to f. On entry, f allocates a frame by simply subtracting the frame size from the stack pointer SP.

The old SP becomes the current *frame pointer* FP. In some frame layouts, FP is a separate register; the old value of FP is saved in memory (in the frame) and the new FP becomes the old SP. When f exits, it just copies FP back to SP and fetches back the saved FP. This arrangement is useful if f's frame size can vary, or if frames are not always contiguous on the stack. But if the frame size is fixed, then for each function f the FP will always differ from SP by a known constant, and it is not necessary to use a register for FP at all – FP is a "fictional" register whose value is always SP+*framesize*.

Why talk about a frame pointer at all? Why not just refer to all variables, parameters, etc. by their offset from SP, if the frame size is constant? The frame size is not known until quite late in the compilation process, when the number of memory-resident temporaries and saved registers is determined. But it is useful to know the offsets of formal parameters and local variables much earlier. So, for convenience, we still talk about a frame pointer. And we put the formals and locals right near the frame pointer at offsets that are known *early*; the temporaries and saved registers go farther away, at offsets that are known *later*.

REGISTERS

A modern machine has a large set of *registers* (typically 32 of them). To make compiled programs run fast, it's useful to keep local variables, intermediate results of expressions, and other values in registers instead of in the stack frame. Registers can be directly accessed by arithmetic instructions; on most machines, accessing memory requires separate *load* and *store* instructions. Even on machines whose arithmetic instructions can access memory, it is faster to access registers.

A machine (usually) has only one set of registers, but many different procedures and functions need to use registers. Suppose a function f is using register r to hold a local variable and calls procedure g, which also uses r for its own calculations. Then r must be saved (stored into a stack frame) before g uses it and restored (fetched back from the frame) after g is finished using it. But is it f's responsibility to save and restore the register, or g's? We say that r is a *caller-save* register if the caller (in this case, f) must save and restore the register, and r is *callee-save* if it is the responsibility of the callee (in this case, g).

On most machine architectures, the notion of caller-save or callee-save register is not something built into the hardware, but is a convention described in the machine's reference manual. On the MIPS computer, for example, registers 16–23 are preserved across procedure calls (callee-save), and all other registers are not preserved across procedure calls (caller-save).

Sometimes the saves and restores are unnecessary. If f knows that the value of some variable x will not be needed after the call, it may put x in a caller-save register *and not save it* when calling g. Conversely, if f has a local variable i that is needed before and after several function calls, it may put i in some callee-save register r_i and, save r_i just once (upon entry to f) and fetch it back just once (before returning from f). Thus, the wise selection of a caller-save or callee-save register for each local variable and temporary can reduce the number of stores and fetches a program executes. We will rely on our register allocator to choose the appropriate kind of register for each local variable and temporary value.

PARAMETER PASSING

On most machines whose calling conventions were designed in the 1970s, function arguments were passed on the stack.[2] But this causes needless memory traffic. Studies of actual programs have shown that very few functions have more than four arguments, and almost none have more then six. Therefore, parameter-passing conventions for modern machines specify that the first k arguments (for $k = 4$ or $k = 6$, typically) of a function are passed in registers $r_p, ..., r_{p+k-1}$, and the rest of the arguments are passed in memory.

Now, suppose $f(a_1, \ldots, a_n)$ (which received its parameters in $r_1, \ldots, r_n$, for example) calls $h(z)$. It must pass the argument z in r_1; so f saves the old contents of r_1 (the value a_1) in its stack frame before calling h. But there is the memory traffic that was supposedly avoided by passing arguments in registers! How has the use of registers saved any time?

---

[2]Before about 1960, they were passed not on the stack but in statically allocated blocks of memory, which precluded the use of recursive functions.

There are four answers, any or all of which can be used at the same time:

1. Some procedures don't call other procedures – these are called *leaf* procedures. What proportion of procedures are leaves? Well, if we make the (optimistic) assumption that the average procedure calls either no other procedures or calls at least two others, then we can describe a "tree" of procedure calls in which there are more leaves than internal nodes. This means that *most* procedures called are leaf procedures.

   Leaf procedures need not write their incoming arguments to memory. In fact, often they don't need to allocate a stack frame at all. This is an important savings.

2. Some optimizing compilers use *interprocedural register allocation*, analyzing all the functions in an entire program at once. Then they assign different procedures different registers in which to receive parameters and hold local variables. Thus $f(x)$ might receive x in r_1, but call $h(z)$ with z in r_7.

3. Even if f is not a leaf procedure, it might be finished with all its use of the argument x by the time it calls h (technically, x is a dead variable at the point where h is called). Then f can overwrite r_1 without saving it.

4. Some architectures have *register windows*, so that each function invocation can allocate a fresh set of registers without memory traffic.

If f needs to write an incoming parameter into the frame, where in the frame should it go? Ideally, f's frame layout should matter only in the implementation of f. A straightforward approach would be for the caller to pass arguments $a_1, ..., a_k$ in registers and $a_{k+1}, ..., a_n$ at the end of its own frame – the place marked *incoming arguments* in Figure 6.2. If the callee needed to write any of these arguments to memory, it would write them to the area marked *local variables*.

The C programming language actually allows you to take the address of a formal parameter and guarantees that all the formal parameters of a function are at consecutive addresses! This is the `varargs` feature that `printf` uses. Allowing programmers to take the address of a parameter can lead to a *dangling reference* if the address outlives the frame – consider `int *f(int x){return &x;}` – and even when it does not lead to bugs, the consecutive-address rule for parameters constrains the compiler and makes stack-frame layout more complicated. To resolve the contradiction that parameters are passed in registers, but have addresses too, the first k parameters are passed in registers; but any parameter whose address is taken must be written to a memory location on entry to the function. To satisfy `printf`, the memory locations into which register arguments are written must all be consecutive with the memory locations in which arguments $k+1, k+2$, etc. are written. Therefore, C programs can't have some of the arguments saved in one place and some saved in another – they must all be saved contiguously.

So in the standard calling convention of many modern machines the *calling* function reserves space for the register arguments in its own frame, next to the place where it writes argument $k+1$. But the calling function does not actually write anything there; that space is written into *by the called function*, and only if the called function needs to write arguments into memory for any reason.

A more dignified way to take the address of a local variable is to use *call-by-reference*. With call-by-reference, the programmer does not explicitly manipulate the address of a variable x. Instead, if x is passed as the argument to $f(y)$ where y is a "by-reference" parameter, the compiler generates code to pass the address of x instead of the contents of x. At any use of y within the function, the compiler generates an extra pointer dereference. With call-by-reference, there can be no "dangling reference," since y must disappear when f returns, and f returns before x's scope ends.

RETURN ADDRESSES

When function g calls function f, eventually f must return. It needs to know where to go back to. If the *call* instruction within g is at address a, then (usually) the right place to return to is $a+1$, the next instruction in g. This is called the *return address*.

On 1970s machines, the return address was pushed on the stack by the *call* instruction. Modern science has shown that it is faster and more flexible to pass the return address in a register, avoiding memory traffic and also avoiding the need to build any particular stack discipline into the hardware.

On modern machines, the *call* instruction merely puts the return address (the address of the instruction after the call) in a designated register. A nonleaf procedure will then have to write it to the stack (unless interprocedural register allocation is used), but a leaf procedure will not.

FRAME-RESIDENT VARIABLES

So a modern procedure-call convention will pass function parameters in registers, pass the return address in a register, and return the function result in a register. Many of the local variables will be allocated to registers, as will the intermediate results of expression evaluation. Values are written to memory (in the stack frame) only when necessary for one of these reasons:

- the variable will be passed by reference, so it must have a memory address (or, in the C language the & operator is anywhere applied to the variable);
- the variable is accessed by a procedure nested inside the current one;[3]
- the value is too big to fit into a single register;[4]
- the variable is an array, for which address arithmetic is necessary to extract components;
- the register holding the variable is needed for a specific purpose, such as parameter passing (as described above), though a compiler may move such values to other registers instead of storing them in memory;
- or there are so many local variables and temporary values that they won't all fit in registers, in which case some of them are "spilled" into the frame.

We will say that a variable *escapes* if it is passed by reference, its address is taken (using C's & operator), or it is accessed from a nested function.

When a formal parameter or local variable is declared, it's convenient to assign it a location – either in registers or in the stack frame – right at that point in processing the program. Then, when occurrences of that variable are found in expressions, they can be translated into machine code that refers to the right location. Unfortunately, the conditions in our list don't manifest themselves early enough. When the compiler first encounters the declaration of a variable, it doesn't yet know whether the variable will ever be passed by reference, accessed in a nested procedure, or have its address taken; and doesn't know how many registers the calculation of expressions will require (it might be desirable to put some local variables in the frame instead of in registers). An industrial-strength compiler must assign provisional locations to all formals and locals, and decide later which of them should really go in registers.

STATIC LINKS

In languages that allow nested function declarations (such as Pascal, ML, and Tiger), the inner functions may use variables declared in outer functions. This language feature is called *block structure*.

For example, in Program 6.3, `write` refers to the outer variable `output`, and `indent` refers to outer variables n and `output`. To make this work, the function `indent` must have access not only to its own frame (for variables i and s) but also to the frames of `show` (for variable n) and `prettyprint` (for variable `output`).

---

[3]However, with register allocation across function boundaries, local variables accessed by inner functions can sometimes go in registers, as long as the inner function knows where to look.

[4]However, some compilers spread out a large value into several registers for efficiency.

```
1        type tree = {key: string, left: tree, right: tree}
2
3        function prettyprint(tree: tree) : string =
4         let
5             var output := ""
6
7             function write(s: string) =
8                 output := concat(output,s)
9
10            function show(n:int, t: tree) =
11                let function indent(s: string) =
12                        (for i := 1 to n
13                            do write(" ");
14                            output := concat(output,s))
15                 in if t=nil then indent(".")
16                    else (indent(t.key);
17                            show(n+1,t.left);
18                            show(n+1,t.right))
19                end
20
21         in show(0,tree); output
22        end
```

PROGRAM 6.3.   Nested functions.

There are several methods to accomplish this:

- Whenever a function f is called, it can be passed a pointer to the frame of the function statically enclosing f; this pointer is the *static link*.
- A global array can be maintained, containing – in position i – a pointer to the frame of the most recently entered procedure whose *static nesting depth* is i. This array is called a *display*.
- When g calls f, each variable of g that is actually accessed by f (or by any function nested inside f) is passed to f as an extra argument. This is called *lambda lifting*.

I will describe in detail only the method of static links. Which method should be used in practice? See Exercise 6.7.

Whenever a function f is called, it is passed a pointer to the stack frame of the "current" (most recently entered) activation of the function g that *immediately encloses* f in the text of the program.

For example, in Program 6.3:

Line #

21 prettyprint calls show, passing prettyprint's own frame pointer as show's static link.

10 `show` stores its static link (the address of `prettyprint`'s frame) into its own frame.

15 `show` calls `indent`, passing its own frame pointer as `indent`'s static link.

17 `show` calls `show`, passing its own static link (not its own frame pointer) as the static link.

12 `indent` uses the value n from `show`'s frame. To do so, it fetches at an appropriate offset from `indent`'s static link (which points at the frame of `show`).

13 `indent` calls `write`. It must pass the frame pointer of `prettyprint` as the static link. To obtain this, it first fetches at an offset from its own static link (from `show`'s frame), the static link that had been passed to `show`.

14 `indent` uses the variable `output` from `prettyprint`'s frame. To do so it starts with its own static link, then fetches `show`'s, then fetches `output`.[5]

So on each procedure call or variable access, a chain of zero or more fetches is required; the length of the chain is just the *difference* in static nesting depth between the two functions involved.

6.2   FRAMES IN THE Tiger COMPILER

What sort of stack frames should the Tiger compiler use? Here we face the fact that every target machine architecture will have a different standard stack frame layout. If we want Tiger functions to be able to call C functions, we should use the standard layout. But we don't want the specifics of any particular machine intruding on the implementation of the semantic analysis module of the Tiger compiler.

Thus we must use *abstraction*. Just as the `Symbol` module provides a clean interface, and hides the internal representation of `Symbol.Table` from its clients, we must use an abstract representation for frames.

The frame interface will look something like this:

```
package Frame;
import Temp.Temp; import Temp.Label;

public abstract class Access { ⋯ }
public abstract class AccessList {⋯head;⋯tail;⋯ }
```

---

[5]This program would be cleaner if `show` called `write` here instead of manipulating `output` directly, but it would not be as instructive.

```
public abstract class Frame {
   abstract public Frame newFrame(Label name,
                                    Util.BoolList formals);
   abstract public Label name;
   abstract public AccessList formals;
   abstract public Access allocLocal(boolean escape);
    /* ... other stuff, eventually ... */
}
```

The abstract class `Frame` is implemented by a module specific to the target machine. For example, if compiling to the MIPS architecture, there would be

```
package Mips;
class Frame extends Frame.Frame { ··· }
```

In general, we may assume that the machine-independent parts of the compiler have access to this implementation of `Frame`; for example,

```
// in class Main.Main:
Frame.Frame frame = Mips.Frame(···);
```

In this way the rest of the compiler may access `frame` without knowing the identity of the target machine (except an occurrence of the word Mips here and there).

The class `Frame` holds information about formal parameters and local variables allocated in this frame. To make a new frame for a function f with k formal parameters, call `newFrame`(f, l), where l is a list of k booleans: `true` for each parameter that escapes and `false` for each parameter that does not. The result will be a `Frame` object. For example, consider a three-argument function named g whose first argument escapes (needs to be kept in memory). Then

```
frame.newFrame(g, new BoolList(true,
                    new BoolList(false,
                      new BoolList(false, null))))
```

returns a new frame object.

The `Access` class describes formals and locals that may be in the frame or in registers. This is an *abstract data type*, so its implementation as a pair of subclasses is visible only inside the `Frame` module:

```
package Mips;
class InFrame extends Frame.Access {int offset; ··· }
class InReg   extends Frame.Access {Temp temp; ··· }
```

InFrame(X) indicates offset X from the frame pointer; InReg(t_{84}) indicates that it will be held in "register" t_{84}. Frame.Access is an abstract data type, so outside of the module the InFrame and InReg constructors are not visible. Other modules manipulate accesses using interface functions to be described in the next chapter.

The formals field is a list of k "accesses" denoting the locations where the formal parameters will be kept at run time, as seen from inside the callee. Parameters may be seen differently by the caller and the callee. For example, if parameters are passed on the stack, the caller may put a parameter at offset 4 from the stack pointer, but the callee sees it at offset 4 from the frame pointer. Or the caller may put a parameter into register 6, but the callee may want to move it out of the way and always access it from register 13. On the Sparc architecture, with register windows, the caller puts a parameter into register o1, but the save instruction shifts register windows so the callee sees this parameter in register i1.

Because this "shift of view" depends on the calling conventions of the target machine, it must be handled by the Frame module, starting with newFrame. For each formal parameter, newFrame must calculate two things:

- How the parameter will be seen from inside the function (in a register, or in a frame location);
- What instructions must be produced to implement the "view shift."

For example, a frame-resident parameter will be seen as "memory at offset X from the frame pointer," and the view shift will be implemented by copying the stack pointer to the frame pointer on entry to the procedure.

REPRESENTATION OF FRAME DESCRIPTIONS

The implementation module Frame is supposed to keep the representation of Frame objects secret from any clients of the Frame module. But really it's an object holding:

- the locations of all the formals,
- instructions required to implement the "view shift,"
- the number of locals allocated so far,
- and the label at which the function's machine code is to begin (see page 136).

Table 6.4 shows the formals of the three-argument function g (see page 131) as newFrame would allocate them on three different architectures: the Pentium, MIPS, and Sparc. The first parameter escapes, so it needs to be InFrame

		Pentium	MIPS	Sparc
	1	$\text{InFrame}(8)$	$\text{InFrame}(0)$	$\text{InFrame}(68)$
Formals	2	$\text{InFrame}(12)$	$\text{InReg}(t_{157})$	$\text{InReg}(t_{157})$
	3	$\text{InFrame}(16)$	$\text{InReg}(t_{158})$	$\text{InReg}(t_{158})$
View		$M[\text{sp} + 0] \leftarrow fp$	$\text{sp} \leftarrow \text{sp} - K$	$\text{save } \%\text{sp}, -K, \%\text{sp}$
Shift		$\text{fp} \leftarrow \text{sp}$	$M[\text{sp} + K + 0] \leftarrow \text{r2}$	$M[\text{fp} + 68] \leftarrow \text{i0}$
		$\text{sp} \leftarrow \text{sp} - K$	$t_{157} \leftarrow \text{r4}$	$t_{157} \leftarrow \text{i0}$
			$t_{158} \leftarrow \text{r5}$	$t_{158} \leftarrow \text{i1}$

TABLE 6.4. Formal parameters for g on different machines.

on all three machines. The remaining parameters are InFrame on the Pentium, but InReg on the other machines.

The freshly created temporaries t_{157} and t_{158}, and the *move* instructions that copy r4 and r5 into them (or on the Sparc, i0 and i1) may seem superfluous. Why shouldn't the body of g just access these formals directly from the registers in which they arrive? To see why not, consider

```
function m(x:int, y:int) =  (h(y,y); h(x,x))
```

If x stays in "parameter register 1" throughout g, and y is passed to h in parameter register 1, then there is a problem.

The register allocator will eventually choose which machine register should hold t_{157}. If there is no interference of the type shown in function m, then (on the MIPS) the allocator will take care to choose register r4 to hold t_{157} and r5 to hold t_{158}. Then the *move* instructions will be unnecessary and will be deleted at that time.

See also pages 166 and 252 for more discussion of the view shift.

LOCAL VARIABLES

Some local variables are kept in the frame; others are kept in registers. To allocate a new local variable in a frame f, the semantic analysis phase calls

```
f.allocLocal(true)
```

This returns an InFrame access with the appropriate offset from the frame pointer. For example, to allocate two local variables on the Sparc, allocLocal would be called twice, returning successively InFrame(-4) and InFrame(-8), which are standard Sparc frame-pointer offsets for local variables.

The boolean argument to `allocLocal` specifies whether the new variable escapes and needs to go in the frame; if it is false, then the variable can be allocated in a register. Thus, `f.allocLocal(false)` might create $\text{InReg}(t_{481})$.

The calls to `allocLocal` need not come immediately after the frame is created. In a language such as Tiger or C, there may be variable-declaration blocks nested inside the body of a function. For example,

```
function f() =                    void f()
let var v := 6                    {int v=6;
 in print(v);                      print(v);
    let var v := 7                 {int v=7;
     in print (v)                   print(v);
    end;                           }
    print(v);                      print(v);
    let var v := 8                 {int v=8;
     in print (v)                   print(v);
    end;                           }
    print(v)                       print(v);
end                               }
```

In each of these cases, there are three different variables v. Either program will print the sequence 6 7 6 8 6. As each variable declaration is encountered in processing the Tiger program, `allocLocal` will be called to allocate a temporary or new space in the frame, associated with the name v. As each `end` (or closing brace) is encountered, the association with v will be forgotten – but the space is still reserved in the frame. Thus, there will be a distinct temporary or frame slot for every variable declared within the entire function.

The register allocator will use as few registers as possible to represent the temporaries. In this example, the second and third v variables (initialized to 7 and 8) could be held in the same temporary. A clever compiler might also optimize the size of the frame by noticing when two frame-resident variables could be allocated to the same slot.

CALCULATING ESCAPES

Local variables that do not escape can be allocated in a register; escaping variables must be allocated in the frame. A `FindEscape` function can look for escaping variables and record this information in the `escape` fields of the abstract syntax. The simplest way is to traverse the entire abstract syntax tree, looking for escaping uses of every variable. This phase must occur before semantic analysis begins, since `Semant` needs to know whether a variable escapes *immediately* upon seeing that variable for the first time.

The traversal function for `FindEscape` will be a mutual recursion on abstract syntax `exp`'s and `var`'s, just like the type-checker. And, just like the type-checker, it will use environments that map variables to bindings. But in this case the binding will be very simple: it will be the boolean flag that is to be set if the particular variable escapes:

```
package FindEscape;

class Escape {
    int depth;
    abstract void setEscape();
}
class FormalEscape extends Escape {
  Absyn.FieldList fl;
  FormalEscape(int d, Abyn.FieldList f) {
        depth=d; fl=f; fl.escape=false;    }
  void setEscape() {f.escape:=true;}
}
class VarEscape extends Escape {
  Absyn.VarDec vd;
  VarEscape(int d; Abyn.VarDec v) {
        depth=d; vd=v; vd.escape=false;
  }
  void setEscape() {vd.escape:=true;}
}


public class FindEscape {
  Symbol.Table escEnv = new Symbol.Table();
                  // escEnv maps Symbol to Escape
  void traverseVar(int depth, Absyn.Var v) { ··· }
  void traverseExp(int depth, Absyn.Exp e) { ··· }
  void traverseDec(int depth, Absyn.Dec d) { ··· }
  public FindEscape(Absyn.Exp e) traverseExp(0,e);
}
```

Whenever a variable or formal-parameter declaration is found at static function-nesting depth d, such as

$$x \; = \; \text{VarDec}\{name=symbol(\text{``}a\text{''}), escape=r,...\}$$

then a new `VarEscape(d,x)` is entered into the environment.

This new environment is used in processing expressions within the scope of the variable; whenever a is used at depth $> d$, then `setEscape()` is called, which sets the `escape` field of x back to `true`.

For a language where addresses of variables can be taken explicitly by the programmer, or where there are call-by-reference parameters, a similar FindEscape can find variables that escape in those ways.

TEMPORARIES AND LABELS

The compiler's semantic analysis phase will want to choose registers for parameters and local variables, and choose machine-code addresses for procedure bodies. But it is too early to determine exactly which registers are available, or exactly where a procedure body will be located. We use the word *temporary* to mean a value that is temporarily held in a register, and the word *label* to mean some machine-language location whose exact address is yet to be determined – just like a label in assembly language.

Temps are abstract names for local variables; labels are abstract names for static memory addresses. The Temp module manages these two distinct sets of names.

```
package Temp;
public class Temp {
  public String toString();
  public Temp();
}
public class Label {
  public String toString();
  public Label();
  public Label(String s);
  public Label(Symbol s);
}
public class TempList   {···}
public class LabelList  {···}
```

new Temp.Temp() returns a new temporary from an infinite set of temps. new Temp.Label() returns a new label from an infinite set of labels. And new Temp.Label(*string*) returns a new label whose assembly-language name is *string*.

When processing the declaration function f(···), a label for the address of f's machine code can be produced by new Temp.Label(). It's tempting to call new Temp.Label("f") instead – the assembly-language program will be easier to debug if it uses the label f instead of L213 – but unfortunately there could be two different functions named f in different scopes.

TWO LAYERS OF ABSTRACTION

Our Tiger compiler will have two layers of abstraction between semantic analysis and frame-layout details:

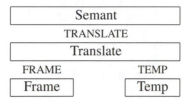

The `Frame` and `Temp` packages provide machine-independent views of memory-resident and register-resident variables. The `Translate` module augments this by handling the notion of nested scopes (via static links), providing the interface TRANSLATE to the `Semant` module.

It is essential to have an abstraction layer at FRAME, to separate the source-language semantics from the machine-dependent frame layout. Separating `Semant` from `Translate` at the TRANSLATE interface is not absolutely necessary: we do it to avoid a huge, unwieldy module that does both type-checking and semantic translation.

In Chapter 7, we will see how `Translate` provides Java functions that are useful in producing intermediate representation from abstract syntax. Here, we need to know how `Translate` manages local variables and static function nesting for `Semant`.

```
package Translate;

public class Access { ··· }
public class AccessList { ··· }
public class Level {
  Frame.Frame frame;   // not public!
  public AccessList formals;
  public Level(Level parent, Symbol name, BoolList fmls);
  public Level(Frame.Frame f);
  public Access allocLocal(boolean escape);
}
```

In the semantic analysis phase of the Tiger compiler, `transDec` creates a new "nesting level" for each function body by constructing

```
new Level(parent,name,formals);
```

the `Level` constructor in turn calls `Frame.newFrame` to make a new frame. `Semant` keeps this `level` in its `FunEntry` data structure for the function, so that when it comes across a function call it can pass the called function's `level` back to `Translate`. The `FunEntry` also needs the `label` of the function's machine-code entry point:

```
/* new versions of VarEntry and FunEntry */
class VarEntry extends Entry {
   Translate.Access access;
   Types.Type ty;
   VarEntry(Translate.Access a, Types.Type t) {···}
}

class FunEntry extends Entry {
  public Translate.Level level;
  public Temp.Label label;
  public Types.RECORD formals;
  public Types.Type result;
  public FunEntry(Translate.Level v, Temp.Label l,
                  Types.RECORD f, Types.Type r) {
    level=v; label=l; formals=f; result=r;
  }
}
```

When `Semant` processes a local variable declaration at level `lev`, it calls `lev.allocLocal(esc)` to create the variable in this level; the argument `esc` specifies whether the variable escapes. The result is a `Translate.Access`, which is an abstract data type (not the same as `Frame.Access`, since it must know about static links). Later, when the variable is used in an expression, `Semant` can hand this `access` back to `Translate` in order to generate the machine code to access the variable. Meanwhile, `Semant` records the access in each `VarEntry` in the value-environment.

The abstract data type `Translate.Access` can be implemented as a pair consisting of the variable's `level` and its `Frame.access`:

```
package Translate;
public class Access {
  Level home;
  Frame.Access acc;
  Access(Level h, Frame.Access a) {home=h; acc=a; }
}
```

so that `Level.allocLocal` calls `Frame.allocLocal`, and also remembers what level the variable lives in. The level information will be necessary later for calculating static links, when the variable is accessed from a (possibly) different level.

MANAGING STATIC LINKS

The `Frame` module should be independent of the specific source language being compiled. Many source languages do not have nested function declarations; thus, `Frame` should not know anything about static links. Instead, this is the responsibility of `Translate`.

`Translate` knows that each frame contains a static link. The static link is passed to a function in a register and stored into the frame. Since the static link behaves so much like a formal parameter, we will treat it as one (as much as possible). For a function with k "ordinary" parameters, let l be the list of booleans signifying whether the parameters escape. Then

$$l' = \text{new BoolList(true, } l)$$

is a new list; the extra `true` at the front signifies that the static link "extra parameter" does escape. Then $\text{newFrame}(label, l')$ makes the frame whose formal parameter list includes the "extra" parameter.

Suppose, for example, function $f(x, y)$ is nested inside function g, and the `level` (previously created) for g is called level_g. Then `Semant.transDec` can call

```
new Translate.Level(level_g, f, new BoolList(false,
                            new BoolList(false, null)))
```

assuming that neither x nor y escapes. Then `Level(parent,name,fmls)` adds an extra element to the formal-parameter list (for the static link), and calls

```
parent.frame.newFrame(name,new BoolList(true, fmls))
```

What comes back is a `Frame`. In this frame are three frame-offset values, accessible as `frame.formals`. The first of these is the static-link offset; the other two are the offsets for x and y. When `Semant` calls `Translate.formals(level)`, it will get these two offsets, suitably converted into `access` values.

KEEPING TRACK OF LEVELS

With every call to `new Level(···)`, `Semant` must pass the enclosing `level` value. When creating the level for the "main" Tiger program (one not within any Tiger function), `Semant` should pass a special "outermost" level value, created as `new Translate.Level(frame)`. This is not the level of the Tiger main program, it is the level within which that program is nested. All "library" functions (described in Section 5.2) are declared at this outermost level, which does not contain a frame or formal parameter list.

The function `transDec` will make a new level for each Tiger function declaration. But `Level(···)` must be told the enclosing function's `level`. This means that `transDec` must know, while processing each declaration, the current static nesting level.

This is easy: `transDec` will now get an additional argument (in addition to the type and value environments) that is the current `level` as given by the appropriate call to `newLevel`. And `transExp` will also require this argument, so that `transDec` can pass a `level` to `transExp`, which passes it in turn to `transDec` to process declarations of nested functions. For similar reasons, `transVar` will also need a `level` argument.

Instead of passing an extra level argument and a new "break scope" to every function call, it's simpler to make a `level` field and a `breakScope` field of the `Semant` class. Then, at each function definition, `Semant` can create a new version of itself by calling

```
Semant newsem = new Semant(env,translate,new_lev,new_brk);
```

and then use `newsem` for processing the function body.

PROGRAM FRAMES

Augment `Semant/*.java` to allocate locations for local variables, and to keep track of the nesting level. To keep things simple, assume every variable escapes.

Implement the `Translate` module as `Translate/*`.

If you are compiling for the Sparc, implement the `Sparc` package containing `Sparc/Frame.java`. If compiling for the MIPS, implement the `Mips` package, and so on.

Try to keep *all* the machine-specific details in your machine-dependent `Frame` module, not in `Semant` or `Translate`.

To keep things simple, handle *only* escaping parameters. That is, when implementing `newFrame`, handle only the case where all "escape" indicators are `true`.

If you are working on a RISC machine (such as MIPS or Sparc) that passes the first k parameters in registers and the rest in memory, keep things simple by handling *only* the case where there are k or fewer parameters.

Optional: Implement `FindEscape`, the module that sets the `escape` field of every variable in the abstract syntax. Modify your `transDec` function to allocate nonescaping variables and formal parameters in registers.

Optional: Handle functions with more than k formal parameters.
Supporting files available in `$TIGER/chap6` include:

`Temp/*` the module supporting temporaries and labels.
`Util/BoolList.java` the class for lists of booleans.

EXERCISES

6.1 Using the C compiler of your choice (or a compiler for another language), compile some small test functions into assembly language. On Unix this is usually done by `cc -S`. Turn on all possible compiler optimizations. Then evaluate the compiled programs by these criteria:

a. Are local variables kept in registers?

b. If local variable b is live across more than one procedure call, is it kept in a callee-save register? Explain how doing this would speed up the program.

```
int f(int a) {int b; b=a+1; g(); h(b); return b+2;}
```

c. If local variable x is never live across a procedure call, is it properly kept in a caller-save register? Explain how doing this would speed up the program.

```
void h(int y) {int x; x=y+1; f(y); f(2);}
```

6.2 If you have a RISC machine, use your C compiler to generate assembly language for this function

```
extern void h(int, int);
void m(int x, int y) {h(y,y); h(x,x);}
```

and explain when and how it moves x out of the parameter-1 register so as to call $h(y, y)$.

6.3 For each of the variables a, b, c, d, e in this C program, say whether the variable should be kept in memory or a register, and why.

```
int f(int a, int b)
{ int c[3], d, e;
  d=a+1;
  e=g(c, &b);
  return e+c[1]+b;
}
```

6.4 How much memory should this program use?

```
int f(int i) {int j,k; j=i*i; k=i?f(i-1):0; return k+j;}
void main() {f(100000);}
```

a. Imagine a compiler that passes parameters in registers, wastes no space providing "backup storage" for parameters passed in registers, does not use static links, and in general makes stack frames as small as possible. How big should each stack frame for f be, in words?

b. What is the maximum memory use of this program, with such a compiler?

c. Using your favorite C compiler, compile this program to assembly language and report the size of f's stack frame.

d. Calculate the total memory use of this program with the real C compiler.

e. Quantitatively and comprehensively explain the discrepancy between (a) and (c).

f. Comment on the likelihood that the designers of this C compiler considered deeply recursive functions important in real programs.

6.5 Some Tiger functions do not need static links, because they do not make use of a particular feature of the Tiger language.

a. Characterize precisely those functions that do not need a static link passed to them.

b. Give an algorithm (perhaps similar to `FindEscape`) that marks all such functions.

6.6 Instead of (or in addition to) using static links, there are other ways of getting access to nonlocal variables. One way is just to leave the variable in a register!

```
function f() : int =
  let var a := 5
      function g() : int =
          (a+1)
    in g()+g()
    end
```

If a is left in register r_7 (for example) while g is called, then g can just access it from there.

What properties must a local variable, the function in which it is defined, and the functions in which it is used, have for this trick to work?

6.7   A *display* is a data structure that may be used as an alternative to static links for maintaining access to nonlocal variables. It is an array of frame pointers, indexed by static nesting depth. Element D_i of the display always points to the most recently called function whose static nesting depth is i.

The bookkeeping performed by a function f, whose static nesting depth is i, looks like:

> Copy D_i to *save location* in stack frame
> Copy frame pointer to D_i
> $\cdots$ body of f $\cdots$
> Copy *save location* back to D_i

In Program 6.3, function `prettyprint` is at depth 1, `write` and `show` are at depth 2, and so on.

a. Show the sequence of machine instructions required to fetch the variable `output` into a register at line 14 of Program 6.3, using static links.

b. Show the machine instructions required if a display were used instead.

c. When variable x is declared at depth d_1 and accessed at depth d_2, how many instructions does the static-link method require to fetch x?

d. How many does the display method require?

e. How many instructions does static-link maintenance require for a procedure entry and exit (combined)?

f. How many instructions does display maintenance require for procedure entry and exit?

Should we use displays instead of static links? Perhaps; but the issue is more complicated. For languages such as Pascal and Tiger with block structure but no function variables, displays work well.

But the full expressive power of block structure is obtained when functions can be returned as results of other functions, as in Scheme and ML. For such languages, there are more issues to consider than just variable-access time and procedure entry-exit cost. The best solution is neither displays nor static links; see Chapter 15.

7

Translation to Intermediate Code

trans-late: to turn into one's own or another language

Webster's Dictionary

The semantic analysis phase of a compiler must translate abstract syntax into abstract machine code. It can do this after type-checking, or at the same time.

Though it is possible to translate directly to real machine code, this hinders portability and modularity. Suppose we want compilers for N different source languages, targeted to M different machines. In principle this is $N \cdot M$ compilers (Figure 7.1a), a large implementation task.

An *intermediate representation* (IR) is a kind of abstract machine language that can express the target-machine operations without committing to too much machine-specific detail. But it is also independent of the details of the source language. The *front end* of the compiler does lexical analysis, parsing, semantic analysis, and translation to intermediate representation. The *back end* does optimization of the intermediate representation and translation to machine language.

A portable compiler translates the source language into IR and then translates the IR into machine language, as illustrated in Figure 7.1b. Now only N front ends and M back ends are required. Such an implementation task is more reasonable.

Even when only one front end and one back end are being built, a good IR can modularize the task, so that the front end is not complicated with machine-specific details, and the back end is not bothered with source-language-specific information. Many different kinds of IR are used in compilers; for this compiler I have chosen simple expression trees.

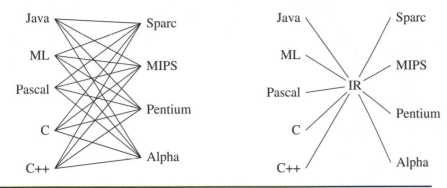

FIGURE 7.1.   Compilers for five languages and four target machines:
(left) without an IR, (right) with an IR.

7.1   INTERMEDIATE REPRESENTATION TREES

The intermediate representation tree language is defined by the package
`Tree`, containing abstract classes `Stm` and `Exp` and their subclasses, as shown
in Figure 7.2.

A good intermediate representation has several qualities:

- It must be convenient for the semantic analysis phase to produce.
- It must be convenient to translate into real machine language, for all the desired
  target machines.
- Each construct must have a clear and simple meaning, so that optimizing transformations that rewrite the intermediate representation can easily be specified
  and implemented.

Individual pieces of abstract syntax can be complicated things, such as
array subscripts, procedure calls, and so on. And individual "real machine"
instructions can also have a complicated effect (though this is less true of
modern RISC machines than of earlier architectures). Unfortunately, it is not
always the case that complex pieces of the abstract syntax correspond exactly
to the complex instructions that a machine can execute.

Therefore, the intermediate representation should have individual components that describe only extremely simple things: a single fetch, store, add,
move, or jump. Then any "chunky" piece of abstract syntax can be translated
into just the right set of abstract machine instructions; and groups of abstract
machine instructions can be clumped together (perhaps in quite different
clumps) to form "real" machine instructions.

```
package Tree;

abstract class Exp
 CONST(int value)
 NAME(Label label)
 TEMP(Temp.Temp temp)
 BINOP(int binop, Exp left, Exp right)
 MEM(Exp exp)
 CALL(Exp func, ExpList args)
 ESEQ(Stm stm, Exp exp)

abstract class Stm
 MOVE(Exp dst, Exp src)
 EXP(Exp exp)
 JUMP(Exp exp, Temp.LabelList targets)
 CJUMP(int relop, Exp left, Exp right, Label iftrue, Label iffalse)
 SEQ(Stm left, Stm right)
 LABEL(Label label)
```

other classes:
ExpList(Exp head, ExpList tail)
StmList(Stm head, StmList tail)

other constants:
```
final static int BINOP.PLUS, BINOP.MINUS, BINOP.MUL, BINOP.DIV, BINOP.AND,
    BINOP.OR, BINOP.LSHIFT, BINOP.RSHIFT, BINOP.ARSHIFT, BINOP.XOR;

final static int RELOP.EQ, RELOP.NE, RELOP.LT, RELOP.GT, RELOP.LE,
        RELOP.GE, RELOP.ULT, RELOP.ULE, RELOP.UGT, RELOP.UGE;
```

FIGURE 7.2.   Intermediate representation trees.

Here is a description of the meaning of each tree operator. First, the expressions (Exp), which stand for the computation of some value (possibly with side effects):

CONST(i) The integer constant i.

NAME(n) The symbolic constant n (corresponding to an assembly language label).

TEMP(t) Temporary t. A temporary in the abstract machine is similar to a register in a real machine. However, the abstract machine has an infinite number of temporaries.

BINOP(o, e_1, e_2) The application of binary operator o to operands e_1, e_2. Subexpression e_1 is evaluated before e_2. The integer arithmetic operators are PLUS, MINUS, MUL, DIV; the integer bitwise logical operators are AND, OR, XOR; the integer logical shift operators are LSHIFT, RSHIFT; the integer arithmetic right-shift is ARSHIFT. The Tiger language has no logical operators, but the intermediate language is meant to be independent of any source language; also, the logical operators might be used in implementing other features of Tiger.

MEM(e) The contents of *wordSize* bytes of memory starting at address e (where *wordSize* is defined in the `Frame` module). Note that when MEM is used as the left child of a MOVE, it means "store," but anywhere else it means "fetch."

CALL(f, l) A procedure call: the application of function f to argument list l. The subexpression f is evaluated before the arguments which are evaluated left to right.

ESEQ(s, e) The statement s is evaluated for side effects, then e is evaluated for a result.

The statements (`stm`) of the tree language perform side effects and control flow:

MOVE(TEMP t, e) Evaluate e and move it into temporary t.

MOVE(MEM(e_1, k), e_2) Evaluate e_1, yielding address a. Then evaluate e_2, and store the result into k bytes of memory starting at a.

EXP(e) Evaluate e and discard the result.

JUMP($e, labs$) Transfer control (jump) to address e. The destination e may be a literal label, as in NAME(lab), or it may be an address calculated by any other kind of expression. For example, a C-language `switch(i)` statement may be implemented by doing arithmetic on i. The list of labels `labs` specifies all the possible locations that the expression e can evaluate to; this is necessary for dataflow analysis later. The common case of jumping to a known label l is written as JUMP(NAME l, new `ExpList`(l, null)), but the JUMP class has an extra constructor so that this can be abbreviated as JUMP(l).

CJUMP(o, e_1, e_2, t, f) Evaluate e_1, e_2 in that order, yielding values a, b. Then compare a, b using the relational operator o. If the result is `true`, jump to t; otherwise jump to f. The relational operators are EQ and NE for integer equality and nonequality (signed or unsigned); signed integer inequalities LT, GT, LE, GE; and unsigned integer inequalities ULT, ULE, UGT, UGE.

SEQ(s_1, s_2) The statement s_1 followed by s_2.

LABEL(n) Define the constant value of name n to be the current machine code address. This is like a label definition in assembly language. The value NAME(n) may be the target of jumps, calls, etc.

It is almost possible to give a formal semantics to the `Tree` language. However, there is no provision in this language for procedure and function definitions – we can specify only the body of each function. The procedure entry and exit sequences will be added later as special "glue" that is different for each target machine.

7.2 TRANSLATION INTO TREES

Translation of abstract syntax expressions into intermediate trees is reasonably straightforward; but there are many cases to handle.

KINDS OF EXPRESSIONS

What should the representation of an abstract syntax expression `Absyn.Exp` be in the `Tree` language? At first it seems obvious that it should be `Tree.Exp`. However, this is true only for certain kinds of expressions, the ones that compute a value. Expressions that return no value (such as some procedure calls, or **while** expressions in the Tiger language) are more naturally represented by `Tree.Stm`. And expressions with Boolean values, such as $a > b$, might best be represented as a conditional jump – a combination of `Tree.Stm` and a pair of destinations represented by `Temp.Label`s.

It is better instead to ask, "how might the expression be used?" Then we can make the right kind of *methods* for an object-oriented interface to expressions. We end up with `Translate.Exp`, not the same class as `Tree.Exp`, having three methods:

```
package Translate;
public abstract class Exp {
   abstract Tree.Exp unEx();
   abstract Tree.Stm unNx();
   abstract Tree.Stm unCx(Temp.Label t, Temp.Label f);
}
```

`Ex` stands for an "expression," represented as a `Tree.Exp`.

`Nx` stands for "no result," represented as a `Tree` statement.

`Cx` stands for "conditional," represented as a function from label-pair to statement. If you pass it a true-destination and a false-destination, it will make a statement that evaluates some conditionals and then jumps to one of the destinations (the statement will never "fall through").

For example, the Tiger expression   `a>b|c<d` might translate to a `Translate.Exp` whose unCx method is roughly like

```
Tree.Stm unCx(Label t, Label f) {
  Label z = new Label();
  return new SEQ(new CJUMP(CJUMP.GT,a,b,t,z),
               new SEQ(new LABEL(z),
                   new CJUMP(CJUMP.LT,c,d,t,f)));
}
```

The abstract class `Translate.Exp` can be instantiated by several subclasses: `Ex` for an ordinary expression that yields a single value, `Nx` for an expression that yields no value, and `Cx` for a "conditional" expression that jumps to either t or f:

```
class Ex extends Exp {
   Tree.Exp exp;
   Ex(Tree.Exp e) {exp=e;}
   Tree.Exp unEx() {return exp;}
   Tree.Stm unNx() { ···?··· }
   Tree.Stm unCx(Label t, Label f) { ···?··· }
}
class Nx extends Exp {
   Tree.Stm stm;
   Nx(Tree.Stm s) {stm=s;}
   Tree.Exp unEx() { ···?··· }
   Tree.Stm unNx() {return stm;}
   Tree.Stm unCx(Label t, Label f) { ···?··· }
}
```

But what does the unNx method of an `Ex` do? We have a simple `Tree.Exp` that yields a value, and we are asked to produce a `Tree.Stm` that produces no value. There is a conversion operator `Tree.EXP`, and unNx must apply it:

```
class Ex extends Exp {
  Tree.Exp exp;
    .
    .
    .
  Tree.Stm unNx() {return new Tree.EXP(exp); }
    .
    .
    .
}
```

Each kind of `Translate.Exp` class must have similar conversion methods. For example, the Tiger statement

```
flag := (a>b | c<d)
```

requires the unEx method of a `Cx` object so that a 1 (for true) or 0 (for false) can be stored into `flag`.

Program 7.3 shows the class `Cx`. The unEx method is of particular interest. To convert a "conditional" into a "value expression," we invent a new temporary r and new labels t and f. Then we make a `Tree.Stm` that moves the value 1 into r, and a conditional jump $unCx(t, f)$ that implements the conditional. If the condition is false, then 0 is moved into r; if true, then execution

```
abstract class Cx extends Exp {
  Tree.Exp unEx() {
    Temp r = new Temp();
    Label t = new Label();
    Label f = new Label();

    return new Tree.ESEQ(
            new Tree.SEQ(new Tree.MOVE(new Tree.TEMP(r),
                                       new Tree.CONST(1)),
                    new Tree.SEQ(unCx(t,f),
                      new Tree.SEQ(new Tree.LABEL(f),
                        new Tree.SEQ(new Tree.MOVE(new Tree.TEMP(r),
                                                   new Tree.CONST(0)),
                          new Tree.LABEL(t))))),
                    new Tree.TEMP(r));
  }

  abstract Tree.Stm unCx(Label t, Label f);

  Tree.Stm unNx() { ··· }
}
```

PROGRAM 7.3.   The Cx class.

---

proceeds at t and the second move is skipped. The result of the whole thing is just the temporary r containing zero or one.

The unCx method is still abstract: I will discuss this later, with the translation of Tiger comparison operators. But the unEx and unNx methods can still be implemented in terms of the unCx method. I have shown unEx; I will leave unNx (which is simpler) as an exercise.

The unCx method of class Ex is left as an exercise. It's helpful to have unCx treat the cases of CONST 0 and CONST 1 specially, since they have particularly simple and efficient translations. Class Nx's unEx and unCx methods need not be implemented, since these cases should never occur in compiling a well typed Tiger program.

SIMPLE VARIABLES

The semantic analysis phase has a function that type-checks a variable in the context of a type environment tenv and a value environment env. This function transVar returns an ExpTy containing a Translate.Exp and a Types.Type. In Chapter 5 the exp was merely a place-holder, but now Semant must be modified so that each exp holds the intermediate-representation translation of each Tiger expression.

For a simple variable v declared in the current procedure's stack frame, we translate it as

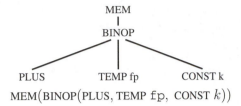

$$\text{MEM}(\text{BINOP}(\text{PLUS}, \text{TEMP fp}, \text{CONST } k))$$

where k is the offset of v within the frame and TEMP fp is the frame pointer register. For the Tiger compiler we make the simplifying assumption that all variables are the same size – the natural word size of the machine.

Interface between Translate and Semant. The type `Translate.Exp` is an abstract data type, whose `Ex` and `Nx` constructors are visible only within `Translate`.

The manipulation of MEM nodes should all be done in the `Translate` module, not in `Semant`. Doing it in `Semant` would clutter up the readability of that module and would make `Semant` dependent on the `Tree` representation. We add a function

```
public Exp simpleVar(Access, Level)
```

to the `Translate` interface. Now `Semant` can pass the `access` of x (obtained from `Translate.allocLocal`) and the `level` of the function in which x is used and get back a `Translate.Exp`.

With this interface, `Semant` never gets its hands dirty with a `Tree.Exp` at all. In fact, this is a good rule of thumb in determining the interface between `Semant` and `Translate`: the `Semant` module should not contain any direct reference to the `Tree` or `Frame` module. Any manipulation of IR trees should be done by `Translate`.

The `Frame` class holds all machine-dependent definitions; here we add to it a frame-pointer register `FP` and a constant whose value is the machine's natural word size:

```
package Frame;
public class Frame {
       ⋮
    abstract public Temp FP();
    abstract public int wordSize();
}
public abstract class Access {
    public abstract Tree.Exp exp(Tree.Exp framePtr);
}
```

In this and later chapters, I will abbreviate BINOP(PLUS, e_1, e_2) as $+(e_1, e_2)$, so the tree above would be shown as

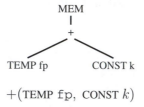

$+($TEMP $\texttt{fp}$, CONST $k)$

The $\texttt{exp}$ method of $\texttt{Frame.Access}$ is used by $\texttt{Translate}$ to turn a $\texttt{Frame.Access}$ into the $\texttt{Tree}$ expression. The $\texttt{Tree.Exp}$ argument is the address of the stack frame that the $\texttt{Access}$ lives in. Thus, for an access a such as $\texttt{InFrame}(k)$, we have

```
a.exp(new TEMP(frame.FP())) =
            MEM(BINOP(PLUS,TEMP(frame.FP()),CONST(k)))
```

Why bother to pass the tree expression $\texttt{TEMP(frame.FP())}$ as an argument? The answer is that the address of the frame is the same as the current frame pointer *only* when accessing the variable from its own level. When accessing a from an inner-nested function, the frame address must be calculated using static links, and the result of this calculation will be the $\texttt{Tree.Exp}$ argument to $a.\texttt{exp()}$.

If a is a register access such as $\texttt{InReg}(t_{832})$, then the frame-address argument to $a.\texttt{exp()}$ will be discarded, and the result will be simply TEMP t_{832}.

An l-value such as v or $a[i]$ or $p.next$ can appear either on the left side or the right side of an assignment statement – l stands for *left*, to distinguish from r-values that can appear only on the right side of an assignment. Fortunately, only MEM and TEMP nodes can appear on the left of a MOVE node.

FOLLOWING STATIC LINKS

When a variable x is declared at an outer level of static scope, static links must be used. The general form is

$$\text{MEM}(+(\text{CONST } k_n, \text{ MEM}(+(\text{CONST } k_{n-1}, | \ldots \\ \text{MEM}(+(\text{CONST } k_1, \text{ TEMP FP}))\ldots))))$$

where the $k_1, ..., k_{n-1}$ are the various static link offsets in nested functions, and k_n is the offset of x in its own frame.

To construct this expression, we need the `level` l_f of the function f in which x is used, and the `level` l_g of the function g in which x is declared. As we strip levels from l_f, we use the static link offsets $k_1, k_2, ...$ from these levels to construct the tree. Eventually we reach l_g, and we can stop.

`Translate.simpleVar` must produce a chain of MEM and + nodes to fetch static links for all frames between the level of use (the `level` passed to `simpleVar`) and the level of definition (the `level` within the variable's `access`).

ARRAY VARIABLES

For the rest of this chapter I will not specify all the interface functions of `Translate`, as I have done for `simpleVar`. But the rule of thumb just given applies to all of them; there should be a `Translate` function to handle array subscripts, one for record fields, one for each kind of expression, and so on.

Different programming languages treat array-valued variables differently.

In Pascal, an array variable stands for the contents of the array – in this case all twelve integers. The Pascal program

```
var a,b : array[1..12] of integer
begin
      a := b
end;
```

copies the contents of array a into array b.

In C, there is no such thing as an array variable. There are pointer variables; arrays are like "pointer constants." Thus, this is illegal:

```
{int a[12], b[12];
 a = b;
}
```

but this is quite legal:

```
{int a[12], *b;
 b = a;
}
```

The statement b=a does not copy the elements of a; instead, it means that b now points to the beginning of the array a.

In Tiger (as in Java and ML), array variables behave like pointers. Tiger has no named array constants as in C, however. Instead, new array values are created (and initialized) by the construct $t_a[n]$ of i, where t_a is the name of an array type, n is the number of elements, and i is the initial value of each element. In the program

```
let
  type intArray = array of int
  var a := intArray[12] of 0
  var b := intArray[12] of 7
in a := b
end
```

the array variable a ends up pointing to the same 12 sevens as the variable b; the original 12 zeros allocated for a are discarded.

Tiger record values are also pointers. Record assigment, like array assignment, is pointer assigment and does not copy all the fields. This is also true of modern object-oriented and functional programming languages, which try to blur the syntactic distinction between pointers and objects. In C or Pascal, however, a record value is "big," and record assigment means copying all the fields.

STRUCTURED L-VALUES

An l-value is the result of an expression that can occur on the *left* of an assignment statement, such as x or p.y or a[i+2]. An r-value is one that can only appear on the *right* of an assignment, such as a+3 or f(x). That is, an l-value denotes a *location* that can be assigned to, and an r-value does not.

Of course, an l-value can occur on the right of an assignment statement; in this case the *contents* of the location are implicitly taken.

We say that an integer or pointer value is a "scalar," since it has only one component. Such a value occupies just one word of memory and can fit in a register. All the variables and l-values in Tiger are scalar. Even a Tiger array or record variable is really a pointer (a kind of scalar); the *Tiger Language Reference Manual* does not say so explicitly, because it is talking about Tiger semantics instead of Tiger implementation.

In C or Pascal there are structured l-values – structs in C, arrays and records in Pascal – that are not scalar. To implement a language with "large" variables such as the arrays and records in C or Pascal requires a bit of extra work. In a C compiler, the `access` type would require information about the size of the variable. Then, the MEM operator of the TREE intermediate language would need to be extended with a notion of size:

```
package Tree;
abstract class Exp
 MEM(Exp exp, int size)
```

The translation of a local variable into an IR tree would look like

$$\text{MEM}(+(\text{TEMP fp, CONST } k_n), \ S)$$

where the S indicates the size of the object to be fetched or stored (depending on whether this tree appears on the left or right of a MOVE).

Leaving out the size on MEM nodes makes the Tiger compiler easier to implement, but limits the generality of its intermediate representation.

SUBSCRIPTING AND FIELD SELECTION

To subscript an array in Pascal or C (to compute $a[i]$), just calculate address of the ith element of a: $(i - l) \times s + a$, where l is the lower bound of the index range, s is the size (in bytes) of each array element, and a is the base address of the array elements. If a is global, with a compile-time constant address, then the subtraction $a - s \times l$ can be done at compile time.

Similarly, to select field f of a record l-value a (to calculate $a.f$), simply add the constant field offset of f to the address a.

An array variable a is an l-value; so is an array subscript expression $a[i]$, even if i is not an l-value. To calculate the l-value $a[i]$ from a, we do arithmetic on the address of a. Thus, in a Pascal compiler, the translation of an l-value (particularly a structured l-value) should *not* be something like

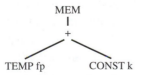

but should instead be the `Tree` expression representing the base address of the array:

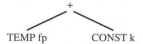

What could happen to this l-value?

- A particular element might be subscripted, yielding a (smaller) l-value. A "+" node would add the index times the element size to the l-value for the base of the array.
- The l-value (representing the entire array) might be used in a context where an r-value is required (e.g., passed as a by-value parameter, or assigned to another array variable). Then the l-value is *coerced* into an r-value by applying the MEM operator to it.

In the Tiger language, there are no structured, or "large," l-values. This is because all record and array values are really pointers to record and array structures. The "base address" of the array is really the contents of a pointer variable, so MEM is required to fetch this base address.

Thus, if a is a memory-resident array variable represented as MEM(e), then the contents of address e will be a one-word pointer value p. The contents of addresses $p, p+W, p+2W, ...$ (where W is the word size) will be the elements of the array (all elements are one word long). Thus, $a[i]$ is just

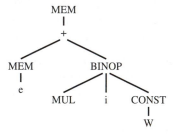

$$\text{MEM}(+(\text{MEM}(e),\ \text{BINOP}(\text{MUL},\ i,\ \text{CONST}\ W)))$$

L-values and MEM nodes. Technically, an l-value (or *assignable variable*) should be represented as an *address* (without the top MEM node in the diagram above). Converting an l-value to an r-value (when it is used in an expression) means *fetching* from that address; assigning to an l-value means *storing* to that address. We are attaching the MEM node to the l-value before knowing whether it is to be fetched or stored; this works only because in the `Tree` intermediate representation, MEM means both *store* (when used as the left child of a MOVE) and *fetch* (when used elsewhere).

A SERMON ON SAFETY

Life is too short to spend time chasing down irreproducible bugs, and money is too valuable to waste on the purchase of flaky software. When a program has a bug, it should detect that fact as soon as possible and announce that fact (or take corrective action) before the bug causes any harm.

Some bugs are very subtle. But it should not take a genius to detect an out-of-bounds array subscript: if the array bounds are $L..H$, and the subscript is i, then $i < L$ or $i > H$ is an array bounds error. Furthermore, computers are well-equipped with hardware able to compute the condition $i > H$. For several decades now, we have known that compilers can automatically emit the code to test this condition. There is no excuse for a compiler that is unable to emit code for checking array bounds. Optimizing compilers can often *safely* remove the checks by compile-time analysis; see Section 17.4.

One might say, by way of excuse, "but the language in which I program has the kind of address arithmetic that makes it impossible to know the bounds of an array." Yes, and the man who shot his mother and father threw himself upon the mercy of the court because he was an orphan.

In some rare circumstances, a portion of a program demands blinding speed, and the timing budget does not allow for bounds checking. In such a case, it would be best if the optimizing compiler could analyze the subscript expressions and prove that the index will always be within bounds, so that an explicit bounds check is not necessary. If that is not possible, perhaps it is reasonable in these rare cases to allow the programmer to explicitly specify an unchecked subscript operation. But this does not excuse the compiler from checking all the other subscript expressions in the program.

Needless to say, the compiler should check pointers for `nil` before dereferencing them, too.

ARITHMETIC

Integer arithmetic is easy to translate: each `Absyn` arithmetic operator corresponds to a `Tree` operator.

The `Tree` language has no unary arithmetic operators. Unary negation of integers can be implemented as subtraction from zero; unary complement can be implemented as XOR with all ones.

Unary floating-point negation cannot be implemented as subtraction from zero, because many floating-point representations allow a *negative zero*. The negation of negative zero is positive zero, and vice versa. Some numerical programs rely on identities such as $-0 < 0$. Thus, the `Tree` language does not support unary negation very well.

Fortunately, the Tiger language doesn't support floating-point numbers; but in a real compiler, a new operator would have to be added for floating negation.

CONDITIONALS

The result of a comparison operator will be a Cx expression: a statement s that will jump to any true-destination and false-destination you specify.

Making "simple" Cx expressions from Absyn comparison operators is easy with the CJUMP operator. However, the whole point of the Cx representation is that conditional expressions can be combined easily with the Tiger operators & and |. Therefore, an expression such as x<5 will be translated as $\text{Cx}(s_1)$ where

$$s_1(t, f) = \text{CJUMP}(\text{LT}, x, \text{CONST}(5), t, f)$$

for any labels t and f.

To do this, we extend the Cx class to make a subclass RelCx that has private fields to hold the left and right expressions (in this case x and 5) and the comparison operator (in this case Tree.CJUMP.LT). Then we override the unCx method to generate the CJUMP from these data. It is not necessary to make unEx and unNx methods, since these will be inherited from the parent Cx class.

The & and | operators of the Tiger language, which combine conditionals with short-circuit conjunction and disjunction (*and* and *or*) respectively, have already been translated into if-expressions in the abstract syntax.

The most straightforward thing to do with an if-expression

if e_1 **then** e_2 **else** e_3

is to treat e_1 as a Cx expression, and e_2 and e_3 as Ex expressions. That is, use the unCx method of e_1 and the unEx of e_2 and e_3. Make two labels t and f to which the conditional will branch. Allocate a temporary r, and after label t, move e_2 to r; after label f, move e_3 to r. Both branches should finish by jumping to a newly created "join" label.

This will produce perfectly correct results. However, the translated code may not be very efficient at all. If e_2 and e_3 are both "statements" (expressions that return no value), then their representation is likely to be Nx, not Ex. Applying unEx to them will work – a coercion will automatically be applied – but it might be better to recognize this case specially.

Even worse, if e_2 or e_3 is a Cx expression, then applying the unEx coercion to it will yield a horrible tangle of jumps and labels. It is much better to recognize this case specially.

For example, consider

if $x < 5$ **then** $a > b$ **else** 0

As shown above, $x < 5$ translates into $\text{Cx}(s_1)$; similarly, $a > b$ will be translated as $\text{Cx}(s_2)$ for some s_2. The whole if-statement should come out approximately as

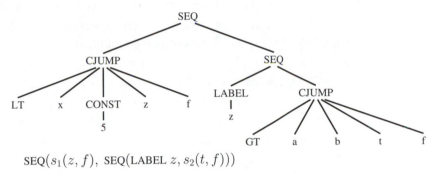

$$\text{SEQ}(s_1(z, f), \ \text{SEQ}(\text{LABEL}\ z, s_2(t, f)))$$

for some new label z.

Therefore, the translation of an **if** requires a new subclass of Exp:

```
class IfThenElseExp extends Exp {
    Exp cond, a, b;
    Label t = new Label();
    Label f = new Label();
    Label join = new Label();
    IfThenElseExp(Exp cc, Exp aa, Exp bb) {
            cond=cc; a=aa; b=bb;
    }
    Tree.Stm unCx(Label tt, Label ff) {  ...  }
    Tree.Exp unEx() {  ...  }
    Tree.Stm unNx() {  ...  }
}
```

The labels t and f indicate the beginning of the then-clause and else-clause, respectively. The labels tt and ff are quite different: these are the places to which conditions inside the then-clause (or else-clause) must jump, depending on the truth of those subexpressions.

String comparison. Because the string equality operator is complicated (it must loop through the bytes checking byte-for-byte equality), the compiler should call a runtime-system function `stringEqual` that implements it. This function returns a 0 or 1 value (false or true), so the CALL tree is naturally contained within an Ex expression. String not-equals can be implemented by generating `Tree` code that complements the result of the function call.

STRINGS

A string literal in the Tiger (or C) language is the constant address of a segment of memory initialized to the proper characters. In assembly language a label is used to refer to this address from the middle of some sequence of instructions. At some other place in the assembly-language program, the *definition* of that label appears, followed by the assembly-language pseudo-instruction to reserve and initialize a block of memory to the appropriate characters.

For each string literal `lit`, the `Translate` module makes a new label `lab`, and returns the tree `Tree.NAME(lab)`. It also puts the assembly-language fragment `frame.string(lab,lit)` onto a global list of such fragments to be handed to the code emitter. "Fragments" are discussed further on page 166; translation of string fragments to assembly language, on page 252.

All string operations are performed in functions provided by the runtime system; these functions heap-allocate space for their results, and return pointers. Thus, the compiler (almost) doesn't need to know what the representation is, as long as it knows that each string pointer is exactly one word long. I say "almost" because string literals must be represented.

But how are strings represented in Tiger? In Pascal, they are fixed-length arrays of characters; literals are padded with blanks to make them fit. This is not very useful. In C, strings are pointers to variable-length, zero-terminated sequences. This is much more useful, though a string containing a zero byte cannot be represented.

Tiger strings should be able to contain arbitrary 8-bit codes (including zero). A simple representation that serves well is to have a string pointer point to a one-word integer containing the length (number of characters), followed immediately by the characters themselves. Then the `string` function in the machine-specific `Frame` module (`Mips.Frame`, `Sparc.Frame`, `Pentium.Frame`, etc.) can make a string with a label definition, an assembly-language pseudo-instruction to make a word containing the integer length, and a pseudo-instruction to emit character data.

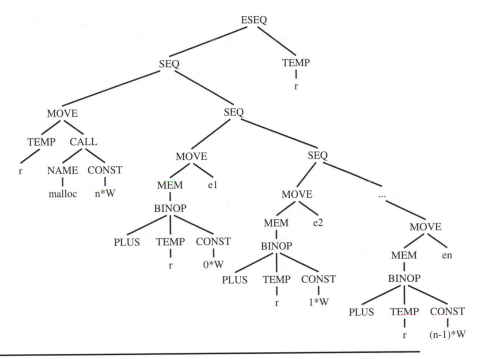

FIGURE 7.4.   Record allocation.

RECORD AND ARRAY CREATION

The Tiger language construct $a\{f_1 = e_1, f_2 = e_2, ..., f_n = e_n\}$ creates an n-element record initialized to the values of expressions e_i. Such a record may outlive the procedure activation that creates it, so it cannot be allocated on the stack. Instead, it must be allocated on the *heap*. There is no provision for freeing records (or strings); industrial-strength Tiger systems should have a *garbage collector* to reclaim unreachable records (see Chapter 13).

The simplest way to create a record is to call an external memory-allocation function that returns a pointer to an n-word area into a new temporary r. Then a series of MOVE trees can initialize offsets $0, 1W, 2W, ..., (n-1)W$ from r with the translations of expressions e_i. Finally the result of the whole expression is TEMP(r), as shown in Figure 7.4.

In an industrial compiler, calling `malloc` (or its equivalent) on every record creation might be too slow; see Section 13.7.

Array creation is very much like record creation, except that all the fields are initialized to the same value. The external `initArray` function can take the array length and the initializing value as arguments.

Calling runtime-system functions. To call an external function named init-Array with arguments a, b, simply generate a CALL such as

```
static Label initArray = new Label("initArray");
new CALL(new NAME(initArray),
         new Tree.ExpList(a, new Tree.ExpList(b, null)));
```

This refers to an external function initArray which is written in a language such as C or assembly language – it cannot be written in Tiger because Tiger has no mechanism for manipulating raw memory.

But on some operating systems, the C compiler puts an underscore at the beginning of each label; and the calling conventions for C functions may differ from those of Tiger functions; and C functions don't expect to receive a static link, and so on. All these target-machine-specific details should be encapsulated into a function provided by the Frame structure:

```
public abstract class Frame {
   ⋮
   abstract public Tree.Exp externalCall(String func,
                                          Tree.ExpList args);
}
```

where externalCall takes the name of the external procedure and the arguments to be passed.

The implementation of externalCall depends on the relationship between Tiger's procedure-call convention and that of the external function. The simplest possible implementation looks like

```
Tree.Exp externalCall(String s, Tree.ExpList args) {
    return new Tree.CALL(new Tree.NAME(new Temp.Label(s)),
                         args);
}
```

but may have to be adjusted for static links, or underscores in labels, and so on. Also, calling new Label(s) repeatedly with the same s makes several label objects that all mean the same thing; this may confuse other parts of the compiler, so it might be useful to maintain a string-to-label table to avoid duplication.

WHILE LOOPS

The general layout of a **while** loop is

test:

      if not(*condition*) goto *done*
      body
      goto *test*

done:

If a **break** statement occurs within the *body* (and not nested within any interior **while** statements), the translation is simply a JUMP to *done*.

So that `transExp` can translate **break** statements, it will have a new formal parameter `break` that is the *done* label of the nearest enclosing loop. In translating a **while** loop, `transExp` is called upon *body* with the *done* label passed as the `break` parameter. When `transExp` is recursively calling itself in nonloop contexts, it can simply pass down the same `break` parameter that was passed to it.

The `break` argument must also be added to the `transDec` function.

FOR LOOPS

A **for** statement can be expressed using other kinds of statements:

for i : = *lo* **to** *hi*
  do *body*

let var i : = *lo*
  var *limit* : = *hi*
in while i <= *limit*
    do *(body; i := i+1)*
end

A very straightforward approach to the translation of **for** statements is to rewrite the *abstract syntax* into the abstract syntax of the **let/while** expression shown, and then call `transExp` on the result.

This is almost right, but consider the case where *limit=maxint*. Then $i + 1$ will overflow; either a hardware exception will be raised, or $i \leq limit$ will always be true! The solution is to put the test at the *bottom* of the loop, where $i < limit$ can be tested *before* the increment. Then an extra test will be needed before entering the loop to check $lo \leq hi$.

FUNCTION CALL

Translating a function call $f(a_1, ...a_n)$ is simple, except that the static link must be added as an implicit extra argument:

CALL(NAME l_f, $[sl, e_1, e_2, ..., e_n]$)

Here l_f is the label for f, and sl is the static link, computed as described in Chapter 6. To do this computation, both the `level` of f and the `level` of the function calling f are required. A chain of (zero or more) offsets found in successive `level` descriptors is fetched, starting with the frame pointer TEMP(FP) defined by the `Frame` module.

7.3 DECLARATIONS

The clause to type-check **let** expressions was shown on page 114. It is not hard to augment this clause to translate into `Tree` expressions. `TransExp` and `transDec` now take more arguments than before (as described elsewhere in this chapter), and `transDec` must now return an extra result – the `Translate.Exp` resulting from the evaluation of the declaration (this will be explained below).

The call to `transDec` will not only return a result record (containing a new type environment, value environment, and `Translate.Exp`), but also will have side effects: for each variable declaration within the declaration, additional space will be reserved in the current level's `frame`. Also, for each function declaration, a new "fragment" of `Tree` code will be kept for the function's body.

VARIABLE DEFINITION

The `transDec` function, described in Chapter 5, updates the value environment and type environment that are used in processing the body of a **let** expression.

However, the initialization of a variable translates into a `Tree` expression that must be put just before the body of the **let**. Therefore, `transDec` must return a `Translate.Exp` containing assignment expressions that accomplish these initializations.

If `transDec` is applied to function and type declarations, the `Translate.Exp` will be a "no-op" expression such as Ex(CONST(0)).

FUNCTION DEFINITION

Each Tiger function is translated into a segment of assembly language with a *prologue*, a *body*, and an *epilogue*. The body of a Tiger function is an expression, and the *body* of the translation is simply the translation of that expression.

The *prologue*, which precedes the body in the assembly-language version of the function, contains

1. pseudo-instructions, as needed in the particular assembly language, to announce the beginning of a function;
2. a label definition for the function name;
3. an instruction to adjust the stack pointer (to allocate a new frame);
4. instructions to save "escaping" arguments – including the static link – into the frame, and to move nonescaping arguments into fresh temporary registers;
5. store instructions to save any callee-save registers – including the return address register – used within the function.

Then comes

6. the function *body*.

The *epilogue* comes after the body and contains

7. an instruction to move the return value (result of the function) to the register reserved for that purpose;
8. load instructions to restore the callee-save registers;
9. an instruction to reset the stack pointer (to deallocate the frame);
10. a *return* instruction (JUMP to the return address);
11. pseudo-instructions, as needed, to announce the end of a function.

Some of these items (1, 3, 9, and 11) depend on exact knowledge of the frame size, which will not be known until after the register allocator determines how many local variables need to be kept in the frame because they don't fit in registers. So these instructions should be generated very late, in a FRAME function called procEntryExit3 (see also page 252). Item 2 (and 10), nestled between 1 and 3 (and 9 and 11, respectively) are also handled at that time.

To implement 7, the Translate phase should generate a move instruction

MOVE(RV, body)

that puts the result of evaluating the body in the return value (RV) location specified by the machine-specific frame structure:

```
package Frame;
public abstract class Frame {
    ⋮
    abstract public Temp RV();
}
```

Item 4 (moving incoming formal parameters), and 5 and 8 (the saving and restoring of callee-save registers), should be done by a function in the `Frame` module:

```
package Frame;
public abstract class Frame {
    ⋮
    abstract public Tree.Stm procEntryExit1(Tree.Stm body);
}
```

The implementation of this function will be discussed on page 252 (see also page 132). `Translate` should apply it to each procedure body (items 5–7) as it is translated.

FRAGMENTS

Given a Tiger function definition comprising a `level` and an already-translated `body` expression, the `Translate` phase should produce a descriptor for the function containing this necessary information:

frame: The frame descriptor containing machine-specific information about local variables and parameters;
body: The result returned from `procEntryExit1`.

Call this pair a *fragment* to be translated to assembly language. It is the second kind of fragment we have seen; the other was the assembly-language pseudo-instruction sequence for a string literal. Thus, it is useful to define (in the `Translate` interface) a `frag` datatype:

```
package Translate;
public class Frag {  public Frag next; }
public ProcFrag(Tree.Stm body, Frame.Frame frame);
public DataFrag(String data);


public class Translate {
    ⋮
  private Frag frags;    // linked list of accumulated fragments
  public void procEntryExit(Level level, Exp body);
  public Frag getResult();
}
```

The semantic analysis phase calls upon `new Translate.Level(···)` in processing a function header. Later it calls other methods of `Translate` to translate the body of the Tiger function; this has the side effect of remembering

DataFrag fragments for any string literals encountered. Finally the semantic analyzer calls procEntryExit, which has the *side effect* of remembering a ProcFrag.

All the remembered fragments go into a private fragment list within Translate; then getResult can be used to extract the fragment list.

PROGRAM   TRANSLATION TO TREES

Design a set of methods for the Translate class, and rewrite the Semant structure to call upon Translate appropriately. The result of calling Semant.transProg should be a Translate.Frag linked list.

To keep things simpler (for now), keep all local variables in the frame; do not bother with FindEscape, and assume that every variable escapes.

In the Frame module, a "dummy" implementation

```
public Tree.Stm procEntryExit1(Tree.Stm body) {
        return body;
}
```

is suitable for preliminary testing of Translate.

Supporting files in $TIGER/chap7 include:

Tree/* Data types for the Tree language
Tree/Print.java Functions to display trees for debugging

and other files as before.

A simpler Translate. To simplify the implementation of Translate, you may do without the Ex, Nx, Cx constructors. The entire Translate module can be done with ordinary value-expressions. This means, basically, that there is only one Translate.Exp class (no subclasses); this class contains a Tree.Exp field and only an unEx() method. Instead of $\text{Nx}(s)$, use $\text{Ex}(\text{ESEQ}(s, \text{CONST } 0))$. For conditionals, instead of a Cx, use an expression that just evaluates to 1 or 0.

The intermediate representation trees produced from this kind of naive translation will be bulkier and slower than a "fancy" translation. But they *will* work correctly, and in principle a fancy back-end optimizer might be able to clean up the clumsiness. In any case, a clumsy but correct Translate module is better than a fancy one that doesn't work.

EXERCISES

7.1 Using the C compiler of your choice (or a compiler for another language), translate some functions to assembly language. On Unix this is done with the -S option to the C compiler.

Then identify all the components of the calling sequence (items 1–11), and explain what each line of assembly language does (especially the pseudo-instructions that comprise items 1 and 11). Try one small function that returns without much computation (a *leaf* function), and one that calls another function before eventually returning.

7.2 The Tree intermediate language has no operators for floating-point variables. Show how the language would look with new binops for floating-point arithmetic, and new relops for floating-point comparisons. You may find it useful to introduce a variant of MEM nodes to describe fetching and storing floating-point values.

*7.3 The Tree intermediate language has no provision for data values that are not exactly one word long. The C programming language has signed and unsigned integers of several sizes, with conversion operators among the different sizes. Augment the intermediate language to accommodate several sizes of integers, with conversions among them.

Hint: Do not distinguish signed values from unsigned values in the intermediate trees, but do distinguish between signed operators and unsigned operators. See also Fraser and Hanson [1995], sections 5.5 and 9.1.

8

Basic Blocks and Traces

ca-non-i-cal: reduced to the simplest or clearest schema possible

Webster's Dictionary

The trees generated by the semantic analysis phase must be translated into assembly or machine language. The operators of the `Tree` language are chosen carefully to match the capabilities of most machines. However, there are certain aspects of the tree language that do not correspond exactly with machine languages, and some aspects of the `Tree` language interfere with compile-time optimization analyses.

For example, it's useful to be able to evaluate the subexpressions of an expression in any order. But the subexpressions of `Tree.exp` can contain side effects – ESEQ and CALL nodes that contain assignment statements and perform input/output. If tree expressions did not contain ESEQ and CALL nodes, then the order of evaluation would not matter.

Some of the mismatches between `Trees` and machine-language programs are:

- The CJUMP instruction can jump to either of two labels, but real machines' conditional jump instructions fall through to the next instruction if the condition is false.
- ESEQ nodes within expressions are inconvenient, because they make different orders of evaluating subtrees yield different results.
- CALL nodes within expressions cause the same problem.
- CALL nodes within the argument-expressions of other CALL nodes will cause problems when trying to put arguments into a fixed set of formal-parameter registers.

Why does the `Tree` language allow ESEQ and two-way CJUMP, if they are so troublesome? Because they make it much more convenient for the Translate (translation to intermediate code) phase of the compiler.

We can take any tree and rewrite it into an equivalent tree without any of the cases listed above. Without these cases, the only possible parent of a SEQ node is another SEQ; all the SEQ nodes will be clustered at the top of the tree. This makes the SEQs entirely uninteresting; we might as well get rid of them and make a linear list of Tree.Stms.

The transformation is done in three stages: First, a tree is rewritten into a list of *canonical trees* without SEQ or ESEQ, nodes; then this list is grouped into a set of *basic blocks*, which contain no internal jumps or labels; then the basic blocks are ordered into a set of *traces* in which every CJUMP is immediately followed by its false label.

Thus the module Canon has these tree-rearrangement functions:

```
package Canon;
public class Canon {
 static public Tree.StmList linearize(Tree.Stm s);
}
public class BasicBlocks {
  public StmListList blocks;
  public Temp.Label done;
  public BasicBlocks(Tree.StmList stms);
}
StmListList(Tree.StmList head, StmListList tail);
public class TraceSchedule {
  public TraceSchedule(BasicBlocks b);
  public Tree.StmList stms;
}
```

Linearize removes the ESEQs and moves the CALLs to top level. BasicBlocks groups statements into sequences of straight-line code. And TraceSchedule orders the blocks so that every CJUMP is followed by its false label.

8.1 CANONICAL TREES

Let us define *canonical trees* as having these properties:

1. No SEQ or ESEQ.
2. The parent of each CALL is either EXP(...) or MOVE(TEMP t, ...).

TRANSFORMATIONS ON ESEQ

How can the ESEQ nodes be eliminated? The idea is to lift them higher and higher in the tree, until they can become SEQ nodes.

Figure 8.1 gives some useful identities on trees.

Identity (1) is obvious. So is identity (2): Statement s is to be evaluated; then e_1; then e_2; then the sum of the expressions is returned. If s has side effects that affect e_1 or e_2, then either the left-hand side or the right-hand side of the first equation will execute those side effects before the expressions are evaluated.

Identity (3) is more complicated, because of the need not to interchange the evaluations of s and e_1. For example, if s is MOVE(MEM(x), y) and e_1 is BINOP(PLUS, MEM(x), z), then the program will compute a different result if s is evaluated before e_1 instead of after. Our goal is simply to pull s out of the BINOP expression; but now (to preserve the order of evaluation) we must pull e_1 out of the BINOP with it. To do so, we assign e_1 into a new temporary t, and put t inside the BINOP.

It may happen that s causes no side effects that can alter the result produced by e_1. This will happen if the temporaries and memory locations assigned by s are not referenced by e_1 (and s and e_1 don't both perform external I/O). In this case, identity (4) can be used.

We cannot always tell if two expressions commute. For example, whether MOVE(MEM(x), y) commutes with MEM(z) depends on whether $x = z$, which we cannot always determine at compile time. So we *conservatively approximate* whether statements commute, saying either "they definitely do commute" or "perhaps they don't commute." For example, we know that any statement "definitely commutes" with the expression CONST(n), so we can use identity (4) to justify special cases like

$$\text{BINOP}(op, \text{CONST}(n), \text{ESEQ}(s, e)) = \text{ESEQ}(s, \text{BINOP}(op, \text{CONST}(n), e)).$$

GENERAL REWRITING RULES

In general, for each kind of `Tree` statement or expression we can identify the subexpressions. Then we can make rewriting rules, similar to the ones in Figure 8.1, to pull the ESEQs out of the statement or expression.

Step one is to make a "subexpression-extraction" method for each kind. Step two is to make a "subexpression-insertion" method: given an ESEQ-clean version of each subexpression, this builds a new version of the expression or statement.

(1)

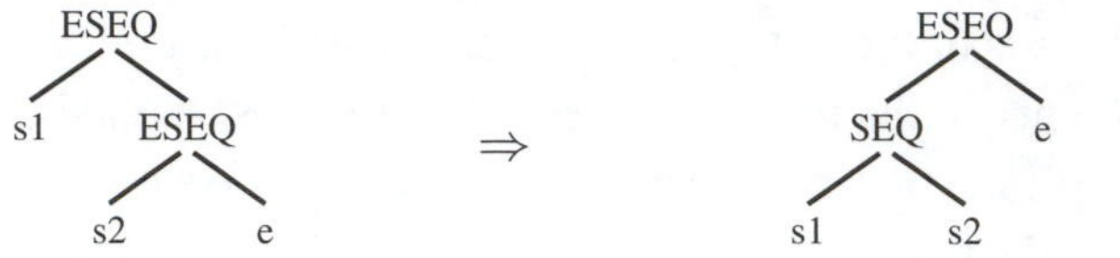

$$\text{ESEQ}(s_1, \text{ESEQ}(s_2, e)) \quad = \quad \text{ESEQ}(\text{SEQ}(s_1, s_2), e)$$

(2)

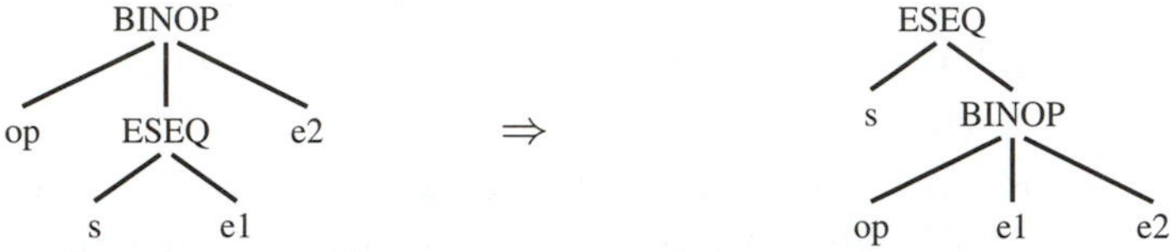

$$\text{BINOP}(op, \text{ESEQ}(s, e_1), e_2) \quad = \quad \text{ESEQ}(s, \text{BINOP}(op, e_1, e_2))$$

$$\text{MEM}(\text{ESEQ}(s, e_1)) \quad = \quad \text{ESEQ}(s, \text{MEM}(e_1))$$

$$\text{JUMP}(\text{ESEQ}(s, e_1)) \quad = \quad \text{SEQ}(s, \text{JUMP}(e_1))$$

$$\text{CJUMP}(op, \text{ESEQ}(s, e_1), e_2, l_1, l_2) \quad = \quad \text{SEQ}(s, \text{CJUMP}(op, e_1, e_2, l_1, l_2))$$

(3)

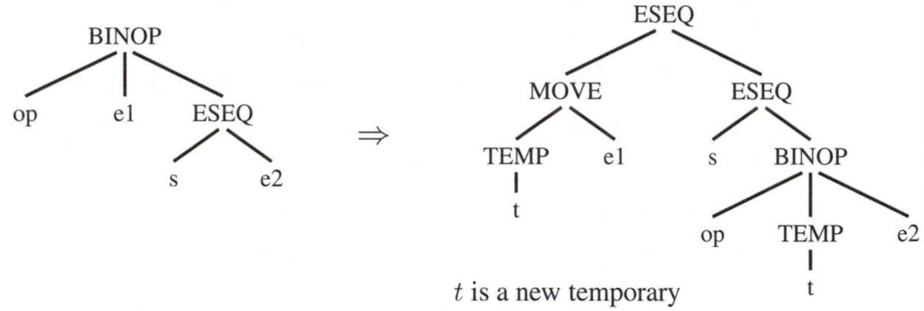

t is a new temporary

$$\text{BINOP}(op, e_1, \text{ESEQ}(s, e_2)) \quad = \quad \text{ESEQ}(\text{MOVE}(\text{TEMP } t, e_1), \text{ESEQ}(s, \text{BINOP}(op, \text{TEMP } t, e_2)))$$

$$\text{CJUMP}(op, e_1, \text{ESEQ}(s, e_2), l_1, l_2) \quad = \quad \text{SEQ}(\text{MOVE}(\text{TEMP}t, e_1), \text{SEQ}(s, \text{CJUMP}(op, \text{TEMP}t, e_2, l_1, l_2)))$$

(4)

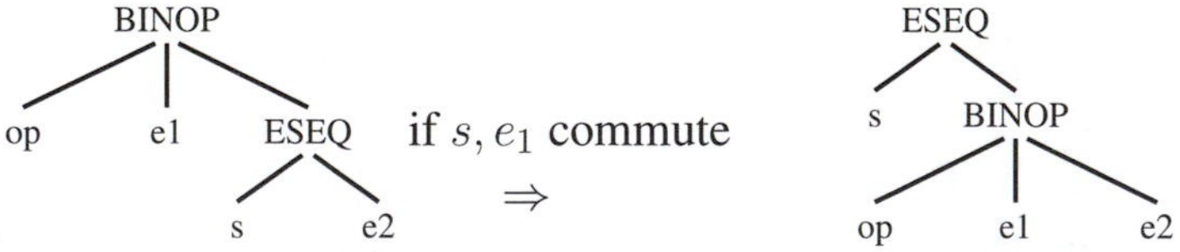

if s, e_1 commute

$$\text{BINOP}(op, e_1, \text{ESEQ}(s, e_2)) \quad = \quad \text{ESEQ}(s, \text{BINOP}(op, e_1, e_2))$$

$$\text{CJUMP}(op, e_1, \text{ESEQ}(s, e_2), l_1, l_2) \quad = \quad \text{SEQ}(s, \text{CJUMP}(op, e_1, e_2, l_1, l_2))$$

FIGURE 8.1. Identities on trees.

These will be methods of the `Tree.Exp` and `Tree.Stm` classes:

```
package Tree;
abstract public class Exp {
        abstract public ExpList kids();
        abstract public Exp build(ExpList kids);
}
abstract public class Stm {
        abstract public ExpList kids();
        abstract public Stm build(ExpList kids);
}
```

Each subclass `Exp` or `Stm` must implement the methods; for example,

```
package Tree;
public class BINOP extends Exp {
  public int binop;
  public Exp left, right;
  public BINOP(int b, Exp l, Exp r) {binop=b; ···}
  public final static int PLUS=0, MINUS=1, MUL=2, DIV=3,
           AND=4,OR=5,LSHIFT=6,RSHIFT=7,ARSHIFT=8,XOR=9;
  public ExpList kids() {return new ExpList(left,
                                 new ExpList(right,null));}
  public Exp build(ExpList kids) {
    return new BINOP(binop,kids.head,kids.tail.head);
  }
}
```

Other subclasses have similar (or even simpler) `kids` and `build` methods. Using these `build` methods, we can write functions

```
static Tree.Stm do_stm(Tree.Stm s)
static Tree.ESEQ do_exp (Tree.Exp e)
```

that pull all the ESEQs out of a statement or expression, respectively. That is, `do_stm` uses `s.kids()` to get the immediate subexpressions of `s`, which will be an expression-list l. It then pulls all the ESEQs out of l recursively, yielding a clump of side-effecting statements s_1 and a cleaned-up list l'. Then $\text{SEQ}(s_1, \text{s.build}(l'))$ constructs a new statement, like the original `s` but with no ESEQs. These functions rely on auxiliary functions `reorder_stm` and `reorder_exp` for help; see also Exercise 8.1.

The left-hand operand of the MOVE statement is not considered a subexpression, because it is the *destination* of the statement – its value is not used by the statement. However, if the destination is a memory location, then the *address* acts like a source. Thus we have,

```
public class MOVE extends Stm {
  public Exp dst, src;
  public MOVE(Exp d, Exp s) {dst=d; src=s;}
  public ExpList kids() {
    if (dst instanceof MEM)
        return new ExpList(((MEM)dst).exp,
                                new ExpList(src,null));
    else return new ExpList(src,null);
  }
  public Stm build(ExpList kids) {
    if (dst instanceof MEM)
     return new MOVE(new MEM(kids.head), kids.tail.head);
    else return new MOVE(dst, kids.head);
  }
}
```

Now, given a list of "kids," we simply pull the ESEQs out, from right to left. For example, in $[e_1, e_2, \text{ESEQ}(s, e_3)]$, the statement s must be pulled leftward past e_2 and e_1. If they commute, we have $(s; [e_1, e_2, e_3])$. But suppose e_2 does not commute with s; then we must have

$$(\text{SEQ}(\text{MOVE}(t_1, e_1), \text{SEQ}(\text{MOVE}(t_2, e_2), s)); \quad [\text{TEMP}(t_1), \text{TEMP}(t_2), e_3])$$

Or if e_2 commutes with s but e_1 does not, we have

$$(\text{SEQ}(\text{MOVE}(t_1, e_1), s); \quad [\text{TEMP}(t_1), e_2, e_3])$$

The `reorder` function takes a list of expressions and returns a pair of (statement, expression-list). The statement contains all the things that must be executed before the expression-list. As shown in these examples, this includes all the statement-parts of the ESEQs, as well as any expressions to their left with which they did not commute. When there are no ESEQs at all we will use EXP(CONST 0), which does nothing, as the statement.

The following function estimates (very naively) whether two expressions commute:

```
static boolean isNop(Tree.Stm a) {
  return a instanceof Tree.EXP
         && ((Tree.EXP)a).exp instanceof Tree.CONST;
}
static boolean commute(Tree.Stm a, Tree.Exp b) {
    return isNop(a)
         || b instanceof Tree.NAME
         || b instanceof Tree.CONST;
}
```

A constant commutes with any statement, and the empty statement commutes with any expression. Anything else is assumed not to commute.

MOVING CALLS TO TOP LEVEL

The `Tree` language permits CALL nodes to be used as subexpressions. However, the actual implementation of CALL will be that each function returns its result in the same dedicated return-value register TEMP(RV). Thus, if we have

$$\text{BINOP}(\text{PLUS}, \text{CALL}(\ldots), \text{CALL}(\ldots))$$

the second call will overwrite the RV register before the PLUS can be executed.

We can solve this problem with a rewriting rule. The idea is to assign each return value immediately into a fresh temporary register, that is

$$\text{CALL}(fun, args) \quad \rightarrow \quad \text{ESEQ}(\text{MOVE}(\text{TEMP } t, \text{CALL}(fun, args)), \text{TEMP } t)$$

Now the ESEQ-eliminator will percolate the MOVE up outside of its containing BINOP (etc.) expressions.

This technique will generate a few extra MOVE instructions, which the register allocator (Chapter 11) can clean up.

The rewriting rule is implemented as follows: `reorder` replaces any CALL($f, args$) by

$$\text{ESEQ}(\text{MOVE}(\text{TEMP } t_{\text{new}}, \text{CALL}(f, args)), \; \text{TEMP } t_{\text{new}})$$

and calls itself again on the ESEQ. But `do_stm` recognizes the pattern

$$\text{MOVE}(\text{TEMP } t_{\text{new}}, \text{CALL}(f, args)),$$

and does not call `reorder` on the CALL node in that case, but treats the f and $args$ as the children of the MOVE node. Thus, `reorder` never "sees" any CALL that is already the immediate child of a MOVE. The pattern EXP(CALL($f, args$)) is treated similarly.

A LINEAR LIST OF STATEMENTS

Once an entire function body s_0 is processed with `do_stm`, the result is a tree s_0' where all the SEQ nodes are near the top (never underneath any other kind of node). The `linearize` function repeatedly applies the rule

$$\text{SEQ}(\text{SEQ}(a, b), c) = \text{SEQ}(a, seq(b, c))$$

The result is that s_0' is linearized into an expression of the form

$$\text{SEQ}(s_1, \text{SEQ}(s_2, \ldots, \text{SEQ}(s_{n-1}, s_n) \ldots))$$

Here the SEQ nodes provide no structuring information at all, and we can just consider this to be a simple list of statements,

$$s_1, s_2, \ldots, s_{n-1}, s_n$$

where none of the s_i contain SEQ or ESEQ nodes.

These rewrite rules are implemented by `linearize`, with an auxiliary function `linear`:

```
static Tree.StmList linear(Tree.SEQ s, Tree.StmList l) {
  return linear(s.left,linear(s.right,l));
}
static Tree.StmList linear(Tree.Stm s, Tree.StmList l) {
  if (s instanceof Tree.SEQ) return linear((Tree.SEQ)s,l);
  else return new Tree.StmList(s,l);
}
static public Tree.StmList linearize(Tree.Stm s) {
  return linear(do_stm(s), null);
}
```

8.2 TAMING CONDITIONAL BRANCHES

Another aspect of the `Tree` language that has no direct equivalent in most machine instruction sets is the two-way branch of the CJUMP instruction. The `Tree` language CJUMP is designed with two target labels for convenience in translating into trees and analyzing trees. On a real machine, the conditional jump either transfers control (on a `true` condition) or "falls through" to the next instruction.

To make the trees easy to translate into machine instructions, we will rearrange them so that every CJUMP($cond, l_t, l_f$) is immediately followed by LABEL(l_f), its "false branch." Each such CJUMP can be directly implemented on a real machine as a conditional branch to label l_t.

We will make this transformation in two stages: first, we take the list of canonical trees and form them into *basic blocks*; then we order the basic blocks into a *trace*. The next sections will define these terms.

BASIC BLOCKS

In determining where the jumps go in a program, we are analyzing the program's *control flow*. Control flow is the sequencing of instructions in a program, ignoring the data values in registers and memory, and ignoring the arithmetic calculations. Of course, not knowing the data values means we cannot know whether the conditional jumps will go to their true or false labels; so we simply say that such jumps can go either way.

In analyzing the control flow of a program, any instruction that is not a jump has an entirely uninteresting behavior. We can lump together any sequence of non-branch instructions into a basic block and analyze the control flow between basic blocks.

A *basic block* is a sequence of statements that is always entered at the beginning and exited at the end, that is:

- The first statement is a LABEL.
- The last statement is a JUMP or CJUMP.
- There are no other LABELs, JUMPs, or CJUMPs.

The algorithm for dividing a long sequence of statements into basic blocks is quite simple. The sequence is scanned from beginning to end; whenever a LABEL is found, a new block is started (and the previous block is ended); whenever a JUMP or CJUMP is found, a block is ended (and the next block is started). If this leaves any block not ending with a JUMP or CJUMP, then a JUMP to the next block's label is appended to the block. If any block has been left without a LABEL at the beginning, a new label is invented and stuck there.

We will apply this algorithm to each function-body in turn. The procedure "epilogue" (which pops the stack and returns to the caller) will not be part of this body, but is intended to follow the last statement. When the flow of program execution reaches the end of the last block, the epilogue should follow. But it is inconvenient to have a "special" block that must come last and that has no JUMP at the end. Thus, we will invent a new label done – intended to mean the beginning of the epilogue – and put a JUMP(NAME done) at the end of the last block.

In the Tiger compiler, the class `Canon.BasicBlocks` implements this simple algorithm.

TRACES

Now the basic blocks can be arranged in any order, and the result of executing the program will be the same – every block ends with a jump to the appropriate place. We can take advantage of this to choose an ordering of the blocks satisfying the condition that each CJUMP is followed by its false label.

At the same time, we can also arrange that many of the unconditional JUMPs are immediately followed by their target label. This will allow the deletion of these jumps, which will make the compiled program run a bit faster.

A *trace* is a sequence of statements that could be consecutively executed during the execution of the program. It can include conditional branches. A program has many different, overlapping traces. For our purposes in arranging CJUMPs and false-labels, we want to make a set of traces that exactly covers the program: each block must be in exactly one trace. To minimize the number of JUMPs from one trace to another, we would like to have as few traces as possible in our covering set.

A very simple algorithm will suffice to find a covering set of traces. The idea is to start with some block – the beginning of a trace – and follow a possible execution path – the rest of the trace. Suppose block b_1 ends with a JUMP to b_4, and b_4 has a JUMP to b_6. Then we can make the trace b_1, b_4, b_6.

But suppose b_6 ends with a conditional jump CJUMP($cond, b_7, b_3$). We cannot know at compile time whether b_7 or b_3 will be next. But we can assume that some execution will follow b_3, so let us imagine it is that execution that we are simulating. Thus, we append b_3 to our trace and continue with the rest of the trace after b_3. The block b_7 will be in some other trace.

Algorithm 8.2 orders the blocks into traces is as follows: It starts with some block and follows a chain of jumps, marking each block and appending it to the current trace. Eventually it comes to a block whose successors are all marked, so it ends the trace and picks an unmarked block to start the next trace.

FINISHING UP

An efficient compiler will keep the statements grouped into basic blocks, because many kinds of analysis and optimization algorithms run faster on (relatively few) basic blocks than on (relatively many) individual statements. For the Tiger compiler, however, we seek simplicity in the implementation of later phases. So we will flatten the ordered list of traces back into one long list of statements.

At this point, most (but not all) CJUMPs will be followed by their true or false label. We perform some minor adjustments:

- Any CJUMP immediately followed by its false label we let alone (there will be many of these).

Put all the blocks of the program into a list Q.

while Q is not empty

    Start a new (empty) trace, call it T.

    Remove the head element b from Q.

    while b is not marked

        Mark b; append b to the end of the current trace T.

        Examine the successors of b (the blocks to which b branches);

        if there is any unmarked successor c

            $b \leftarrow c$

    (All the successors of b are marked.)

    End the current trace T.

ALGORITHM 8.2. Generation of traces.

- For any CJUMP followed by its true label, we switch the true and false labels and negate the condition.
- For any CJUMP($cond, a, b, l_t, l_f$) followed by neither label, we invent a new false label l_f' and rewrite the single CJUMP statement as three statements, just to achieve the condition that the CJUMP is followed by its false label:

    CJUMP($cond, a, b, l_t, l_f'$)

    LABEL l_f'

    JUMP(NAME l_f)

The trace-generating algorithm will tend to order the blocks so that many of the unconditional JUMPs are immediately followed by their target labels. We can remove such jumps.

OPTIMAL TRACES

For some applications of traces, it is important that any frequently executed sequence of instructions (such as the body of a loop) should occupy its own trace. This helps not only to minimize the number of unconditional jumps, but also may help with other kinds of optimization such as register allocation and instruction scheduling.

Figure 8.3 shows the same program organized into traces in different ways. Figure 8.3a has a CJUMP and a JUMP in every iteration of the **while**-loop; Figure 8.3b uses a different trace covering, also with CJUMP and a JUMP in every iteration. But 8.3b shows a better trace covering, with no JUMP in each iteration.

prologue statements	prologue statements	prologue statements
~~JUMP(NAME *test*)~~	~~JUMP(NAME *test*)~~	JUMP(NAME *test*)
LABEL(*test*)	LABEL(*test*)	LABEL(*body*)
CJUMP($>, i, N, done, body$)	CJUMP($\leq, i, N, body, done$)	loop body statements
LABEL(*body*)	LABEL(*done*)	~~JUMP(NAME *test*)~~
loop body statements	epilogue statements	LABEL(*test*)
JUMP(NAME *test*)	LABEL(*body*)	CJUMP($>, i, N, done, body$)
LABEL(*done*)	loop body statements	LABEL(*done*)
epilogue statements	JUMP(NAME *test*)	epilogue statements
(a)	(b)	(c)

FIGURE 8.3. Different trace coverings for the same program.

The Tiger compiler's `Canon` module doesn't attempt to optimize traces around loops, but it is sufficient for the purpose of cleaning up the `Tree`-statement lists for generating assembly code.

EXERCISES

8.1 The directory `$TIGER/chap8` contains an implementation of every algorithm described in this chapter. Read and understand it. Then write down all the rewriting rules implemented within `linearize` (Figure 8.1 is a start).

8.2 A primitive form of the *commute* test is shown on page 174. This function is conservative: if interchanging the order of evaluation of the expressions will change the result of executing the program, this function will definitely return false; but if an interchange is harmless, `commute` might return true or false.

Write a more powerful version of commute that returns true in more cases, but is still conservative. Document your program by drawing pictures of (pairs of) expression trees on which it will return true.

8.3 Break this program into basic blocks.

1	$m \leftarrow 0$		9	$x \leftarrow M[r]$
2	$v \leftarrow 0$		10	$s \leftarrow s + x$
3	if $v \geq n$ goto 15		11	if $s \leq m$ goto 13
4	$r \leftarrow v$		12	$m \leftarrow s$
5	$s \leftarrow 0$		13	$r \leftarrow r + 1$
6	if $r < n$ goto 9		14	goto 6
7	$v \leftarrow v + 1$		15	return m
8	goto 3			

9

Instruction Selection

in-struc-tion: a code that tells a computer to perform a
particular operation

Webster's Dictionary

The intermediate representation (`Tree`) language expresses only one operation in each tree node: memory fetch or store, addition or subtraction, conditional jump, and so on. A real machine instruction can often perform several
of these primitive operations. For example, almost any machine can perform
an add and a fetch in the same instruction, corresponding to the tree

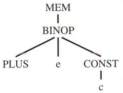

Finding the appropriate machine instructions to implement a given intermediate representation tree is the job of the *instruction selection* phase of a
compiler.

TREE PATTERNS

We can express a machine instruction as a fragment of an IR tree, called a *tree
pattern*. Then instruction selection becomes the task of tiling the tree with a
minimal set of tree patterns.

For purposes of illustration, we invent an instruction set: the *Jouette* architecture. The arithmetic and memory instructions of *Jouette* are shown in
Figure 9.1. On this machine, register r_0 always contains zero.

Name	*Effect*
—	r_i
ADD	$r_i \leftarrow r_j + r_k$
MUL	$r_i \leftarrow r_j \times r_k$
SUB	$r_i \leftarrow r_j - r_k$
DIV	$r_i \leftarrow r_j / r_k$
ADDI	$r_i \leftarrow r_j + c$
SUBI	$r_i \leftarrow r_j - c$
LOAD	$r_i \leftarrow M[r_j + c]$
STORE	$M[r_j + c] \leftarrow r_i$
MOVEM	$M[r_j] \leftarrow M[r_i]$

Trees

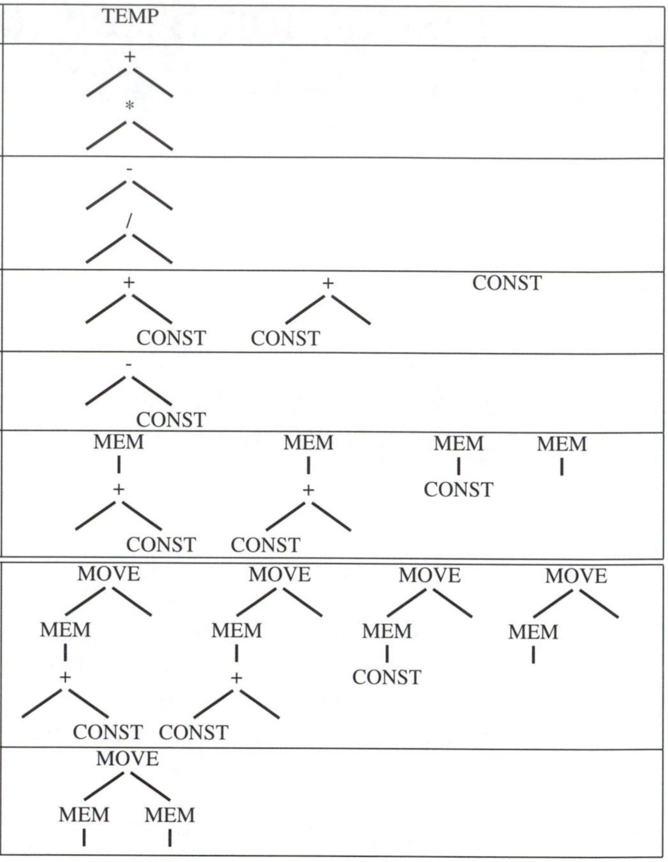

FIGURE 9.1. Arithmetic and memory instructions. The notation $M[x]$ denotes the memory word at address x.

Each instruction above the double line in Figure 9.1 produces a result in a register. The very first entry is not really an instruction, but expresses the idea that a TEMP node is implemented as a register, so it can "produce a result in a register" without executing any instructions at all. The instructions below the double line do not produce results in registers, but are executed only for side effects on memory.

For each instruction, the tree-patterns it implements are shown. Some instructions correspond to more than one tree pattern; the alternate patterns are obtained for commutative operators (+ and *), and in some cases where a register or constant can be zero (LOAD and STORE). In this chapter we abbreviate

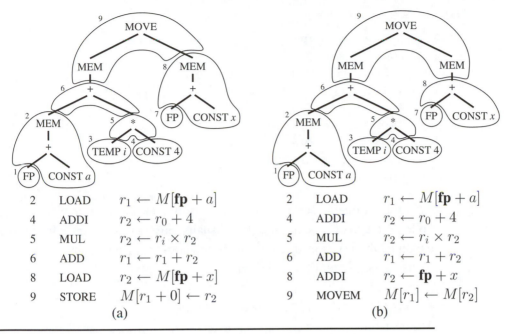

2	LOAD	$r_1 \leftarrow M[\mathbf{fp} + a]$
4	ADDI	$r_2 \leftarrow r_0 + 4$
5	MUL	$r_2 \leftarrow r_i \times r_2$
6	ADD	$r_1 \leftarrow r_1 + r_2$
8	LOAD	$r_2 \leftarrow M[\mathbf{fp} + x]$
9	STORE	$M[r_1 + 0] \leftarrow r_2$

(a)

2	LOAD	$r_1 \leftarrow M[\mathbf{fp} + a]$
4	ADDI	$r_2 \leftarrow r_0 + 4$
5	MUL	$r_2 \leftarrow r_i \times r_2$
6	ADD	$r_1 \leftarrow r_1 + r_2$
8	ADDI	$r_2 \leftarrow \mathbf{fp} + x$
9	MOVEM	$M[r_1] \leftarrow M[r_2]$

(b)

FIGURE 9.2.   A tree tiled in two ways.

the tree diagrams slightly: BINOP(PLUS, x, y) nodes will be written as $+(x, y)$, and the actual values of CONST and TEMP nodes will not always be shown.

The fundamental idea of instruction selection using a tree-based intermediate representation is *tiling* the IR tree. The *tiles* are the set of tree patterns corresponding to legal machine instructions, and the goal is to cover the tree with nonoverlapping tiles.

For example, the Tiger-language expression such as $a[i] := x$, where i is a register variable and a and x are frame-resident,[6] results in a tree that can be tiled in many different ways. Two tilings, and the corresponding instruction sequences, are shown in Figure 9.2. In each case, tiles 1, 3, and 7 do not correspond to any machine instructions, because they are just registers (TEMPs) already containing the right values.

Finally – assuming a "reasonable" set of tile-patterns – it is always possible to tile the tree with tiny tiles, each covering only one node. In our example, such a tiling looks like this:

---

[6]Remember that a is really a pointer to an array.

ADDI	$r_1 \leftarrow r_0 + a$
ADD	$r_1 \leftarrow \mathbf{fp} + r_1$
LOAD	$r_1 \leftarrow M[r_1 + 0]$
ADDI	$r_2 \leftarrow r_0 + 4$
MUL	$r_2 \leftarrow r_i \times r_2$
ADD	$r_1 \leftarrow r_1 + r_2$
ADDI	$r_2 \leftarrow r_0 + x$
ADD	$r_2 \leftarrow \mathbf{fp} + r_2$
LOAD	$r_2 \leftarrow M[r_2 + 0]$
STORE	$M[r_1 + 0] \leftarrow r_2$

For a reasonable set of patterns, it is sufficient that each individual Tree node correspond to some tile. It is usually possible to arrange for this; for example, the LOAD instruction can be made to cover just a single MEM node by using a constant of 0, and so on.

OPTIMAL AND OPTIMUM TILINGS

The best tiling of a tree corresponds to an instruction sequence of least cost: the shortest sequence of instructions. Or if the instructions take different amounts of time to execute, the least-cost sequence has the lowest total time.

Suppose we could give each kind of instruction a cost. Then we could define an *optimum* tiling as the one whose tiles sum to the lowest possible value. An *optimal* tiling is one where no two adjacent tiles can be combined into a single tile of lower cost. If there is some tree pattern that can be split into several tiles of lower combined cost, then we should remove that pattern from our catalog of tiles before we begin.

Every *optimum* tiling is also *optimal*, but not vice versa. For example, suppose every instruction costs one unit, except for MOVEM which costs m units. Then either Figure 9.2a is optimum (if $m > 1$) or Figure 9.2b is optimum (if $m < 1$) or both (if $m = 1$); but both trees are optimal.

9.1 ALGORITHMS FOR INSTRUCTION SELECTION

There are good algorithms for finding optimum and optimal tilings, but the algorithms for optimal tilings are simpler, as you might expect.

Complex Instruction Set Computers (CISC) have instructions that accomplish several operations each. The tiles for these instructions are quite large, and the difference between optimum and optimal tilings – while never very large – is at least sometimes noticeable.

Most architectures of modern design are *Reduced Instruction Set Computers (RISC)*. Each RISC instruction accomplishes just a small number of operations (all the *Jouette* instructions except MOVEM are typical RISC instructions). Since the tiles are small and of uniform cost, there is usually no difference at all between optimum and optimal tilings. Thus, the simpler tiling algorithms suffice.

MAXIMAL MUNCH

The algorithm for optimal tiling is called *Maximal Munch*. It is quite simple. Starting at the root of the tree, find the largest tile that fits. Cover the root node – and perhaps several other nodes near the root – with this tile, leaving several subtrees. Now repeat the same algorithm for each subtree.

As each tile is placed, the instruction corresponding to that tile is generated. The Maximal Munch algorithm generates the instructions *in reverse order* – after all, the instruction at the root is the first to be generated, but it can only execute after the other instructions have produced operand values in registers.

The "largest tile" is the one with the most nodes. For example, the tile for ADD has one node, the tile for SUBI has two nodes, and the tiles for STORE and MOVEM have three nodes each.

If two tiles of equal size match at the root, then the choice between them is arbitrary. Thus, in the tree of Figure 9.2, STORE and MOVEM both match, and either can be chosen.

Maximal Munch is quite straightforward to implement in Java. Simply write two recursive functions, munchStm for statements and munchExp for expressions. Each clause of munchExp will match one tile. The clauses are ordered in order of tile preference (biggest tiles first).

Program 9.3 is a partial example of a *Jouette* code-generator based on the Maximal Munch algorithm. Executing this program on the tree of Figure 9.2 will match the first clause of munchStm; this will call munchExp to emit all the instructions for the operands of the STORE, followed by the STORE itself. Program 9.3 does not show how the registers are chosen and operand syntax is specified for the instructions; we are concerned here only with the pattern-matching of tiles.

If, for each node-type in the Tree language, there exists a single-node tile pattern, then Maximal Munch cannot get "stuck" with no tile to match some subtree.

```
void munchMove(MEM dst, Exp src) {
  // MOVE(MEM(BINOP(PLUS, e₁, CONST(i))), e₂)
  if (dst.exp instanceof BINOP && ((BINOP)dst.exp).oper==BINOP.PLUS
          && ((BINOP)dst.exp).right instanceof CONST)
     {munchExp(((BINOP)dst.exp).left); munchExp(src); emit("STORE");}
  // MOVE(MEM(BINOP(PLUS, CONST(i), e₁)), e₂)
  else if (dst.exp instanceof BINOP && ((BINOP)dst.exp).oper==BINOP.PLUS
          && ((BINOP)dst.exp).left instanceof CONST)
     {munchExp(((BINOP)dst.exp).right); munchExp(src); emit("STORE");}
  // MOVE(MEM(e₁), MEM(e₂))
  else if (src instanceof MEM)
     {munchExp(dst.exp); munchExp(((MEM)src).exp); emit("MOVEM");}
  // MOVE(MEM(e₁), e₂)
  else
     {munchExp(dst.exp); munchExp(src); emit("STORE");}
}
void munchMove(TEMP dst, Exp src) {
  // MOVE(TEMP(t₁), e)
  munchExp(src); emit "ADD";
}
void munchMove(Exp dst, Exp src) {
  // MOVE(d, e)
  if (dst instanceof MEM) munchMove((MEM)dst,src);
  else if (dst instanceof TEMP) munchMove((TEMP)dst,src);
}
void munchStm(Stm s) {
  if (s instanceof MOVE) munchMove(((MOVE)s).dst, ((MOVE)s).src);
  ⋮  // CALL, JUMP, CJUMP unimplemented here
}

void munchExp(Exp)
MEM(BINOP(PLUS, e₁, CONST(i)))  ⇒ munchExp(e₁); emit("LOAD");
MEM(BINOP(PLUS, CONST(i), e₁))  ⇒ munchExp(e₁); emit("LOAD");
MEM(CONST(i))  ⇒ emit("LOAD");
MEM(e₁)  ⇒ munchExp(e₁); emit("LOAD");
BINOP(PLUS, e₁, CONST(i))  ⇒ munchExp(e₁); emit("ADDI");
BINOP(PLUS, CONST(i), e₁)  ⇒ munchExp(e₁); emit("ADDI");
CONST(i)  ⇒ munchExp(e₁); emit("ADDI");
BINOP(PLUS, e₁, CONST(i))  ⇒ munchExp(e₁); emit("ADD");
TEMP(t)  ⇒ {}
```

PROGRAM 9.3.   Maximal Munch in Java.

DYNAMIC PROGRAMMING

Maximal Munch always finds an optimal tiling, but not necessarily an optimum. A dynamic-programming algorithm can find the optimum. In general, dynamic programming is a technique for finding optimum solutions for a whole problem based on the optimum solution of each subproblem; here the subproblems are the tilings of the subtrees.

The dynamic-programming algorithm assigns a *cost* to every node in the tree. The cost is the sum of the instruction-costs of the best instruction sequence that can tile the subtree rooted at that node.

This algorithm works bottom-up, in contrast to Maximal Munch, which works top-down. First, the costs of all the children (and grandchildren, etc.) of node n are found recursively. Then, each tree-pattern (tile kind) is matched against node n.

Each tile has zero or more *leaves*. In Figure 9.1 the leaves are represented as edges whose bottom ends are not labeled by any node. The leaves of a tile are places where subtrees can be attached.

For each tile t of cost c that matches at node n, there will be zero or more subtrees s_i corresponding to the leaves of the tile. The cost c_i of each subtree has already been computed (because the algorithm works bottom-up). So the cost of matching tile t is just $c + \sum c_i$.

Of all the tiles t_j that match at node n, the one with the minimum-cost match is chosen, and the (minimum) cost of node n is thus computed. For example, consider this tree:

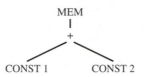

The only tile that matches CONST 1 is an ADDI instruction with cost 1. Similarly, CONST 2 has cost 1. Several tiles match the + node:

Tile	Instruction	Tile Cost	Leaves Cost	Total Cost
+	ADD	1	1+1	3
+ CONST	ADDI	1	1	2
CONST +	ADDI	1	1	2

The ADD tile has two leaves, but the ADDI tile has only one leaf. In matching the first ADDI pattern, we are saying "though we computed the cost of tiling CONST 2, we are not going to use that information." If we choose to use the first ADDI pattern, then CONST 2 will not be the root of any tile, and its cost will be ignored. In this case, either of the two ADDI tiles leads to the minimum cost for the + node, and the choice is arbitrary. The + node gets a cost of 2.

Now, several tiles match the MEM node:

Tile	Instruction	Tile Cost	Leaves Cost	Total Cost
MEM |	LOAD	1	2	3
MEM | + /\	LOAD	1	1+1	3
MEM | + /\ CONST	LOAD	1	1	2
MEM | + /\ CONST	LOAD	1	1	2

Either of the last two matches will be optimum.

Once the cost of the root node (and thus the entire tree) is found, the *instruction emission* phase begins. The algorithm is as follows:

Emission(node n): for each leaves l_i of the tile selected at node n, perform Emission(l_i). Then emit the instruction matched at node n.

Emission(n) does *not* recur on the children of node n, but on the *leaves of the tile* that matched at n. For example, after the dynamic programming algorithm finds the optimum cost of the simple tree above, the Emission phase emits

ADDI $r_1 \leftarrow r_0 + 1$
LOAD $r_1 \leftarrow M[r_1 + 2]$

but no instruction is emitted for any tile rooted at the + node, because this was not a leaf of the tile matched at the root.

TREE GRAMMARS

For machines with complex instruction sets and several classes of registers and addressing modes, there is a useful generalization of the dynamic-programming algorithm.

Suppose we make a brain-damaged version of *Jouette* with two classes of registers: *a* registers for addressing, and *d* registers for "data." The instruction set of the *Schizo-Jouette* machine (loosely based on the Motorola 68000) is shown in Figure 9.4.

The root and leaves of each tile must be marked with a or d to indicate which kind of register is implied. Now, the dynamic programming algorithm must keep track, for each node, of the min-cost match as an a register, *and also* the min-cost match as a d register.

At this point it is useful to use a context-free grammar to describe the tiles; the grammar will have nonterminals s (for statements), a (for expressions calculated into an a register), and d (for expressions calculated into a d register). Section 3.1 describes the use of context-free grammars for source-language syntax; here we use them for quite a different purpose.

The grammar rules for the LOAD, MOVEA, and MOVED instructions might look like this:

$$d \rightarrow \text{MEM}(+(a, \text{CONST}))$$
$$d \rightarrow \text{MEM}(+(\text{CONST}, a))$$
$$d \rightarrow \text{MEM}(\text{CONST})$$
$$d \rightarrow \text{MEM}(a)$$
$$d \rightarrow a$$
$$a \rightarrow d$$

Such a grammar is highly ambiguous: there are many different parses of the same tree (since there are many different instruction sequences implementing the same expression). For this reason, the parsing techniques described in Chapter 3 are not very useful in this application. However, a generalization of the dynamic programming algorithm works quite well: the minimum-cost match at each node *for each nonterminal of the grammar* is computed.

Though the dynamic programming algorithm is conceptually simple, it becomes messy to write down directly in a general-purpose programming language such as Java. Thus, several tools have been developed. These *code-generator generators* process grammars that specify machine instruction sets; for each rule of the grammar, a cost and an action are specified. The costs are used to find the optimum tiling, and then the actions of the matched rules are

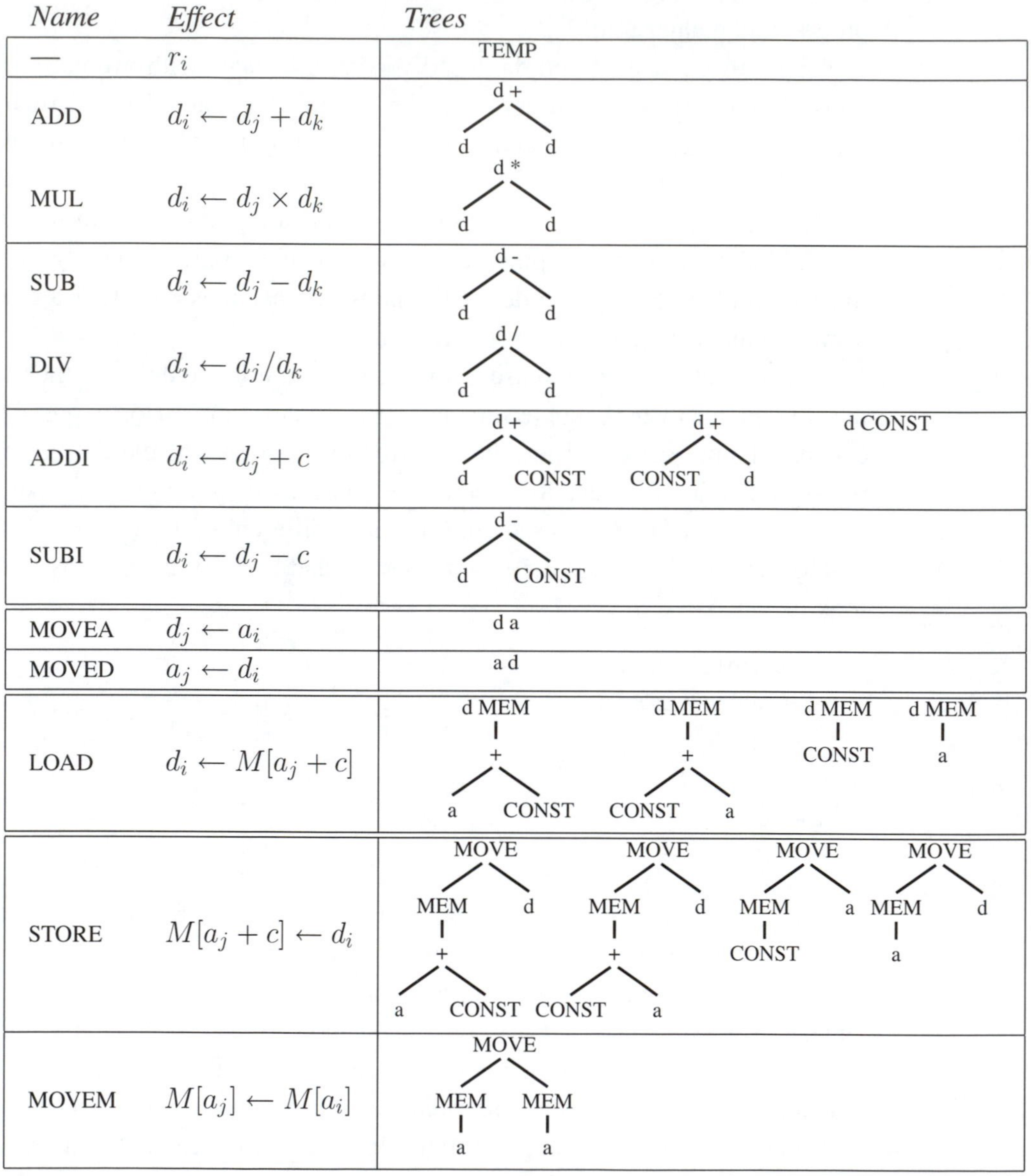

Name	Effect	Trees
—	r_i	TEMP
ADD	$d_i \leftarrow d_j + d_k$	d + (d, d)
MUL	$d_i \leftarrow d_j \times d_k$	d * (d, d)
SUB	$d_i \leftarrow d_j - d_k$	d - (d, d)
DIV	$d_i \leftarrow d_j / d_k$	d / (d, d)
ADDI	$d_i \leftarrow d_j + c$	d + (d, CONST) d + (CONST, d) d CONST
SUBI	$d_i \leftarrow d_j - c$	d - (d, CONST)
MOVEA	$d_j \leftarrow a_i$	d a
MOVED	$a_j \leftarrow d_i$	a d
LOAD	$d_i \leftarrow M[a_j + c]$	d MEM (+ (a, CONST)) d MEM (+ (CONST, a)) d MEM (CONST) d MEM (a)
STORE	$M[a_j + c] \leftarrow d_i$	MOVE (MEM (+ (a, CONST)), d) MOVE (MEM (+ (CONST, a)), d) MOVE (MEM (CONST), a) MOVE (MEM (a), d)
MOVEM	$M[a_j] \leftarrow M[a_i]$	MOVE (MEM (a), MEM (a))

FIGURE 9.4. The *Schizo-Jouette* architecture.

used in the *emission* phase.

Like Yacc and Lex, the output of a code-generator generator is usually a program in C or Java that operates a table-driven matching engine with the action fragments (written in C or Java) inserted at the appropriate points.

Such tools are quite convenient. Grammars can specify addressing modes of treelike CISC instructions quite well. A typical grammar for the VAX has 112 rules and 20 nonterminal symbols; and one for the Motorola 68020 has 141 rules and 35 nonterminal symbols. However, instructions that produce more than one result – such as autoincrement instructions on the VAX – are difficult to express using tree patterns.

Code-generator generators are probably overkill for RISC machines. The tiles are quite small, there aren't very many of them, and there is little need for a grammar with many nonterminal symbols.

FAST MATCHING

Maximal Munch and the dynamic programming algorithm must examine, for each node, all the tiles that match at that node. A tile matches if each nonleaf node of the tile is labeled with the same operator (MEM, CONST, etc.) as the corresponding node of the tree.

The naive algorithm for matching would be to examine each tile in turn, checking each node of the tile against the corresponding part of the tree. However, there are better approaches. To match a tile at node n of the tree, the label at n can be used in a `case` statement:

```
match(n) {
  switch (label(n)) {
    case MEM: · · ·
    case BINOP: · · ·
    case CONST: · · ·
  }
}
```

Once the clause for one label (such as MEM) is selected, only those patterns rooted in that label remain in consideration. Another `case` statement can use the label of the child of n to begin distinguishing among those patterns.

The organization and optimization of decision trees for pattern matching is beyond the scope of this book. However, for better performance the naive sequence of clauses in function `munchExp` should be rewritten as a sequence of comparisons that never looks twice at the same tree node.

EFFICIENCY OF TILING ALGORITHMS

How expensive are the Maximal Munch and the dynamic programming algorithms?

Let us suppose that there are T different tiles, and that the average matching tile contains K nonleaf (labeled) nodes. Let K' be the largest number of nodes that ever need to be examined to see which tiles match at a given subtree; this is approximately the same as the size of the largest tile. And suppose that, on the average, T' different patterns (tiles) match at each tree node. For a typical RISC machine we might expect $T = 50$, $K = 2$, $K' = 4$, $T' = 5$.

Suppose there are N nodes in the input tree. Then Maximal Munch will have to consider matches at only N/K nodes because, once a "munch" is made at the root, no pattern-matching needs to take place at the nonleaf nodes of the tile.

To find all the tiles that match at one node, at most K' tree-nodes must be examined; but (with a sophisticated decision tree) each of these nodes will be examined only once. Then each of the successful matches must be compared to see if its cost is minimal. Thus, the matching at each node costs $K' + T'$, for a total cost proportional to $(K' + T')N/K$.

The dynamic programming algorithm must find all the matches at *every* node, so its cost is proportional to $(K' + T')N$. However, the constant of proportionality is higher than that of Maximal Munch, since dynamic programming requires two tree-walks instead of one.

If the "grammar" version of the dynamic programming algorithm is used, then the best cost for each nonterminal at each node must be computed. However, each grammar rule defines only one nonterminal. The cost of examining each success match is T', just as before, so this version of the dynamic programming algorithm runs in time proportional to $(K' + T')N/K$.

Since K, K', and T' are constant, the running time of all of these algorithms is linear. In practice, measurements show that these instruction selection algorithms run very quickly compared to the other work performed by a real compiler – even lexical analysis is likely to take more time than instruction selection.

9.2   CISC MACHINES

A typical modern RISC machine has

1. 32 registers,

2. only one class of integer/pointer registers,

3. arithmetic operations only between registers,

4. "three-address" instructions of the form $r_1 \leftarrow r_2 \oplus r_3$,

5. load and store instructions with only the M[reg+const] addressing mode,

6. every instruction exactly 32 bits long,

7. one result or effect per instruction.

Many machines designed between 1970 and 1985 are *Complex Instruction Set Computers* (CISC). Such computers have more complicated addressing modes that encode instructions in fewer bits, which was important when computer memories were smaller and more expensive. Typical features found on CISC machines include

1. few registers (16, or 8, or 6),

2. registers divided into different classes, with some operations available only on certain registers,

3. arithmetic operations can access registers or memory through "addressing modes,"

4. "two-address" instructions of the form $r_1 \leftarrow r_1 \oplus r_2$,

5. several different addressing modes,

6. variable-length instructions, formed from variable-length opcode plus variable-length addressing modes,

7. instructions with side effects such as "auto-increment" addressing modes.

Most computer architectures designed since 1990 are RISC machines, but most general-purpose computers installed since 1990 are CISC machines: the Intel 80386 and its descendants (486, Pentium).

The Pentium, in 32-bit mode, has six general-purpose registers, a stack pointer, and a frame pointer. Most instructions can operate on all six registers, but the multiply and divide instructions operate only on the `eax` register. In contrast to the "3-address" instructions found on RISC machines, Pentium arithmetic instructions are generally "2-address," meaning that the destination register must be the same as the first source register. Most instructions can have either two register operands ($r_1 \leftarrow r_1 \oplus r_2$), or one register and one memory operand, for example $M[r_1 + c] \leftarrow M[r_1 + c] \oplus r_2$ or $r_1 \leftarrow r_1 \oplus M[r_2 + c]$, but not $M[r_1 + c_1] \leftarrow M[r_1 + c_1] \oplus M[r_2 + c_2]$

We will cut through these Gordian knots as follows:

1. Few registers: we continue to generate TEMP nodes freely, and assume that the register allocator will do a good job.

2. Classes of registers: The multiply instruction on the Pentium requires that its left operand (and therefore destination) must be the `eax` register. The high-order bits of the result (useless to a Tiger program) are put into register edx. The solution is to move the operands and result explicitly; to implement $t_1 \leftarrow t_2 \times t_3$:

mov eax, t_1	$\text{eax} \leftarrow t_1$
mul t_2	$\text{eax} \leftarrow \text{eax} \times t_2$; $\text{edx} \leftarrow \textit{garbage}$
mov t_3, eax	$t_3 \quad \leftarrow \text{eax}$

This looks very clumsy; but one job that the register allocator performs is to eliminate as many move instructions as possible. If the allocator can assign t_1 or t_3 (or both) to register eax, then then it can delete one or both of the move instructions.

3. **Two-address instructions:** We solve this problem in the same way as we solve the previous one: by adding extra move instructions. To implement $t_1 \leftarrow t_2 + t_3$ we produce

mov t_1, t_2	$t_1 \leftarrow t_2$
add t_2, t_3	$t_2 \leftarrow t_2 + t_3$

Then we hope that the register allocator will be able to allocate t_1 and t_2 to the same register, so that the move instruction will be deleted.

4. **Arithmetic operations can address memory:** The instruction selection phase turns every TEMP node into a "register" reference. Many of these "registers" will actually turn out to be memory locations. The *spill* phase of the register allocator must be made to handle this case efficiently; see Chapter 11.

   The alternative to using memory-mode operands is simply to fetch all the operands into registers before operating and store them back to memory afterwards. For example, these two sequences compute the same thing:

mov eax, $[\text{ebp} - 8]$	
add eax, ecx	add $[\text{ebp} - 8]$, ecx
mov $[\text{ebp} - 8]$, eax	

The sequence on the right is more concise (and takes less machine-code space), but *the two sequences are equally fast*. The load, register-register add, and store take 1 cycle each, and the memory-register add takes 3 cycles. On a highly pipelined machine such as the Pentium Pro, simple cycle counts are not the whole story, but the result will be the same: the processor has to perform the load, add, and store, no matter how the instructions specify them.

   The sequence on the left has one significant disadvantage: it trashes the value in register eax. Therefore, we should try to use the sequence on the right when possible. But the issue here turns into one of register allocation, not of instruction speed; so we defer its solution to the register allocator.

5. **Several addressing modes:** An addressing mode that accomplishes six things typically takes six steps to execute. Thus, these instructions are often no faster

than the multi-instruction sequences they replace. They have only two advantages: they "trash" fewer registers (such as the register eax in the previous example), and they have a shorter instruction encoding. With some work, tree-matching instruction selection can be made to select CISC addressing modes, but programs can be just as fast using the simple RISC-like instructions.

6. **Variable-length instructions:** This is not really a problem for the compiler; once the instructions are selected, it is a trivial (though tedious) matter for the assembler to emit the encodings.

7. **Instructions with side effects:** Some machines have an "autoincrement" memory-fetch instruction whose effect is

$$r_2 \leftarrow M[r_1]; \quad r_1 \leftarrow r_1 + 4$$

This instruction is difficult to model using tree patterns, since it produces two results. There are three solutions to this problem:

(a) Ignore the autoincrement instructions, and hope they go away. This is an increasingly successful solution, as few modern machines have multiple-side-effect instructions.

(b) Try to match special idioms in an ad hoc way, within the context of a tree pattern-matching code generator.

(c) Use a different instruction algorithm entirely, one based on DAG-patterns instead of tree-patterns.

Several of these solutions depend critically on the register allocator to eliminate move instructions and to be smart about spilling; see Chapter 11.

9.3   INSTRUCTION SELECTION FOR THE Tiger COMPILER

Pattern-matching of "tiles" is simple (if tedious) in Java, as shown in Figure 9.3. But this figure does not show what to do with each pattern match. It is all very well to print the name of the instruction, but which registers should these instructions use?

In a tree tiled by instruction patterns, the root of each tile will correspond to some intermediate result held in a register. Register allocation is the act of assigning register-numbers to each such node.

The instruction selection phase can simultaneously do register allocation. However, many aspects of register allocation are independent of the particular target-machine instruction set, and it is a shame to duplicate the register-allocation algorithm for each target machine. Thus, register allocation should come either before or after instruction selection.

Before instruction selection, it is not even known which tree nodes will need registers to hold their results, since only the roots of tiles (and not other labeled nodes within tiles) require explicit registers. Thus, register allocation before instruction selection cannot be very accurate. But some compilers do it anyway, to avoid the need to describe machine instructions without the real registers filled in.

We will do register allocation after instruction selection. The instruction selection phase will generate instructions without quite knowing which registers the instructions use.

ABSTRACT ASSEMBLY-LANGUAGE INSTRUCTIONS

We will invent a data type for "assembly language instruction without register assignments," called Assem.Instr:

```
package Assem;
import Temp.TempList;

public abstract class Instr {
  public String assem;
  public abstract TempList use();
  public abstract TempList def();
  public abstract Targets jumps();
  public String format(Temp.TempMap m);
}

public Targets(Temp.LabelList labels);

public OPER(String assem, TempList dst, TempList src,
            Temp.LabelList jump);
public OPER(String assem, TempList dst, TempList src);
public MOVE(String assem, Temp dst, Temp src);
public LABEL(String assem, Temp.Label label);
```

An OPER holds an assembly-language instruction assem, a list of operand registers src, and a list of result registers dst. Either of these lists may be empty. Operations that always fall through to the next instruction are constructed with OPER(assem,dst,src) and the jumps() method will return null; other operations have a list of "target" labels to which they may jump (this list must explicitly include the next instruction if it is possible to fall through to it). The use() method returns the src list, and the def() method returns the dst list, either of which may be null.

A LABEL is a point in a program to which jumps may go. It has an assem component showing how the label will look in the assembly-language program, and a `label` component identifying which label-symbol was used.

A MOVE is like an OPER, but must perform only data transfer. Then, if the `dst` and `src` temporaries are assigned to the same register, the MOVE can later be deleted. The `use()` method returns a singleton list `src`, and the `def()` method returns a singleton list `dst`.

Calling $i.\text{format}(m)$ formats an assembly instruction as a string; m is an object implementing the `TempMap` interface, which contains a method to give the register assignment (or perhaps just the name) of every temp.

```
package Temp;
public interface TempMap {
    public String tempMap(Temp.Temp t);
}
```

Machine-independence. The `Assem.Instr` class is *independent* of the chosen target-machine assembly language (though it is tuned for machines with only one class of register). If the target machine is a Sparc, then the `assem` strings will be Sparc assembly language. I will use *Jouette* assembly language for illustration.

For example, the tree

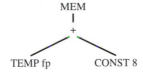

could be translated into *Jouette* assembly language as

```
new OPER("LOAD 'd0 <- M['s0+8]",
         new TempList(new Temp(), null),
         frame.FP());
```

This instruction needs some explanation. The actual assembly language of *Jouette*, after register allocation, might be

```
LOAD r1 <- M[r27+8]
```

assuming that register r_{27} is the frame pointer `fp` and that the register allocator decided to assign the new temp to register r_1. But the `Assem` instruction does not know about register assignments; instead, it just talks of the sources and destination of each instruction. This LOAD instruction has one source register, which is referred to as `'s0`; and one destination register, referred to as `'d0`.

Another example will be useful. The tree

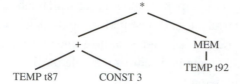

could be translated as

assem	dst	src
ADDI `d0 <- `s0+3	t908	t87
LOAD `d0 <- M[`s0+0]	t909	t92
MUL `d0 <- `s0*`s1	t910	t908,t909

where t908, t909, and t910 are temporaries newly chosen by the instruction selector.

After register allocation the assembly language might look like:

```
ADDI   r1 <- r12+3
LOAD   r2 <- M[r13+0]
MUL    r1 <- r1 * r2
```

The `string` of an `instr` may refer to *source registers* `s0, `s1, ... `s$(k-1)$, and *destination* registers `d0, `d1, etc. Jumps are OPER instructions that refer to labels `j0, `j1, etc. Conditional jumps, which may branch away or fall through, typically have two labels in the `jump` list but refer to only one of them in the `assem` string.

Two-address instructions. Some machines have arithmetic instructions with two operands, where one of the operands is both a source and a destination. The instruction add t1, t2, which has the effect of $t_1 \leftarrow t_1 + t_2$, can be described as

assem	dst	src
add `d0, `s1	t1	t1, t2

where `s0 is implicitly, but not explicitly, mentioned in the `assem` string.

PRODUCING ASSEMBLY INSTRUCTIONS

Now it is a simple matter to write the right-hand sides of the pattern-matching clauses that "munch" Tree expressions into Assem instructions. I will show some examples from the *Jouette* code generator, but the same ideas apply to code generators for real machines.

```
TempList L(Temp h, TempList t) {return new TempList(h,t);}

munchStm(SEQ(a,b))
     {munchStm a; munchStm b;}
munchStm(MOVE(MEM(BINOP(PLUS,e1,CONST(i))),e2))
     emit(new OPER("STORE M['s0+" ^ int i ^ "] <- 's1\n",
               null, L(munchExp e1, L(munchExp e2, null))));
munchStm(MOVE(MEM(BINOP(PLUS,CONST(i),e1)),e2))
     emit(new OPER("STORE M['s0+" ^ int i ^ "] <- 's1\n",
               null, L(munchExp e1, L(munchExp e2, null))));
munchStm(MOVE(MEM(e1),MEM(e2)))
     emit(new OPER("MOVE  M['s0] <- M['s1]\n",
               null, L(munchExp e1, L(munchExp e2, null))));
munchStm(MOVE(MEM(CONST(i)),e2))
     emit(new OPER("STORE M[r0+" ^ int i ^ "] <- 's0\n",
               null, L(munchExp e2, null)));
munchStm(MOVE(MEM(e1),e2))
     emit(new OPER("STORE M['s0] <- 's1\n",
               null, L(munchExp e1, L(munchExp e2, null))));
munchStm(MOVE(TEMP(i), e2))
     emit(new OPER("ADD   'd0 <- 's0 + r0\n",
               L(i,null), L(munchExp e2, null)));
munchStm(LABEL(lab))
     emit(new Assem.LABEL(lab.toString() + ":\n", lab));
```

PROGRAM 9.5.   Assem-instructions for munchStm.

The functions munchStm and munchExp will produce Assem instructions, bottom-up, as side effects. MunchExp returns the temporary in which the result is held.

```
Temp.Temp munchExp(Tree.Exp e);
void      munchStm(Tree.Stm s);
```

The "actions" of the munchExp clauses of Program 9.3 can be written as shown in Programs 9.5 and 9.6.

The emit function just accumulates a list of instructions to be returned later, as shown in Program 9.7.

PROCEDURE CALLS

Procedure calls are represented by EXP(CALL($f, args$)), and function calls by MOVE(TEMP t, CALL($f, args$)). These trees can be matched by tiles such as

```
munchExp(MEM(BINOP(PLUS,e1,CONST(i))))
    Temp r = new Temp();
    emit(new OPER("LOAD `d0 <- M['s0+" + int i + "]\n",
                  L(r,null), L(munchExp(e1),null)));
    return r;
munchExp(MEM(BINOP(PLUS,CONST(i),e1)))
    Temp r = new Temp();
    emit(new OPER("LOAD `d0 <- M['s0+" + int i + "]\n",
                  L(r,null), L(munchExp(e1),null)));
    return r;
munchExp(MEM(CONST(i)))
    Temp r = new Temp();
    emit(new OPER("LOAD `d0 <- M[r0+" + int i + "]\n",
              L(r,null), null));
    return r;
munchExp(MEM(e1))
    Temp r = new Temp();
    emit(new OPER("LOAD `d0 <- M['s0+0]\n",
                  L(r,null), L(munchExp(e1),null)));
    return r;
munchExp(BINOP(PLUS,e1,CONST(i)))
    Temp r = new Temp();
    emit(new OPER("ADDI `d0 <- 's0+" + int i + "\n",
                  L(r,null), L(munchExp(e1),null)));
    return r;
munchExp(BINOP(PLUS,CONST(i),e1))
    Temp r = new Temp();
    emit(new OPER("ADDI `d0 <- 's0+" + int i + "\n",
                  L(r,null), L(munchExp(e1),null)));
    return r;
munchExp(CONST(i))
    Temp r = new Temp();
    emit(new OPER("ADDI `d0 <- r0+" + int i + "\n",
                  null, L(munchExp(e1),null)));
    return r;
munchExp(BINOP(PLUS,e1,e2))
    Temp r = new Temp();
    emit(new OPER("ADD  `d0 <- 's0+'s1\n",
                  L(r,null), L(munchExp(e1),L(munchExp(e2),null))));
    return r;
munchExp(TEMP(t))
    return t;
```

PROGRAM 9.6.   Assem-instructions for munchExp.

```
package Jouette;
public class Codegen {
  Frame frame;
  public Codegen(Frame f) {frame=f;}

  private Assem.InstrList ilist=null, last=null;

  private void emit(Assem.Instr inst) {
     if (last!=null)
        last = last.tail = new Assem.InstrList(inst,null);
     else last = ilist = new Assem.InstrList(inst,null);
  }

  void       munchStm(Tree.Stm s) { ··· }
  Temp.Temp munchExp(Tree.Exp s) { ··· }

  Assem.InstrList codegen(Tree.Stm s) {
        Assem.InstrList l;
        munchStm(s);
        l=ilist;
        ilist=last=null;
        return l;
  }
}

package Frame;
public class Frame {
   ...
  public Assem.InstrList codegen(Tree.Stm stm); {
        return (new Codegen(this)).codegen(stm);
  }
}
```

PROGRAM 9.7.   The Codegen class.

```
munchStm(EXP(CALL(e,args)))
    {Temp r = munchExp(e); TempList l = munchArgs(0,args);
      emit(new OPER("CALL 's0\n",L(r,l),calldefs);}
```

In this example, munchArgs generates code to move all the arguments to their correct positions, in outgoing parameter registers and/or in memory. The integer parameter to munchArgs is i for the ith argument; munchArgs will recur with $i + 1$ for the next argument, and so on.

What munchArgs returns is a list of all the temporaries that are to be passed to the machine's CALL instruction. Even though these temps are never written down explicitly in assembly language, it's useful to list them as "sources" of the instruction, so that liveness analysis (Chapter 10) can see that their values need to be kept up to the point of call.

A CALL is expected to "trash" certain registers – the caller-save registers, the return-address register, and the return-value register. This list of calldefs should be listed as "destinations" of the CALL, so that the later phases of the compiler know that something happens to them here.

In general, any instruction that has the side effect of writing to another register requires this treatment. For example, the Pentium's multiply instruction writes to register edx with useless high-order result bits, so edx and eax are both listed as destinations of this instruction. (The high-order bits can be very useful for programs written in assembly language to do multiprecision arithmetic, but most programming languages do not support any way to access them.)

IF THERE'S NO FRAME POINTER

In a stack frame layout such as the one shown in Figure 6.2, the frame pointer points at one end of the frame and the stack pointer points at the other. At each procedure call, the stack pointer register is copied to the frame pointer register, and then the stack pointer is incremented by the size of the new frame.

Many machines' calling conventions do not use a frame pointer. Instead, the "virtual frame pointer" is always equal to stack pointer plus frame size. This saves time (no copy instruction) and space (one more register usable for other purposes). But our Translate phase has generated trees that refer to this fictitious frame pointer. The codegen function must replace any reference to FP+k with SP + k + fs, where fs is the frame size. It can recognize these patterns as it munches the trees.

However, to replace them it must know the value of fs, which cannot yet be known because register allocation is not known. Assuming the function f is to be emitted at label L14 (for example), codegen can just put sp+L14_framesize in its assembly instructions and hope that the prologue for f will include a definition of the assembly-language constant L14_framesize. Codegen is passed the frame argument (Program 9.7) so that it can learn the name L14.

Implementations that have a "real" frame pointer won't need this hack and can ignore the frame argument to codegen. But why would an implementation use a real frame pointer when it wastes time and space to do so? The answer is that this permits the frame size to grow and shrink even after it is first created; some languages have permitted dynamic allocation of arrays within the stack frame (e.g., using `alloca` in C). Calling-convention designers now tend to avoid dynamically adjustable frame sizes, however.

PROGRAM   INSTRUCTION SELECTION

Implement the translation to Assem-instructions for your favorite instruction set (let μ stand for *Sparc, Mips, Alpha, Pentium,* etc.) using Maximal Munch.

First write the class μ.Codegen implementing the "Maximal Munch" translation algorithm from IR trees to the `Assem` data structure.

Use the `Canon` module (described in Chapter 8) to simplify the trees before applying your `Codegen` module to them. Use the `format` function to translate the resulting `Assem` trees to μ assembly language. Since you won't have done register assignment, just pass `new Temp.DefaultMap()` to `format` as the translation function from temporaries to strings.

```
package Temp;
public class DefaultMap implements TempMap {
        public String tempMap(Temp.Temp t) {
            return t.toString();
        }
}
```

This will produce "assembly" language that does not use register names at all: the instructions will use names such as `t3`, `t283`, and so on. But some of these temps are the "built-in" ones created by the `Frame` module to stand for particular machine registers (see page 151), such as `Frame.FP`. The assembly language will be easier to read if these registers appear with their natural names (e.g., `fp` instead of `t1`).

The `Frame` module must provide a mapping from the special temps to their names, and nonspecial temps to `null`:

```
package Frame;
public class Frame implements Temp.TempMap {
    ⋮
    abstract public String tempMap(Temp temp);
}
```

Then, for the purposes of displaying your assembly language prior to register allocation, make a new `TempMap` function that first tries `frame.tempMap`, and if that returns `null`, resorts to `Temp.toString()`.

REGISTER LISTS

Make the following lists of registers; for each register, you will need a string for its assembly-language representation and a `Temp.Temp` for referring to it in `Tree` and `Assem` data structures.

`specialregs` a list of μ registers used to implement "special" registers such as RV and FP and also the stack pointer SP, the return-address register RA, and (on some machines) the zero register ZERO. Some machines may have other special registers;

`argregs` a list of μ registers in which to pass outgoing arguments (including the static link);

`calleesaves` a list of μ registers that the called procedure (callee) must preserve unchanged (or save and restore);

`callersaves` a list of μ registers that the callee may trash.

The four lists of registers must not overlap, and must include any register that might show up in `Assem` instructions. These lists are not `public`, but they are useful internally for both `Frame` and `Codegen` – for example, to implement `munchArgs` and to construct the `calldefs` list.

Implement the `procEntryExit2` function of the μ.`Frame` class.

```
package Frame;
class Frame implements Temp.TempMap {
    ⋮
    abstract public Assem.InstrList procEntryExit2(
                                   Assem.InstrList body);
}
```

This function appends a "sink" instruction to the function body to tell the register allocator that certain registers are live at procedure exit. In the case of the Jouette machine, this is simply:

```
package Jouette;
class Frame extends Frame.Frame {
    ⋮
    static TempList returnSink =
                       L(ZERO, L(RA, L(SP, calleeSaves)));
```

```
static Assem.InstrList append(Assem.InstrList a,
                              Assem.InstrList b) {
    if (a==null) return b;
    else {Assem.InstrList p;
         for(p=a; p.tail!=null; p=p.tail) {}
         p.tail=b;
         return a;
    }
}


public Assem.InstrList procEntryExit2(
                            Assem.InstrList body) {
  return append(body,
    new Assem.InstrList(
         new Assem.OPER("", null, returnSink),null));
}
}
```

meaning that the temporaries *zero*, *return-address*, *stack-pointer*, and all the callee-saves registers are still live at the end of the function. Having *zero* live at the end means that it is live throughout, which will prevent the register allocator from trying to use it for some other purpose. The same trick works for any other special registers the machine might have.

Files available in $TIGER/chap9 include:

Canon/* Canonicalization and trace-generation.
Assem/* The Assem module.
Main/Main.java A Main module that you may wish to adapt.

Your code generator will handle only the body of each procedure or function, but not the procedure entry/exit sequences. Use a "scaffold" version of Frame.procEntryExit3 function:

```
package μ;
class Frame extends Frame.Frame {
   ⋮
   public Frame.Proc procEntryExit3(Assem.InstrList body) {
       return new Frame.Proc(
           "PROCEDURE " + name.toString() + "\n",
            body,
           "END " + name.toString() + "\n");
   }
}
```

EXERCISES

9.1 Consider a machine with the following instruction:
```
mult const1(src1), const2(src2), dst3
```
$r_3 \leftarrow M[r_1 + \text{const}_1] * M[r_2 + \text{const}_2]$

On this machine, register zero is always zero, and memory location 1 always contains 1.

a. Draw all the tree patterns corresponding to this instruction (and its special cases).

b. Pick **one** of the bigger patterns and show how to write a Java if-statement to match it, with the `Tree` intermediate representation used for the Tiger compiler.

10

Liveness Analysis

live: of continuing or current interest

Webster's Dictionary

The front end of the compiler translates programs into an intermediate language with an unbounded number of temporaries. This program must run on a machine with a bounded number of registers. Two temporaries a and b can fit into the same register, if a and b are never "in use" at the same time. Thus, many temporaries can fit in few registers; if they don't all fit, the excess temporaries can be kept in memory.

Therefore, the compiler needs to analyze the intermediate-representation program to determine which temporaries are in use at the same time. We say a variable is *live* if it holds a value that may be needed in the future, so this analysis is called *liveness* analysis.

To perform analyses on a program, it is often useful to make a *control-flow graph*. Each statement in the program is a node in the flow graph; if statement x can be followed by statement y, there is an edge from x to y. Graph 10.1 shows the flow graph for a simple loop.

Let us consider the liveness of each variable (Figure 10.2). A variable is live if its current value will be used in the future, so we analyze liveness by working from the future to the past. Variable b is used in statement 4, so b is live on the $3 \rightarrow 4$ edge. Since statement 3 does not assign into b, then b is also live on the $2 \rightarrow 3$ edge. Statement 2 assigns into b. That means that the contents of b on the $1 \rightarrow 2$ edge are not needed by anyone; b is dead on this edge. So the *live range* of b is $\{2 \rightarrow 3, 3 \rightarrow 4\}$.

The variable a is an interesting case. It's live from $1 \rightarrow 2$, and again from $4 \rightarrow 5 \rightarrow 2$, but not from $2 \rightarrow 3 \rightarrow 4$. Although a has a perfectly well defined

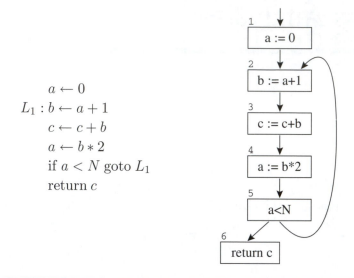

$$a \leftarrow 0$$
$$L_1 : b \leftarrow a + 1$$
$$c \leftarrow c + b$$
$$a \leftarrow b * 2$$
$$\text{if } a < N \text{ goto } L_1$$
$$\text{return } c$$

GRAPH 10.1. Control-flow graph of a program.

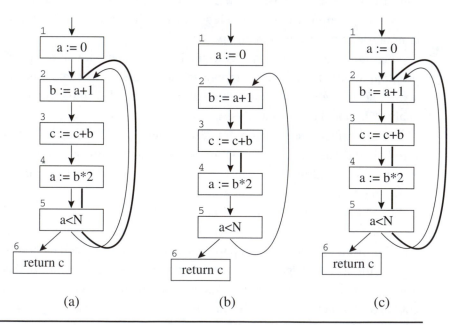

(a)   (b)   (c)

FIGURE 10.2. Liveness of variables a, b, c.

value at node 3, that value will not be needed again before a is assigned a new value.

The variable c is live on entry to this program. Perhaps it is a formal parameter. If it is a local variable, then liveness analysis has detected an uninitialized variable; the compiler could print a warning message for the programmer.

Once all the live ranges are computed, we can see that only two registers are needed to hold a, b, and c, since a and b are never live at the same time. Register 1 can hold both a and b, and register 2 can hold c.

10.1   SOLUTION OF DATAFLOW EQUATIONS

Liveness of variables "flows" around the edges of the control-flow graph; determining the live range of each variable is an example of a *dataflow* problem. Chapter 16 will discuss several other kinds of dataflow problems.

Flow graph terminology. A flow-graph node has *out-edges* that lead to *successor* nodes, and *in-edges* that come from *predecessor* nodes. The set $pred[n]$ is all the predecessors of node n, and $succ[n]$ is the set of successors.

In Graph 10.1 the out-edges of node 5 are $5 \rightarrow 6$ and $5 \rightarrow 2$, and $succ[5] = \{2, 6\}$. The in-edges of 2 are $5 \rightarrow 2$ and $1 \rightarrow 2$, and $pred[2] = \{1, 5\}$.

Uses and defs. An assignment to a variable or temporary *defines* that variable. An occurrence of a variable on the right-hand side of an assignment (or in other expressions) *uses* the variable. We can speak of the *def* of a variable as the set of graph nodes that define it; or the *def* of a graph node as the set of variables that it defines; and similarly for the *use* of a variable or graph node. In Graph 10.1, $def(3) = \{c\}$, $use(3) = \{b, c\}$.

Liveness. A variable is *live* on an edge if there is a directed path from that edge to a *use* of the variable that does not go through any *def*. A variable is *live-in* at a node if it is live on any of the in-edges of that node; it is *live-out* at a node if it is live on any of the out-edges of the node.

If a variable is in $use[n]$, then it is *live-in* at node n. That is, if a statement uses a variable, the variable is live on entry to that statement.

If a variable is *live-in* at a node n, then it is *live-out* at all nodes m in $pred[n]$.

If a variable is *live-out* at node n, and not in $def[n]$, then the variable is also *live-in* at n. That is, if someone needs the value of a at the end of statement n, and n does not provide that value, then a has a needed value even on entry to n.

CALCULATION OF LIVENESS

$$in[n] = use[n] \cup (out[n] - def[n])$$
$$out[n] = \bigcup_{s \in succ[n]} in[s]$$

EQUATIONS 10.3. Dataflow equations for liveness analysis.

These three statements can be written as equations on sets of variables. The live-in sets are an array $in[n]$ indexed by node, and the live-out sets are an array $out[n]$. That is, $in[n]$ is all the variables in $use[n]$, plus all the variables in $out[n]$ and not in $def[n]$. And $out[n]$ is the union of the live-in sets of all successors of n.

Algorithm 10.4 finds a solution to these equations by iteration. As usual, we initialize $in[n]$ and $out[n]$ to the the empty set ϕ, for all n, then repeatedly treat the equations as assignment statements until a fixed point is reached.

for each n
    $in[n] \leftarrow \phi;\ out[n] \leftarrow \phi$
repeat
    for each n
        $in'[n] \leftarrow in[n];\ out'[n] \leftarrow out[n]$
        $in[n] \leftarrow use[n] \cup (out[n] - def[n])$
        $out[n] \leftarrow \bigcup_{s \in succ[n]} in[s]$
until $in'[n] = in[n]$ and $out'[n] = out[n]$ for all n

ALGORITHM 10.4. Computation of liveness by iteration.

Table 10.5 shows the results of running the algorithm on Graph 10.1. The columns 1st, 2nd, etc. are the values of in and out on successive iterations of the **repeat** loop. Since the 7th column is the same as the 6th, the algorithm terminates.

We can speed the convergence of this algorithm significantly by ordering the nodes properly. Suppose there is an edge $3 \rightarrow 4$ in the graph. Since $in[4]$

	use	def	1st in	1st out	2nd in	2nd out	3rd in	3rd out	4th in	4th out	5th in	5th out	6th in	6th out	7th in	7th out
1		a				a		a		ac	c	ac	c	ac	c	ac
2	a	b	a		a	bc	ac	bc	ac	bc	ac	bc	ac	bc	ac	bc
3	bc	c	bc		bc	b	bc	b	bc	c	bc	b	bc	bc	bc	bc
4	b	a	b		b	a	b	a	b	ac	bc	ac	bc	ac	bc	ac
5	a		a	a	a	ac	ac	ac	ac	ac	ac	ac	ac	ac	ac	ac
6	c		c		c		c		c		c		c		c	

TABLE 10.5. Liveness calculation following forward control-flow edges.

	use	def	1st out	1st in	2nd out	2nd in	3rd out	3rd in
6	c			c		c		c
5	a		c	ac	ac	ac	ac	ac
4	b	a	ac	bc	ac	bc	ac	bc
3	bc	c	bc	bc	bc	bc	bc	bc
2	a	b	bc	ac	bc	ac	bc	ac
1		a	ac	c	ac	c	ac	c

TABLE 10.6. Liveness calculation following reverse control-flow edges.

is computed from $out[4]$, and $out[3]$ is computed from $in[4]$, and so on, we should compute the in and out sets in the order $out[4] \rightarrow in[4] \rightarrow out[3] \rightarrow in[3]$. But in Table 10.5, just the opposite order is used in each iteration! We have waited as long as possible (in each iteration) to make use of information gained from the previous iteration.

Table 10.6 shows the computation, in which each **for** loop iterates from 6 to 1 (approximately following the *reversed* direction of the flow-graph arrows), and in each iteration the out sets are computed before the in sets. By the end of the second iteration, the fixed point has been found; the third iteration just confirms this.

When solving dataflow equations by iteration, the order of computation should follow the "flow." Since liveness flows *backward* along control-flow arrows, and from "out" to "in," so should the computation.

Ordering the nodes can be done easily by depth-first search, as shown in Section 16.4.

Basic blocks. Flow-graph nodes that have only one predecessor and one successor are not very interesting. Such nodes can be merged with their predecessors and successors; what results is a graph with many fewer nodes, where each node represents a basic block. The algorithms that operate on flow graphs, such as liveness analysis, go much faster on the smaller graphs. Chapter 16 explains how to adjust the dataflow equations to use basic blocks. In this chapter we keep things simple.

One variable at a time. Instead of doing dataflow "in parallel" using set equations, it can be just as practical to compute dataflow for one variable at a time as information about that variable is needed. For liveness, this would mean repeating the dataflow traversal once for each temporary. Starting from each *use* site of a temporary t, and tracing backward (following *predecessor* edges of the flow graph) using depth-first search, we note the liveness of t at each flow-graph node. The search stops at any definition of the temporary. Although this might seem expensive, many temporaries have very short live ranges, so the searches terminate quickly and do not traverse the entire flow graph for most variables.

REPRESENTATION OF SETS

There are at least two good ways to represent sets for dataflow equations: as arrays of bits or as sorted lists of variables.

If there are N variables in the program, the bit-array representation uses N bits for each set. Calculating the union of two sets is done by *or*-ing the corresponding bits at each position. Since computers can represent K bits per word (with $K = 32$ typical), one set-union operation takes N/K operations.

A set can also be represented as a linked list of its members, sorted by any totally ordered key (such as variable name). Calculating the union is done by merging the lists (discarding duplicates). This takes time proportional to the size of the sets being unioned.

Clearly, when the sets are sparse (fewer than N/K elements, on the average), the sorted-list representation is asymptotically faster; when the sets are dense, the bit-array representation is better.

TIME COMPLEXITY

How fast is iterative dataflow analysis?

A program of size N has at most N nodes in the flow graph, and at most N variables. Thus, each live-in set (or live-out set) has at most N elements;

	use	def	X in	X out	Y in	Y out	Z in	Z out
			X		Y		Z	
1		a	c	ac	cd	acd	c	ac
2	a	b	ac	bc	acd	bcd	ac	b
3	bc	c	bc	bc	bcd	bcd	b	b
4	b	a	bc	ac	bcd	acd	b	ac
5	a		ac	ac	acd	acd	ac	ac
6	c		c		c		c	

TABLE 10.7. X and Y are solutions to the liveness equations; Z is not a solution.

each set-union operation to compute live-in (or live-out) takes $O(N)$ time.

The **for** loop computes a constant number of set operations per flow-graph node; there are $O(N)$ nodes; thus, the **for** loop takes $O(N^2)$ time.

Each iteration of the **repeat** loop can only make each in or out set larger, never smaller. This is because the in and out sets are *monotonic* with respect to each other. That is, in the equation $in[n] = use[n] \cup (out[n] - def[n])$, a larger $out[n]$ can only make $in[n]$ larger. Similarly, in $out[n] = \bigcup_{s \in succ[n]} in[s]$, a larger $in[s]$ can only make $out[n]$ larger.

Each iteration must add something to the sets; but the sets cannot keep growing infinitely; at most every set can contain every variable. Thus, the sum of the sizes of all in and out sets is $2N^2$, which is the most that the repeat loop can iterate.

Thus, the worst-case run time of this algorithm is $O(N^4)$. Ordering the nodes using depth-first search usually brings the number of **repeat**-loop iterations to two or three, and the live-sets are often sparse, so the algorithm runs between $O(N)$ and $O(N^2)$ in practice.

Chapter 16 discusses more sophisticated ways of solving dataflow equations quickly.

LEAST FIXED POINTS

Table 10.7 illustrates two solutions (and a nonsolution!) to the Equations 10.3; assume there is another program variable d not used in this fragment of the program.

In solution Y, the variable d is carried uselessly around the loop. But in fact, Y satisfies Equations 10.3 just as X does. What does this mean? Is d live or not?

The answer is that any solution to the dataflow equations is a *conservative approximation*. If the value of variable a will truly be needed in some execution of the program when execution reaches node n of the flow graph, then we can be assured that a is live-out at node n in any solution of the equations. But the converse is not true; we might calculate that d is live-out, but that doesn't mean that its value will really be used.

Is this acceptable? We can answer that question by asking what use will be made of the dataflow information. In the case of liveness analysis, if a variable is *thought to be live* then we will make sure to have its value in a register. A conservative approximation of liveness is one that may erroneously believe a variable is live, but will never erroneously believe it is dead. The consequence of a conservative approximation is that the compiled code might use more registers than it really needs; but it will compute the right answer.

Consider instead the live-in sets Z, which fail to satisfy the dataflow equations. Using this Z we think that b and c are never live at the same time, and we would assign them to the same register. The resulting program would use an optimal number of registers but *compute the wrong answer*.

A dataflow equation used for compiler optimization should be set up so that any solution to it provides conservative information to the optimizer; imprecise information may lead to suboptimal but never incorrect programs.

Theorem. Equations 10.3 have more than one solution.

Proof. X and Y are both solutions.

Theorem. All solutions to Equations 10.3 contain solution X. That is, if $in_X[n]$ and $in_Y[n]$ are the live-in sets for some node n in solutions X and Y, then $in_X[n] \subseteq in_Y[n]$.

Proof. See Exercise 10.2.

We say that X is the *least solution* to Equations 10.3. Clearly, since a bigger solution will lead to using more registers (producing suboptimal code), we want to use the least solution. Fortunately, Algorithm 10.4 always computes the least fixed point.

STATIC VS. DYNAMIC LIVENESS

A variable is live "if its value will be used in the future." In Graph 10.8, we know that $b \times b$ must be nonnegative, so that the test $c \geq b$ will be true. Thus,

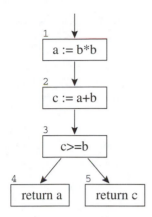

GRAPH 10.8. Standard static dataflow analysis will not take advantage of the fact that node 4 can never be reached.

node 4 will never be reached, and a's value will not be used after node 2; a is not live-out of node 2.

But Equations 10.3 say that a is live-in to node 4, and therefore live-out of nodes 3 and 2. The equations are ignorant of which way the conditional branch will go. "Smarter" equations would permit a and c to be assigned the same register.

Although we can prove here that $b * b > 0$, and we could have the compiler look for arithmetic identities, no compiler can ever fully understand how all the control flow in every program will work. This is a fundamental mathematical theorem, derivable from the halting problem.

Theorem. There is no program H that takes as input any program P and input X and (without infinite-looping) returns true if $P(X)$ halts and false if $P(X)$ infinite-loops.

Proof. Suppose that there were such a program H; then we could arrive at a contradiction as follows. From the program H, construct the function F,

$$F(Y) = \textbf{if } H(Y, Y) \textbf{ then } (\textbf{while } \text{true } \textbf{do } ()) \textbf{ else } \text{true}$$

By the definition of H, if $F(F)$ halts, then $H(F, F)$ is true; so the **then** clause is taken; so the **while** loop executes forever; so $F(F)$ does not halt. But if $F(F)$ loops forever, then $H(F, F)$ is false; so the **else** clause is taken; so $F(F)$ halts. The program $F(F)$ halts if it doesn't halt, and doesn't halt if it halts:

a contradiction. Thus there can be no program H that tests whether another program halts (and always halts itself).

Corollary. No program $H'(X, L)$ can tell, for any program X and label L within X, whether the label L is ever reached on an execution of X.

Proof. From H' we could construct H. In some program that we want to test for halting, just let L be the end of the program, and replace all instances of the **halt** command with **goto** L.

Conservative approximation. This theorem does not mean that we can *never* tell if a given label is reached or not, just that there is not a general algorithm that can *always* tell. We could improve our liveness analysis with some special-case algorithms that, in some cases, calculate more information about run-time control flow. But any such algorithm will come up against many cases where it simply cannot tell exactly what will happen at run time.

Because of this inherent limitation of program analysis, no compiler can really tell if a variable's value is truly needed – whether the variable is truly live. Instead, we have to make do with a conservative approximation. We assume that any conditional branch goes both ways. Thus, we have a dynamic condition and its static approximation:

Dynamic liveness A variable a is dynamically live at node n if some execution of the program goes from n to a use of a without going through any definition of a.

Static liveness A variable a is statically live at node n if there is some path of control-flow edges from n to some use of a that does not go through a definition of a.

Clearly, if a is dynamically live it is also statically live. An optimizing compiler must allocate registers, and do other optimizations, on the basis of static liveness, because (in general) dynamic liveness cannot be computed.

SPECIAL TREATMENT OF MOVE INSTRUCTIONS

In static liveness analysis, we can give MOVE instructions special consideration. It is important not to create artifical interferences between the source and destination of a move. Consider the program:

$$t \leftarrow s \qquad\qquad (copy)$$

$$\vdots$$

$$x \leftarrow \ldots s \ldots \qquad\qquad (use\ of\ s)$$

$$\vdots$$

$$y \leftarrow \ldots t \ldots \qquad\qquad (use\ of\ t)$$

After the copy instruction both s and t are live, and normally we would make an interference edge (s, t) since t is being defined at a point where s is live. But we do not need separate registers for s and t, since they contain the same value. The solution is just not to add an interference edge (t, s) in this case. Of course, if there is a later (nonmove) definition of t while s is still live, that will create the interference edge (t, s).

Therefore, the way to add inteference edges for each new definition is:

1. At any nonmove instruction that *defines* a variable a, where variables $b_1, \ldots, b_j$ are live, add inteference edges $(a, b_1), \ldots, (a, b_j)$.
2. At a move instruction $a \leftarrow c$, where variables $b_1, \ldots, b_j$ are live, add inteference edges $(a, b_1), \ldots, (a, b_j)$ for any b_i that is *not* the same as c.

10.2   LIVENESS IN THE Tiger COMPILER

Liveness information is used for several kinds of optimization in a compiler. For some optimizations, we need to know exactly which variables are live at each node in the flow graph.

But for the Tiger compiler, we will use liveness only to allocate temporaries to machine registers. For register allocation, all we need to know, for each pair of variables a, b, is whether a and b are live at the same time.

A condition that prevents a and b being allocated to the same register is called an *interference*. For example, when a and b are live at the same time, or when a must be generated by an instruction that cannot address register b, then a and b interfere.

Interference information can be expressed as a matrix; Figure 10.9a has an **x** marking interferences of the variables in Graph 10.1. The interference matrix can also be expressed as an undirected graph (Figure 10.9b), with a node for each variable, and edges connecting variables that interfere.

The flow analysis for the Tiger compiler is done in two stages: first, the control flow of the Assem program is analyzed, producing a control-flow

	a	b	c
a			x
b			x
c	x	x	

(a) Matrix

(b) Graph

FIGURE 10.9. Representations of interference.

```
package Graph;

public class Graph {
  public Graph();
  public NodeList nodes();
  public Node newNode();
  public void addEdge(Node from, Node to);
  public void rmEdge(Node from, Node to);
  public void show(java.io.PrintStream out);
}

public class Node {
    public Node(Graph g);
    public NodeList succ();
    public NodeList pred();
    public NodeList adj();
    public int outDegree();
    public int inDegree();
    public int degree();
    public boolean goesTo(Node n);
    public boolean comesFrom(Node n);
    public boolean adj(Node n);
    public String toString();
}
```

PROGRAM 10.10. The Graph abstract data type.

graph; then, the liveness of variables in the control-flow graph is analyzed, producing an interference graph.

GRAPHS

To represent both kinds of graphs, let's make a Graph abstract data type (Program 10.10).

The constructor Graph() creates an empty directed graph; g.newNode() makes a new node within a graph g. A directed edge from n to m is created by `g.addEdge(n,m)`; after that, m will be found in the list `n.succ()` and n will be in `m.pred()`. When working with undirected graphs, the function `adj` is useful: $m.\mathrm{adj}() = m.\mathrm{succ}() \cup m.\mathrm{pred}()$.

To delete an edge, use `rmEdge`. To test whether m and n are the same node, use `m==n`.

When using a graph in an algorithm, we want each node to represent something (an instruction in a program, for example). To make mappings from nodes to the things they are supposed to represent, we use a `Hashtable`. The following idiom associates information x with node n in a mapping `mytable`.

```
java.util.Dictionary mytable = new java.util.Hashtable();
   ...   mytable.put(n,x);
```

CONTROL-FLOW GRAPHS

The `FlowGraph` package manages control-flow graphs. Each instruction (or basic block) is represented by a node in the flow graph. If instruction m can be followed by instruction n (either by a jump or by falling through), then there will be an edge (m, n) in the graph.

```
public abstract class FlowGraph extends Graph.Graph {
    public abstract TempList def(Node node);
    public abstract TempList use(Node node);
    public abstract boolean isMove(Node node);
    public void show(java.io.PrintStream out);
}
```

Each `Node` of the flow graph represents an instruction (or, perhaps, a basic block). The `def()` method tells what temporaries are defined at this node (destination registers of the instruction). `use()` tells what temporaries are used at this node (source registers of the instruction). `isMove` tells whether this instruction is a MOVE instruction, one that could be deleted if the `def` and `use` were identical.

The `AssemFlowGraph` class provides an implementation of `FlowGraph` for `Assem` instructions.

```
package FlowGraph;
public class AssemFlowGraph extends FlowGraph {
    public Instr instr(Node n);
    public AssemFlowGraph(Assem.InstrList instrs);
}
```

The constructor `AssemFlowGraph` takes a list of instructions and returns a flow graph. In making the flow graph, the `jump` fields of the `instrs` are used in creating control-flow edges, and the `use` and `def` information is attached to the nodes by means of the `use` and `def` methods of the `flowgraph`.

Information associated with the nodes. For a flow graph, we want to associate some *use* and *def* information with each node in the graph. Then the liveness-analysis algorithm will also want to remember *live-in* and *live-out* information at each node. We could make room in the `Node` class to store all of this information. This would work well and would be quite efficient. However, it may not be very modular. Eventually we may want to do other analyses on flow graphs, which remember other kinds of information about each node. We may not want to modify the data structure (which is a widely used interface) for each new analysis.

Instead of storing the information *in* the nodes, a more modular approach is to say that a graph is a graph, and that a flow graph is a graph along with separately packaged auxiliary information (tables, or functions mapping nodes to whatever). Similarly, a dataflow algorithm on a graph does not need to modify dataflow information *in* the nodes, but modifies its own privately held mappings.

There may be a trade-off here between efficiency and modularity, since it may be faster to keep the information *in* the nodes, accessibly by a simple pointer-traversal instead of a hash-table or search-tree lookup.

LIVENESS ANALYSIS

The `RegAlloc` package has an abstract class `InterferenceGraph` to indicate which pairs of temporaries cannot share a register:

```
package RegAlloc;
abstract public class InterferenceGraph extends Graph.Graph{
    abstract public Graph.Node tnode(Temp.Temp temp);
    abstract public Temp.Temp gtemp(Node node);
    abstract public MoveList moves();
    public int spillCost(Node node);
}
```

The method `tnode` relates a `Temp` to a `Node`, and `gtemp` is the inverse map. The method `moves` tells what MOVE instructions are associated with this graph (this is a hint about what pairs of temporaries to try to allocate to the same register). The `spillCost(n)` is an estimate of how many extra instructions would be executed if n were kept in memory instead of in registers; for a naive spiller, it suffices to return 1 for every n.

The class `Liveness` produces an interference graph from a flow graph:

```
package RegAlloc;
public class Liveness extends InterferenceGraph {
    public Liveness(FlowGraph flow);
}
```

In the implementation of the `Liveness` module, it is useful to maintain a data structure that remembers what is live at the exit of each flow-graph node:

```
private java.util.Dictionary liveMap =
                        new java.util.Hashtable();
```

where the keys are nodes and objects are `TempLists`. Given a flow-graph node n, the set of live temporaries at that node can be looked up in a global `liveMap`.

Having calculated a complete `liveMap`, we can now construct an interference graph. At each flow node n where there is a newly defined temporary $d \in def(n)$, and where temporaries $\{t_1, t_2, \ldots\}$ are in the `liveMap`, we just add interference edges $(d, t_1), (d, t_2), \ldots$.

What if a newly defined temporary is not live just after its definition? This would be the case if a variable is defined but never used. It would seem that there's no need to put it in a register at all; thus it would not interfere with any other temporaries. But if the defining instruction is going to execute (perhaps it is necessary for some other side effect of the instruction), then it *will* write to some register, and that register had better not contain any other live variable. Thus, zero-length live ranges *do* interfere with any live ranges that overlap them.

PROGRAM CONSTRUCTING FLOW GRAPHS

Implement the `AssemFlowGraph` class that turns a list of `Assem` instructions into a flow graph. Use the abstract classes `Graph.Graph` and `Flow-Graph.FlowGraph` provided in `$TIGER/chap10`.

PROGRAM LIVENESS

Implement the `Liveness` module. Use either the set-equation algorithm with the array-of-boolean or sorted-list-of-temporaries representations of sets, or the one-variable-at-a-time method.

EXERCISES

10.1 Perform flow analysis on the program of Exercise 8.3:

a. Draw the control-flow graph.

b. Calculate live-in and live-out at each statement.

c. Construct the register interference graph.

*10.2 Prove that Algorithm 10.4 always computes the least fixed point.

Hint: We know it computes *some* fixed point, because it refuses to terminate until it has a fixed point. The question is whether it computes the smallest possible fixed point. Show by induction that at any time, the *in* and *out* sets are subsets of the least fixed point. This is clearly true initially, when *in* and *out* are both empty; show that each step of the algorithm preserves the invariant.

10.3 Analyze the asymptotic complexity of the one-variable-at-a-time method of computing dataflow information.

10.4 Analyze the worst-case asymptotic complexity of making an interference graph, for a program of size N (with at most N variables and at most N control-flow nodes). Assume the dataflow analysis is already done and that *use*, *def*, and *live-out* information for each node can be queried in constant time. What representation of graph adjacency matrices should be used for efficiency?

11

Register Allocation

reg-is-ter: a device for storing small amounts of data
al-lo-cate: to apportion for a specific purpose

Webster's Dictionary

The `Translate`, `Canon`, and `Codegen` phases of the compiler assume that there are an infinite number of registers to hold temporary values and that MOVE instructions cost nothing. The job of the register allocator is to assign the many temporaries to a small number of machine registers, and, where possible, to assign the source and destination of a MOVE to the same register so that the MOVE can be deleted.

From an examination of the control and dataflow graph, we derive an *interference graph*. Each node in the inteference graph represents a temporary value; each edge (t_1, t_2) indicates a pair of temporaries that cannot be assigned to the same register. The most common reason for an interference edge is that t_1 and t_2 are live at the same time. Interference edges can also express other constraints; for example, if a certain instruction $a \leftarrow b \oplus c$ cannot produce results in register r_{12} on our machine, we can make a interfere with r_{12}.

Next we *color* the interference graph. We want to use as few colors as possible, but no pair of nodes connected by an edge may be assigned the same color. Graph coloring problems derive from the old mapmakers' rule that adjacent countries on a map should be colored with different colors. Our "colors" correspond to registers: if our target machine has K registers, and we can K-color the graph (color the graph with K colors), then the coloring is a valid register assignment for the inteference graph. If there is no K-coloring, we will have to keep some of our variables and temporaries in memory instead of registers; this is called *spilling*.

```
live-in: k j
        g := mem[j+12]
        h := k - 1
        f := g * h
        e := mem[j+8]
        m := mem[j+16]
        b := mem[f]
        c := e + 8
        d := c
        k := m + 4
        j := b
live-out: d k j
```

GRAPH 11.1. Interference graph for a program. Dotted lines are not interference edges but indicate move instructions.

11.1 COLORING BY SIMPLIFICATION

The principal phases of a graph-coloring register allocator are **Build**, **Simplify**, **Spill**, and **Select**.

Build: Construct the interference graph. We use dataflow analysis to compute the set of registers that are simultaneously live at each program point, and we add an edge to the graph for each pair of registers in the set. We repeat this for all program points.

Simplify: We color the graph using a simple heuristic. Suppose the graph G contains a node m with fewer than K neighbors, where K is the number of registers on the machine. Let G' be the graph $G - \{m\}$ obtained by removing m. If G' can be colored, then so can G, for when m is added to the colored graph G', the neighbors of m have at most $K - 1$ colors among them so a free color can always be found for m. This leads naturally to a stack-based (or recursive) algorithm for coloring: we repeatedly remove (and push on a stack) nodes of degree less than K. Each such simplification will decrease the degrees of other nodes, leading to more opportunity for simplification.

Spill: Suppose at some point during simplification the graph G has nodes only of *significant degree*, that is, nodes of degree $\geq K$. Then the *simplify* heuristic fails, and we mark some node for spilling. That is, we choose some node in the graph (standing for a temporary variable in the program) and decide to represent it in memory, not registers, during program execution. An optimistic approximation to the effect of spilling is that the spilled node does not interfere with any of the other nodes remaining in the graph. It can therefore be removed and pushed on the stack, and the simplify process continued.

Select: We assign colors to nodes in the graph. Starting with the empty graph, we rebuild the original graph by repeatedly adding a node from the top of the stack. When we add a node to the graph, there must be a color for it, as the premise for removing it in the simplify phase was that it could always be assigned a color provided the remaining nodes in the graph could be successfully colored.

When *potential spill* node n that was pushed using the *Spill* heuristic is popped, there is no guarantee that it will be colorable: its neighbors in the graph may be colored with K different colors already. In this case, we have an *actual spill*. We do not assign any color, but we continue the *Select* phase to identify other actual spills.

But perhaps some of the neighbors are the same color, so that among them there are fewer than K colors. Then we can color n, and it does not become an actual spill. This technique is known as *optimistic coloring*.

Start over: If the **Select** phase is unable to find a color for some node(s), then the program must be rewritten to fetch them from memory just before each use, and store them back after each definition. Thus, a spilled temporary will turn into several new temporaries with tiny live ranges. These will interfere with other temporaries in the graph. So the algorithm is repeated on this rewritten program. This process iterates until *simplify* succeeds with no spills; in practice, one or two iterations almost always suffice.

EXAMPLE

Graph 11.1 shows the interferences for a simple program. The nodes are labeled with the temporaries they represent, and there is an edge between two nodes if they are simultaneously live. For example, nodes d, k, and j are all connected since they are live simultaneously at the end of the block. Assuming that there are four registers available on the machine, then the simplify phase can start with the nodes g, h, c, and f in its working set, since they have less than four neighbors each. A color can always be found for them if the remaining graph can be successfully colored. If the algorithm starts by

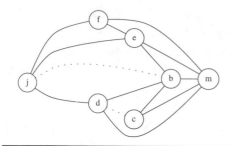

GRAPH 11.2. After removal of h, g, k.

(a) stack	(b) assignment
m	1
c	3
b	2
f	2
e	4
j	3
d	4
k	1
h	2
g	4

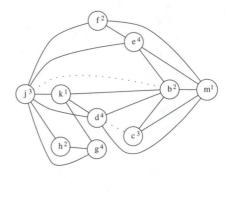

FIGURE 11.3. Simplification stack, and a possible coloring.

removing h and g and all their edges, then node k becomes a candidate for removal and can be added to the work-list. Graph 11.2 remains after nodes g, h, and k have been removed. Continuing in this fashion a possible order in which nodes are removed is represented by the stack shown in Figure 11.3a, where the stack grows upward.

The nodes are now popped off the stack and the original graph reconstructed and colored simultaneously. Starting with m, a color is chosen arbitrarily since the graph at this point consists of a singleton node. The next node to be put into the graph is c. The only constraint is that it be given a color different from m, since there is an edge from m to c. A possible assignment of colors for the reconstructed original graph is shown in Figure 11.3b.

11.2   COALESCING

It is easy to eliminate redundant move instructions with an interference graph. If there is no edge in the interference graph between the source and destination of a move instruction, then the move can be eliminated. The source and destination nodes are *coalesced* into a new node whose edges are the union of those of the nodes being replaced.

In principle, any pair of nodes not connected by an interference edge could be coalesced. This aggressive form of copy propagation is very successful at eliminating move instructions. Unfortunately, the node being introduced is more constrained than those being removed, as it contains a union of edges. Thus, it is quite possible that a graph, colorable with K colors before coalescing, may no longer be K-colorable after reckless coalescing.

If some nodes are *precolored* – assigned to specific machine registers before register allocation (because they are used in calling conventions, for example), they cannot be spilled. Some coloring problems with precolored nodes have no solution: if a temporary interferes with K precolored nodes (all of different colors), then the temporary must be spilled. But there is no register into which it can be fetched back for computation! We say such a graph is uncolorable; reckless coalescing often leads to uncolorable graphs.

We can address this problem by a *conservative* coalescing strategy. If the node being coalesced has fewer than K neighbors of significant degree, then coalescing is guaranteed not to turn a K-colorable graph into a non-K-colorable graph. The proof of the guarantee is simple: after the simplify phase has removed all the insignificant-degree nodes from the graph, the coalesced node will be adjacent only to those neighbors that were of significant degree. Since these are less than K in number, *simplify* can remove the coalesced node from the graph. Thus if the original graph was colorable, the conservative coalescing strategy does not alter the colorability of the graph.

There are cases where coalesing t_1 and t_2 will result in a node with more than K neighbors of significant degree, but the graph might still be K-colorable. We call the coalescing strategy conservative because it will be too timid to coalesce such nodes.

Interleaving simplification steps with conservative coalescing eliminates most move instructions, while still guaranteeing not to introduce spills. The coalesce, simplify, and spill procedures should be alternated until the graph is empty, as shown in Figure 11.4.

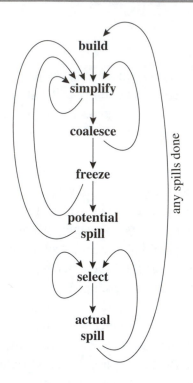

build

simplify

coalesce

freeze

potential spill

select

actual spill

any spills done

FIGURE 11.4.
Graph coloring with coalescing.

These are the phases of a register allocator with coalescing:

Build: Construct the interference graph, and categorize each node as either *move-related* or *non-move-related*. A move-related node is one that is the either the source or destination of a move instruction.

Simplify: One at a time, remove non-move-related nodes of low ($< K$) degree from the graph.

Coalesce: Perform conservative coalescing on the reduced graph obtained in the simplification phase. Since the degrees of many nodes have been reduced by *simplify*, the conservative strategy is likely to find many more moves to coalesce than it would have in the initial interference graph. After two nodes have been coalesced (and the move instruction deleted), if the resulting node is no longer move-related it will be available for the next round of simplification. *Simplify* and *coalesce* are repeated until only significant-degree or move-related nodes remain.

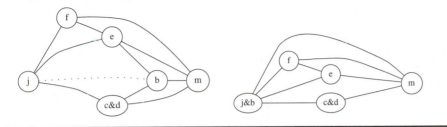

GRAPH 11.5.   (a) after coalescing c and d;   (b) after coalescing b and j.

Freeze: If neither *simplify* nor *coalesce* applies, we look for a move-related node of low degree. We *freeze* the moves in which this node is involved: that is, we give up hope of coalescing those moves. This causes the node (and perhaps other nodes related to the frozen moves) to be considered non-move-related, which should enable more simplification. Now, *simplify* and *coalesce* are resumed.

Spill: If there are no low-degree nodes, we select a high-degree node for potential spilling and push it on the stack.

Select: Pop the entire stack, assigning colors.

Consider Graph 11.1; nodes b, c, d, and j are the only move-related nodes. The initial work-list used in the simplify phase must contain only non-move-related nodes and consists of nodes g, h, and f. Once again, after removal of g, h, and k we obtain Graph 11.2.

We could continue the simplification phase further; however, if we invoke a round of coalescing at this point, we discover that c and d are indeed coalesceable as the coalesced node has only two neighbors of significant degree: m and b. The resulting graph is shown in Graph 11.5a, with the coalesced node labeled as c&d.

From Graph 11.5a we see that it is possible to coalesce b and j as well. Nodes b and j are adjacent to two neighbors of significant degree, namely m and e. The result of coalescing b and j is shown in Graph 11.5b.

After coalescing these two moves, there are no more move-related nodes, and therefore no more coalescing is possible. The simplify phase can be invoked one more time to remove all the remaining nodes. A possible assignment of colors is shown in Figure 11.6.

Some moves are neither coalesced nor frozen. Instead, they are *constrained*. Consider the graph X, Y, Z, where (X, Z) is the only interference edge and there are two moves $X \leftarrow Y$ and $Y \leftarrow Z$. Either move is a candidate for

stack	coloring
e	1
m	2
f	3
j&b	4
c&d	1
k	2
h	2
g	1

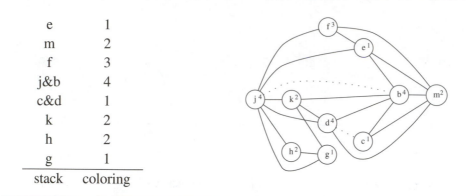

FIGURE 11.6.   A coloring, with coalescing, for Graph 11.1.

coalescing. But after X and Y are coalesced, the remaining move $XY \leftarrow Z$ cannot be coalesced because of the interference edge (XY, Z). We say this move is *constrained*, and we remove it from further consideration: it no longer causes nodes to be treated as move-related.

SPILLING

If spilling is necessary, *build* and *simplify* must be repeated on the whole program. The simplest version of the algorithm discards any coalescences found if *build* must be repeated. Then it is easy to see that coalescing does not increase the number of spills in any future round of *build*. A more efficient algorithm preserves any coalescences done *before the first potential spill was discovered*, but discards (uncoalesces) any coalescences done after that point.

PRECOLORED NODES

Some temporaries are *precolored* – they represent machine registers. The front end generates these when interfacing to standard calling conventions across module boundaries, for example. Ordinary temporaries can be assigned the same colors as precolored registers, as long as they don't interfere, and in fact this is quite common. Thus, a standard calling-convention register can be re-used inside a procedure as a temporary.

Precolored nodes are, in effect, the first to be colored; thus they must be removed from the graph last. In fact, the algorithm works by calling *simplify, coalesce,* and *spill* until only the precolored nodes remain, and then the *select* phase can start adding the other nodes (and coloring them). All the precolored nodes are assumed to interfere with each other.

$$\text{enter} : \text{def}(r_7)$$

$$\vdots$$

$$\text{exit} : \quad \text{use}(r_7)$$

$$\text{enter} : \text{def}(r_7)$$
$$t_{231} \leftarrow r_7$$

$$\vdots$$

$$r_7 \leftarrow t_{231}$$
$$\text{exit} : \quad \text{use}(r_7)$$

FIGURE 11.7. Moving a callee-save register to a fresh temporary.

Precolored nodes may be coalesced with other (non-precolored) nodes using conservative coalescing.

Precolored nodes should not be spilled. Spilling a node means removing it from the graph, and precolored nodes must remain until all other nodes are removed. Because precolored nodes do not spill, the front end must be careful to keep their live ranges short. It can do this by generating MOVE instructions to move values to and from precolored nodes. For example, suppose r_7 is a callee-save register; it is "defined" at procedure entry and "used" at procedure exit. Instead of being kept in a precolored register throughout the procedure as shown at left below, it can be moved into a fresh temporary and then moved back, as shown in Figure 11.7. If there is *register pressure* (a high demand for registers) in this function, t_{231} will spill; otherwise it will be coalesced with r_7 and the MOVE instructions eliminated.

CALLER-SAVE AND CALLEE-SAVE REGISTERS

A local variable or compiler temporary that is not live across any procedure call should usually be allocated to a caller-save register, because in this case no saving and restoring of the register will be necessary at all. On the other hand, any variable that is live across several procedure calls should be kept in a callee-save register, since then only one save/restore will be necessary (on entry/exit from the calling procedure).

The register allocator should allocate variables to registers using this criterion. Fortunately, a graph-coloring allocator with spilling can do this very easily. The CALL instructions in the Assem language have been annotated to *define* (interfere with) all the caller-save registers. If a variable is not live across a procedure call, it will tend to be allocated to a caller-save register.

If a variable x is live across a procedure call, then it interferes with all the caller-save (precolored) registers, *and* it interferes with all the new temporaries (such as t_{231} in Figure 11.7) created for callee-save registers. Thus, a spill will occur. Using the common spill-cost heuristic that spills a node with high degree but few uses, the node chosen for spilling will not be x but t_{231}. Since t_{231} is spilled, r_7 will be available for coloring x (or some other variable). Thus, the most basic of spill heuristics achieves the effect of allocating variables live across calls to callee-save registers.

11.3 GRAPH COLORING IMPLEMENTATION

The graph coloring algorithm needs to query the inteference-graph data structure frequently. There are two kinds of queries:

1. Get all the nodes adjacent to node X; and
2. Tell if X and Y are adjacent.

An adjacency list (per node) can answer query 1 quickly, but not query 2 if the lists are long. A two-dimensional bit matrix indexed by node numbers can answer query 2 quickly, but not query 1. Therefore, we need both data structures to (redundantly) represent the interference graph.

If the graph is very sparse, a hash table of integer pairs may be better than a bit matrix.

The adjacency lists of machine registers can be very large; because they're used in standard calling conventions they interfere with many temporaries. Furthermore, the adjacency lists are mainly used in the *select* phase; and since machine registers are precolored, their adjacency lists are not necessary for *select*. Therefore, it will save space and time if we do not explicitly represent the adjacency lists of the machine registers. The time savings is significant: when X is coalesced to Y, and X interferes with a machine register, then the long adjacency list for the machine register must be traversed to remove X and add Y.

In the absence of adjacency lists for machine registers, a simple heuristic is used to coalesce temporaries with machine registers. A non-precolored temporary X can be coalesced to a machine register R, if for every T that is a neighbor of X, the coalescing does not increase the number of T's significant-degree neighbors from $< K$ to $\geq K$.

Any of the following conditions will suffice:

1. T already interferes with R. Then the set of T's neighbors gains no nodes.
2. T is a machine register. Since we already assume that all machine registers mutually interfere, this implies condition 1.

3. Degree$(T) < K$. Since T will lose the neighbor R and gain the neighbor T, then degree(T) will continue to be $< K$.

The third condition can be weakened to require T to have fewer than $K - 1$ neighbors of significant degree. This test would coalesce more liberally while still ensuring that the graph retains its colorability; but it would be more expensive to implement.

Associated with each move-related node is a count of the moves it is involved in. This count is easy to maintain and is used to test if a node is no longer move-related. Associated with all nodes is a count of the number of neighbors currently in the graph. This is used to determine whether a node is of significant degree during coalescing, and whether a node can be removed from the graph during simplification.

To make the algorithm efficient, it is important to be able to quickly perform each *simplify* step (removing a low-degree non-move-related node), each *coalesce* step, and each *freeze* step. To do this, we maintain four work-lists:

- Low-degree non-move-related nodes *(simplifyWorklist)*;
- Coalesce candidates: move-related nodes that have not been proved uncoalesceable *(worklistMoves)*;
- Low-degree move-related nodes *(freezeWorklist)*;
- High-degree nodes *(spillWorklist)*.

Maintenance of these work-lists avoids quadratic time blowup in finding coalesceable nodes.

MOVE-WORK-LIST MANAGEMENT
When a node X changes from significant to low degree, the moves associated with its neighbors must be added to the move work-list. Moves that were blocked with too many significant neighbors (including X) might now be enabled for coalescing. Moves are added to the move work-list in only a few places:

- During simplify the degree of a node X might make the transition as a result of removing another node. Moves associated with neighbors of X are added to the *worklistMoves*.
- When U and V are coalesced, there may be a node X that interferes with both U and V. The degree of X is decremented as it now interferes with the single coalesced node. Moves associated with neighbors of X are added. If X is move-related, then moves associated with X itself are also added as both U and V may have been significant degree nodes.

- When U is coalesced into V, moves associated with U are added to the move work-list. This will catch other moves from U to V.

DATA STRUCTURES

The algorithm maintains these data structures to keep track of graph nodes and move edges:

Node work-lists, sets, and stacks

precolored: machine registers, preassigned a color.

initial: temporary registers, not preassigned a color and not yet processed by the algorithm.

simplifyWorklist: list of low-degree non-move-related nodes.

freezeWorklist: low-degree move-related nodes.

spillWorklist: high-degree nodes.

spilledNodes: nodes marked for spilling during this round; initially empty.

coalescedNodes: registers that have been coalesced; when the move $u \leftarrow v$ is coalesced, one of u or v is added to this set, and the other is put back on some work-list.

coloredNodes: nodes successfully colored.

selectStack: stack containing temporaries removed from the graph.

Invariant: These lists and sets are always *mutually disjoint* and every node is always in exactly one of the sets or lists. Since membership in these sets is often tested, the representation of each node should contain an enumeration value telling which set it is in.

Implementation: Since nodes must frequently be added to and removed from these sets, each set can be represented by a doubly linked list of nodes.

Precondition: Initially (on entry to Main), and on exiting RewriteProgram, only the sets *precolored* and *initial* are nonempty.

Move sets There are five sets of move instructions:

coalescedMoves: moves that have been coalesced.

constrainedMoves: moves whose source and target interfere.

frozenMoves: moves that will no longer be considered for coalescing.

worklistMoves: moves enabled for possible coalescing.

activeMoves: moves not yet ready for coalescing.

Move Invariant: Every move is in exactly one of these sets (after Build through the end of Main). Like the node work-lists, the move sets should be implemented as doubly linked lists, with each move containing an enumeration value identifying which set it belongs to.

Others

adjSet: the set of interference edges (u, v) in the graph. If $(u, v) \in$ adjSet then $(v, u) \in$ adjSet.

adjList: adjacency list representation of the graph; for each non-precolored temporary u, adjList$[u]$ is the set of nodes that interfere with u.

degree: an array containing the current degree of each node.

Degree Invariant.

For any $u \in$ simplifyWorklist $\cup$ freezeWorklist $\cup$ spillWorklist

it will always be the case that

$$\text{degree}(u) = |\text{adjList}(u) \cap (\text{precolored} \cup \text{simplifyWorklist}$$
$$\cup \text{freezeWorklist} \cup \text{spillWorklist})|$$

- **moveList:** a mapping from a node to the list of moves it is associated with.
- **alias:** when a move (u, v) has been coalesced, and v put in coalescedNodes, then alias$(v) = u$.
- **color:** the color chosen by the algorithm for a node; for precolored nodes this is initialized to the given color.

simplifyWorklist Invariant.

$$(u \in \text{simplifyWorklist}) \Rightarrow$$
$$\text{degree}(u) < K$$
$$\wedge \text{ moveList}[u] \cap (\text{activeMoves} \cup \text{worklistMoves}) = \{\}$$

freezeWorklist Invariant.

$$(u \in \text{freezeWorklist}) \Rightarrow$$
$$\text{degree}(u) < K$$
$$\wedge \text{ moveList}[u] \cap (\text{activeMoves} \cup \text{worklistMoves}) \neq \{\}$$

spillWorklist Invariant.

$$(u \in \text{spillWorklist}) \Rightarrow \text{degree}(u) \geq K$$

PROGRAM CODE

The algorithm is invoked using the procedure Main, which loops (via tail recursion) until no spills are generated.

procedure Main()
    LivenessAnalysis()
    Build()
    MakeWorklist()
    repeat
        if simplifyWorklist $\neq$ {} **then** Simplify()
        else if worklistMoves $\neq$ {} **then** Coalesce()
        else if freezeWorklist $\neq$ {} **then** Freeze()
        else if spillWorklist $\neq$ {} **then** SelectSpill()
    until simplifyWorklist = {} $\wedge$ worklistMoves = {}
        $\wedge$ freezeWorklist = {} $\wedge$ spillWorklist = {}
    AssignColors()
    if spilledNodes $\neq$ {} **then**
        RewriteProgram(spilledNodes)
        Main()

If AssignColors produces spills, then RewriteProgram allocates memory locations for the spilled temporaries and inserts store and fetch instructions to access them. These stores and fetches are to newly created temporaries (with tiny live ranges), so the main loop must be performed on the altered graph.

procedure Build ()
    forall $b \in$ blocks in program
        let live = liveOut(b)
        forall $I \in$ instructions(b) in reverse order
            if isMoveInstruction(I) **then**
                live $\leftarrow$ live\use(I)
                forall $n \in$ def(I) $\cup$ use(I)
                    moveList[n] $\leftarrow$ moveList[n] $\cup$ {I}
                worklistMoves $\leftarrow$ worklistMoves $\cup$ {I}
            live $\leftarrow$ live $\cup$ def(I)
            forall $d \in$ def(I)
                forall $l \in$ live
                  AddEdge(l, d)
            live $\leftarrow$ use(I) $\cup$ (live\def(I))

Procedure Build constructs the interference graph (and bit matrix) using the results of static liveness analysis, and also initializes the worklistMoves to contain all the moves in the program.

procedure AddEdge(u, v)
    if $((u, v) \notin \text{adjSet}) \wedge (u \neq v)$ **then**
        adjSet $\leftarrow$ adjSet $\cup \{(u, v), (v, u)\}$
        if $u \notin$ precolored **then**
            adjList[u] $\leftarrow$ adjList[u] $\cup \{v\}$
            degree[u] $\leftarrow$ degree[u] + 1
        if $v \notin$ precolored **then**
            adjList[v] $\leftarrow$ adjList[v] $\cup \{u\}$
            degree[v] $\leftarrow$ degree[v] + 1

function Adjacent(n)
    adjList[n] \ (selectStack $\cup$ coalescedNodes)

function NodeMoves (n)
    moveList[n] $\cap$ (activeMoves $\cup$ worklistMoves)

function MoveRelated(n)
    NodeMoves(n) $\neq \{\}$

procedure MakeWorklist()
    forall $n \in$ initial
        initial $\leftarrow$ initial \ $\{n\}$
        if degree[n] $\geq K$ **then**
            spillWorklist $\leftarrow$ spillWorklist $\cup \{$n$\}$
        else if MoveRelated(n) **then**
            freezeWorklist $\leftarrow$ freezeWorklist $\cup \{$n$\}$
        else
            simplifyWorklist $\leftarrow$ simplifyWorklist $\cup \{$n$\}$

procedure Simplify()
    let $n \in$ simplifyWorklist
    simplifyWorklist $\leftarrow$ simplifyWorklist \ $\{n\}$
    push(n, selectStack)
    forall m $\in$ Adjacent(n)
        DecrementDegree(m)

Removing a node from the graph involves decrementing the degree of its *current* neighbors. If the `degree` of a neighbor is already less than $K - 1$ then the neighbor must be move-related, and is not added to the `simplify-Worklist`. When the degree of a neigbor transitions from K to $K - 1$, moves associated with *its* neighbors may be enabled.

procedure DecrementDegree(m)
    let d = degree[m]
    degree[m] ← d-1
    if $d = K$ **then**
        EnableMoves($\{m\}$ ∪ Adjacent(m))
        spillWorklist ← spillWorklist $\setminus \{m\}$
        if MoveRelated(m) **then**
            freezeWorklist ← freezeWorklist ∪ $\{m\}$
        else
            simplifyWorklist ← simplifyWorklist ∪ $\{m\}$

procedure EnableMoves(nodes)
    forall n ∈ nodes
        forall m ∈ NodeMoves(n)
            if m ∈ activeMoves **then**
                activeMoves ← activeMoves $\setminus \{m\}$
                worklistMoves ← worklistMoves ∪ $\{m\}$

procedure Coalesce()
    let $m_{(=copy(x,y))}$ ∈ worklistMoves
    x ← GetAlias(x)
    y ← GetAlias(y)
    if y ∈ precolored **then**
        let $(u, v) = (y, x)$
    else
        let $(u, v) = (x, y)$
    worklistMoves ← worklistMoves $\setminus \{m\}$
    if $(u = v)$ **then**
        coalescedMoves ← coalescedMoves ∪ $\{m\}$
        AddWorkList(u)
    else if v ∈ precolored ∨ (u, v) ∈ adjSet **then**
        constrainedMoves ← constrainedMoves ∪ $\{m\}$
        AddWorkList(u)
        AddWorkList(v)
    else if u ∈ precolored ∧ $(\forall t$ ∈ Adjacent(v), OK(t, u))
            ∨ u ∉ precolored ∧
                Conservative(Adjacent(u) ∪ Adjacent(v)) **then**
        coalescedMoves ← coalescedMoves ∪ $\{m\}$
        Combine(u,v)
        AddWorkList(u)
    else
        activeMoves ← activeMoves ∪ $\{m\}$

Only moves in the `worklistMoves` are considered in the coalesce phase. When a move is coalesced, it may no longer be move-related and can be added to the simplify work-list by the procedure `AddWorkList`. OK implements the heuristic used for coalescing a precolored register. `Conservative` implements the conservative coalescing heuristic.

procedure AddWorkList(u)
    if ($u \notin$ precolored $\land$ not(MoveRelated(u)) $\land$ degree[u] < K) **then**
        freezeWorklist $\leftarrow$ freezeWorklist $\setminus \{u\}$
        simplifyWorklist $\leftarrow$ simplifyWorklist $\cup \{u\}$

function OK(t,r)
    degree[t] < K $\lor$ $t \in$ precolored $\lor$ $(t, r) \in$ adjSet

function Conservative(nodes)
    let $k = 0$
    forall $n \in$ nodes
        if degree[n] $\geq K$ **then** $k \leftarrow k + 1$
    return $(k < K)$

function GetAlias (n)
    if $n \in$ coalescedNodes **then**
        GetAlias(alias[n])
    else n

procedure Combine(u,v)
    if $v \in$ freezeWorklist **then**
        freezeWorklist $\leftarrow$ freezeWorklist $\setminus \{v\}$
    else
        spillWorklist $\leftarrow$ spillWorklist $\setminus \{v\}$
    coalescedNodes $\leftarrow$ coalescedNodes $\cup \{v\}$
    alias[v] $\leftarrow u$
    nodeMoves[u] $\leftarrow$ nodeMoves[u] $\cup$ nodeMoves[v]
    forall $t \in$ Adjacent(v)
        AddEdge(t,u)
        DecrementDegree(t)
    if degree[u] $\geq K \land u \in$ freezeWorkList
        freezeWorkList $\leftarrow$ freezeWorkList $\setminus \{u\}$
        spillWorkList $\leftarrow$ spillWorkList $\cup \{u\}$

procedure Freeze()
    let $u \in$ freezeWorklist
    freezeWorklist $\leftarrow$ freezeWorklist $\setminus \{u\}$
    simplifyWorklist $\leftarrow$ simplifyWorklist $\cup \{u\}$
    FreezeMoves(u)

procedure FreezeMoves(u)
    forall $m(=$ copy(u,v) or copy(v,u)$) \in$ NodeMoves(u)
        if $m \in$ activeMoves **then**
            activeMoves $\leftarrow$ activeMoves $\setminus \{m\}$
        else
            worklistMoves $\leftarrow$ worklistMoves $\setminus \{m\}$
        frozenMoves $\leftarrow$ frozenMoves $\cup \{m\}$
        if NodeMoves(v) $= \{\} \wedge$ degree[v] $< K$ **then**
            freezeWorklist $\leftarrow$ freezeWorklist $\setminus \{v\}$
            simplifyWorklist $\leftarrow$ simplifyWorklist $\cup \{v\}$

procedure SelectSpill()
    let $m \in$ spillWorklist *selected using favorite heuristic*
        Note: avoid choosing nodes that are the tiny live ranges
        resulting from the fetches of previously spilled registers
    spillWorklist $\leftarrow$ spillWorklist $\setminus \{m\}$
    simplifyWorklist $\leftarrow$ simplifyWorklist $\cup \{m\}$
    FreezeMoves(m)

procedure AssignColors()
    while SelectStack not empty
        let $n =$ pop(SelectStack)
        okColors $\leftarrow \{0, \ldots, K\text{-}1\}$
        forall $w \in$ adjList[n]
            if GetAlias(w) $\in$ (coloredNodes $\cup$ precolored) **then**
                okColors $\leftarrow$ okColors $\setminus \{$color[GetAlias(w)]$\}$
        if okColors $= \{\}$ **then**
            spilledNodes $\leftarrow$ spilledNodes $\cup \{n\}$
        else
            coloredNodes $\leftarrow$ coloredNodes $\cup \{n\}$
            let $c \in$ okColors
            color[n] $\leftarrow c$
    forall $n \in$ coalescedNodes
        color[n] $\leftarrow$ color[GetAlias(n)]

procedure RewriteProgram()
    Allocate memory locations for each $v \in$ spilledNodes,
    Create a new temporary v_i for each definition and each use,
    In the program *(instructions)*, insert a store after each
    definition of a v_i, a fetch before each use of a v_i.
    Put all the v_i into a set newTemps.
    spilledNodes $\leftarrow \{\}$
    initial $\leftarrow$ coloredNodes $\cup$ coalescedNodes $\cup$ newTemps
    coloredNodes $\leftarrow \{\}$
    coalescedNodes $\leftarrow \{\}$

We show a variant of the algorithm in which all coalesces are discarded if the program must be rewritten to incorporate spill fetches and stores. For a faster algorithm, keep all the coalesces found before the first call to `SelectSpill` and rewrite the program to eliminate the coalesced move instructions and temporaries.

In principle, a heuristic could be used to select the freeze node; the `Freeze` shown above picks an arbitrary node from the freeze work-list. But freezes are not common, and a selection heuristic is unlikely to make a significant difference.

11.4   REGISTER ALLOCATION FOR TREES

Register allocation for expression trees is much simpler than for arbitrary flow graphs. We do not need global dataflow analysis or interference graphs. Suppose we have a tiled tree such as in Figure 9.2a. This tree has two *trivial* tiles, the TEMP nodes *fp* and *i*, which we assume are already in registers r_{fp} and r_i. We wish to label the roots of the nontrivial tiles (the ones corresponding to instructions, i.e. 2,4,5,6,8) with registers from the list $r_1, r_2, \ldots, r_k$.

Algorithm 11.8 traverses the tree in postorder, assigning a register to the root of each tile. With n initialized to zero, this algorithm applied to the root (tile 9) produces the allocation $\{$tile2 $\mapsto r_1$, tile4 $\mapsto r_2$, tile5 $\mapsto r_2$, tile6 $\mapsto r_1$, tile8 $\mapsto r_2$, tile9 $\mapsto r_1\}$. The algorithm can be combined with Maximal Munch, since both algorithms are doing the same bottom-up traversal.

But this algorithm will not always lead to an optimal allocation. Consider the following tree, where each tile is shown as a single node:

function SimpleAlloc(t)
    for each nontrivial tile u that is a child of t
        SimpleAlloc(u)
    for each nontrivial tile u that is a child of t
        $n \leftarrow n - 1$
    $n \leftarrow n + 1$
    assign r_n to hold the value at the root of t

ALGORITHM 11.8. Simple register allocation on trees.

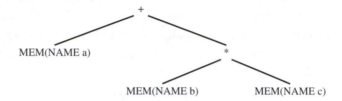

The SimpleAlloc function will use three registers for this expression (as shown at left below), but by reordering the instructions we can do the computation using only two registers (as shown at right):

$r_1 \leftarrow M[a]$	$r_1 \leftarrow M[b]$
$r_2 \leftarrow M[b]$	$r_2 \leftarrow M[c]$
$r_3 \leftarrow M[c]$	$r_1 \leftarrow r_1 \times r_2$
$r_2 \leftarrow r_2 \times r_3$	$r_2 \leftarrow M[a]$
$r_1 \leftarrow r_1 + r_2$	$r_1 \leftarrow r_2 + r_1$

Using dynamic programming, we can find the optimal ordering for the instructions. The idea is to label each tile with the number of registers it needs during its evaluation. Suppose a tile t has two nontrivial children u_{left} and u_{right} that require n and m registers, respectively, for their evaluation. If we evaluate u_{left} first, and hold its result in one register while we evaluate u_{right}, then we have needed $\max(n, 1 + m)$ registers for the whole expression rooted at t. Conversely, if we evaluate u_{right} first, then we need $\max(1 + n, m)$ registers. Clearly, if $n > m$ we should evaluate u_{left} first, and if $n < m$ we should evaluate u_{right} first. If $n = m$ we will need $n + 1$ registers no matter which subexpression is evaluated first.

function Label(t)
    for each tile u that is a child of t
        Label(u)
    if t is trivial
        then $need[t] \leftarrow 0$
    else if t has two children, u_{left} and u_{right}
        then if $need[u_{\text{left}}] = need[u_{\text{right}}]$
            then $need[t] \leftarrow 1 + need[u_{\text{left}}]$
            else $need[t] \leftarrow \max(1, need[u_{\text{left}}], need[u_{\text{right}}])$
    else if t has one child, u
        then $need[t] \leftarrow \max(1, need[u])$
    else if t has no children
        then $need[t] \leftarrow 1$

ALGORITHM 11.9. Sethi-Ullman labeling algorithm.

Algorithm 11.9 labels each tile t with $need[t]$, the number of registers needed to evaluate the subtree rooted at t. It can be generalized to handle tiles with more than two children. Maximal Munch should identify – but not emit – the tiles, simultaneously with the labeling of Algorithm 11.9. The next pass emits Assem instructions for the tiles; wherever a tile has more than one child, the subtrees must be emitted in decreasing order of register *need*.

Algorithm 11.9 can profitably be used in a compiler that uses graph-coloring register allocation. Emitting the subtrees in decreasing order of *need* will minimize the number of simultaneously live temporaries and reduce the number of spills.

In a compiler without graph-coloring register allocation, Algorithm 11.9 is used as a pre-pass to Algorithm 11.10, which assigns registers as the trees are emitted and also handles spilling cleanly. This takes care of register allocation for the internal nodes of expression trees; allocating registers for explicit TEMPs of the Tree language would have to be done in some other way. In general, such a compiler would keep almost all program variables in the stack frame, so there would not be many of these explicit TEMPs to allocate.

function SethiUllman(t)
   if t has two children, u_{left} and u_{right}
      if $need[u_{\text{left}}] \geq K \;\wedge\; need[u_{\text{right}}] \geq K$
         SethiUllman(t_{right})
         $n \leftarrow n - 1$
         spill: emit instruction to store $reg[t_{\text{right}}]$
         SethiUllman(t_{left})
         unspill: emit instruction to fetch $reg[t_{\text{right}}]$
      else if $need[u_{\text{left}}] \geq need[u_{\text{right}}]$
         SethiUllman(t_{left})
         SethiUllman(t_{right})
         $n \leftarrow n - 1$
      else $need[u_{\text{left}}] < need[u_{\text{right}}]$
         SethiUllman(t_{right})
         SethiUllman(t_{left})
         $n \leftarrow n - 1$
      $reg[t] \leftarrow \text{``}r_n\text{''}$
      emit OPER($instruction[t], \; reg[t], \; [\, reg[t_{\text{left}}], \; reg[t_{\text{right}}]\,]$)
   else if t has one child, u
      SethiUllman(u)
      $reg[t] \leftarrow \text{``}r_n\text{''}$
      emit OPER($instruction[t], \; reg[t], \; [reg[u]]$)
   else if t is nontrivial but has no children
      $n \leftarrow n + 1$
      $reg[t] \leftarrow \text{``}r_n\text{''}$
      emit OPER($instruction[t], \; reg[t], \; [\,]$)
   else if t is a trivial node TEMP(r_i)
      $reg[t] \leftarrow \text{``}r_i\text{''}$

ALGORITHM 11.10. Sethi-Ullman register allocation for trees.

PROGRAM GRAPH COLORING

Implement graph coloring register allocation as two modules: `Color`, which does just the graph coloring itself, and `RegAlloc`, which manages spilling and calls upon `Color` as a subroutine. To keep things simple, do not implement spilling or coalescing; this simplifies the algorithm considerably.

```
package RegAlloc;

public class RegAlloc implements Temp.TempMap {
   public Assem.InstrList instrs;
   public String tempMap(Temp temp);
   public RegAlloc(Frame.Frame f, Assem.InstrList il);
}

class Color implements TempMap {
   public TempList spills();
   public String tempMap(Temp t);
   public Color(InterferenceGraph ig,
                TempMap initial,
                TempList registers);
}
```

Given an interference graph, an `initial` allocation (precoloring) of some temporaries imposed by calling conventions, and a list of colors (`registers`), `color` produces an extension of the `initial` allocation. The resulting allocation assigns all temps used in the flow graph, making use of registers from the `registers` list.

The `initial` allocation is the `frame` (which implements a `TempMap` describing precolored temporaries); the `registers` argument is just the list of all machine registers, `Frame.registers` (see page 252). The registers in the `initial` allocation can also appear in the `registers` argument to `Color`, since it's OK to use them to color other nodes as well.

The result of `Color` is a `TempMap` (that is, `Color` implements `TempMap`) describing the register allocation, along with a list of spills. The result of `RegAlloc` – if there were no spills – is an identical `TempMap`, which can be used in final assembly-code emission phase as an argument to `Assem.format`.

A better `Color` interface would have a `spillCost` argument that specifies the spilling cost of each temporary. This can be just the number of uses and defs, or better yet, uses and defs weighted by occurrence in loops and nested loops. A naive `spillCost` that just returns 1 for every temporary will also work.

A simple implementation of the coloring algorithm without coalescing requires only one work-list: the simplifyWorklist, which contains all non-precolored, nonsimplified nodes of degree less than K. Obviously, no freezeWorklist is necessary. No spillWorklist is necessary either, if we are willing to look through all the nodes in the original graph for a spill candidate every time the simplifyWorklist becomes empty.

With only a simplifyWorklist, the doubly linked representation is not necessary: this work-list can be implemented as a singly linked list or a stack, since it is never accessed "in the middle."

ADVANCED PROJECT: SPILLING

Implement spilling, so that no matter how many parameters and locals a Tiger program has, you can still compile it.

ADVANCED PROJECT: COALESCING

Implement coalescing, to eliminate practically all the MOVE instructions from the program.

FURTHER READING

Kempe [1879] invented the simplification algorithm that colors graphs by removing vertices of degree $< K$. Chaitin [1982] formulated register allocation as a graph-coloring problem – using Kempe's algorithm to color the graph – and performed copy propagation by (nonconservatively) coalescing non-interfering move-related nodes before coloring the graph. Briggs et al. [1994] improved the algorithm with the idea of optimistic spilling, and also avoided introducing spills by using the conservative coalescing heuristic before coloring the graph. George and Appel [1996] found that there are more opportunities for coalescing if conservative coalescing is done during simplification instead of beforehand, and developed the worklist algorithm presented in this chapter.

Ershov [1958] developed the algorithm for optimal register allocation on expression trees; Sethi and Ullman [1970] generalized this algorithm and showed how it should handle spills.

11.1 The table below represents a register-interference graph. Nodes 1–6 are pre-colored (with colors 1–6), and nodes A–H are ordinary (non-precolored). Every pair of precolored nodes interferes, and each ordinary node interferes with nodes where there is an x in the table.

	1	2	3	4	5	6	A	B	C	D	E	F	G	H
A	x	x	x	x	x	x								
B	x		x	x	x	x								
C			x	x	x	x				x	x	x	x	x
D	x		x	x	x				x		x	x	x	x
E	x		x		x	x			x	x		x	x	x
F	x		x	x		x			x	x	x		x	x
G									x	x	x	x		
H	x			x	x	x			x	x	x	x		

The following pairs of nodes are related by MOVE instructions:

$$(A, 3) \ (H, 3) \ (G, 3) \ (B, 2) \ (C, 1) \ (D, 6) \ (E, 4) \ (F, 5)$$

Assume that register allocation must be done for an 8-register machine.

a. Ignoring the MOVE instructions, and without using the *coalesce* heuristic, color this graph using *simplify* and *spill*. Record the sequence (stack) of *simplify* and *potential-spill* decisions, show which potential spills become actual spills, and show the coloring that results.

b. Color this graph using coalescing. Record the sequence of *simplify, coalesce, freeze,* and *spill* decisions. Show how many MOVE instructions remain.

c. Another coalescing heuristic is *biased coloring*. Instead of using the *conservative coalescing* heuristic, run the *simplify-spill* part of the algorithm as in part (a), but in the *select*-color part of the algorithm,

   i.   When selecting a color for node X that is move-related to node Y, when a color for Y has already been selected, use the same color if possible (to eliminate the MOVE).

  ii. When selecting a color for node X that is move-related to node Y, when a color for Y has not yet been selected, use a color that is *not* the same as the color of any of Y's neighbors (to increase the chance of heuristic (i) working when Y is colored).

Conservative coalescing (in the *simplify* phase) has been found more effective than biased coloring, in general; but it might not be on this particular graph. Since the two coalescing algorithms are used in different phases, they can both be used in the same register allocator.

d. Use both conservative coalescing and biased coloring in allocating registers. Show where biased coloring helps make the right decisions.

11.2 *Conservative coalescing* (page 227) is so called because it will not introduce any (potential) spills. But consider this graph, where the solid edges represent interferences and the dashed edge represents a MOVE:

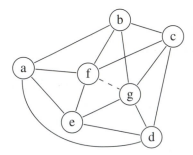

a. 4-color the graph without coalescing. Is there a potential spill?

b. 4-color the graph with conservative coalescing. Is there a potential spill?

c. Explain more precisely why it is called conservative coalescing.

11.3 It has been proposed that the conservative coalescing heuristic could be simplified. In testing whether MOVE(a, b) can be coalesced, instead of asking whether the combined node ab is adjacent to $< K$ nodes of significant degree, we could simply test whether ab is adjacent to $< K$ nodes of any degree. The theory is that if ab is adjacent to many low-degree nodes, they will be removed by simplification anyway.

a. Show that this kind of coalescing cannot create any new potential spills.

b. Demonstrate the algorithm on this graph (with $K = 3$):

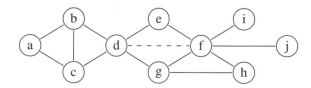

c. Show that this test is less effective than standard conservative coalescing. Hint: use the graph of Exercise 11.2, with $K = 4$.

12

Putting It All Together

de-bug: to eliminate errors in or malfunctions of

Webster's Dictionary

Chapters 2–11 have described the fundamental components of a good compiler: a *front end*, which does lexical analysis, parsing, construction of abstract syntax, type-checking, and translation to intermediate code; and a *back end*, which does instruction selection, dataflow analysis, and register allocation.

What lessons have we learned? I hope that the reader has learned about the algorithms used in different components of a compiler and the interfaces used to connect the components. But the author has also learned quite a bit from the exercise.

My goal was to describe a good compiler that is, to use Einstein's phrase, "as simple as possible – but no simpler." I will now discuss the thorny issues that arose in designing Tiger and its compiler.

Nested functions. Tiger has nested functions, requiring some mechanism (such as static links) for implementing access to nonlocal variables. But many programming languages in widespread use – C, C++, Java – do not have nested functions or static links. The Tiger compiler would become simpler without nested functions, for then variables would not escape, and the `FindEscape` phase would be unnecessary. But there are two reasons for explaining how to compile nonlocal variables. First, there are programming languages where nested functions are extremely useful – these are the *functional* languages described in Chapter 15. And second, escaping variables and the mechanisms necessary to handle them are also found in languages where addresses can be taken (such as C) or with call-by-reference (such as C++).

Structured l-values. Tiger has no record or array variables, as C, C++, and Pascal do. Instead, all record and array values are really just pointers to heap-allocated data. This omission is really just to keep the compiler simple; implementing structured l-values requires some care but not too many new insights.

Tree intermediate representation. The `Tree` language has a fundamental flaw: it does not describe procedure entry and exit. These are handled by opaque procedures inside the `Frame` module that generate `Tree` code. This means that a program translated to `Trees` using, for example, the `Pentium-Frame` version of `Frame` will be different from the same program translated using `SparcFrame` – the `Tree` representation is not completely machine independent.

Also, there is not enough information in the trees themselves to simulate the execution of an entire program, since the *view shift* (page 132) is partly done implicitly by procedure prologues and epilogues that are not represented as `Trees`. Consequently, there is not enough information to do whole-program optimization (across function boundaries).

The `Tree` representation is useful as a *low-level* intermediate representation, useful for instruction selection and intraprocedural optimization. A *high-level* intermediate representation would preserve more of the source-program semantics, including the notions of nested functions, nonlocal variables, record creation (as distinguished from an opaque external function call), and so on. Such a representation would be more tied to a particular family of source languages than the general-purpose `Tree` language is.

Register allocation. Graph-coloring register allocation is widely used in real compilers, but does it belong in a compiler that is supposed to be "as simple as possible"? After all, it requires the use of global dataflow (liveness) analysis, construction of interference graphs, and so on. This makes the back end of the compiler significantly bigger.

It is instructive to consider what the Tiger compiler would be like without it. We could keep all local variables in the stack frame (as we do now for variables that escape), fetching them into temporaries only when they are used as operands of instructions. The redundant loads within a single basic block can be eliminated by a simple intrablock liveness analysis. Internal nodes of `Tree` expressions could be assigned registers using Algorithms 11.9 and 11.8. But other parts of the compiler would become much uglier: The

```
package Frame;
import Temp.Temp;

public abstract class Frame implements Temp.TempMap {
abstract public Temp RV();       (see page 165)
abstract public Temp FP();       (page 151)
abstract public Temp.TempList registers();
abstract public String tempMap(Temp temp);
abstract public int wordSize();  (p. 151)
abstract public Tree.Exp externalCall(String func, Tree.ExpList args);  (p. 162)
abstract public Frame newFrame(Temp.Label name,
                               Util.BoolList formals);   (p. 130)
public AccessList formals;       (p. 132)
public Temp.Label name;          (p. 130)
abstract public Access allocLocal(boolean escape);   (p. 130)
abstract public String string(Temp.Label label, String value);   (p. 252)
abstract public Tree.Stm procEntryExit1(Tree.Stm body);  (p. 252)
abstract public Assem.InstrList procEntryExit2(Assem.InstrList body);   (p. 204)
abstract public Proc procEntryExit3(Assem.InstrList body);
abstract public Assem.InstrList codegen(Tree.Stm stm);   (p. 201)
}
```

PROGRAM 12.1. Package Frame.

TEMPs introduced in canonicalizing the trees (eliminating ESEQs) would have to be dealt with in an ad hoc way, by augmenting the Tree language with an operator that provides explicit scope for temporary variables; the Frame interface, which mentions registers in many places, would now have to deal with them in more complicated ways. To be able to create arbitrarily many temps and moves, and rely on the register allocator to clean them up, greatly simplifies procedure calling sequences and code generation.

PROGRAM

PROCEDURE ENTRY/EXIT

Implement the rest of the Frame module, which contains all the machine-dependent parts of the compiler: register sets, calling sequences, activation record (frame) layout.

Program 12.1 shows the Frame class. Most of this interface has been described elsewhere. What remains is:

registers A list of all the register names on the machine, which can be used as "colors" for register allocation.

tempMap For each machine register, the Frame module maintains a particular Temp that serves as the "precolored temporary" that stands for the register.

These temps appear in the `Assem` instructions generated from CALL nodes, in procedure entry sequences generated by `procEntryExit1`, and so on. The `tempMap` tells the "color" of each of these precolored temps.

procEntryExit1 For each incoming register parameter, move it to the place from which it is seen from within the function. This could be a frame location (for escaping parameters) or a fresh temporary. One good way to handle this is for `newFrame` to create a sequence of `Tree.MOVE` statements as it creates all the formal parameter "accesses." `newFrame` can put this into the `frame` data structure, and `procEntryExit1` can just concatenate it onto the procedure body.

Also concatenated to the body are statements for saving and restoring of callee-save registers (including the return-address register). If your register allocator does not implement spilling, all the callee-save (and return-address) registers should be written to the frame at the beginning of the procedure body and fetched back afterward. Therefore, `procEntryExit1` should call `allocLocal` for each register to be saved, and generate `Tree.MOVE` instructions to save and restore the registers. With luck, saving and restoring the callee-save registers will give the register allocator enough headroom to work with, so that some nontrivial programs can be compiled. Of course, some programs just cannot be compiled without spilling.

If your register allocator implements spilling, then the callee-save registers should not always be written to the frame. Instead, if the register allocator needs the space, it may choose to spill only some of the callee-save registers. But "precolored" temporaries are never spilled; so `procEntryExit1` should make up new temporaries for each callee-save (and return-address) register. On entry, it should move all these registers to their new temporary locations, and on exit, it should move them back. Of course, these moves (for nonspilled registers) will be eliminated by register coalescing, so they cost nothing.

procEntryExit3 Creates the procedure prologue and epilogue assembly language. First (for some machines) it calculates the size of the *outgoing parameter space* in the frame. This is equal to the maximum number of outgoing parameters of any CALL instruction in the procedure body. Unfortunately, after conversion to `Assem` trees the procedure calls have been separated from their arguments, so the outgoing parameters are not obvious. Either `procEntryExit2` should scan the body and record this information in some new component of the `frame` type, or `procEntryExit3` should use the maximum legal value.

Once this is known, the assembly language for procedure entry, stack-pointer adjustment, and procedure exit can be put together; these are the `prologue` and `epilogue`.

string A string literal in Tiger, translated into a STRING fragment, must eventually be translated into machine-dependent assembly language that reserves and initializes a block of memory. The `Frame.string` function returns a string containing the assembly-language instructions required to define and initialize a string literal.

PROGRAM MAKING IT WORK

Make your compiler generate working code that runs.

The file `$TIGER/chap12/runtime.c` is a C-language file containing several external functions useful to your Tiger program. These are generally reached by `externalCall` from code generated by your compiler. You may modify this as necessary.

Write a module `Main` that calls on all the other modules to produce an assembly language file `prog.s` for each input program `prog.tig`. This assembly language program should be assembled (producing `prog.o`) and linked with `runtime.o` to produce an executable file.

Programming projects

After your Tiger compiler is done, here are some ideas for further work:

12.1 Write a garbage collector (in C) for your Tiger compiler. You will need to make some modifications to the compiler itself to add descriptors to records and stack frames.

12.2 Implement first-class function values in Tiger (so that functions can be passed as arguments, returned as results, etc.).

12.3 Make the Tiger language object-oriented, so that instead of records there are objects with methods. Make a compiler for this object-oriented Tiger.

12.4 Figure out other approaches to improving the assembly-language generated by your compiler. Discuss; perhaps implement.

12.5 Implement instruction scheduling to fill branch-delay and load-delay slots in the assembly language. Or discuss how such a module could be integrated into the existing compiler; what interfaces would have to change, and in what ways?

12.6 Implement "software pipelining" (instruction scheduling around loop iterations) in your compiler.

12.7 Analyze how adequate the Tiger language itself would be for writing a compiler. What are the smallest possible additions/changes that would make it a much more useful language?

12.8 In the Tiger language, some record types are recursive and *must* be implemented as pointers; others are not recursive and could be implemented without pointers. Modify your compiler to take advantage of this by keeping nonrecursive, nonescaping records in the stack frame instead of on the heap.

12.9 Similarly, some arrays have bounds known at compile time, are not recursive, and are not assigned to other array variables. Modify your compiler so that these arrays are implemented right in the stack frame.

12.10 Implement in-line expansion of functions.

12.11 Suppose an ordinary Tiger program were to run on a parallel machine (a multiprocessor)? How could the compiler automatically make a parallel program out of the original sequential one? Research the approaches.

PART TWO
Advanced Topics

13

Garbage Collection

gar-bage: unwanted or useless material

Webster's Dictionary

Heap-allocated records that are not reachable by any chain of pointers from program variables are *garbage*. The memory occupied by garbage should be reclaimed for use in allocating new records. This process is called *garbage collection*, and is performed not by the compiler but by the runtime system (the support programs linked with the compiled code).

Ideally, we would say that any record that is not dynamically live (will not be used in the future of the computation) is garbage. But, as Section 10.1 explains, it is not always possible to know whether a variable is live. So we will use a conservative approximation: we will require the compiler to guarantee that any *live* record is *reachable*; we will ask the compiler to minimize the number of reachable records that are *not* live; and we will preserve all reachable records, even if some of them might not be live.

Figure 13.1 shows a Tiger program ready to undergo garbage collection (at the point marked *garbage-collect here*). There are only three program variables in scope: p, q, and r.

13.1   MARK-AND-SWEEP COLLECTION

Program variables and heap-allocated records form a directed graph. The variables are *roots* of this graph. A node n is reachable if there is a path of directed edges $r \rightarrow \cdots \rightarrow n$ starting at some root r. A graph-search algorithm such as *depth-first search* (Algorithm 13.2) can *mark* all the reachable nodes.

```
let
    type list = {link: list,
                 key: int}
    type tree = {key: int,
                 left: tree,
                 right: tree}
    function maketree() = ···
    function showtree(t: tree) = ···
in
    let var x := list{link=nil,key=7}
        var y := list{link=x,key=9}
    in x.link := y
    end;
    let var p := maketree()
        var r := p.right
        var q := r.key
    in  garbage-collect here
        showtree(r)
    end
end
```

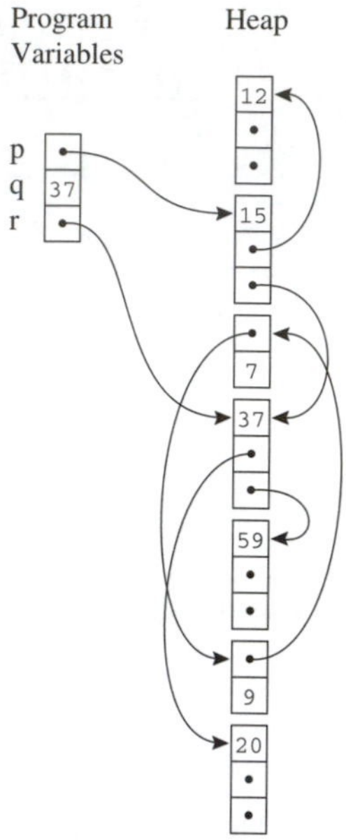

Program Variables | Heap

FIGURE 13.1.   A heap to be garbage collected.

function DFS(x)
    if x is a pointer into the heap
        if record x is not marked
            mark x
            for each field f_i of record x
                DFS($x.f_i$)

ALGORITHM 13.2. Depth-first search.

Any node not marked must be garbage, and should be reclaimed. This can be done by a *sweep* of the entire heap, from its first address to its last, looking for nodes that are not marked (Algorithm 13.3). These are garbage and can be linked together in a linked list (the *freelist*). The sweep phase should also unmark all the marked nodes, in preparation for the next garbage collection.

After the garbage collection, the compiled program resumes execution. Whenever it wants to heap-allocate a new record, it gets a record from the freelist. When the freelist becomes empty, that is a good time to do another garbage collection to replenish the freelist.

Mark phase:
  for each root v
    DFS(v)

Sweep phase:
  $p \leftarrow$ first address in heap
  while $p <$ last address in heap
    if record p is marked
      unmark p
    else let f_1 be the first field in p
      $p.f_1 \leftarrow$ `freelist`
      `freelist` $\leftarrow p$
    $p \leftarrow p+$(size of record p)

ALGORITHM 13.3. Mark-and-sweep garbage collection.

Cost of garbage collection. Depth-first search takes time proportional to the number of nodes it marks, that is, time proportional to the amount of reachable data. The sweep phase takes time proportional to the size of the heap. Suppose there are R words of reachable data in a heap of size H. Then the cost of one garbage collection is $c_1 R + c_2 H$ for some constants c_1 and c_2; for example, c_1 might be 10 instructions and c_2 might be 3 instructions.

The "good" that collection does is to replenish the freelist with $H - R$ words of usable memory. Therefore, we can compute the *amortized cost* of collection by dividing the *time spent collecting* by the *amount of garbage reclaimed*. That is, for every word that the compiled program allocates, there is an eventual garbage-collection cost of

$$\frac{c_1 R + c_2 H}{H - R}$$

If R is close to H, this cost becomes very large: each garbage collection reclaims only a few words of garbage. If H is much larger than R, then the cost per allocated word is approximately c_2, or about three instructions of garbage-collection cost per word allocated.

The garbage collector can measure H (the heap size) and $H - R$ (the freelist size) directly. After a collection, if R/H is larger than 0.5 (or some other criterion), the collector should increase H by asking the operating system for more memory. Then the cost per allocated word will be approximately $c_1 + 2c_2$, or perhaps 16 instructions per word.

Using an explicit stack. The DFS algorithm is recursive, and the maximum depth of its recursion is as long as the longest path in the graph of reachable

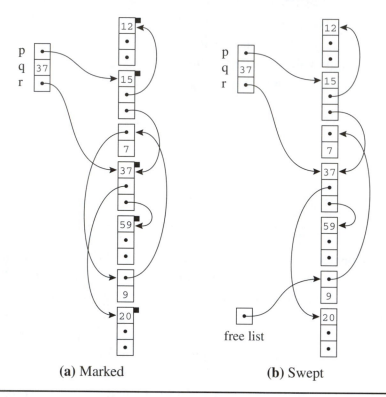

(a) Marked   **(b)** Swept

FIGURE 13.4.   Mark-and-sweep collection.

data. There could be a path of length H in the worst case, meaning that the stack of activation records would be larger than the entire heap!

To attack this problem, we use an explicit stack (instead of recursion), as in Algorithm 13.5. Now the stack could still grow to size H, but at least this is H words and not H activation records. Still, it is unacceptable to require auxiliary stack memory as large as the heap being collected.

Pointer reversal. After the contents of field $x.f_i$ has been pushed on the stack, Algorithm 13.5 will never again look the original location $x.f_i$. This means we can use $x.f_i$ to store one element of the stack itself! This all-too-clever idea is called *pointer reversal*, because $x.f_i$ will be made to point back to the record from which x was reached. Then, as the stack is popped, the field $x.f_i$ will be restored to its original value.

Algorithm 13.6 requires a field in each record called *done*, which indicates how many fields in that record have been processed. This takes only a few

function DFS(x)
  if x is a pointer and record x is not marked
  $t \leftarrow 1$
  stack$[t] \leftarrow x$
  while $t > 0$
       $x \leftarrow$ stack$[t]$; $t \leftarrow t - 1$
       for each field f_i of record x
          if $x.f_i$ is a pointer and record $x.f_i$ is not marked
          mark $x.f_i$
          $t \leftarrow t + 1$; stack$[t] \leftarrow x.f_i$

ALGORITHM 13.5. Depth-first search using an explicit stack.

bits per record (and it can also serve as the mark field).

The variable t serves as the top of the stack; every record x on the stack is already marked, and if $i = $ done$[x]$ then $x.f_i$ is the "stack link" to the next node down. When popping the stack, $x.f_i$ is restored to its original value.

An array of freelists. The sweep phase is the same no matter which marking algorithm is used: it just puts the unmarked records on the freelist, and unmarks the marked records. But if records are of many different sizes, a simple linked list will not be very efficient for the allocator. When allocating a record of size n, it may have to search a long way down the list for a free block of that size.

A good solution is to have an array of several freelists, so that freelist$[i]$ is a linked list of all records of size i. The program can allocate a node of size i just by taking the head of freelist$[i]$; the sweep phase of the collector can put each node of size j at the head of freelist$[j]$.

If the program attempts to allocate from an empty freelist$[i]$, it can try to grab a larger record from freelist$[j]$ (for $j > i$) and split it (putting the unused portion back on freelist$[j - i]$). If this fails, it is time to call the garbage collector to replenish the freelists.

Fragmentation. It can happen that the program wants to allocate a record of size n, and there are many free records smaller than n but none of the right size. This is called *external fragmentation*. On the other hand, *internal fragmentation* occurs when the program uses a too-large record without splitting it, so that the unused memory is inside the record instead of outside.

function DFS(x)
  if x is a pointer and record x is not marked
    $t \leftarrow$ nil
  mark x; done$[x] \leftarrow 0$
  while true
      $i \leftarrow$ done$[x]$
    if $i <$ # of fields in record x
      $y \leftarrow x.f_i$
      if y is a pointer and record y is not marked
        $x.f_i \leftarrow t$; $t \leftarrow x$; $x \leftarrow y$
        mark x; done$[x] \leftarrow 0$
      else
        done$[x] \leftarrow i + 1$
    else
      $y \leftarrow x$; $x \leftarrow t$
      if $x =$ nil **then return**
      $i \leftarrow$ done$[x]$
      $t \leftarrow x.f_i$; $x.f_i \leftarrow y$
      done$[x] \leftarrow i + 1$

ALGORITHM 13.6. Depth-first search using pointer reversal.

13.2   REFERENCE COUNTS

One day a student came to Moon and said: "I understand how to make a better garbage collector. We must keep a reference count of the pointers to each cons."
Moon patiently told the student the following story:
    "One day a student came to Moon and said: 'I understand how to make a better garbage collector ...' "

(MIT-AI koan by Danny Hillis)

Mark-sweep collection identifies the garbage by first finding out what is reachable. Instead, it can be done directly by keeping track of how many pointers point to each record: this is the *reference count* of the record, and it is stored with each record.

The compiler emits extra instructions so that whenever p is stored into $x.f_i$, the reference count of p is incremented, and the reference count of what $x.f_i$ previously pointed to is decremented. If the decremented reference count of some record r reaches zero, then r is put on the freelist and all the other records that r points to have their reference counts decremented.

Instead of decrementing the counts of $r.f_i$ when r is put on the freelist, it is better to do this "recursive" decrementing when r is removed from the freelist, for two reasons:

1. It breaks up the "recursive decrementing" work into shorter pieces, so that the program can run more smoothly (this is important only for interactive or real-time programs).

2. The compiler must emit code (at each decrement) to check whether the count has reached zero and put the record on the freelist, but the recursive decrementing will be done only in one place, in the allocator.

Reference counting seems simple and attractive. But there are two major problems:

1. Cycles of garbage cannot be reclaimed. In Figure 13.1, for example, there is a loop of list cells (whose keys are 7 and 9) that are not reachable from program variables; but each has a reference count of 1.

2. Incrementing the reference counts is very expensive indeed. In place of the single machine instruction $x.f_i \leftarrow p$, the program must execute

$$
\begin{aligned}
z \quad & \leftarrow x.f_i \\
c \quad & \leftarrow z.\text{count} \\
c \quad & \leftarrow c - 1 \\
z.\text{count} & \leftarrow c \\
\text{if } c & = 0 \text{ goto } putOnFreelist \\
x.f_i \quad & \leftarrow p \\
c \quad & \leftarrow p.\text{count} \\
c \quad & \leftarrow c + 1 \\
p.\text{count} & \leftarrow c
\end{aligned}
$$

A naive reference counter will increment and decrement the counts on every assignment to a program variable. Because this would be extremely expensive, many of the increments and decrements are eliminated using dataflow analysis: As a pointer value is fetched and then propagated through local variables, the compiler can aggregate the many changes in the count to a single increment, or (if the net change is zero) no extra instructions at all. However, even with this technique there are many ref-count increments and decrements that remain, and their cost is very high.

There are two possible solutions to the "cycles" problem. The first is simply to require the programmer to explicitly break all cycles when she is done with a data structure. This is less annoying than putting explicit *free* calls (as would be necessary without any garbage collection at all), but it is hardly elegant. The other solution is to combine reference counting (for eager and nondisruptive reclamation of garbage) with an occasional mark-sweep collection (to reclaim the cycles).

On the whole, the problems with reference counting outweigh its advantages, and it is rarely used for automatic storage management in programming language environments.

13.3   COPYING COLLECTION

The reachable part of the heap is a directed graph, with records as nodes, and pointers as edges, and program variables as roots. Copying garbage collection traverses this graph (in a part of the heap called *from-space*), building an isomorphic copy in a fresh area of the heap (called *to-space*). The to-space copy is *compact*, occupying contiguous memory without fragmentation (that is, without free records interspersed with the reachable data). The roots are made to point at the to-space copy; then the entire from-space (garbage, plus the previously reachable graph) is unreachable.

Figure 13.7 illustrates the situation before and after a copying collection. Before the collection, from-space is full of reachable nodes and garbage; there is no place left to allocate, since next has reached limit. After the collection, the area of to-space between next and limit is available for the compiled program to allocate new records. Because the new-allocation area is contiguous, allocating a new record of size n into pointer p is very easy: just copy next to p, and increment next by n. Copying collection does not have a fragmentation problem.

Eventually, the program will allocate enough that next reaches limit; then another garbage collection is needed. The roles of from-space and to-space are swapped, and the reachable data are again copied.

Initiating a collection. To start a new collection, the pointer next is initialized to point at the beginning of to-space; as each reachable record in from-space is found, it is copied to to-space at position next, and next incremented by the size of the record.

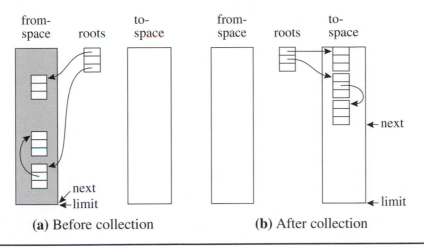

(a) Before collection   **(b)** After collection

FIGURE 13.7.   Copying collection.

---

function Forward(p)
    if p points to from-space
        then if $p.f_1$ points to to-space
            then return $p.f_1$
            else for each field f_i of p
                next.f_i ← $p.f_i$
              $p.f_1$ ← next
              next ← next$+$ size of record p
            return $p.f_1$
    else **return** p

ALGORITHM 13.8. Forwarding a pointer.

Forwarding. The basic operation of copying collection is *forwarding* a pointer; that is, given a pointer p that points to from-space, make p point to to-space (Algorithm 13.8).

There are three cases:

1. If p points to a from-space record that has already been copied, then $p.f_1$ is a special *forwarding pointer* that indicates where the copy is. The forwarding pointer can be identified just by the fact that it points within the to-space, as no ordinary from-space field could point there.

2. If p points to a from-space record that has not yet been copied, then it is copied to location next; and the forwarding pointer is installed into $p.f_1$. It's all right

scan ← next ← beginning of to-space
for each root r
　　$r \leftarrow \text{Forward}(r)$
while scan < next
　　for each field f_i of record at scan
　　　　$\text{scan}.f_i \leftarrow \text{Forward}(\text{scan}.f_i)$
　　scan ← scan+ size of record at scan

ALGORITHM 13.9. Breadth-first copying garbage collection.

---

to overwrite the f_1 field of the old record, because all the data have already been copied to the to-space at next.

3. If p is not a pointer at all, or if it points outside from-space (to a record outside the garbage-collected arena, or to to-space), then forwarding p does nothing.

Cheney's algorithm. The simplest algorithm for copying collection uses breadth-first search to traverse the reachable data (Algorithm 13.9, illustrated in Figure 13.10). First, the roots are forwarded. This copies a few records (those reachable *directly* from root pointers) to to-space, thereby increment-ing next.

The area between scan and next contains records that have been copied to to-space, but whose fields have not yet been forwarded: in general, these fields point to from-space. The area between the beginning of to-space and scan contains records that have been copied *and* forwarded, so that all the pointers in this area point to to-space. The **while** loop of (Algorithm 13.9) moves scan toward next, but copying records will cause next to move also. Eventually, scan catches up with next after all the reachable data are copied to to-space.

Cheney's algorithm requires no external stack, and no pointer reversal: it uses the to-space area between scan and next as the queue of its breadth-first search. This makes it considerably simpler to implement than depth-first search with pointer reversal.

Locality of reference. However, pointer data structures copied by breadth-first have poor locality of reference: If a record at address a points to another record at address b, it is likely that a and b will be far apart. Conversely, the record at $a+8$ is likely to be unrelated to the one at a. Records that are copied near each other are those whose distance from the roots are equal.

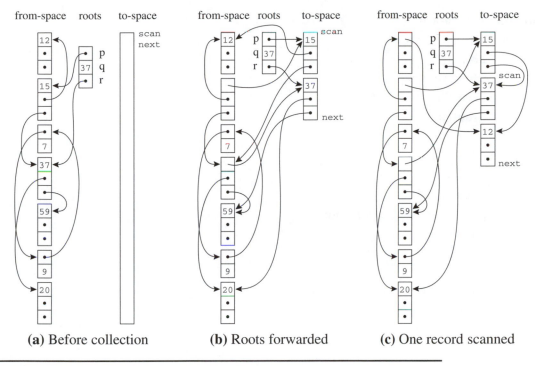

(a) Before collection   **(b)** Roots forwarded   **(c)** One record scanned

FIGURE 13.10.   Breadth-first copying collection.

In a computer system with virtual memory, or with a memory cache, good locality of reference is important. After the program fetches address a, then the memory subsystem expects addresses near a to be fetched soon. So it ensures that the entire page or cache line containing a and nearby addresses can be quickly accessed.

Suppose the program is fetching down a chain of n pointers in a linked list. If the records in the list are scattered around memory, each on a page (or cache line) containing completely unrelated data, then we expect n difference pages or cache lines to be active. But if successive records in the chain are at adjacent addresses, then only n/k pages (cache lines) need to be active, where k records fit on each page (cache line).

Depth-first copying gives better locality, since each object a will tend to be adjacent to its first child b; unless b is adjacent to another "parent" a'. Other children of a may not be adjacent to a, but if the subtree b is small, then they should be nearby.

But depth-first copy requires pointer-reversal, which is inconvenient and

function Forward(p)

   if p points to from-space

     then if $p.f_1$ points to to-space

        then return $p.f_1$

        else Chase(p); **return** $p.f_1$

     else **return** p

function Chase(p)

   repeat

     $q \leftarrow$ next

     next $\leftarrow$ next$+$ size of record p

     $r \leftarrow$ nil

     for each field f_i of record p

        $q.f_i \leftarrow p.f_i$

        if $q.f_i$ points to from-space **and** $q.f_i.f_1$ does not point to to-space

        then $r \leftarrow q.f_i$

     $p.f_1 \leftarrow q$

     $p \leftarrow r$

   until $p =$ nil

ALGORITHM 13.11. Semi-depth-first forwarding.

---

slow. A hybrid, partly depth-first and partly breadth-first algorithm can provide acceptable locality. The basic idea is to use breadth-first copying, but whenever an object is copied, see if some child can be copied near it (Algorithm 13.11).

Cost of garbage collection. Breadth-first search (or the semi-depth-first variant) takes time proportional to the number of nodes it marks; that is, $c_3 R$ for some constant c_3 (perhaps equal to 10 instructions). There is no sweep phase, so $c_3 R$ is the total cost of collection. The heap is divided into two semi-spaces, so each collection reclaims $H/2 - R$ words that can be allocated before the next collection. The amortized cost of collection is thus

$$\frac{c_3 R}{\frac{H}{2} - R}$$

instructions per word allocated.

As H grows much larger than R, this cost approaches zero. That is, *there is no inherent lower bound to the cost of garbage collection.* In a more realistic

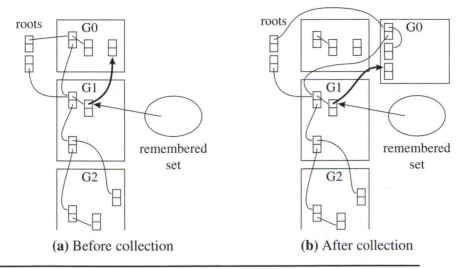

(a) Before collection   **(b)** After collection

FIGURE 13.12.   Generational collection. The bold arrow is one of the rare pointers from an older generation to a newer one.

setting, where $H = 4R$, the cost would be about 10 instructions per word allocated. This is rather costly in space and time: it requires four times as much memory as reachable data, and requires 40 instructions of overhead for every 4-word object allocated. To reduce both space and time costs significantly, we use *generational* collection.

13.4   GENERATIONAL COLLECTION

In many programs, newly created objects are likely to die soon; but an object that is still reachable after many collections will probably survive for many collections more. Therefore the collector should concentrate its effort on the "young" data, where there is a higher proportion of garbage.

We divide the heap into *generations*, with the youngest objects in generation G_0; every object in generation G_1 is older than any object in G_0; everything in G_2 is older than anything in G_1 and so on.

To collect (by mark-and-sweep or by copying) just G_0, just start from the roots and do either depth-first marking or breadth-first copying (or semi-depth-first copying). But now the roots are not just program variables: they include any pointer within $G_1, G_2, \ldots$ that points into G_0. If there are too many of these, then processing the roots will take longer than the traversal of reachable objects within G_0!

Fortunately, it is rare for an older object to point to a much younger object. In many common programming styles, when an object a is created its fields are immediately initialized; for example, they might be made to point to b and c. But b and c already exist; they are older than a. So we have a newer object pointing to an older object. The only way that an older object b could point to a newer object a is if some field of b is updated long after b is created; this turns out to be rare.

To avoid searching all of $G_1, G_2, \ldots$ for roots of G_0, we make the compiled program *remember* where there are pointers from old objects to new ones. There are several ways of remembering:

Remembered list: The compiler generates code, after each *update* store of the form $b.f_i \leftarrow a$, to put b into a vector of *updated objects*. Then, at each garbage collection, the collector scans the remembered list looking for old objects b that point into G_0.

Remembered set: Like the remembered list, but uses a bit within object b to record that b is already in the vector. Then the code generated by the compiler can check this bit to avoid duplicate references to b in the vector.

Card marking: Divide memory into logical "cards" of size 2^k bytes. An object can occupy part of a card or can start in the middle of one card and continue onto the next. Whenever address b is updated, the card containing that address is *marked*. There is an array of bytes that serve as marks; the byte index can be found by shifting address b right by k bits.

Page marking: This is like card marking, but if 2^k is the page size, then the computer's virtual memory system can be used instead of extra instructions generated by the compiler. An update to an old generation sets a *dirty bit* for that page. If the operating system does not make dirty bits available to user programs, then the user program can sometimes implement this by write-protecting the page and asking the operating system to refer protection violations to a user-mode fault handler that records the dirtiness and unprotects the page.

When a garbage collection begins, the remembered set tells which old-generation objects (or cards, or pages) can possibly contain pointers into G_0; these are scanned for roots.

Algorithm 13.3 or 13.9 can be used to collect G_0: "heap" or "from-space" means G_0, "to-space" means a new area big enough to hold the reachable objects in G_0, and "roots" include program variables *and* the remembered set. Pointers to older generations are left unchanged: the marking algorithm does not mark old-generation records, and the copying algorithm copies them verbatim without forwarding them.

After several collections of G_0, generation G_1 may have accumulated a significant amount of garbage that should be collected. Since G_0 may contain many pointers into G_1, it is best to collect G_0 and G_1 together. As before, the remembered set must be scanned for roots contained in $G_2, G_3, \ldots$. Even more rarely, G_2 will be collected, and so on.

Each older generation should be exponentially bigger than the previous one. If G_0 is half a megabyte, then G_1 should be two megabytes, G_2 should be eight megabytes, and so on. An object should be promoted from G_i to G_{i+1} when it survives two or three collections of G_i.

Cost of generational collection. Without detailed empirical information about the distribution of object lifetimes, we cannot analyze the behavior of generational collection. In practice, however, it is common for the youngest generation to be less than 10% live data. With a copying collector, this means that H/R is 10 *in this generation*, so that the amortized cost per word reclaimed is $c_3 R/(10R - R)$, or about 1 instruction. If the amount of reachable data in G_0 is about 50 to 100 kilobytes, then the amount of space "wasted" by having $H = 10R$ in the youngest generation is about a megabyte. In a 50-megabyte multigeneration system, this is a small space cost.

Collecting the older generations can be more expensive. To avoid using too much space, a smaller H/R ratio can be used for older generations. This increases the time cost of an older-generation collection, but these are sufficiently rare that the overall amortized time cost is still good.

Maintaining the remembered set also takes time, approximately 10 instructions per pointer update to enter an object into the remembered set and then process that entry in the remembered set. If the program does many more updates than fresh allocations, then generational collection may be more expensive than nongenerational collection.

13.5   INCREMENTAL COLLECTION

Even if the overall garbage collection time is only a few percent of the computation time, the collector will occasionally interrupt the program for long periods. For interactive or real-time programs this is undesirable. Incremental or concurrent algorithms interleave the garbage collection work with the execution of the program, to avoid long interruptions.

while there are any grey objects
　　select a grey record p
　　for each field f_i of p
　　　　if record $p.f_i$ is white
　　　　　　color record $p.f_i$ grey
　　color record p black

ALGORITHM 13.13. Basic tricolor marking.

Terminology. The *collector* tries to collect the garbage; meanwhile, the compiled program keeps changing (mutating) the graph of reachable data, so it is called the *mutator*. An *incremental* algorithm is one in the collector operators only when the mutator requests it; in a *concurrent* algorithm the collector can operate between or during any instructions executed by the mutator.

Tricolor marking. In a mark-sweep or copying garbage collection, there are three classes of records:

White objects are not yet visited by the depth-first or breadth-first search.
Grey objects have been visited (marked or copied), but their children have not yet been examined. In mark-sweep collection, these objects are on the stack; in Cheney's copying collection, they are between scan and next.
Black objects have been marked, and their children also marked. In mark-sweep collection, they have already been popped off the stack; in Cheney's algorithm, have already been scanned.

The collection starts with all objects white; the collector executes Algorithm 13.13, blackening grey objects and greying their white children. Implicit in changing an object from grey to black is *removing it from the stack or queue*; implicit in greying an object is *putting it into the stack or queue*. When there are no grey objects, then all white objects must be garbage.

Algorithm 13.13 generalizes all of the mark-sweep and copying algorithms shown so far: Algorithms 13.2, 13.3, 13.5, 13.6, and 13.9.

All these algorithms preserve two natural invariants:

1. No black object points to a white object.
2. Every grey object is on the collector's (stack or queue) data structure (which we will call the *grey-set*).

While the collector operates, the mutator creates new objects (of what color?) and updates pointer fields of existing objects. If the mutator breaks one of the invariants, then the collection algorithm will not work.

Most incremental and concurrent collection algorithms are based on techniques to allow the mutator to get work done while preserving the invariants. For example:

Dijkstra, Lamport, et al. Whenever the mutator stores a white pointer a into a black object b, it colors a grey. (The compiler generates extra instructions at each store to check for this.)

Steele Whenever the mutator stores a white pointer a into a black object b, it colors b grey (using extra instructions generated by the compiler).

Boehm, Demers, Shenker All-black pages are marked read-only in the virtual memory system. Whenever the mutator stores *any* value into an all-black page, a page fault marks all objects on that page grey (and makes the page writable).

Baker Whenever the mutator fetches a pointer b to a grey or white object, it colors b grey. The mutator never possesses a pointer to a white object, so it cannot violate invariant 1. The instructions to check the color of b are generated by the compiler after every fetch.

Appel, Ellis, Li Whenever the mutator fetches a pointer b from any virtual-memory page containing any nonblack object, a page-fault handler colors every object on the page black (making children of these objects grey). Thus the mutator never possesses a pointer to a white object.

The first three of these are *write-barrier* algorithms, meaning that each *write* (store) by the mutator must be checked to make sure an invariant is preserved. The last two are *read-barrier* algorithms, meaning that *read* (fetch) instructions are the ones that must be checked. We have seen write barriers before, for generational collection: remembered lists, remembered sets, card marking, and page marking are all different implementations of the write barrier. Similarly, the read barrier can be implemented in software (as in Baker's algorithm) or using the virtual-memory hardware.

Any implementation of a write or read barrier must synchronize with the collector. For example, a Dijkstra-style collector might try to change a white node to grey (and put it into the grey-set) at the same time the mutator is also greying the node (and putting it into the grey-set). Thus, software implementations of the read or write barrier will need to use explicit synchronization instructions, which can be expensive.

But implementations using virtual-memory hardware can take advantage of the synchronization implicit in a page fault: if the mutator faults on a page, the operating system will ensure that no other process has access to that page before processing the fault.

13.6   BAKER'S ALGORITHM

Baker's algorithm illustrates the details of incremental collection. It is based on Cheney's copying collection algorithm, so it forwards reachable objects from from-space to to-space. Baker's algorithm is compatible with generational collection, so that the from-space and to-space might be for generation G_0, or might be $G_0 + \cdots + G_k$.

To initiate a garbage collection (which happens when an *allocate* request fails for lack of unused memory), the roles of the (previous) from-space and to-space are swapped, and all the roots are forwarded; this is called the *flip*. Then the mutator is resumed; but each time the mutator calls the allocator to get a new record, a few pointers at scan are scanned, so that scan advances toward next. Then a new record is allocated *at the end of the to-space* by decrementing limit by the appropriate amount.

The invariant is that the mutator has pointers only to to-space (never to from-space). Thus, when the mutator allocates and initializes a new record, that record need not be scanned; when the mutator stores a pointer into an old record, it is only storing a to-space pointer.

If the mutator fetches a field of a record, it might break the invariant. So each fetch is followed by two or three instructions that check whether the fetched pointer points to from-space. If so, that pointer must be *forwarded* immediately, using the standard *forward* algorithm.

For every word allocated, the allocator must advance scan by at least one word. When scan=next, the collection terminates until the next time the allocator runs out of space. If the heap is divided into two semi-spaces of size $H/2$, and $R < H/4$, then scan will catch up with next before next reaches halfway through the to-space; also by this time, no more than half the to-space will be occupied by newly allocated records.

Baker's algorithm copies no more data than is live at the flip. Records allocated during collection are not scanned, so they do not add to the cost of collection. The collection cost is thus $c_3 R$. But there is also a cost to check (at every allocation) whether incremental scanning is necessary; this is proportional to $H/2 - R$.

But the largest cost of Baker's algorithm is the extra instructions after every fetch, required to maintain the invariant. If one in every 10 instructions fetches from a heap record, and each of these fetches requires two extra instructions to test whether it is a from-space pointer, then there is at least a 20% overhead cost just to maintain the invariant. All of the incremental or concurrent algorithms that use a software write or read barrier will have a significant cost in overhead of ordinary mutator operations.

13.7   INTERFACE TO THE COMPILER

The compiler for a garbage-collected language interacts with the garbage collector by allocating new records, by describing locations of roots for each garbage-collection cycle, and by describing the layout of data records on the heap. For some versions of incremental collection, the compiler must also generate instructions to implement a read barrier or write barrier.

FAST ALLOCATION

Some programming languages, and some programs, allocate heap data (and generate garbage) very rapidly. This is especially true of programs in functional languages, where updating old data is discouraged.

The most allocation (and garbage) one could imagine a reasonable program generating is one word of allocation per store instruction; this is because each word of a heap-allocated record is usually initialized. Empirical measurements show that about one in every seven instructions executed is a store, almost regardless of programming language or program. Thus, we have (at most) $\frac{1}{7}$ word of allocation per instruction executed.

Supposing that the cost of garbage collection can be made small by proper tuning of a generational collector, there may still be a considerable cost to create the heap records. To minimize this cost, *copying collection* should be used so that the allocation space is a contiguous free region; the next free location is next and the end of the region is limit. To allocate one record of size N, the steps are:

1. Call the allocate function.
2. Test next $+ N <$ limit ? (If the test fails, call the garbage collector.)
3. Move next into result
4. Clear $M[\text{next}], M[\text{next} + 1], \ldots, M[\text{next} + \text{N} - 1]$
5. next $\leftarrow$ next $+ N$
6. Return from the allocate function.
A. Move result into some computationally useful place.
B. Store useful values into the record.

Steps 1 and 6 should be eliminated by *inline expanding* the allocate function at each place where a record is allocated. Step 3 can often be eliminated by combining it with step A, and step 4 can be eliminated in favor of step B (steps A and B are not numbered because they are part of the useful computation; they are not allocation overhead).

Steps 2 and 5 cannot be eliminated, but if there is more than one allocation in the same basic block (or in the same *trace*, see Section 8.2) the comparison and increment can be shared among multiple allocations. By keeping `next` and `limit` in registers, steps 2 and 5 can be done in a total of three instructions.

By this combination of techniques, the cost of allocating a record – and then eventually garbage collecting it – can be brought down to about four instructions. This means that programming techniques such as the *persistent binary search tree* (page 104) can be efficient enough for everyday use.

DESCRIBING DATA LAYOUTS

The collector must be able to operate on records of all types: `list`, `tree`, or whatever the program has declared. It must be able to determine the number of fields in each record, and whether each field is a pointer.

For statically typed languages such as Tiger or Pascal, or for object-oriented languages such as Java or Modula-3, the simplest way to identify heap objects is to have the first word of every object point to a special type- or class-descriptor record. This record tells the total size of the object and the location of each pointer field.

For statically typed languages this is an overhead of one word per record to serve the garbage collector. But object-oriented languages need this descriptor-pointer in every object just to implement dynamic method lookup, so that there is no additional overhead attributable to garbage collection.

The type- or class-descriptor must be generated by the compiler from the static type information calculated by the semantic analysis phase of the compiler. The descriptor-pointer will be the argument to the runtime system's `alloc` function.

In addition to describing every heap record, the compiler must identify to the collector every pointer-containing temporary and local variable, whether it is in a register or in an activation record. Because the set of live temporaries can change at every instruction, the *pointer map* is different at every point in the program. Therefore, it is simpler to describe the pointer map only at points where a new garbage collection can begin. These are at calls to the `alloc` function; and also, since any function-call might be calling a function which in turn calls `alloc`, the pointer map must be described at each function call.

The pointer map is best keyed by return addresses: a function call at location a is best described by its return address immediately after a, because the return address is what the collector will see in the very next activation record. The data structure maps return addresses to live-pointer sets; for each pointer that is live immediately after the call, the pointer map tells its register or frame location.

To find all the roots, the collector starts at the top of the stack and scans downward, frame by frame. Each return address keys the pointer-map entry that describes the next frame. In each frame, the collector marks (or forwards, if copying collection) from the pointers in that frame.

Callee-save registers need special handling. Suppose function f calls g, which calls h. Function h knows that it saved some of the callee-save registers in its frame and mentions this fact in its pointer map; but h *does not know which of these registers are pointers*. Therefore the pointer map for g must describe which of its callee-save registers contain pointers at the call to h and which are "inherited" from f.

DERIVED POINTERS

Sometimes a compiled program has a pointer into the middle of a heap record, or pointing before or after the record. For example, the expression a[2000-i] can be calculated internally as M[a+2000-i]:

$$t_1 \leftarrow a + 2000$$
$$t_2 \leftarrow t_1 - i$$
$$t_3 \leftarrow M[t_2]$$

If the expression a[2000-i] occurs inside a loop, the compiler might choose to hoist $t_1 \leftarrow a - 2000$ outside the loop to avoid recalculating it in each iteration. If the loop also contains an alloc, and a garbage collection occurs while t_1 is live, will the collector be confused by a pointer t_1 that does not point to the beginning of an object, or (worse yet) points to an unrelated object?

We say that the t_1 is *derived* from the *base* pointer a. The pointer map must identify each *derived pointer* and tell the base pointer from which it is derived. Then, when the collector relocates a to address a', it must adjust t_1 to point to address $t_1 + a' - a$.

Of course, this means that a must remain live as long as t_1 is live. Consider the loop at left, implemented as shown at right:

```
let
    var a := intarray[100] of 0


  in
   for i := 1930 to 1990
     do f(a[i-2000])

end
```

$$r_1 \leftarrow 100$$
$$r_2 \leftarrow 0$$
call alloc
$$a \leftarrow r_1$$
$$t_1 \leftarrow a - 2000$$
$$i \leftarrow 1930$$
$$L_1: r_1 \leftarrow M[t_1 + i]$$
call f
$$L_2: \text{if } i \leq 1990 \text{ goto } L_1$$

If there are no other uses of a, then the temporary a appears dead after the assignment to t_1. But then the pointer map associated with the return address L_2 would not be able to "explain" t_1 adequately. Therefore, for purposes of the compiler's liveness analysis, *a derived pointer implicitly keeps its base pointer live*.

PROGRAM DESCRIPTORS

Implement record descriptors and pointer maps for the Tiger compiler.

For each record-type declaration, make a string literal to serve as the record descriptor. The length of the string should be equal to the number of fields in the record. The ith byte of the string should be p if the ith field of the record is a pointer (string, record, or array); or n if the ith field is a nonpointer.

The allocRecord function should now take the record descriptor string (pointer) instead of a length; the allocator can obtain the length from the string literal. Then allocRecord should store this descriptor pointer at field zero of the record. Modify the runtime system appropriately.

The user-visible fields of the record will now be at offsets $1, 2, 3, \ldots$ instead of $0, 1, 2, \ldots$; adjust the compiler appropriately.

Design a descriptor format for arrays, and implement it in the compiler and runtime system.

Implement a temp-map with a boolean for each temporary: is it a pointer or not? Also make a similar map for the offsets in each stack frame, for frame-resident pointer variables. You will not need to handle derived pointers, as your Tiger compiler probably does not keep derived pointers live across function calls.

For each procedure call, put a new return-address label L_{ret} immediately after the call instruction. For each one, make a data fragment of the form

$$L_{\text{ptrmap327}}: \quad \begin{array}{lll} .\text{word} & L_{\text{ptrmap326}} & \textit{link to previous ptr-map entry} \\ .\text{word} & L_{\text{ret327}} & \textit{key for this entry} \\ .\text{word} & \dots & \textit{pointer map for} \\ & & \quad \textit{this return address} \\ \vdots \end{array}$$

and then the runtime can traverse this linked list of pointer-map entries, and perhaps build it into a data structure of its own choosing for fast lookup of return addresses. The data-layout pseudo-instructions (.word, etc.) are, of course, machine dependent.

PROGRAM

GARBAGE COLLECTION

Implement a mark-sweep or copying garbage collector in the C language, and link it into the runtime system. Invoke the collector from allocRecord or initArray when the free space is exhausted.

FURTHER READING

Reference counting [Collins 1960] and mark-sweep collection [McCarthy 1960] are almost old as languages with pointers. The pointer-reversal idea is attributed by Knuth [1967] to Peter Deutsch and to Herbert Schorr and W. M. Waite.

Fenichel and Yochelson [1969] designed the first two-space copying collector, using depth-first search; Cheney [1970] designed the algorithm that uses the unscanned nodes in to-space as the queue of a breadth-first search, and also the semi-depth-first copying that improves the locality of a linked list.

Steele [1975] designed the first concurrent mark-and-sweep algorithm. Dijkstra et al. [1978] formalized the notion of tricolor marking, and designed a concurrent algorithm that they could prove correct, trying to keep the synchronization requirements as weak as possible. Baker [1978] invented the incremental copying algorithm in which the mutator sees only to-space pointers.

Generational garbage collection, taking advantage of the fact that newer objects die quickly and that there are few old-to-new pointers, was invented by Lieberman and Hewitt [1983]; Ungar [1986] developed a simpler and more efficient *remembered set* mechanism.

The Symbolics Lisp Machine [Moon 1984] had special hardware to assist with incremental and generational garbage collection. The microcoded memory-fetch instructions enforced the invariant of Baker's algorithm; the microcoded memory-store instructions maintained the remembered set for generational collection. This collector was the first to explicitly improve locality of reference by keeping related objects on the same virtual-memory page.

As modern computers rarely use microcode, and a modern general-purpose processor embedded in a general-purpose memory hierarchy tends to be an order of magnitude faster and cheaper than a computer with special-purpose instructions and memory tags, attention turned in the late 1980s to algorithms that could be implemented with standard RISC instructions and standard virtual-memory hardware. Appel et al. [1988] use virtual memory to implement a read barrier in a truly concurrent variant of Baker's algorithm. Shaw [1988] uses virtual memory *dirty bits* to implement a write barrier for generational collection, and Boehm et al. [1991] make the same simple write barrier serve for concurrent generational mark-and-sweep. Write barriers are cheaper to implement than read barriers, because stores to old pages are rarer than fetches from to-space, and a write barrier merely needs to set a dirty bit and continue with minimal interruption of the mutator. Sobalvarro [1988] invented the card marking technique, which uses ordinary RISC instructions without requiring interaction with the virtual-memory system.

Appel and Shao [1996] describe techniques for fast allocation of heap records and discuss several other efficiency issues related to garbage-collected systems.

Branquart and Lewi [1971] describe pointer maps communicated from a compiler to its garbage collector; Diwan et al. [1992] tie pointer maps to return addresses, show how to handle derived pointers, and compress the maps to save space.

Boehm and Weiser [1988] describe *conservative collection*, where the compiler does not inform the collector which variables and record-fields contain pointers, so the collector must "guess." Any bit-pattern pointing into the allocated heap is assumed to be a possible pointer and keeps the pointed-to record live. However, since the bit-pattern might really be meant as an integer, the object cannot be moved (which would change the possible integer), and some garbage objects may not be reclaimed. Wentworth [1990] points out that such an integer may (coincidentally) point to the root of a huge garbage data structure, which therefore will not be reclaimed; so conservative collection will occasionally suffer from a disastrous space leak. Boehm [1993] describes several techniques for making these disasters unlikely: for example, if the collector ever finds an integer pointing to address X that is not a currently allocated object, it should *blacklist* that address so that the allocator will never allocate an object there. Boehm [1996] points out that even a conservative collector needs some amount of compiler assistance: if a derived pointer can point outside the bounds of an object, then its base pointer must be kept live as long as the derived pointer exists.

Cohen [1981] comprehensively surveys the first two decades of garbage-collection research; Wilson [1997] describes and discusses more recent work. Jones and Lins [1996] offer a comprehensive textbook on garbage collection.

EXERCISES

13.1 Analyze the cost of mark-sweep versus copying collection. Assume that every record is exactly two words long, and every field is a pointer. Some pointers may point outside the collectible heap, and these are to be left unchanged.

a. Analyze Algorithm 13.6 to estimate c_1, the cost (in instructions per reachable word) of depth-first marking.

b. Analyze Algorithm 13.3 to estimate c_2, the cost (in instructions per word in the heap) of sweeping.

c. Analyze Algorithm 13.9 to estimate c_3, the cost per reachable word of copying collection.

d. There is some ratio γ so that with $H = \gamma R$ the cost of copying collection equals the cost of mark-sweep collection. Find γ.

e. For $H > \gamma R$, which is cheaper, mark-sweep or copying collection?

13.2 Run Algorithm 13.6 (pointer reversal) on the heap of Figure 13.1. Show the state of the heap, the done flags, and variables t, x, and y at the time the node containing 59 is first marked.

13.3 Assume main calls f with callee-save registers all containing 0. Then f saves the callee-save registers it is going to use; puts pointers into some callee-save registers, integers into others, and leaves the rest untouched; then calls g. Now g saves some of the callee-save registers, puts some pointers and integers into them, and calls alloc, which starts a garbage collection.

a. Write functions f and g matching this description.

b. Illustrate the pointer maps of functions f and g.

c. Show the steps that the collector takes to recover the exact locations of all the pointers.

13.4 Every object in the Java language supports a `hashCode()` method that returns a "hash code" for that object. Hash codes need not be unique – different objects can return the same hash code – but each object must return the same hash code every time it is called, and two objects selected at random should have only a small chance of having the same hash code.

The Java language specification says that "This is typically implemented by converting the address of the object to an integer, but this implementation technique is not required by the Java language."

Explain the problem in implementing `hashCode()` this way in a Java system with copying garbage collection, and propose a solution.

14

Object-oriented Languages

ob-ject: to feel distaste for something

Webster's Dictionary

A useful software-engineering principle is *information hiding* or *encapsulation*. A module may provide values of a given type, but the representation of that type is known only to the module. Clients of the module may manipulate the values only through *operations* provided by the module. In this way, the module can assure that the values always meet consistency requirements of its own choosing.

Object-oriented programming languages are designed to support information hiding. Because the "values" may have internal state that the operations will modify, it makes sense to call them *objects*. Because a typical "module" manipulates only one type of object, we can eliminate the notion of module and (syntactically) treat the operations as fields of the objects, where they are called *methods*.

Another important characteristic of object-oriented languages is the notion of *extension* or *inheritance*. If some program context (such as the formal parameter of a function or method) expects an object that supports methods m_1, m_2, m_3, then it will also accept an object that supports m_1, m_2, m_3, m_4.

14.1   CLASSES

Not all object-oriented languages are class based, but to illustrate the techniques of compiling object-oriented languages I will use a simple class-based object-oriented language called Object-Tiger.

We extend the Tiger language with new declaration syntax to create classes:

$dec \rightarrow classdec$

$classdec \rightarrow$ **class** *class-id* **extends** *class-id* { {*classfield*} }

$classfield \rightarrow vardec$

$classfield \rightarrow method$

$method \rightarrow$ **method** *id(tyfields)* = *exp*

$method \rightarrow$ **method** *id(tyfields)* : *type-id* = *exp*

The declaration class B extends A { ⋯ } declares a new class B that extends the class A. This declaration must be in the scope of the let-expression that declares A. All the fields and methods of A implicitly belong to B. Some of the A methods may be *overridden* (have new declarations) in B, but the fields may not be overridden. The parameter and result types of an overriding method must be identical to those of the overridden method.

There is a predefined class identifier Object with no fields or methods.

Methods are much like functions, with formal parameters and bodies. However, each method within B has an implicit formal parameter self of type B. But self is not a reserved word, it is just an identifier automatically bound in each method.

The responsibility for initializing object data fields rests with the class, not with the client. Thus, object-field declarations look more like variable declarations than like record-field declarations.

We make new expression syntax to create objects and invoke methods:

$exp \rightarrow$ **new** *class-id*

$\rightarrow lvalue$. *id()*

$\rightarrow lvalue$. *id(exp{, exp})*

The expression new B makes a new object of type B; the data fields are initialized by evaluating their respective initialization expressions from the class declaration of B.

The *l*-value b.x, where b is an *l*-value of type B, denotes the field x of object b; this is similar to record-field selection and requires no new syntax.

The expression b.f(x,y), where b is an *l*-value of type B, denotes a call to the f method of object b with explicit actual parameters x and y, and the value b for the implicit self parameter of f.

Program 14.1 illustrates the use of the Object-Tiger language. Every Vehicle is an Object; every Car is a Vehicle; thus every Car is also an

```
let start := 10

    class Vehicle extends Object {
       var position := start
       method move(int x) = (position := position + x)
    }
    class Car extends Vehicle {
       int passengers := 0
       method await(v: Vehicle) =
           if (v.position < position)
                then v.move(position - v.position);
           else self.move(10);
    }
    class Truck extends Vehicle {
       method move(int x) =
           if x <= 55 then position := position + x
    }

    var t := new Truck;
    var c := new Car;
    var v : Vehicle = c;
 in
    c.passengers := 2;
    c.move(60);
    v.move(70);
    c.await(t)
 end
```

PROGRAM 14.1. An object-oriented program.

Object. Every Vehicle (and thus every Car and Truck) has an integer position field and a move method.

In addition, a Car has an integer passengers field and an await method. The variables in scope on entry to await are

start by normal Tiger language scoping rules.
passengers because it is a field of Car.
position because it is (implicitly) a field of Car.
v because it is a formal parameter of await.
self because it is (implicitly) a formal parameter of await.

In the main program, the expression new Truck has type Truck, so the type of t is Truck (in the normal manner of variable declarations in Tiger). Variable c has type Car, and variable v is explicitly declared to have type Vehicle. It is legal to use c (of type Car) in a context where type Vehicle is required (the initialization of v), because class Car is a subclass of Vehicle.

```
class A extends Object {
                  var a := 0}
class B extends A {var b := 0
                  var c := 0}
class C extends A {var d := 0}
class D extends B {var e := 0}
```

A		B		C		D
a		a		a		a
		b		d		b
		c				c
						e

FIGURE 14.2. Single inheritance of data fields.

Class Truck overrides the move method of Vehicle, so that any attempt to move a truck "faster" than 55 has no effect.

At the call to c.await(t), the truck t is bound to the formal parameter v of the await method. Then when v.move is called, this activates the Truck_move method body, not Vehicle_move.

We use the notation A_m to indicate a *method instance* m declared within a class A. This is not part of the Object-Tiger syntax, it is just for use in discussing the semantics of Object-Tiger programs. Each different declaration of a method is a different method instance. Two different method instances could have the same method name if, for example, one overrides the other.

14.2 SINGLE INHERITANCE OF DATA FIELDS

To evaluate the expression v.position, where v belongs to class Vehicle, the compiler must generate code to fetch the field position from the object (record) that v points to.

This seems simple enough: the environment entry for variable v contains (among other things) a pointer to the type (class) description of Vehicle; this has a list of fields and their offsets. But at run time the variable v could also contain a pointer to a Car or Truck; where will the position field be in a Car or Truck object?

Single inheritance. For *single-inheritance* languages, in which each class extends just one parent class, the simple technique of *prefixing* works well. Where B extends A, those fields of B that are inherited from A are laid out in a B record *at the beginning, in the same order they appear in A records*. Fields of B not inherited from A are placed afterward, as shown in Figure 14.2.

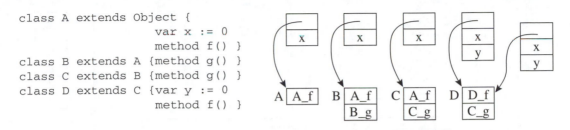

```
class A extends Object {
                var x := 0
                method f() }
class B extends A {method g() }
class C extends B {method g() }
class D extends C {var y := 0
                method f() }
```

PROGRAM 14.3. Class descriptors for dynamic method lookup.

METHODS

A method instance is compiled much like a function: it turns into machine code that resides at a particular address in the instruction space. Let us say, for example, that the method instance `Truck_move` has an entry point at machine-code label `Truck_move`. In the semantic-analysis phase of an object-oriented program, each variable's environment entry contains a pointer to its class descriptor; each class descriptor contains a pointer to its parent class, and also a list of method instances; each method instance has a machine-code label.

Static methods. Some object-oriented languages allow some methods to be declared *static*. Static methods cannot be overridden. To compile a method-call of the form `c.f()`, the compiler finds the class of `c`; let us suppose it is class `C`. Then it searches in class `C` for a method `f`; suppose none is found. Then it searches the parent class of `C`, class `B`, for a method `f`; then the parent class of `B`; and so on. Suppose in some ancestor class `A` it finds a static method `f`; then it can compile a function call to label `A_f`.

Dynamic methods. But this technique will not work for dynamic methods. If method `f` in `A` is a dynamic method, then it might be overridden in some class `D` which is a subclass of `C` (see Figure 14.3). But there is no way to tell at compile time if the variable `c` is pointing to an object of class `D` (in which case `D_f` should be called) or class `C` (in which case `A_f` should be called).

To solve this problem, the class descriptor must contain a vector with a method instance for each (nonstatic) method name. When class `B` inherits from `A`, the method table *starts with* entries for all method names known to `A`, and then continues with `new` methods declared by `B`. This is very much like the arrangement of fields in objects with inheritance.

Figure 14.3 shows what happens when class `D` overrides method `f`. Al-though the entry for `f` is at the beginning of `D`'s method table, as it is also at

```
class A extends Object {var a := 0}
class B extends Object {var b := 0
                        var c := 0}
class C extends A {var d := 0}
class D extends A,B,C {var e := 0}
```

A		B		C		D
a				a		a
		b				b
		c				c
				d		d
						e

FIGURE 14.4. Multiple inheritance of data fields.

the beginning of the ancestor class A's method table, it points to a different method-instance label because f has been overridden.

To execute c.f(), where f is a dynamic method, the compiled code must execute these instructions:

1. Fetch the class descriptor d at offset 0 from object c.
2. Fetch the method-instance pointer p from the (constant) f offset of d.
3. Jump to address p, saving return address (that is, call p).

14.3 MULTIPLE INHERITANCE

In languages that permit a class D to extend several parent classes A,B,C (that is, where A is not a subclass of B or vice versa), finding field offsets and method instances is more difficult. It is impossible to put all the A fields at the beginning of D *and* to put all the B fields at the beginning of D.

Global graph coloring. One solution to this problem is to statically analyze all classes at once, finding some offset for each field name that can be used in every record containing that field. We can model this as a graph-coloring problem: there is a node for each distinct field name, and an edge for any two fields which coexist (perhaps by inheritance) in the same class.[7] The offsets $0, 1, 2, \ldots$ are the colors. Figure 14.4 shows an example.

The problem with this approach is that it leaves empty slots in the middle of objects, since it cannot always color the N fields of each class with colors with the first N colors. To eliminate the empty slots in objects, we pack the fields of each object and have the class descriptor tell where each field is. Figure 14.5 shows an example. We have done graph coloring on all the field names, as before, but now the "colors" are not the offsets of those fields within

---

[7]*Distinct field name* does not mean simple equivalence of strings. Each fresh declaration of field or method x (where it is not overriding the x of a parent class) is really a distinct name.

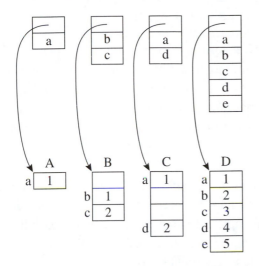

FIGURE 14.5.   Field offsets in descriptors for multiple inheritance.

the *objects* but within the *descriptors*. To fetch a field a of object x, we fetch the a-word from x's descriptor; this word contains a small integer telling the position of the actual a data within x.

Thus, each data-fetch requires two load instructions instead of one (and a data-store requires a load and a store instruction). Class descriptors have empty slots, but the objects do not; this is acceptable because a system with millions of objects is likely to have only dozens of class descriptors.

Method lookup. Finding method instances in a language with multiple inheritance is just as complicated as finding field offsets. The global graph-coloring approach works well: the method names can be mixed with the field names to form nodes of a large interference graph. Descriptor entries for fields give locations within the objects; descriptor entries for methods give machine-code addresses of method instances.

Problems with dynamic linking. Any global approach suffers from the problem that the coloring (and layout of class descriptors) can be done only at link-time; the job is certainly within the capability of a special-purpose linker.

However, many object-oriented systems have the capability to load new classes into a running system; these classes may be extensions (subclasses) of classes already in use. Link-time graph coloring poses many problems for a system that allows dynamic incremental linking.

Hashing. Instead of global graph coloring, we can put a hash table in each class descriptor, mapping field names to offsets and method names to method instances. This works well with separate compilation and dynamic linking.

The characters of the field names are not hashed at run time. Instead, each field name a is hashed at compile time to an integer hash_a in the range $[0, N-1]$. Also, for each field name a unique run-time record (pointer) ptr_a is made for each field.

Each class descriptor has a field-offset table Ftab of size N containing field-offsets and method instances, and (for purposes of collision detection) a parallel *key* table Ktab containing field-name pointers. If the class has a field x, then field-offset-table slot number hash_x contains the offset for x, and key-table slot number hash_x contains the pointer ptr_x.

To fetch a field x of object c, the compiler generates code to

1. Fetch the class descriptor d at offset 0 from object c.
2. Fetch the field-name f from the address offset $d + \mathtt{Ktab} + \mathrm{hash}_x$.
3. Test whether $f = \mathrm{ptr}_x$; if so
4. Fetch the field offset k from $d + \mathtt{Ftab} + \mathrm{hash}_x$.
5. Fetch the contents of the field from $c + k$.

This algorithm has four instructions of overhead, which may still be tolerable. A similar algorithm works for dynamic method-instance lookup.

The algorithm as described does not say what to do if the test at line 3 fails. Any hash-table collision-resolution technique can be used.

14.4 TESTING CLASS MEMBERSHIP

Some object-oriented languages allow the program to test membership of an object in a class at run time, as summarized in Table 14.6.

Since each object points to its class descriptor, the address of the class descriptor can serve as a "type-tag." However, if x is an instance of D, and D extends C, then x is also an instance of C. Assuming there is no multiple inheritance, a simple way to implement x instanceof C is to generate code that performs the following loop at run time:

$$t_1 \leftarrow x.\text{descriptor}$$
$$L_1: \quad \textbf{if } t_1 = C \textbf{ goto } true$$
$$t_1 \leftarrow t_1.\text{super}$$

	Modula-3	Java
Test whether object x belongs class C, or to any subclass of C.	ISTYPE(x,C)	x instanceof C
Given a variable x of class C, where X actually points to an object of class D that extends C, yield an expression whose compile-time type is class D.	NARROW(x,D)	(D)x

TABLE 14.6. Facilities for type testing and safe casting.

> **if** t_1 = nil **goto** *false*
> **goto** L_1

where t_1.super is the superclass (parent class) of class t_1.

However, there is a faster approach using a *display* of parent classes. Assume that the class nesting depth is limited to some constant, such as 20. Reserve a 20-word block in each class descriptor. In the descriptor for a class D whose nesting depth is j, put a pointer to descriptor D in the jth slot, a pointer to D.super in the $(j-1)$th slot, a pointer to D.super.super in slot $j-2$, and so on up to Object in slot 0. In all slots numbered greater than j, put nil.

Now, if x is an instance of D, or of any subclass of D, then the jth slot of x's class descriptor will point to the class descriptor D. Otherwise it will not. So x instanceof D requires

1. Fetch the class descriptor d at offset 0 from object c.
2. Fetch the jth class-pointer slot from d.
3. Compare with the class descriptor D.

This works because the class-nesting depth of D is known at compile time.

Type coercions. Given a variable c of type C, it is always legal to treat c as any supertype of C – if C extends B, and variable b has type B, then the assignment $b \leftarrow c$ is legal and safe.

But the reverse is not true. The assignment $c \leftarrow b$ is safe only if b is really (at run time) an instance of C, which is not always the case. If we have $b \leftarrow$ new B, $c \leftarrow b$, followed by fetching some field of c that is part of class C but not class B, then this fetch will lead to unpredictable behavior.

Thus, safe object-oriented languages (such as Modula-3 and Java) accompany any coercion from a superclass to a subclass with a run-time type-check that raises an exception unless the run-time value is really an instance of the subclass (e.g. unless b instanceof C).

It is a common idiom to write

Modula-3:
```
IF ISTYPE(b,C)
  THEN f(NARROW(b,C))
  ELSE ...
```

Java:
```
if (b instanceof C)
    f((C)b)
else ...
```

Now there are two consecutive, identical type tests: one explicit (ISTYPE or instanceof) and one implicit (in NARROW or the cast). A good compiler will do enough flow analysis to notice that the **then**-clause is reached only if b is in fact an instance of C, so that the type-check in the narrowing operation can be eliminated.

C++ is an unsafe object-oriented language. It does not (as of this writing) have a standard mechanism for testing whether an object is an instance of a class, or for type-safe narrowing. When C++ programmers need to cast from a superclass to a subclass, they do so without the benefit of run-time safety.

Typecase. Explicit instanceof testing, followed by a narrowing cast to a subclass, is not a wholesome "object-oriented" style. Instead of using this idiom, programmers are expected to use dynamic methods that accomplish the right thing in each subclass. Nevertheless, the test-then-narrow idiom is fairly common.

Modula-3 has a **typecase** facility that makes the idiom more beautiful and efficient (but not any more "object-oriented"):

TYPECASE $expr$
OF C_1 (v_1) => S_1
| C_2 (v_2) => S_2
⋮
| C_n (v_n) => S_n
ELSE S_0
END

If the $expr$ evaluates to an instance of class C_i, then a new variable v_i of type C_i points to the result of the $expr$, and statement S_i is executed. The declaration of v_i is implicit in the TYPECASE, and its scope covers only S_i.

If more than one of the C_i match (which can happen if, for example, one is a superclass of another), then only the first matching clause is taken. If none of the C_i match, then the ELSE clause is taken (statement S_0 is executed).

Typecase can be converted straightforwardly to a chain of **else-if**s, with each **if** doing an instance test, a narrowing, and a local variable declaration.

However, if there are very many clauses, then it can take a long time to go through all the **else-if**s. Therefore it is attractive to treat it like a case (switch) statement on integers, using an indexed jump (computed goto).

That is, an ordinary case statement on integers:

ML:
```
case i
  of 0 => s₀
   | 1 => s₁
   | 2 => s₂
   | 3 => s₃
   | 4 => s₄
   | _ => s_d
```

C, Java:
```
switch (i) {
  case 0: s₀; break;
  case 1: s₁; break;
  case 2: s₂; break;
  case 3: s₃; break;
  case 4: s₄; break;
  default: s_d;
}
```

is compiled as follows: first a range-check comparison is made to ensure that i is within the range of case labels (0–4, in this case); then the address of the ith statement is fetched from the ith slot of a table, and control jumps to s_i.

This approach will not work for **typecase**, because of subclassing. That is, even if we could make class descriptors be small integers instead of pointers, we cannot do an indexed jump based on the class of the object, because we will miss clauses that match superclasses of that class. Thus, Modula-3 **typecase** is implemented as chain of **else-if**s.

Assigning integers to classes is not trivial, because separately compiled modules can each define their own classes, and we do not want the integers to clash. But a sophisticated linker might be able to assign the integers at link time.

If all the classes in the **typecase** were `final` classes (in the sense used by Java, that they cannot be extended), then this problem would not apply. Modula-3 does not have final classes; and Java does not have **typecase**. But a clever Java system might be able to recognize a chain of **else-if**s that do **instanceof** tests for a set of final classes, and generate a indexed jump.

14.5 PRIVATE FIELDS AND METHODS

True object-oriented languages can protect fields of objects from direct manipulation by other objects' methods. A *private* field is one that cannot be fetched or updated from any function or method declared outside the object; a private method is one that cannot be called from outside the object.

Privacy is enforced by the type-checking phase of the compiler. In the symbol table of C, along with each field offset and method offset, is a boolean flag indicating whether the field is private. When compiling the expression c.f() or c.x, it is a simple matter to check that field and reject accesses to private fields from any method outside the object declaration.

There are many varieties of privacy and protection. Different languages allow

- Fields and methods which are accessible only to the class that declares them.
- Fields and methods accessible to the declaring class, and to any subclasses of that class.
- Fields and methods accessible only within the same module (package, namespace) as the declaring class.
- Fields that are read-only from outside the declaring class, but writable by methods of the class.

In general, these varieties of protection can be statically enforced by compile-time type-checking, for class-based languages.

14.6 CLASSLESS LANGUAGES

Some object-oriented languages do not use the notion of **class** at all. In such a language, each object implements whatever methods and has whatever data fields it wants. Type-checking for such languages is usually *dynamic* (done at run time) instead of *static* (done at compile time).

Many objects are created by *cloning*: copying an existing object (or *template* object) and then modifying some of the fields. Thus, even in a classless language there will be groups ("pseudo-classes") of similar objects that can share descriptors. When b is created by cloning a, it can share a descriptor with a. Only if a new field is added or a method field is updated (overridden) does b require a new descriptor.

The techniques used in compiling classless languages are similar to those for class-based languages with multiple inheritance and dynamic linking: pseudo-class descriptors contain hash tables that yield field offsets and method instances.

The same kinds of global program analysis and optimization that are used for class-based languages – finding which method instance will be called from a (dynamic) method call site – are just as useful for classless languages.

OPTIMIZING OBJECT-ORIENTED PROGRAMS

An optimization of particular importance to object-oriented languages (which also benefit from most optimizations that apply to programming languages in general) is conversion of dynamic method calls to static method-instance calls.

Compared with an ordinary function call, at each method call site there is a dynamic method lookup to determine the method instance. For single-inheritance languages, method lookup takes only two instructions. This seems like a small cost, but:

- Modern machines can jump to constant addresses more efficiently than to addresses fetched from tables. When the address is manifest in the instruction stream, the processor is able to pre-fetch the instruction cache at the destination and direct the instruction-issue mechanism to fetch at the target of the jump. Unpredictable jumps stall the instruction-issue and -execution pipeline for several cycles.
- An optimizing compiler that does interprocedural analysis will have trouble analyzing the consequences of a call if it doesn't even know which method instance is called at a given site.

For multiple-inheritance and classless languages, the dynamic method-lookup cost is even higher.

Thus, optimizing compilers for object-oriented languages do global program analysis to determine those places where a method call is always calling the same method instance; then the dynamic method call can be replaced by a static function call.

For a method call c.f(), where c is of class C, *type hierarchy analysis* is used to determine which subclasses of C contain methods f that may override C_f. If there is no such method, then the method instance must be C_f.

This idea is combined with *type propagation*, a form of static dataflow analysis similar to *reaching definitions* (see Section 16.2). After an assignment $c \leftarrow \text{new } C$, the exact class of c is known. This information can be propagated through the assignment $d \leftarrow c$, and so on. When d.f() is encountered, the type-propagation information limits the range of the type hierarchy that might contribute method instances to d.

Suppose a method f defined in class C calls method g on self. But g is a dynamic method and may be overridden, so this call requires a dynamic method lookup. An optimizing compiler may make a different copy of a method instance C_f for each subclass (e.g. D, E) that extends C. Then when the (new copy) D_f calls g, the compiler knows to call the instance D_g without a dynamic method lookup.

PROGRAM OBJECT-Tiger

Implement the Object-Tiger object-oriented extensions to your Tiger compiler.

This chapter's description of the Object-Tiger language leaves many things unspecified: if method f is declared before method g, can f call g? Can a method access all the class variables, or just the ones declared above it? Can the initializer of a class variable (field) call a method of the class (and can the method therefore see an unitialized field)? You will need to refine and document the definition of the Object-Tiger language.

FURTHER READING

Dahl and Nygaard's Simula-67 language [Birtwistle et al. 1973] introduced the notion of classes, objects, single inheritance, static methods, instance testing, typecase, and the *prefix* technique to implement static single inheritance. In addition it had coroutines and garbage collection.

Cohen [1991] suggested the *display* for constant-time testing of class membership.

Dynamic methods and multiple inheritance appeared in Smalltalk [Goldberg et al. 1983], a classless language, but the first implementations used slow searches of parent classes to find method instances. Rose [1988] and Connor et al. [1989] discuss fast hash-based field- and method-access algorithms for multiple inheritance. The use of graph coloring in implementing multiple inheritance is due to Dixon et al. [1989].

Chambers et al. [1991] describe several techniques to make classless, dynamically typed languages perform efficiently: pseudo-class descriptors, multiple versions of method instances, and other optimizations. Diwan et al. [1996] describe optimizations for statically typed languages that can replace dynamic method calls by static function calls.

Conventional object-oriented languages choose a method instance for a call a.f(x,y) based only on the class of the method *receiver* (a) and not other arguments (x,y). Languages with *multimethods* [Bobrow et al. 1989] allow dynamic method lookup based on the types of all arguments. This would solve the problem of *orthogonal directions of modularity* discussed on page 90. Chambers and Leavens [1995] show how to do static type-checking for multimethods; Amiel et al. [1994] and Chen and Turau [1994] show how to do efficient dynamic multimethod lookup.

EXERCISES

14.1 A problem with the *display* technique (as explained on page 291) for testing class membership is that the maximum class nesting depth N must be fixed in advance, and every class descriptor needs N words of space even if most classes are not deeply nested. Design a variant of the *display* technique that does not suffer from these problems; it will be a couple of instructions more costly than the one described on page 291.

14.2 The hash-table technique for finding field offsets and method instances in the presence of multiple inheritance is shown incompletely on page 290 – the case of $f \neq \text{ptr}_x$ is not resolved. Choose a collision-resolution technique, explain how it works, and analyze the extra cost (in instructions) in the case that $f = \text{ptr}_x$ (no collision) and $f \neq \text{ptr}_x$ (collision).

14.3 Consider the following class hierarchy, which contains five method-call sites. The task is to show which of the method-call sites call known method instances, and (in each case) show which method instance. For example, you might say that "method-instance X_g always calls Y_f; method Z_g may call more than one instance of f."

```
class A extends Object { method f() = print("1") }
class B extends A      { method g() = (f(); print("2")) }
class C extends B      { method f() = (g(); print("3")) }
class D extends C      { method g() = (f(); print("4")) }
class E extends A      { method g() = (f(); print("5")) }
class F extends E      { method g() = (f(); print("6")) }
```

Do this analysis for each of the following assumptions:

a. This is the entire program, and there are no other subclasses of these modules.

b. This is part of a large program, and any of these classes may be extended elsewhere.

c. Classes C and E are local to this module, and cannot be extended elsewhere; the other classes may be extended.

14.4 Use *method replication* to improve your analysis of the program in Exercise statmeths. That is, make *every* class override f and g. For example, in class B (which does not already override f), put a copy oi method A_f, and in D put a copy of C_F:

```
class B extends A      { ... method f() = (print("1")) }
class D extends C      { ... method f() = (g(); print("3")) }
```

Similarly, add new instances E_f, F_f, and C_g. Now, for each set of assumptions (a), (b), and (c), show which method calls go to known static instances.

*14.5 Devise an efficient implementation mechanism for any **typecase** that only mentions final classes. A final class is one that cannot be extended. (In Java, there is a final keyword; but even in other object-oriented languages, a class that is not exported from a module is effectively final, and a link-time whole-program analysis can discover which classes are never extended, whether declared final or not.)

You may make any of the following assumptions, but state which assumptions you need to use:

a. The linker has control over the placement of class-descriptor records.

b. Class descriptors are integers managed by the linker that index into a table of descriptor records.

c. The compiler explicitly marks final classes (in their descriptors).

d. Code for **typecase** can be generated at link time.

e. After the program is running, no other classes and subclasses are dynamically linked into the program.

15

Functional Programming Languages

func-tion: a mathematical correspondence that assigns exactly one element of one set to each element of the same or another set

Webster's Dictionary

The mathematical notion of function is that if $f(x) = a$ "this time," then $f(x) = a$ "next time"; there is no other value equal to $f(x)$. This allows the use of *equational reasoning* familiar from algebra: that if $a = f(x)$ then $g(f(x), f(x))$ is equivalent to $g(a, a)$. *Pure functional* programming languages encourage a kind of programming in which equational reasoning works, as it does in mathematics.

Imperative programming languages have similar syntax: $a \leftarrow f(x)$. But if we follow this by $b \leftarrow f(x)$ there is no guarantee that $a = b$; the function f can have *side effects* on global variables that make it return a different value each time. Furthermore, a program might assign into variable x between calls to $f(x)$, so $f(x)$ really means a different thing each time.

Higher-order functions. Functional programming languages also allow functions to be passed as arguments to other functions, or returned as results. Functions that take functional arguments are called *higher-order* functions.

Higher-order functions become particularly interesting if the language also supports *nested functions* with *lexical scope* (also called *block structure*). As in Tiger, lexical scope means that each function can refer to variables and parameters of any function in which it is nested. A *higher-order functional language* is one with nested scope and higher-order functions.

What is the essence of functional programming: is it equational reasoning or is it higher-order functions? There is no clear agreement about the an-

swer to this question. In this chapter I will discuss three different flavors of
"functional" language:

Fun-Tiger The Tiger language with higher-order functions. Because side effects
are still permitted (and thus, equational reasoning won't work), this is an
impure, higher order functional language; other such languages are Scheme,
ML, and Smalltalk.

PureFun-Tiger A language with higher-order functions and no side effects, cap-
turing the essence of *strict, pure functional languages* (like the pure-functional
subset of ML).

Lazy-Tiger A *non-strict, pure functional language* that uses lazy evaluation like
the language Haskell. Non-strict pure functional languages support equational
reasoning very well.

A *first-order, pure functional language* such as SISAL supports equational
reasoning but not higher-order functions.

A SIMPLE FUNCTIONAL LANGUAGE

To make the new language Fun-Tiger, we add *function types* to Tiger:

$$
\begin{aligned}
ty &\rightarrow& ty \rightarrow ty \\
&\rightarrow& (\, ty \, \{, \, ty \, \} \,) \rightarrow ty \\
&\rightarrow& (\,) \rightarrow ty
\end{aligned}
$$

The type `int->string` is the type of all functions that take a single integer
argument and return a string result. The type `(int,string)->intarray`
describes functions that take two arguments (one integer, one string) and
return an `intarray` result. The `getchar` function has type `()->string`.

Any variable can have a functional type; functions can be passed as arguments and returned as results. Thus, the type `(int->int)->int->int`
is perfectly legal; the `->` operator is right-associative, so this is the type of
functions that take an `int->int` argument and return an `int->int` result.

We also modify the format of a CALL expression, so that the function being
called is an arbitrary expression, not just an identifier:

$$exp \rightarrow exp \, (\, exp \,)$$

```
let
    type intfun = int -> int

    function add(n: int) : intfun =
        let function h(m: int) : int = n+m
          in h
        end

    var addFive : intfun := add(5)
    var addSeven : intfun := add(7)
    var twenty := addFive(15)
    var twentyTwo := addSeven(15)

    function twice(f: intfun) : intfun =
        let function g(x: int) : int = f(f(x))
          in g
        end

    var addTen : intfun := twice(addFive)

    var seventeen := twice(add(5))(7)
    var addTwentyFour := twice(twice(add(6)))

  in addTwentyFour(seventeen)
end
```

PROGRAM 15.1. A Fun-Tiger program.

Program 15.1 illustrates the use of function types. The function add takes an integer argument n and returns a function h. Thus, addFive is a version of h whose n variable is 5, but addSeven is a function $h(x) = 7 + x$. The need for each different instance of h to "remember" the appropriate value for a *nonlocal* variable n motivates the implementation technique of *closures*, which is described later.

The function twice takes an argument f that is a function from int to int, and the result of twice(f) is a function g that applies f twice. Thus, twice(addTen) is a function $g(x) = $ addFive(addFive(x)). Each instance of $g(x)$ needs to remember the right f value, just as each instance of h needs to remember n.

15.2 CLOSURES

In languages (such as C) without nested functions, the run-time representation of a function value can be the address of the machine code for that function. This address can be passed as an argument, stored in a variable, and so on; when it is time to call the function, the address is loaded into a machine register, and the "call to address contained in register" instruction is used.

In the Tree intermediate representation, this is easy to express. Suppose the function starts at label L_{123}; we assign the address into a variable t_{57} using

$$\text{MOVE}(\text{TEMP}(t_{57}), \text{NAME}(L_{123}))$$

and then call the function with something like

$$\text{CALL}(\text{TEMP}(t_{57}), \dots parameters \dots).$$

But this will not work for nested functions; if we represent the h function by an address, in what outer frame can it access the variable n? Similarly, how does the g function access the variable f?

The solution is to represent a function-variable as *closure*: a record that contains the machine-code pointer and a way to access the necessary nonlocal variables. One simple kind of closure is just a pair of code pointer and static link; the nonlocal variables can be accessed by following the static link. The portion of the closure giving access to values of variables is often called the *environment*.

Closures need not be based on static links; any other data structure that gives access to nonlocal variables will do. Using static links has some serious disadvantages: it takes a chain of pointer dereferences to get to the outermost variables, and the garbage collector cannot collect the intermediate links along this chain even if the program is going to use only the outermost variables. However, in this chapter I will use static-link closures for simplicity.

HEAP-ALLOCATED ACTIVATION RECORDS

Using static links in closures means that the activation record for add must not be destroyed when add returns, because it still serves as the environment for h. To solve this problem, we could create activation records on the heap instead of on the stack. Instead of explicitly destroying add's frame when add returns, we would wait until the garbage collector determines that it is safe to reclaim the frame; this would happen when all the pointers to h disappear.

A refinement of this technique is to save on the heap only those variables that *escape* (that are used by inner-nested functions). The stack frame will hold spilled registers, return address, and so on, and also a pointer to the *escaping-variable record*. The escaping-variable record holds (1) any local variables that an inner-nested procedure might need and (2) a static link to the environment (escaping-variable record) provided by the enclosing function; see Figure 15.2.

Modifications to the Tiger compiler. In each Fun-Tiger function we make a temporary called the *escaping-variables pointer* or EP that will point to the record of escaping variables. All static link computations, whether to access nonlocal variables or to compute a static link to pass to some other function, will be based on the EP, not the FP. The EP itself is a nonescaping local temporary that will be spilled as needed, just like any other temporary. The static-link formal parameter passed to this function escapes (as does the static link of an ordinary Tiger function) since inner nested functions need to access it; thus, the static link is stored into the escaping-variables record.

In the `Frame` module of the compiler, the interface functions that create formals and locals (`newFrame` and `allocLocal`) must be modified to make accesses (for escaping variables) that are offsets from EP instead of FP. The escaping-variables record must be allocated by instructions produced in `procEntryExit1`.

15.3   IMMUTABLE VARIABLES

The Fun-Tiger language has higher-order functions with nested scope, but it is still not really possible to use *equational reasoning* about Fun-Tiger programs. That is, $f(3)$ may return a different value each time. To remedy this situation, we prohibit *side effects* of functions: when a function is called, it must return a result without changing the "world" in any observable way.

Thus, we make a new *pure functional programming* language PureFun-Tiger, in which the following are prohibited:

⊘ Assignments to variables (except as initializations in `var` declarations);
⊘ Assignments to fields of heap-allocated records;
⊘ Calls to external functions that have visible effects: `print`, `flush`, `getchar`, `exit`.

This seems rather Draconian: how is the program to get any work done?

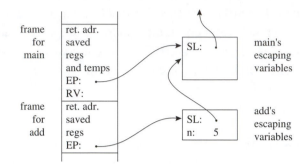

a. Inside `add`

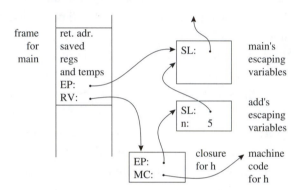

b. Back in `main`

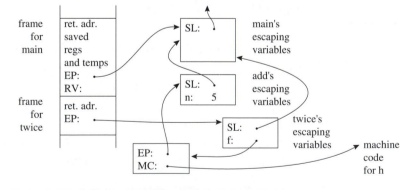

c. Inside `twice`

FIGURE 15.2.   Closures for execution of `twice(add(5))`. SL=static link; RV=return value; EP=escaping-variables-pointer or environment-pointer.

To program without assignments, in a functional style, you produce new values instead of updating old ones. For example, Program 15.3 shows the implementation of binary search trees in imperative and functional styles. As explained in Section 5.1 (page 104), the imperative program updates a tree-node, but the functional program returns a new tree much like the old one, though the path from the root to a "new" leaf has been copied. If we let `t1` be the tree in Figure 5.4a on page 104, we can say

```
var t2 := enter(t1,"mouse",4)
```

and now `t1` and `t2` are both available for the program to use. On the other hand, if the program returns `t2` as the result of a function and discards `t1`, then the root node of `t1` will be reclaimed by the garbage collector (the other nodes of `t1` will not be reclaimed, because they are still in use by tree `t2`).

Similar techniques can allow functional programs to express the same wide variety of algorithms that imperative programs can, and often more clearly, expressively and concisely.

CONTINUATION-BASED I/O

Producing new data structures instead of updating old ones makes it possible to obey the "no assignments" rules, but how is the program to do input/output? The technique of *continuation-based I/O* expresses input/output in a functional framework. As shown in Program 15.4, the predefined types and functions in PureFun-Tiger rely on the notion of an `answer`: this is the "result" returned by the *entire program*.

The built-in `getchar` function does not return a string (as in Tiger); instead, `getchar` takes an argument that is a `stringConsumer` and passes the newly read character to that consumer. Whatever answer the consumer produces will also be the answer of the `getchar`.

Similarly, `print` takes a string to print as well as a *continuation* (`cont`); `print` outputs a string and then calls the `cont` to produce an answer.

The point of these arrangements is to allow input/output while preserving equational reasoning. Interestingly, input/output is now "visible" to the type-checker: any function which does I/O will have `answer` in its result type.

LANGUAGE CHANGES

The following modifications of Fun-Tiger make the new language PureFun-Tiger:

```
type key = string                       type key = string
type binding = int                      type binding = int
type tree = {key: key,                  type tree = {key: key,
             binding: binding,                       binding: binding,
             left: tree,                             left: tree,
             right: tree}                            right: tree}

function look(t: tree, k: key)          function look(t: tree, k: key)
               : binding =                             : binding =
  if k < t.key                            if k < t.key
        then look(t.left,k)                    then look(t.left,k)
  else if k > t.key                       else if k > t.key
        then look(t.right,k)                   then look(t.right,k)
  else t.binding                          else t.binding

function enter(t: tree, k: key,         function enter(t: tree, k: key,
              b: binding) =                           b: binding) : tree =
  if k < t.key                            if k < t.key
    then if t.left=nil                      then
      then t.left :=                          tree{key=t.key,
             tree{key=k,                            binding=t.binding,
                  binding=b,                        left=enter(t.left,k,b),
                  left=nil,                         right=t.right}
                  right=nil}
      else enter(t.left,k,b)              else if k > t.key
  else if k > t.key                         then
    then if t.right=nil                       tree{key=t.key,
      then t.right :=                             binding=t.binding,
             tree{key=k,                          left=t.left,
                  binding=b,                       right=enter(t.right,k,b)}
                  left=nil,                 else tree{key=t.key,
                  right=nil}                       binding=b,
      else enter(t.right,k,b)                      left=t.left,
  else t.binding := b                            right=t.right}
```

    (a) Imperative   (b) Functional

PROGRAM 15.3.   Binary search trees implemented in two ways.

```
type answer
type stringConsumer = string -> answer
type cont = () -> answer

function getchar(c: stringConsumer) : answer
function print(s: string, c: cont) : answer
function flush(c: cont) : answer
function exit() : answer
```

PROGRAM 15.4.   Built-in types and functions for PureFun-Tiger.

- Add the predefined types answer, stringConsumer, and cont; and modify the types of the predefined I/O functions – as shown in Program 15.4.
- A "procedure" (a function without an explicit return type) is now considered to return type answer.
- Assignment statements, **while** loops, **for** loops, and compound statements (with semicolon) are deleted from the language.

Program 15.5 shows a complete PureFun-Tiger program that loops, reading integers and printing the factorial of each integer, until an integer larger than 12 is input.

OPTIMIZATION OF PURE FUNCTIONAL LANGUAGES

Because we have only deleted features from Fun-Tiger, and not added any new ones (except changing some predefined types), our Fun-Tiger compiler can compile PureFun-Tiger right away. And, in general, functional-language compilers can make use of the same kinds of optimizations as imperative-language compilers: inline expansion, instruction selection, loop-invariant analysis, graph-coloring register allocation, copy propagation, and so on. Calculating the control-flow graph can be a bit more complicated, however, because much of the control flow is expressed through function calls, and some of these calls may to be function-variables instead of statically-defined functions.

A PureFun-Tiger compiler can also make several kinds of optimizations that a Fun-Tiger compiler cannot, because it can take advantage of equational reasoning.

Consider this program fragment, which builds a record r and then later fetches fields from it.

```
let
type intConsumer = int -> answer

function isDigit(s : string) : int =
      ord(s)>=ord("0") & ord(s)<=ord("9")

function getInt(done: intConsumer) =
 let function nextDigit(accum: int) =
        let function eatChar(dig: string) =
              if isDigit(dig)
                then nextDigit(accum*10+ord(dig))
                else done(accum)
          in getchar(eatChar)
        end
  in nextDigit(0)
 end

function putInt(i: int, c: cont) =
  if i=0 then c()
  else let var rest := i/10
           var dig := i - rest * 10
           function doDigit() = print(chr(dig), c)
         in putInt(rest, doDigit)
       end

function factorial(i: int) : int =
  if i=0 then 1 else i * factorial(i-1)

function loop(i) =
  if i > 12 then exit()
  else let function next() = getInt(loop)
         in putInt(factorial(i), next)
       end
in
   getInt(loop)
end
```

PROGRAM 15.5. PureFun-Tiger program to read i, print $i!$.

```
type recrd = {a: ···, b: ···}

var a1 := 5
var b1 := 7
var r := recrd{a := a1, b := b1}

var x := f(r)

var y :=  r.a + r.b
```

In a pure functional language, the compiler knows that when the computation of y refers to r.a and r.b, it is going to get the values a1 and b1. In an imperative (or impure functional) language, the computation f(r) might assign new values to the fields of r, but not in PureFun-Tiger.

Thus, within the scope of r every occurrence of r.a can be replaced with a1, and similarly b1 can be substituted for r.b. Also, since no other part of the program can assign any new value to a1, it will contain the same value (5) for all time. Thus, 5 can be substituted for a1 everywhere, and 7 for b1. Thus, we end up with var y := 5+7 which can be turned into var y := 12; thus, 12 can be substituted for y throughout its scope.

The same kind of substitution works for imperative languages too; it's just that a compiler for an imperative language is often not sure whether a field or variable is updated between the point of definition and the point of use. Thus, it must conservatively approximate – assuming that the variable may have been modified – and thus, in most cases, the substitution cannot be performed. See also *alias analysis* (Section 16.5).

The ML language has pure-functional records, which cannot be updated and on which this substitution transformation is always valid, and also has updateable reference cells, which can be assigned to and which behave like records in a conventional imperative language.

15.4   INLINE EXPANSION

Because functional programs tend to use many small functions, and especially because they pass functions from one place to another, an important optimization technique is *inline expansion* of function calls: replacing a function call with a copy of the function body.

For example, in Program 15.6, an observeInt is any function (like the putInt of Program 15.5) that "observes" an integer and then continues. doList is a function that applies an observer f to a list l, and then continues.

In this case, the observer is not putInt but printDouble, which prints i followed by $2i$. Thus, printTable prints a table of integers, each followed by its double.

For comparison, Program 15.7a is a regular Tiger program that does the same thing.

Program 15.6 uses a generic list-traverser, doList, for which any function can be plugged in. Although in this case printDouble is used, the same

```
let
    type list = {head: int, tail: list}
    type observeInt  = (int,cont) -> answer

    function doList(f: observeInt, l: list, c: cont) =
      if l=nil then c()
      else let function doRest() = doList(f, l.tail, c)
            in f(l.head, doRest)
          end

    function double(j: int) : int = j+j

    function printDouble(i: int, c: cont) =
        let function again() = putInt(double(i),c)
         in putInt(i, again)
        end

    function printTable(l: list, c: cont) =
        doList(printDouble, l, c)

    var mylist := ···

  in printTable(mylist, exit)
  end
```

PROGRAM 15.6. `printTable` in PureFun-Tiger.

program could reuse `doList` for other purposes that print or "observe" all the integers in the list. But Program 15.7a lacks this flexibility – it calls `printDouble` directly, because the ordinary Tiger language lacks the ability to pass functions as arguments.

Algorithm 15.8 gives the rules for inline expansion, which can apply to imperative or functional programs. The function body B is used in place of the function call $f(...)$, but within this copy of B, each actual parameter is substituted for the corresponding formal parameter. When the actual parameter is just a variable or a constant, the substitution is very simple (Algorithm 15.8a). But when the actual parameter is a nontrivial expression, we must first assign it to a new variable (Algorithm 15.8b).

For example, in Program 15.6 the function-call `double(i)` can be replaced by a copy of `j+j` in which each `j` is replaced by the actual parameter `i`. Here we have used Algorithm 15.8a, since `i` is a variable, not a more complicated expression.

Suppose we wish to inline expand `double(g(x))`; if we improperly use

```
let                                     
  type list = {head: int,               
               tail: list}              

  function double(j: int): int =        let
        j+j                               type list = {head: int,
                                                       tail:list}
  function printDouble(i: int) =
        (putInt(i);                       function printTable(l: list) =
         putInt(double(i)))                  while l <> nil
                                                do let var i := l.head
  function printTable(l: list) =                 in putInt(i);
     while l <> nil                                 putInt(i+i);
        do (printDouble(l.head);                    l := l.tail
            l := l.tail)                     end

  var mylist := ···                       var mylist := ···

in printTable(mylist)                   in printTable(mylist)
end                                     end
```

         (a) As written   (b) Optimized

PROGRAM 15.7. Regular Tiger `printTable`.

Algorithm 15.8a, we obtain `g(x)+g(x)`, which computes `g(x)` twice. Even though the principle of equational reasoning assures that we will compute the same result each time, we do not wish to slow down the computation by repeating the (potentially expensive) computation `g(x)`. Instead, Algorithm 15.8b yields

```
let i := g(x) in i+i end
```

which computes `g(x)` only once.

In an imperative program, not only is `g(x)+g(x)` slower than

```
let i := g(x) in i+i end
```

but – because `g` may have side effects – it may compute a different result! Again, Algorithm 15.8b does the right thing.

If compiled naively, the pure-functional program – that passed `printDouble` as an argument – will do many more function calls than the imperative program. By using inline expansion and tail-call optimizations (to be described), Program 15.6 can be optimized into machine instructions equivalent to the efficient loop of Program 15.7b.

(a) When the actual parameters are simple variables.
Within the scope of:

function $f(a_1, \ldots, a_n) = B$

the expression

$f(i_1, \ldots, i_n)$

rewrites to

$B[a_1 \mapsto i_1, \ldots, a_n \mapsto i_n]$

(b) When the actual parameters are non-trivial expressions, not just variables.
Within the scope of:

function $f(a_1, \ldots, a_n) = B$

the expression

$f(E_1, \ldots, E_n)$

rewrites to

let var $i_1 := E_1$
$\quad\quad\vdots$
$\quad\quad$ var $i_n := E_n$
in $\quad B[a_1 \mapsto i_1, \ldots, a_n \mapsto i_n]$
end

where $i_1, \ldots, i_n$ are previously unused names.

ALGORITHM 15.8. Inline expansion of function bodies.

Dead function elimination. If all the calls to a function (such as `double`) have been inline expanded, and if the function is not passed as an argument or referenced in any other way, the function itself can be deleted.

Inlining recursive functions. Inlining `doList` into `printTable` yields this new version of `printTable`:

```
function printTable(l: list, c: cont) =
   if l=nil then c()
   else let function doRest() =
                     doList(printDouble, l.tail, c)
          in printDouble(l.head, doRest)
        end
```

This is not so good: `printTable` calls `printDouble` on `l.head`, but to process `l.tail` it calls `doList` as before. Thus, we have inline expanded *only the first iteration of the loop*. We would rather have a fully customized version of `doRest`; therefore, we do not inline expand in this way.

For recursive functions we use a *loop preheader* transformation (Algorithm 15.9). The idea is to split f into two functions: a *prelude* called from

$$\boxed{\begin{array}{l} \texttt{function } f(a_1,\ldots,a_n) = \\ \quad B \end{array}} \quad \rightarrow \quad \boxed{\begin{array}{l} \texttt{function } f(a'_1,\ldots,a'_n) = \\ \quad \texttt{let function } f'(a_1,\ldots,a_n) = \\ \qquad\qquad B[f \mapsto f'] \\ \quad \texttt{in } f'(a'_1,\ldots,a'_n) \\ \quad \texttt{end} \end{array}}$$

ALGORITHM 15.9. Loop-preheader transformation.

outside, and a *loop header* called from inside. Every call to the loop header will be a recursive call from within itself, except for a single call from the prelude. Applying this transformation to `doList` yields

```
function doList(fX: observeInt, lX: list, cX: cont) =
  let function doListX(f: observeInt, l: list, c: cont) =
        if l=nil then c()
        else let function doRest() = doListX(f, l.tail, c)
             in f(l.head, doRest)
             end
    in doListX(fX,lX,cX)
  end
```

where the new `doList` is the prelude, and `doListX` is the loop header. Notice that the prelude function contains the entire loop as an internal function, so that when any call to `doList` is inline expanded, a new copy of `doListX` comes along with it.

Loop-invariant arguments. In this example, the function `doListX` is passing around the values `f` and `c` that are invariant – they are the same in every recursive call. In each case, `f` is `fX` and `c` is `cX`. A *loop-invariant hoisting* transformation (Algorithm 15.10 can replace every use of `f` with `fX`, and `c` with `cX`).

Applying this transformation to `doList` yields

```
function doList(f: observeInt, lX: list, c: cont) =
  let function doListX(l: list) =
        if l=nil then c()
        else let function doRest() = doListX(l.tail)
             in f(l.head, doRest)
             end
    in doListX(lX)
  end
```

Finally, in `printTable` when the call `doList(printDouble,l,c)` is inlined, we obtain:

If every use of f' within B is of the form $f'(E_1, \ldots, E_{i-1}, a_i, E_{i+1}, \ldots, E_n)$ such that the ith argument is always a_i, then rewrite

$$
\boxed{\begin{aligned}
&\text{function } f(a'_1, \ldots, a'_n) = \\
&\quad \text{let function } f'(a_1, \ldots, a_n) = B \\
&\quad \text{in } f'(a'_1, \ldots, a'_n) \\
&\text{end}
\end{aligned}}
\;\longrightarrow\;
\boxed{\begin{aligned}
&\text{function } f(a'_1, \ldots, a'_{i-1}, a_i, a'_{i+1}, \ldots, a'_n) = \\
&\quad \text{let function } f'(a_1, \ldots, a_n) = B \\
&\quad \text{in } f'(a'_1, \ldots, a'_{i-1}, a'_{i+1}, \ldots, a'_n) \\
&\text{end}
\end{aligned}}
$$

where every call $f'(E_1, \ldots, E_{i-1}, a_i, E_{i+1}, \ldots, E_n)$ within B is rewritten as $f'(E_1, \ldots, E_{i-1}, E_{i+1}, \ldots, E_n)$.

ALGORITHM 15.10. Loop-invariant hoisting.

```
function printTable(l: list, c: cont) =
 let function doListX(l: list) =
        if l=nil then c()
        else let function doRest() = doListX(l.tail)
             in printDouble(l.head, doRest)
             end
   in doListX(l)
 end
```

Cascading inlining. In this version of printTable, we have printDouble applied to arguments (instead of just passed to doList), so we can inline expand that call, yielding

```
function printTable(l: list, c: cont) =
 let function doListX(l: list) =
        if l=nil then c()
        else let function doRest() = doListX(l.tail)
             in let var i := l.head
                  in let function again() = putInt(i+i,doRest)
                      in putInt(i,again)
                     end
                end
             end
        end
   in doListX(l)
 end
```

Avoiding code explosion. Inline expansion copies function bodies. This generally makes the program bigger. If done indiscriminantly, the size of the program explodes; in fact, it is easy to construct cases where expanding one function call creates new instances that can also be expanded, ad infinitum.

```
1       function printTable(l: list, c: cont) =
2           let function doListX(l: list) =
3                   if l=nil then c()
4                   else let function doRest() =
5                                   doListX(l.tail)
6                           var i := l.head
7                           function again() =
8                                   putInt(i+i,doRest)
9                       in putInt(i,again)
10              end
11      in doListX(l)
12      end
```

PROGRAM 15.11. `printTable` as automatically specialized.

There are several heuristics that can be used to control inlining:

1. Expand only those function-call sites that are very frequently executed; determine frequency either by static estimation (loop-nest depth) or by feedback from an execution profiler.
2. Expand functions with very small bodies, so that the copied function body is not much larger than the instructions that would have called the function.
3. Expand functions called only once; then *dead function elimination* will delete the original copy of the function body.

Unnesting `let`s. Since the Tiger expression

> let dec_1 in let dec_2 in exp end end

is exactly equivalent to

> let dec_1 dec_2 in exp end

we end up with Program 15.11.

The optimizer has taken a program written with abstraction (general-purpose `doList`) and transformed it into a more efficient, special-purpose program (special-purpose `doListX` that calls `putInt` directly).

15.5   CLOSURE CONVERSION

A function passed as an argument is represented as a *closure*: a combination of a machine-code pointer and a means of accessing the nonlocal variables (also called *free variables*).

Chapter 6 explained the method of static links for accessing free variables, where the static links point directly to the enclosing functions' stack frames. Figure 15.2 shows that the free variables can be kept in a heap-allocated record, separate from the stack frame. Now, for the convenience of the back end of the compiler, we would like to make the creation and access of those free-variable records explicit in the program.

The *closure conversion* phase of a functional-language compiler transforms the program so that none of the functions appears to access free (nonlocal) variables. This is done by turning each free-variable access into a formal-parameter access.

Given a function $f(a_1, \ldots, a_n) = B$ at nesting depth d with escaping local variables (and formal parameters) $x_1, x_2, \ldots, x_n$ and nonescaping variables $y_1, \ldots, y_n$; rewrite into

$$f(a_0, a_1, \ldots, a_n) = \texttt{let var } r := \{a_0, x_1, x_2, \ldots, x_n\} \texttt{ in } B' \texttt{ end}$$

The new parameter a_0 is the static link, now made into an explicit argument. The variable r is a record containing all the escaping variables *and* the enclosing static link. This r becomes the static-link argument when calling functions of depth $d + 1$.

Any use of a nonlocal variable (one that comes from nesting depth $< d$) within B must be transformed into an access of some offset within the record a_0 (in the rewritten function body B').

Function values. Function values are represented as closures, comprising a code pointer and environment. Instead of heap allocating a two-word record to hold these two, when the programmer passes a function as an argument, the compiler should pass the code pointer and environment as two adjacent arguments.

Program 15.12 is the result of closure-converting Program 15.11. We can see that each function creates an explicit record to hold escaping variables. In fact, the function `doListX` creates two different records `r2` and `r3`, because the variables `i` and `doRestC` are not available at the time `r2` must be created. Functions in closure-converted programs access *only* local variables, so that later phases of the compiler need not worry about nonlocal-variable access or static links.

Unknown types of static links in closures. The types of all escaping-variable records are given by record declarations at the top of Program 15.12. But

```
type mainLink = { ··· }
type printTableLink= {SL: mainLink, cFunc: cont, cSL: ?}
type cont = ? -> answer
type doListXLink1 = {SL: printTableLink, l: list}
type doListXLink2 = {SL: doListXLink1, i: int,
                     doRestFunc: cont, doRestSL: doListXLink1}

function printTable(SL: mainLink, l: list, cFunc: cont, cSL: ?) =
    let var r1 := printTableLink{SL=SL,cFunc=cFunc,cSL=cSL}
        function doListX(SL: printTableLink, l: list) =
          let var r2 := doListXLink1{SL: printTableLink, l=l}
          in if r2.l=nil then SL.cFunc(SL.cSL)
             else let function doRest(SL: doListXLink1) =
                            doListX(SL.SL, SL.l.tail)
                      var i := r2.l.head
                      var r3 := doListXLink2{SL=r2, i=i,
                                   doRestFunc=doRest, doRestSL=r2}
                      function again(SL: doListXLink2) =
                            putInt(SL.SL.SL, SL.i+SL.i,
                                         SL.doRest.func, SL.doRestSL)
                  in putInt(SL.SL,i, again,r3)
                  end
    in doListX(r1,l)
    end
```

PROGRAM 15.12. printTable after closure conversion.

what is the type of cont's static link argument? It must be the type of the escaping-variable record of the function that encloses the cont function.

But there are several different functions of type cont:

- the c argument of printTable, which comes from main (examination of Program 15.6 shows that this will in fact be the exit function);
- doRest;
- and again.

Each of these functions has a *different* kind of static link record. Thus, the type of the SL field of contClosure varies, and *cannot always be known* by the caller. The type of the static-link argument of the cont type is shown as a question-mark. That is, although we can write closure-converted Fun-Tiger or PureFun-Tiger programs in Tiger syntax, these programs do not type-check in a conventional sense.

15.6 EFFICIENT TAIL RECURSION

Functional programs tend to express loops and other control flow by function calls. Where Program 15.7b has a **while** loop, Program 15.12 has a function call to doListX. Where Program 15.7b's putInt simply returns to its two points of call within printTable, Program 15.11 has continuation functions. The Fun-Tiger compiler must compile the calls to doListX, doRest, and again as efficently as the Tiger compiler compiles while loops and function returns.

Many of the function calls in Program 15.11 are in *tail position*. A function call $f(x)$ within the body of another function $g(y)$ is in tail position if "calling f is the last thing that g will do before returning." More formally, in each of the following expressions, the B_i are in tail contexts, but the C_i are not:

1. let var x := C_1 in B_1 end
2. $C_1(C_2)$
3. if C_1 then B_1 else B_2
4. C_1 + C_2

For example, C_2 in expression 4 is not in a tail context, even though it seems to be "last," because after C_2 completes there will still need to be an **add** instruction. But B_1 in expression 3 is in a tail context, even though it is not "last" syntactically.

If a function call $f(x)$ is in a tail context with respect to its enclosing expression, and that expression is in a tail context, and so on all the way to the body of the enclosing function definition function $g(y) = B$, then $f(x)$ is a tail call.

Tail calls can be implemented more efficiently than ordinary calls. Given

```
g(y) = let var x := h(y) in f(x) end
```

Then h(y) is not a tail call, but f(x) is. When f(x) returns some result z, then z will also be the result returned from g. Instead of pushing a new return address for f to return to, g could just give f the return address given to g, and have f return there directly.

That is, a tail call can be implemented more like a jump than a call. The steps for a tail call are:

1. Move actual parameters into argument registers;
2. Restore callee-save registers;
3. Pop the stack frame of the calling function, *if it has one;*

printTable:	allocate record `r1`	printTable:	allocate stack frame
	jump to doListX		jump to whileL
doListX:	allocate record `r2`	whileL:	
	if `l=nil` goto doneL		if `l=nil` goto doneL
	`i := r2.l.head`		`i := l.head`
	allocate record `r3`		
	jump to `putInt`		call `putInt`
again:	add `SL.i+SL.i`		add `i+i`
	jump to `putInt`		call `putInt`
doRest:	jump to doListX		jump to whileL
doneL :	jump to `SL.cFunc`	doneL:	return
(a) Functional program		(b) Imperative program	

FIGURE 15.13.   `printTable` as compiled.

4. Jump to the callee.

In many cases, item 1 (moving parameters) is eliminated by the copy-propagation (coalescing) phase of the compiler. Often, items 2 and 3 are eliminated because the calling function has no stack frame – any function that can do all its computation in caller-save registers needs no frame. Thus, a tail call can be as cheap as a jump instruction.

In Program 15.12, *every* call is a tail call! Also, none of the functions in this program needs a stack frame. This need not have been true; for example, the call to `double` in Program 15.6 is not in tail position, and this nontail call only disappeared because the inline expander did away with it.

Tail calls implemented as jumps. The compilation of Programs 15.12 and 15.7b is instructive. Figure 15.13 shows that the pure-functional program and the imperative program are executing almost exactly the same instructions! The figure does not show the functional program's fetching from static-link records; and it does not show the imperative program's saving and restoring callee-save registers.

The remaining inefficiency in the functional program is that it creates three heap-allocated records, `r1,r2,r3`, while the imperative program creates only one stack frame. However, more advanced closure-conversion algorithms can succeed in creating only one record (at the beginning of `printTable`). So the difference between the two programs would be little more than a heap-record creation versus a stack-frame creation.

Allocating a record on the garbage-collected heap may be more expensive than pushing and popping a stack frame. Optimizing compilers for functional languages solve this problem in different ways:

- Compile-time *escape analysis* can identify which closure records do not outlive the function that creates them. These records can be stack-allocated. In the case of `printTable`, this would make the "functional" code almost identical to the "imperative" code.
- Or heap allocation and garbage collection can be made extremely cheap. Then creating (and garbage-collecting) a heap-allocated record takes only four or five instructions, making the functional `printTable` almost as fast as the imperative one (see Section 13.7).

15.7   LAZY EVALUATION

Equational reasoning aids in understanding functional programs. One important principle of equational reasoning is *β-substitution:* if $f(x) = B$ with some function body B then any application $f(E)$ to an expression E is equivalent to B with every occurrence of x replaced with E:

$$f(x) = B \quad \text{implies that} \quad f(E) \equiv B[x \mapsto E]$$

But consider the PureFun-Tiger program fragments,

```
let                                        let
   function loop(z:int):int=                  function loop(z:int):int=
      if z>0 then z                              if z>0 then z
             else loop(z)                               else loop(z)
   function f(x:int):int=                     function f(x:int):int=
      if y>8 then x                              if y>8 then x
             else -y                                    else -y
in                                         in if y>0 then loop(y)
   f(loop(y))                                            else -y
end                                        end
```

If the expression B is `if y>8 then x else -y`, and expression E is `loop(y)`, then clearly the program on the left contains $f(E)$ and the program on the right contains $B[x \mapsto E]$. So these programs are equivalent, using equational reasoning.

However, *the programs do not always behave the same!* If $y = 0$, then the program on the right will return 0, but the program on the right will first get stuck in a call to $loop(0)$, which infinite-loops.

Clearly, if we want to claim that two programs are equivalent then they must behave the same. In PureFun-Tiger, if we obtain program A by doing substition on program B, then A and B will never give different results *if they both halt*; but A or B might not halt on the same set of inputs.

To remedy this (partial) failure of equational reasoning, we can introduce *lazy evaluation* into the programming language. Haskell and Miranda are the most widely used lazy languages. A program compiled with lazy evaluation will not evaluate any expression unless its value is demanded by some other part of the computation. In contrast, *strict* languages such as Tiger, PureFun-Tiger, ML, C, and Java evaluate each expression as the control flow of the program reaches it.

To explore the compilation of lazy functional languages, we will use the Lazy-Tiger language. Its syntax is identical to PureFun-Tiger, and its semantics are almost identical, except that lazy evaluation is used in compiling it.

CALL-BY-NAME EVALUATION

Most programming languages (Pascal, C, ML, Java, Tiger, PureFun-Tiger) use *call-by-value* to pass function arguments: to compute $f(g(x))$, first $g(x)$ is computed, and this value is passed to f. But if f did not actually need to use its argument, then computing $g(x)$ will have been unnecessary.

To avoid computing expressions before their results are needed, we can use *call-by-name* evaluation. Essentially, each variable is not a simple value, but is a *thunk:* a function that computes the value on demand. The compiler replaces each expression of type `int` with a function value of type `()->int`, and similarly for all other types.

At each place where a variable is created, the compiler creates a function value; and everywhere a variable is used, the compiler puts a function application.

Thus the Lazy-Tiger program

```
let var a := 5+7  in   a + 10  end
```

is automatically transformed to

```
let function a() = 5+7  in   a() + 10  end
```

Where are variables created? At `var` declarations and at function-parameter bindings. Thus, each `var` turns into a `function`, and at each function-call site, we need a little `function` declaration for each actual-parameter expression.

```
type tree = {key: ()->key,
             binding: ()->binding,
             left: ()->tree,
             right: ()->tree}

function look(t: ()->tree, k: ()->key) : ()->binding =
  if k() < t().key() then look(t().left,k)
  else if k() > t().key() then look(t().right,k)
  else t().binding
```

PROGRAM 15.14. Call-by-name transformation applied to Program 15.3a.

Program 15.14 illustrates this transformation applied to the `look` function of Program 15.3a.

The problem with call-by-name is that each thunk may be executed many times, each time (redundantly) yielding the same value. For example, suppose there is a tree represented by a thunk `t1`. Each time `look(t1,k)` is called, `t1()` is evaluated, which rebuilds the (identical) tree every time!

CALL-BY-NEED

Lazy evaluation, also called *call-by-need*, is a modification of call-by-name that never evaluates the same thunk twice. Each thunk is equipped with a *memo* slot to store the value. When the thunk is first created, the memo slot is empty. Each evaluation of the thunk checks the memo slot: if full, it returns the *memo-ized* value; if empty, it calls the thunk function.

To streamline this process, we will represent a lazy thunk as a two-element record containing a *thunk function* and a *memo slot*. An *unevaluated* thunk contains an arbitrary thunk function, and the memo slot is a static link to be used in calling the thunk function. An *evaluated* thunk has the previously computed value in its memo slot, and its thunk function just returns the memo-slot value.

For example, the Lazy-Tiger declaration `var twenty:=addFive(15)` (in Program 15.1) is compiled in a context where the environment pointer EP will point to a record containing the `addFive` function. The representation of `addFive(15)` is not a function call that will go and compute the answer *now*, but a thunk that will remember how to compute it on demand, *later*. We might translate this fragment of the Lazy-Tiger program into Fun-Tiger as follows:

```
/*  EP already points to a record containing addFive */
var twenty := intThunk{func=twentyFunc, memo=EP}
```

which is supported by the auxiliary declarations

```
type intThunk = {func: ?->int, memo: ?}
type intfunc = {func: (?,intThunk)->int, SL: ?}
type intfuncThunk = {func: ?->intfunc, memo: ?}

function evaluatedFunc(th: intThunk) : int =
      th.memo

function twentyFunc(mythunk: intThunk) : int =
  let var EP := mythunk.memo
      var add5thunk : intfuncThunk := EP.addFive
      var add5 : intfunc := add5thunk.func(add5thunk)
      var fifteenThunk := intThunk{func=evaluatedFunc, memo=15}
      var result : int := add5.func(add5.SL, fifteenThunk)
   in th.memo := result;
      th.func := evaluatedFunc;
      result
  end
```

To *touch* a lazy thunk `t`, we just compute `t.func(t)`. For `t=twenty`, the first time `t` is touched, `twentyFunc(twenty)` will execute, making `twenty.memo` point at the integer result computed by $addFive(15)$ and making `twenty.func` point to the special function `evaluatedFunc`. Any subsequent time that `twenty` is touched, `evaluatedFunc` will simply return the `twenty.memo` field, which will contain the integer 20.

EVALUATION OF A LAZY PROGRAM

Here is a program that uses the `enter` function of Program 15.3b to build a tree mapping $\{three \mapsto 3!, minusOne \mapsto (-1)!\}$:

```
let function fact(i: int) : int =
        if i=0 then 1 else i * fact(i-1)
    var t1 := enter(nil, "minusOne", fact(-1))
    var t2 := enter(t1,  "three",    fact(3))
 in putInt(look(t2,"three"), exit)
end
```

A curious thing about this program is that `fact(-1)` is undefined. Thus, if this program is compiled by a (strict) PureFun-Tiger compiler, it will infinite-loop (or will eventually overflow the machine's arithmetic as it keeps subtracting 1 from a negative number).

But if compiled by a Lazy-Tiger compiler, the program will succeed, returning three factorial! First, variable `t1` is defined; but this does not actually call `enter` – it merely makes a thunk which will do so on demand. Then, `t2` is defined, which also does nothing but make a thunk. Then a thunk is created for `look(t2,"three")` (but `look` is not actually called).

Finally, a thunk for the expression `putInt(...,exit)` is created. This is the result of the program. But the runtime system then "demands" an `answer` from this program, which can be computed only by calling the outermost thunk. So the body of `putInt` executes, which immediately demands the integer value of its first argument; this causes the `look(t2,"three")` thunk to evaluate.

The body of `look` needs to compare `k` with `t.key`. Since `k` and `t` are each thunks, we can compute an integer by evaluating `k()` and a tree by evaluating `t()`. From the tree we can extract the `key` field, but each field is a thunk, so we must actually do `(t().key)()` to get the integer.

The `t.key` value will turn out to be -1, so `look(t().right,k)` is called. *The program never evaluates the* `binding` *thunk in the* `minusOne` *node,* so `fact(-1)` is never given a chance to infinite-loop.

OPTIMIZATION OF LAZY FUNCTIONAL PROGRAMS

Lazy functional programs are subject to many of the same kinds of optimizations as strict functional programs, or even imperative programs. Loops can be identified (these are simply tail-recursive functions), induction variables can be identified, common subexpressions can be eliminated, and so on.

In addition, lazy compilers can do some kinds of optimizations that strict-functional or imperative compilers cannot, using equational reasoning.

Invariant hoisting. For example, given a loop

```
type intfun = int->int

function f(i: int) : intfun =
  let function g(j: int) = h(i) * j
    in g
  end
```

an optimizer might like to hoist the invariant computation `h(i)` out of the function g. After all, g may be called thousands of times, and it would be better not to recompute i each time. Thus we obtain

```
type intfun = int->int

function f(i: int) : intfun =
  let var hi := h(i)
      function g(j: int) = hi * j
   in g
  end
```

and now each time g is called, it runs faster.

This is valid in a lazy language. But in a strict language, this transformation is invalid! Suppose after var a := f(8) the function a is never called at all; and suppose h(8) infinite-loops; before the "optimization" the program would have terminated successfully, but afterward we get a nonterminating program. Of course, the transformation is also invalid in an impure functional language, because h(8) might have side effects, and we are changing the number of times h(8) is executed.

Dead-code removal. Another subtle problem with strict programming languages is the removal of *dead code*. Suppose we have

```
function f(i: int) : int =
 let var d := g(x)
  in i+2
  end
```

The variable d is never used; it is *dead* at its definition. Therefore, the call to g(x) should be removed. In a conventional programming language, such as Tiger or Fun-Tiger, we cannot remove g(x) because it might have side effects that are necessary to the operation of the program.

In a strict, purely functional language such as PureFun-Tiger, removing the computation g(x) could optimize a nonterminating computation into a terminating one! Though this seems benign, it can be very confusing to the programmer. We do not want programs to change their input/output behavior when compiled with different levels of optimization.

In a lazy language, it is perfectly safe to remove dead computations such as g(x).

Deforestation. In any language, it is common to break a program into one module that produces a data structure and another module that consumes it. Program 15.15 is a simple example; range(i,j) generates a list of the integers from i to j, squares(l) returns the square of each number, and sum(l) adds up all the numbers.

```
type intList = {head: int, tail: intList}
type intfun = int->int
type int2fun = (int,int) -> int

function sumSq(inc: intfun, mul: int2fun, add: int2fun) : int =
let
  function range(i: int, j: int) : intList =
    if i>j then nil else intList{head=i, tail=range(inc(i),j)}

  function squares(l: intList) : intList =
    if l=nil then nil
    else intList{head=mul(l.head,l.head), tail=squares(l.tail)}

  function sum(accum: int, l: intList) : int =
    if l=nil then accum else sum(add(accum,l.head), l.tail)

 in sum(0,squares(range(1,100)))
end
```

PROGRAM 15.15. Summing the squares.

First `range` builds a list of 100 integers; then `squares` builds another list of 100 integers; finally `sum` traverses this list.

It is wasteful to build all three lists. A transformation called *deforestation* removes intermediate lists and trees (hence the name) and does everything in one pass. The deforested `sumSq` program looks like this:

```
function sumSq(inc:intfun, mul:int2fun, add:int2fun):int =
 let function f(accum: int, i: int, j: int) : int =
      if i>j then accum else f(add(accum,mul(i,i)),inc(i))
   in f(0,1,100)
  end
```

In impure functional languages (where functions can have side effects) deforestation is not usually valid. Suppose, for example, that the functions `inc`, `mul`, and `add` alter global variables, or print on an output file. The deforestation transformation has rearranged the order of calling these functions; instead of

$$inc(1), \quad inc(2), \quad \ldots inc(100),$$
$$mul(1,1), mul(2,2), \ldots mul(100,100),$$
$$add(0,1), add(1,4), \ldots add(328350,10000)$$

the functions are called in the order

$$\text{mul}(1,1), \qquad \text{add}(0,1), \qquad \qquad \text{inc}(1),$$
$$\text{mul}(2,2), \qquad \text{add}(1,4), \qquad \qquad \text{inc}(2),$$
$$\vdots$$
$$\text{mul}(100,100), \quad \text{add}(328350,10000), \quad \text{inc}(100)$$

Only in a pure functional language is it always legal to make this transformation.

STRICTNESS ANALYSIS

Although laziness allows certain new optimizations, the overhead of thunk creation and thunk evaluation is very high. If no attention is paid to this problem, then the lazy program will run slowly no matter what other optimizations are enabled.

The solution is to put thunks only where they are needed. If a function $f(x)$ is certain to evaluate its argument x, then there is no need to pass a thunk for x; we can just pass an evaluated x instead. We are trading an evaluation now for a certain eventual evaluation.

Definition of strictness. We say a function $f(x)$ is *strict in x* if, whenever some actual parameter a would fail to terminate, then $f(a)$ would also fail to terminate. A multi-argument function $f(x_1, \ldots, x_n)$ is strict in x_i if, whenever a would fail to terminate, then $f(b_1, \ldots, b_{i-1}, a, b_{i+1}, \ldots, b_n)$ also fails to terminate, regardless of whether the b_j terminate.

Let us take an example:

```
function f(x: int, y: int) : int = x + x + y

function g(x: int, y: int) : int = if x>0 then y else x

function h(x: string, y: int) : tree =
                tree{key=x,binding=y,left=nil,right=nil}

function j(x: int) : int = j(0)
```

The function f is *strict* in its argument x, since if the result f(x,y) is demanded then f will certainly touch (demand the value of) x. Similarly, f is strict in argument y, and g is strict in argument x. But g is not strict in its second argument, because g can sometimes compute its result without touching y.

```
function look(t: tree, k: key) : ()->binding =
  if k < t.key() then look(t.left(),k)
  else if k > t.key() then look(t.right(),k)
  else t.binding
```

PROGRAM 15.16. Partial call-by-name using the results of strictness analysis; compare with Program 15.14.

The function h is not strict in either argument. Even though it appears to "use" both x and y, it does not demand integer values from them; instead it just puts them into a data structure, and it could be that no other part of the program will ever demand integer values from the key or binding fields of that particular tree.

Curiously, by our definition of strictness, the function j is strict in x even though it never uses x. But the purpose of strictness analysis is to determine whether it is safe to evaluate x before passing it to the function j: will this cause a terminating program to become nonterminating? In this case, if j is going to be called, it will infinite-loop anyway, so it doesn't matter if we perform a (possibly nonterminating) evaluation of x beforehand.

Using the result of strictness analysis. Program 15.16 shows the result of transforming the look function (of Program 15.3a) using strictness information. A call-by-name transformation has been applied here, as in Figure 15.14, but the result would be similar using call-by-need. Function look is strict in both its arguments t and key. Thus, when comparing k<t.key, it does not have to *touch* k and t. However, the t.key field still points to a thunk, so it must be touched.

Since look is strict, callers of look are expected to pass evaluated values, not thunks. This is illustrated by the recursive calls, which must explicitly *touch* t.left and t.right to turn them from thunks to values.

Approximate strictness analysis. In some cases, such as the functions f,g,h above, the strictness or nonstrictness of a function is obvious – and easily determined by an optimizing compiler. But in general, exact strictness analysis is not computable – like exact dynamic liveness analysis (see page 214) and many other dataflow problems.

Thus, compilers must use a conservative approximation; where the exact strictness of a function argument cannot be determined, the argument must be assumed nonstrict. Then a thunk will be created for it; this slows down the

Function M:
$$M(7, \sigma) = 1$$
$$M(\mathsf{x}, \sigma) = \mathsf{x} \in \sigma$$
$$M(E_1 + E_2, \sigma) = M(E_1, \sigma) \wedge M(E_2, \sigma)$$
$$M(\mathsf{record}\{E_1, \ldots, E_n\}, \sigma) = 1$$
$$M(\mathsf{if}\ E_1\ \mathsf{then}\ E_2\ \mathsf{else}\ E_3, \sigma) = M(E_1, \sigma) \wedge (M(E_2, \sigma) \vee M(E_3, \sigma))$$
$$M(\mathsf{f}(E_1, \ldots, E_n), \sigma) = (\mathsf{f}, (M(E_1, \sigma), \ldots, M(E_n, \sigma))) \in H$$

Calculation of H:

$H \leftarrow \{\}$

repeat

    $done \leftarrow$ true

    for each function $\mathsf{f}(\mathsf{x}_1, \ldots, \mathsf{x}_n) = B$

        for each sequence $(b_1, \ldots, b_n)$ of booleans (all 2^n of them)

            if $(\mathsf{f}, (b_1, \ldots, b_n)) \notin H$

                $\sigma \leftarrow \{\mathsf{x}_i |\ b_i = 1\}$ *(σ is the set of x's corresponding*

                if $M(B, \sigma)$ *to 1's in the b vector)*

                    $done \leftarrow$ false

                    $H \leftarrow H \cup \{(\mathsf{f}, (b_1, \ldots, b_n))\}$

until *done*

Strictness (after the calculation of H terminates):

f is strict in its ith argument if

$$(\mathsf{f}, (\underbrace{1, 1, \ldots, 1}_{i-1}, 0, \underbrace{1, 1, \ldots, 1}_{n-i})) \notin H$$

ALGORITHM 15.17. First-order strictness analysis.

---

program a bit, but at least the optimizer will not have turned a terminating program into an infinite-looping program.

Algorithm 15.17 shows an algorithm for computing strictness. It maintains a set H of tuples of the form $(\mathsf{f}, (b_1, \ldots, b_n))$, where n is the number of arguments of f and the b_i are booleans. The meaning of a tuple $(\mathsf{f}, (1, 1, 0))$ is this: if f is called with three arguments (thunks), and the first two may halt but the third never halts, then f may halt.

If $(\mathtt{f}, (1, 1, 0))$ is in the set H, then we know that $\mathtt{f}$ is not strict in its third argument. If $(\mathtt{f}, (1, 1, 0))$ is *not* in H, then we are not sure whether $\mathtt{f}$ is not strict in its third argument.

We also need an auxiliary function to calculate whether an *expression* may terminate. Given an expression E and a set of variables σ, we say that $M(E, \sigma)$ means "E may terminate if all the variables in σ may terminate." If E_1 is $\mathtt{i+j}$, and there is some possibility that the thunks $\mathtt{i}$ and $\mathtt{j}$ may halt, then it is also possible that E_1 will halt too: $M(\mathtt{i} + \mathtt{j}, \{\mathtt{i}, \mathtt{j}\})$ is true. But if E_2 is $\mathtt{if\ k\ then\ i\ else\ j}$, where $\mathtt{i}$ and $\mathtt{j}$ could conceivably halt but $\mathtt{k}$ never does, then certainly E_2 will not halt, so $M(E_2, \{\mathtt{i}, \mathtt{j}\})$ is false.

Algorithm 15.17 will not work on the full Lazy-Tiger language, because it does not handle functions passed as arguments or returned as results. But for *first-order* programs (without higher-order functions), it does a good job of computing (static) strictness. More powerful algorithms for strictness analysis handle higher-order functions.

FURTHER READING

Church [1941] developed the λ-calculus, a "programming language" of nested functions that can be passed as arguments and returned as results. He was hampered by having no machines to compile for.

Closures. Landin [1964] showed how to interpret λ-calculus on an abstract machine, using closures allocated on a heap. Steele [1978] used closure representations specialized to different patterns of function usage, so that in many cases nonlocal variables are passed as extra arguments to an inner function to avoid heap allocating a record. Cousineau et al. [1985] showed how closure conversion can be expressed as a transformation back into the source language, so that closure analysis can be cleanly separated from other phases of code generation.

Static links are actually not the best basis for doing closure conversion; for many reasons it is better to consider each nonlocal variable separately, instead of always grouping together all the variables at the same nesting level. Kranz et al. [1986] performed *escape analysis* to determine which closures can be stack-allocated because they do not outlive their creating function and also integrated closure analysis with register allocation to make a high-performance optimizing compiler. Shao and Appel [1994] integrate closures with the use of callee-save registers to minimize the load/store traffic caused by accessing local and nonlocal variables. Appel [1992] has a good overview of closure conversion.

Continuations. Tail calls are particularly efficient and easy to analyze. Strachey and Wadsworth [1974] showed that the control flow of any program (even an imperative one) can be expressed as function calls, using the notion of *continuations*. Steele [1978] transformed programs into *continuation-passing style* early in compilation, turning all function calls into tail calls, to simplify all the analysis and optimization phases of the compiler. Kranz et al. [1986] built an optimizing compiler for Scheme using continuation-passing style; Appel [1992] describes a continuation-based optimizing compiler for ML.

Inline expansion. Cocke and Schwartz [1970] describe inline expansion of function bodies; Scheifler [1977] shows that it is particularly useful for languages supporting data abstraction, where there tend to be many tiny functions implementing operations on an abstract data type. Appel [1992] describes practical heuristics for controlling code explosion.

Continuation-based I/O. Wadler [1995] describes the use of monads to generalize the notion of continuation-based interaction.

Lazy evaluation. Algol-60 [Naur et al. 1963] used call-by-name evaluation for function arguments, implemented using thunks – but also permitted side effects, so programmers needed to know what they were doing! Most of its successors use call-by-value. Henderson and Morris [1976] and Friedman and Wise [1976] independently invented lazy evaluation (call-by-need). Hughes [1989] argues that lazy functional languages permit clearer and more modular programming than imperative languages.

Several lazy pure-functional languages were developed in the 1980s; the community of researchers in this area designed and adopted the language Haskell [Hudak et al. 1992] as a standard. Peyton Jones [1987; 1992] describes many implementation and optimization techniques for lazy functional languages; Peyton Jones and Partain [1993] describe a practical algorithm for higher-order strictness analysis. Wadler [1990] describes deforestation.

PROGRAM **COMPILING FUNCTIONAL LANGUAGES**

    a. Implement Fun-Tiger. A function value can be allocated as a heap-allocated two-element record, containing function-address and static-link fields.

b. Implement PureFun-Tiger. This is just like Fun-Tiger, except that several "impure" features are removed and the predefined functions have different interfaces.

c. Implement optimizations on PureFun-Tiger. This requires changing the Tree intermediate language so that it can represent an entire program, including function entry and exit, in a machine-independent way. After inline expansion (and other) optimizations, the program can be converted into the standard Tree intermediate representation of Chapter 7.

d. Implement Lazy-Tiger.

EXERCISES

15.1 Draw a picture of the closure data structures representing add24 and a in Program 15.1 just at the point where add24(a) is about to be called. Label all the components.

15.2 Figure 15.13 summarizes the instructions necessary to implement printTable in a functional or an imperative style. But it leaves out the MOVE instructions that pass parameters to the calls. Flesh out both the functional and imperative versions with all omitted instructions, writing pseudo-assembly language in the style of the program accompanying Graph 11.1 on page 224. Show which MOVE instructions you expect to be deleted by copy propagation.

15.3 Explain why there are no cycles in the graph of closures and records of a PureFun-Tiger program. Comment on the applicability of reference-count garbage collection to such a program. Hint: Under what circumstances are records or closures updated after they are initialized?

15.4 a. Perform Algorithm 15.9 (loop-preheader transformation) on the look function of Program 15.3a.

b. Perform Algorithm 15.10 (loop-invariant hoisting) on the result.

c. Perform Algorithm 15.8 (inline expansion) on the following call to loop (assuming the previous two transformations have already been applied):

```
look(mytree, a+1)
```

15.5 Perform Algorithm 15.17 (strictness analysis) on the following program, showing the set H on each pass through the **repeat** loop.

```
function f(w: int, x: int, y: int, z: int) =
   if z=0 then w+y else f(x,0,0,z-1) + f(y,y,0,z-1)
```

In which arguments is f strict?

16

Dataflow Analysis

anal-y-sis: an examination of a complex, its elements, and their relations

Webster's Dictionary

An optimizing compiler transforms programs to improve their efficiency without changing their output. There are many transformations that improve efficiency:

Register allocation: Keep two nonoverlapping temporaries in the same register.

Common-subexpression elimimination: If an expression is computed more than once, eliminate one of the computations.

Dead-code elimination: Delete a computation whose result will never be used.

Constant folding: If the operands of an expression are constants, do the computation at compile time.

This is not a complete list of optimizations. In fact, there can never be a complete list.

NO MAGIC BULLET

Computability theory shows that it will always be possible to invent new optimizing transformations.

Let us say that a *fully optimizing compiler* is one that transforms each program P to a program $\mathbf{Opt}(P)$ that is the *smallest* program with the same input/output behavior as P. We could also imagine optimizing for speed instead of program size, but let us choose size to simplify the discussion.

For any program Q that produces no output and never halts, $\mathbf{Opt}(Q)$ is short and easily recognizable:

$L_1:$ **goto** L_1

Therefore, if we had a fully optimizing compiler we could use it to solve the halting problem; to see if there exists an input on which P halts, just see if **Opt**(P) is the one-line infinite loop. But we know that no computable algorithm can always tell whether programs halt, so a fully optimizing compiler cannot be written either.

Since we can't make a *fully* optimizing compiler, we must build *optimizing compilers* instead. An optimizing compiler transforms P into a program P' that always has the same input/output behavior as P, and might be smaller or faster. We hope that P' runs faster than the optimized programs produced by our competitors' compilers.

No matter what optimizing compiler we consider, there must always exist another (usually bigger) optimizing compiler that does a better job. For example, suppose we have an optimizing compiler A. There must be some program P_x which does not halt, such that $A(P_x) \neq$ **Opt**(P_x). If this were not the case, then A would be a fully optimizing compiler, which we could not possibly have. Therefore, there exists a better compiler B:

$$B(P) = \textbf{if } P = P_x \textbf{ then } [\texttt{L : goto L}] \textbf{ else } A(P)$$

Although we don't know what P_x is, it is certainly just a string of source code, and given that string we could trivially construct B.

The optimizing compiler B isn't very useful – it's not worth handling special cases like P_x one at a time. In real life, we improve A by finding some reasonably general program transformation (such as the ones listed at the beginning of the chapter) that improves the performance of many programs. We add this transformation to the optimizer's "bag of tricks" and we get a more competent compiler. When our compiler knows enough tricks, we deem it *mature*.

This theorem, that for any optimizing compiler there exists a better one, is known as the *full employment theorem for compiler writers*.

16.1   INTERMEDIATE REPRESENTATION FOR FLOW ANALYSIS

In this chapter we will consider *intraprocedural global optimization. Intraprocedural* means the analysis stays within a single procedure or function (of a language like Tiger); *global* means that the analysis spans all the statements or basic blocks within that procedure. *Interprocedural* optimization is more global, operating on several procedures and functions at once.

Each of the optimizing transformations listed at the beginning of the chapter can be applied using the following generic recipe:

Dataflow analysis: Traverse the flow graph, gathering information about what may happen at run time (this will necessarily be a conservative approximation).

Transformation: Modify the program to make it faster in some way; the information gathered by analysis will guarantee that the program's result is unchanged.

There are many dataflow analyses that can provide useful information for optimizing transformations. Like the *liveness analysis* described in Chapter 10, most can be described by *dataflow equations*, a set of simultaneous equations derived from nodes in the flow graph.

QUADRUPLES

Chapter 10's liveness analysis operates on Assem instructions, which clearly indicate *uses* and defs but whose actual operations are machine-dependent assembly-language strings. Liveness analysis, and the register allocation based on it, do not need to know what operations the instructions are performing, just their uses and definitions. But for the analyses and optimizations in this chapter, we need to understand the *operations* as well. Therefore, instead of Assem instructions we will use Tree-language terms (Section 7.2), simplified even further by ensuring that each Exp has only a single MEM or BINOP node.

We can easily turn ordinary Tree expressions into simplified ones. Wherever there is a nested expression of one BINOP or MEM inside another, we introduce a new temporary using ESEQ:

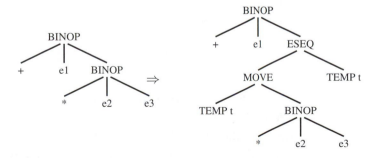

and then apply the Canon module to remove all the ESEQ nodes.

We also introduce new temporaries to ensure that any *store* statement (that is, a MOVE whose left-hand side is a MEM node) has only a TEMP or a CONST on its right-hand side, and only a TEMP or CONST under the MEM.

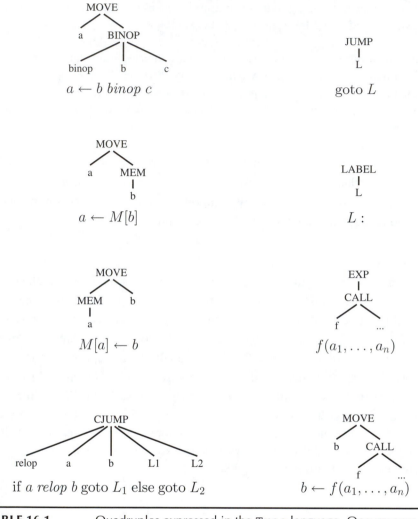

TABLE 16.1. Quadruples expressed in the `Tree` language. Occurrences of a, b, c, f, L denote TEMP, CONST, or LABEL nodes only.

The statements that remain are all quite simple; they take one of the forms shown in Table 16.1.

Because the "typical" statement is $a \leftarrow b \oplus c$ with four components $(a, b, c, \oplus)$, these simple statements are often called *quadruples*. We use $\oplus$ to stand for an arbitrary *binop*.

A more efficient compiler would represent quadruples with a special-purpose data type (instead of using `Tree` data structures), and would translate from trees to quadruples all in one pass.

Intraprocedural optimizations take these quadruples that come out of the Canon phase of the compiler, and transform them into a new set of quadruples. The optimizer may move, insert, delete, and modify the quadruples. The resulting procedure-body must then be fed into the instruction-selection phase of the compiler. However, the tree matching will not be very effective on the "atomized" trees where each expression contains only one BINOP or MOVE. After the optimizations are completed, there will be many MOVE statements that define temporaries that are used only once. It will be necessary to find these and turn them back into nested expressions.

We make a control flow graph of the quadruples, with a directed edge from each node (statement) n to its successors – that is, the nodes that can execute immediately after n.

16.2   VARIOUS DATAFLOW ANALYSES

A dataflow analysis of a control flow graph of quadruples collects information about the execution of the program. One dataflow analysis determines how definitions and uses are related to each other, another estimates what values a variable might have at a given point, and so on. The results of these analyses can be used to make optimizing transformations of the program.

REACHING DEFINITIONS

For many optimizations we need to see if a particular assignment to a temporary t can directly affect on the value of t at another point in the program. We say that an *unambiguous definition* of t is a particular statement (quadruple) in the program of the form $t \leftarrow a \oplus b$ or $t \leftarrow M[a]$. Given such a definition d, we say that d *reaches* a statement u in the program if there is some path of control flow edges from d to u that does not contain any unambiguous definition of t.

An *ambiguous* definition is a statement that might or might not assign a value to t. For example, if t is a global variable, and the statement s is a CALL to a function that sometimes modifies t but sometimes does not, then s is an ambiguous definition. But our Tiger compiler treats escaping variables as memory locations, not as temporaries subject to dataflow analysis. This means that we never have ambiguous definitions; unfortunately, we also lose the opportunity to perform optimizations on escaping variables. For the remainder of this chapter, we will assume all definitions are unambiguous.

Statement s	$gen[s]$	$kill[s]$
$d: t \leftarrow b \oplus c$	$\{d\}$	$defs(t) - \{d\}$
$d: t \leftarrow M[b]$	$\{d\}$	$defs(t) - \{d\}$
$M[a] \leftarrow b$	$\{\}$	$\{\}$
if a relop b goto L_1 else goto L_2	$\{\}$	$\{\}$
goto L	$\{\}$	$\{\}$
$L:$	$\{\}$	$\{\}$
$f(a_1, \ldots, a_n)$	$\{\}$	$\{\}$
$d: t \leftarrow f(a_1, \ldots, a_n)$	$\{d\}$	$defs(t) - \{d\}$

TABLE 16.2. *Gen* and *kill* for reaching definitions.

We can express the calculation of reaching definitions as the solution of dataflow equations. We label every MOVE statement with a definition-ID, and we manipulate sets of definition-IDs. We say that the statement $d_1 : t \leftarrow x \oplus y$ *generates* the definition d_1, because no matter what other definitions reach the beginning of this statement, we know that d_1 reaches the end of it. And we say that this statement *kills* any other definition of t, because no matter what other definitions of t reach the beginning of the statement, they do not reach the end (they cannot directly affect the value of t after this statement).

Let us define $defs(t)$ as the set of all definitions (or definition-IDs) of the temporary t. Table 16.2 summarizes the *generate* and *kill* effects of the different kinds of quadruples.

Using *gen* and *kill*, we can compute $in[n]$ (and $out[n]$) the set of definitions that reach the beginning (and end) of each node n:

$$in[n] = \bigcup_{p \in pred[n]} out[p]$$
$$out[n] = gen[n] \cup (in[n] - kill[n])$$

These equations can be solved by iteration: first $in[n]$ and $out[n]$ are initialized to the empty set, for all n; then the equations are treated as assignment statements and repeatedly executed until there are no changes.

We will take Program 16.3 as an example; it is annotated with statement numbers that will also serve as definition-IDs. In each iteration, we recalculate *in* and *out* for each statement in turn:

```
1 :      a ← 5
2 :      c ← 1
3 : L₁ : if c > a goto L₂
4 :      c ← c + c
5 :      goto L₁
6 : L₂ : a ← c − a
7 :      c ← 0
```

PROGRAM 16.3.

			Iter. 1		Iter. 2		Iter. 3	
n	$gen[n]$	$kill[n]$	$in[n]$	$out[n]$	$in[n]$	$out[n]$	$in[n]$	$out[n]$
1	1	6		1		1		1
2	2	4,7	1	1,2	1	1,2	1	1,2
3			1,2	1,2	1,2,4	1,2,4	1,2,4	1,2,4
4	4	2,7	1,2	1,4	1,2,4	1,4	1,2,4	1,4
5			1,4	1,4	1,4	1,4	1,4	1,4
6	6	1	1,2	2,6	1,2,4	2,4,6	1,2,4	2,4,6
7	7	2,4	2,6	6,7	2,4,6	6,7	2,4,6	6,7

Iteration 3 serves merely to discover that nothing has changed since iteration 2.

Having computed reaching definitions, what can we do with the information? The analysis is useful in several kinds of optimization. As a simple example, we can do *constant propagation:* only one definition of a reaches statement 3, so we can replace the test $c > a$ with $c > 5$.

AVAILABLE EXPRESSIONS

Suppose we want to do *common-subexpression elimination*; that is, given a program that computes $x \oplus y$ more than once, can we eliminate one of the duplicate computations? To find places where such optimizations are possible, indexavailable expressions the notion of *available expressions* is helpful.

An expression $x \oplus y$ is *available* at a node n in the flow graph if, on every path from the entry node of the graph to node n, $x \oplus y$ is computed at least once *and* there are no definitions of x or y since the most recent occurrence of $x \oplus y$ on that path.

We can express this in dataflow equations using *gen* and *kill* sets, where the sets are now sets of expressions.

Any node that computes $x \oplus y$ *generates* $\{x \oplus y\}$, and any definition of x

Statement s	$gen[s]$	$kill[s]$
$t \leftarrow b \oplus c$	$\{b \oplus c\} - kill[s]$	*expressions containing t*
$t \leftarrow M[b]$	$\{M[b]\} - kill[s]$	*expressions containing t*
$M[a] \leftarrow b$	$\{\}$	*expressions of the form $M[x]$*
if $a > b$ goto L_1 else goto L_2	$\{\}$	$\{\}$
goto L	$\{\}$	$\{\}$
$L :$	$\{\}$	$\{\}$
$f(a_1, \ldots, a_n)$	$\{\}$	$\{\}$
$t \leftarrow f(a_1, \ldots, a_n)$	$\{\}$	*expressions containing t*

TABLE 16.4.   *Gen* and *kill* for available expressions.

or y *kills* $x \oplus y$; see Table 16.4.

Basically, $t \leftarrow b + c$ generates the expression $b + c$. But $b \leftarrow b + c$ does not generate $b + c$, because after $b + c$ there is a subsequent definition of b. The statement $gen[s] = \{b \oplus c\} - kill[s]$ takes care of this subtlety.

A *store* instruction ($M[a] \leftarrow b$) might modify any memory location, so it kills any *fetch* expression ($M[x]$). If we were sure that $a \neq x$, we could be less conservative, and say that $M[a] \leftarrow b$ does not kill $M[x]$. This is called *alias analysis*; see Section 16.5.

Given *gen* and *kill*, we compute *in* and *out* almost as for reaching definitions, except that we compute the *intersection* of the *out*-sets of the successors instead of a union. This reflects the fact that an expression is available only if it is computed on *every* path into the node.

$$in[n] = \bigcap_{p \in pred[n]} out[p]$$
$$out[n] = gen[n] \cup (in[n] - kill[n])$$

REACHING EXPRESSIONS

We say that an expression $t \leftarrow x \oplus y$ (in node s of the flow graph) reaches node n if there is a path from s to n that does not go through any assignment to x or y, or through any computation of $x \oplus y$. As usual, we can express *gen* and *kill*; see Exercise 16.1.

In practice, the *reaching expressions* analysis is needed by the *common-subexpression elimination* optimization only for a small subset of all the expressions in a program. Thus, reaching expressions are usually computed ad hoc, by searching backward from node n and stopping whenever a computation $x \oplus y$ is found. Or reaching expressions can be computed during the calculation of available expressions; see Exercise 16.4.

LIVENESS ANALYSIS

Chapter 10 has already covered liveness analysis, but it is useful to note that liveness can also be expressed in terms of *gen* and *kill*. Any use of a variable generates liveness, and any definition kills liveness:

Statement s	$gen[s]$	$kill[s]$
$t \leftarrow b \oplus c$	$\{b, c\} - kill[s]$	$\{t\}$
$t \leftarrow M[b]$	$\{b\} - kill[s]$	$\{t\}$
$M[a] \leftarrow b$	$\{b\}$	$\{\}$
if $a > b$ goto L_1 else goto L_2	$\{a, b\}$	$\{\}$
goto L	$\{\}$	$\{\}$
$L :$	$\{\}$	$\{\}$
$f(a_1, \ldots, a_n)$	$\{a_1, \ldots, a_n\}$	$\{\}$
$t \leftarrow f(a_1, \ldots, a_n)$	$\{a_1, \ldots, a_n\} - kill[s]$	$\{t\}$

The equations for *in* and *out* are similar to the ones for reaching definitions and available expressions, but *backward* because liveness is a *backward* dataflow analysis:

$$in[n] = gen[n] \cup (out[n] - kill[n])$$
$$out[n] = \bigcup_{s \in succ[n]} in[s]$$

16.3   TRANSFORMATIONS USING DATAFLOW ANALYSIS

Using the results of dataflow analysis, the optimizing compiler can improve the program in several ways.

COMMON-SUBEXPRESSION ELIMINATION

Given a flow-graph statement $s : t \leftarrow x \oplus y$, where the expression $x \oplus y$ is *available* at s, the computation within s can be eliminated.

Algorithm. Compute *reaching expressions*, that is, find statements of the form $n : v \leftarrow x \oplus y$, such that the path from n to s does not compute $x \oplus y$

or define x or y.

Choose a new temporary w, and for such n, rewrite as

$$n : w \leftarrow x \oplus y$$
$$n' : v \leftarrow w$$

Finally, modify statement s to be

$$s : \; t \leftarrow w$$

We will rely on copy propagation to remove some or all of the extra assignment quadruples.

CONSTANT PROPAGATION

Suppose we have a statement $d : t \leftarrow c$ where c is a constant, and another statement n that uses t, such as $n : \; y \leftarrow t \oplus x$.

We know that t is constant in n if d reaches n, and no other definitions of t reach n.

In this case, we can rewrite n as $y \leftarrow c \oplus x$.

COPY PROPAGATION

This is like constant propagation, but instead of a constant c we have a variable z.

Suppose we have a statement $d : t \leftarrow z$. and another statement n that uses t, such as $n : \; y \leftarrow t \oplus x$.

If d reaches n, and no other definition of t reaches n, and there is no definition of z on any path from d to n (including a path that goes through n one or more times), then we can rewrite n as $n : \; y \leftarrow z \oplus x$.

A good graph-coloring register allocator will do *coalescing* (see Chapter 11), which is a form of copy propagation. It detects any intervening definitions of z in constructing the interference graph – an assignment to z while d is live makes an interference edge (z, d), rendering d and z uncoalesceable.

If we do copy propagation before register allocation, then we may increase the number of spills. Thus, if our only reason to do copy propagation were to delete redundant MOVE instructions, we should wait until register allocation. However, copy propagation at the quadruple stage may enable the recognition of other optimizations such as common-subexpression elimination. For example, in the program

$$a \leftarrow y + z$$
$$u \leftarrow y$$
$$c \leftarrow u + z$$

the two $+$-expressions are not recognized as common subexpressions until after the copy propagation of $u \leftarrow y$ is performed.

DEAD-CODE ELIMINATION

If there is a quadruple $s : a \leftarrow b \oplus c$ or $s : a \leftarrow M[x]$, such that a is not *live-out* of s, then the quadruple can be deleted.

Some instructions have implicit side effects. For example, if the computer is configured to raise an exception on an arithmetic overflow or divide by zero, then deletion of an exception-causing instruction will change the result of the computation.

The optimizer should never make a change that changes program behavior, even if the change seems benign (such as the removal of a run-time "error"). The problem with such optimizations is that the programmer cannot predict the behavior of the program – and a program debugged with the optimizer enabled may fail with the optimizer disabled.

16.4   SPEEDING UP DATAFLOW ANALYSIS

Many dataflow analyses – including the ones described in this chapter – can be expressed using simultaneous equations on finite sets. So also can many of the algorithms used in constructing finite automata (Chapter 2) and parsers (Chapter 3). The equations can usually be set up so that they can be solved by *iteration*: by treating the equations as assignment statements and repeatedly executing all the assignments until none of the sets changes any more.

There are several ways to speed up the evaluation of dataflow equations.

BIT VECTORS

A set S over a finite domain (that is, where the elements are integers in the range $1 - N$ or can be put in an array indexed by $1 - N$) can be represented by a *bit vector*. The ith bit in the vector is a 1 if the element i is in the set S.

In the bit-vector representation, unioning two sets S and T is done by a bitwise-*or* of the bit vectors. If the word size of the computer is W, and the vectors are N bits long, then a sequence of N/W *or* instructions can union two sets. Of course, $2N/W$ fetches and N/W stores will also be necessary, as well as indexing and loop overhead.

Intersection can be done by bitwise-*and*, set complement can be done by bitwise complement, and so on.

Thus, the bit-vector representation is commonly used for dataflow analysis. It would be inadvisable to use bit vectors for dataflow problems where the sets are expected to be very sparse (so the bit vectors would be almost all zeros), in which case a different implementation of sets would be faster.

BASIC BLOCKS

Suppose we have a node n in the flow graph that has only one predecessor, p, and p has only one successor, n. Then we can combine the *gen* and *kill* effects of p and n and replace nodes n and p with a single node. We will take *reaching definitions* as an example, but almost any dataflow analysis permits a similar kind of combining.

Consider what definitions reach *out* of the node n:

$$out[n] = gen[n] \cup (in[n] - kill[n])$$

We know $in[n]$ is just $out[p]$; therefore

$$out[n] = gen[n] \cup ((gen[p] \cup (in[p] - kill[p])) - kill[n])$$

By using the identity $(A \cup B) - C = (A - C) \cup (B - C)$ and then $A - B - C = A - (B \cup C)$, we have

$$out[n] = gen[n] \cup (gen[p] - kill[n]) \cup (in[p] - (kill[p] \cup kill[n]))$$

If we want to say that node pn combines the effects of p and n, then this last equation says that the appropriate *gen* and *kill* sets for pn are:

$$gen[pn] = gen[n] \cup (gen[p] - kill[n])$$
$$kill[pn] = kill[p] \cup kill[n]$$

We can combine all the statements of a basic block in this way, and agglomerate the *gen* and *kill* effects of the whole block. The control-flow graph of basic blocks is much smaller than the graph of individual statements, so the multi-pass iterative dataflow analysis works much faster on the basic-block graph.

Topological-sort:

$N \leftarrow 0$

for all nodes i

$\quad mark[i] \leftarrow 0$

DFS(*start-node*)

function DFS(i)

$\quad$ **if** $mark[i] = 0$

$\qquad N \leftarrow N + 1$

$\qquad mark[i] \leftarrow N$

$\qquad sorted[N] \leftarrow i$

$\qquad$ **for** each successor s of node i

$\qquad\quad$ DFS(s)

ALGORITHM 16.5. Topological sort by depth-first search.

Once the iterative dataflow analysis algorithm is completed, we may recover the dataflow information of an individual statement (such as n) within a block (such pn in our example) by starting with the *in* set computed for the entire block and – in one pass – applying the *gen* and *kill* sets of the statements that precede n in the block.

ORDERING THE NODES

In a *forward* dataflow problem (such as reaching definitions or available expressions), the information coming *out* of a node goes *in* to the successors. If we could arrange that every node was calculated before its successors, the dataflow analysis would terminate in one pass through the nodes.

This would be possible if the control-flow graph had no cycles. We would *topologically sort* the flow graph – this just gives an ordering where each node comes before its successors – and then compute the dataflow equations in sorted order. But often the graph will have cycles, so this simple idea won't work. Even so, quasi-topologically sorting a cyclic graph by depth-first search helps to reduce the number of iterations required on cyclic graphs; in quasi-sorted order, most nodes come before their successors, so information flows forward quite far through the equations on each iteration.

Depth-first search (Algorithm 16.5) topological-sorts a graph quite efficiently. Using *sorted*, the order computed by depth-first search, the iterative solution of dataflow equations should be computed as

repeat

$\quad$ **for** $i \leftarrow 1$ **to** N

$\qquad n \leftarrow sorted[i]$

$\qquad in \leftarrow \bigcup_{p \in pred[n]} out[p]$

$\qquad out[n] \leftarrow gen[n] \cup (in - kill[n])$

until no *out* set changed in this iteration

$W \leftarrow \{s_0\}$ (where s_0 is the start node)
while W is not empty
  remove a node n from W
  $old \leftarrow out[n]$
  $in \leftarrow \bigcup_{p \in pred[n]} out[p]$
  $out[n] \leftarrow gen[n] \cup (in - kill[n])$
  if $old \neq out[n]$
    for each successor s of n
      if $s \notin W$
        put s into W

ALGORITHM 16.6.   A work-list algorithm for reaching definitions.

There is no need to make *in* a global array, since it is used only locally in computing *out*.

For *backward* dataflow problems such as liveness analysis, we simply use the reverse of the top-sort order.

WORK-LIST ALGORITHMS

If any *out* set changes during an iteration of the **repeat-until** loop of an iterative solver, then all the equations are recalculated. This seems a pity, since most of the equations may not be affected by the change.

A *work-list* algorithm keeps track of just which *out* sets must be recalculated. Whenever node n is recalculated *and its out set is found to change*, all the successors of n are put onto the work-list (if they're not on it already). This is illustrated in Algorithm 16.6.

The coalescing, graph-coloring register allocator described in Chapter 11 is an example of a work-list algorithm with many different work-lists.

INCREMENTAL DATAFLOW ANALYSIS

Using the results of dataflow analysis, the optimizer can perform program transformations: moving, modifying, or deleting instructions. But optimizations can cascade:

- Removal of the dead code $a \leftarrow b \oplus c$ might cause b to become dead in a previous instruction $b \leftarrow x \oplus y$.

- One common-subexpression elimination begets another. In the program

$$x \leftarrow b + c$$
$$y \leftarrow a + x$$
$$u \leftarrow b + c$$
$$v \leftarrow a + u$$

after $u \leftarrow b + c$ is replaced by $u \leftarrow x$, copy propagation changes $a + u$ to $a + x$, which is a common subexpression and can be eliminated.

A simple way to organize a dataflow-based optimizer is to perform a global flow analysis, then make all possible dataflow-based optimizations, then repeat the global flow analysis, then perform optimizations, and so on until no more optimizations can be found. At best this iterates two or three times, so that on the third round there are no more transformations to perform.

But the worst case is very bad indeed. Consider a program in which the statement $z \leftarrow a_1 + a_2 + a_3 + \cdots + a_n$ occurs where z is dead. This translates into the quadruples

$$x_1 \quad \leftarrow a_1 + a_2$$
$$x_2 \quad \leftarrow x_1 + a_3$$
$$\vdots$$
$$x_{n-2} \leftarrow x_{n-3} + a_{n-1}$$
$$z \quad \leftarrow x_{n-2} + a_n$$

Liveness analysis determines that z is dead; then dead-code elimination removes the definition of z. Then another round of liveness analysis determines that x_{n-2} is dead, and then dead-code elimination removes x_{n-2}, and so on. It takes n rounds of analysis and optimization to remove x_1 and then determine that there is no more work to do.

A similar situation occurs with common-subexpression elimination, when there are two occurrences of an expression such as $a_1 + a_2 + a_3 + \cdots + a_n$ in the program.

To avoid the need for repeated, global calculations of dataflow information, there are several strategies:

Cutoff: Perform no more than k rounds of analysis and optimization, for $k = 3$ or so. Later rounds of optimization may not be finding many transformations to do anyway. This is a rather unsophisticated approach, but at least the compilation will terminate in a reasonable time.

Cascading analysis: Design new dataflow analyses that can predict the cascade effects of the optimizations that will be done.

Incremental dataflow analysis: When the optimizer makes a program transformation – which renders the dataflow information invalid – instead of discarding the dataflow information, the optimizer should "patch" it.

Value numbering. The *value numbering* analysis is an example of a cascading analysis that, in one pass, finds all the (cascaded) common subexpressions within a basic block.

The algorithm maintains a table T, mapping *variables* to *value numbers*, and also mapping triples of the form (*value number, operator, value number*) to value numbers. For efficiency, T should be represented as a hash table. There is also a global number N counting how many distinct values have been seen so far.

Using T and N, the value-numbering algorithm (Algorithm 16.7) scans the quadruples of a block from beginning to end. Whenever it sees an expression $b + c$, it looks up the value number of b and the value number of c. It then looks up $\text{hash}(n_b, n_c, +)$ in T; if found, it means that $b + c$ repeats the work of an earlier computation; we mark $b + c$ for deletion, and use the previously computed result. If not found, we leave $b + c$ in the program and also enter it in the hash table.

Figure 16.8 illustrates value numbering on a basic block: (a) is the list of quadruples, and (b) is the table (after the algorithm is finished). We can view the table as a directed acyclic graph (DAG), if we view an entry $(m, \oplus, n) \mapsto q$ as a node q with edges to nodes m and n, as shown in Figure 16.8c.

Value numbering is an example of a single dataflow analysis that calculates the effect of cascaded optimizations: in this case, cascaded common-subexpression elimination. But the optimizer would like to perform a wide variety of transformations – especially when the loop optimizations described in the next chapter are included. It is very hard to design a single dataflow analysis capable of predicting the results of many different optimizations in combination.

Instead, we use a general-purpose dataflow analyzer and a general-purpose optimizer; but when the optimizer changes the program, it must tell the analyzer what information is no longer valid.

Incremental liveness analysis. For example, an incremental algorithm for liveness analysis must keep enough information so that if a statement is inserted or deleted, the liveness information can be efficiently updated.

Suppose we delete this statement $s : a \leftarrow b \oplus c$ from a flow graph on which we have *live-in* and *live-out* information for every node. The changes

$T \leftarrow empty$
$N \leftarrow 0$
for each quadruple $a \leftarrow b \oplus c$ in the block
    if $(b \mapsto k) \in T$ for some k
      $n_b \leftarrow k$
    else
      $N \leftarrow N + 1$
      $n_b \leftarrow N$
      put $b \mapsto n_b$ into T
    if $(c \mapsto k) \in T$ for some k
      $n_c \leftarrow k$
    else
      $N \leftarrow N + 1$
      $n_c \leftarrow N$
      put $c \mapsto n_c$ into T
    if $((n_b, \oplus, n_c) \mapsto m) \in T$ for some m
      put $a \mapsto m$ into T
      mark this quadruple $a \leftarrow b \oplus c$ as a common subexpression
    else
      $N \leftarrow N + 1$
      put $(n_b, \oplus, n_c) \mapsto N$ into T
      put $a \mapsto N$ into T

ALGORITHM 16.7. Value numbering.

---

to the dataflow information are as follows:

1. a is no longer defined here. Therefore, if a is *live-out* of this node, it will now be *live-in* where it was not before.

2. b is no longer used here. Therefore, if b is not *live-out* of this node, it will no longer be *live-in*. We must propagate this change backwards, and do the same for c.

A work-list algorithm will be useful here, since we can just add the predecessor of s to the work-list and run until the work-list is empty; this will often terminate quickly.

Propagating change (1) does the same kind of thing that the original (non-

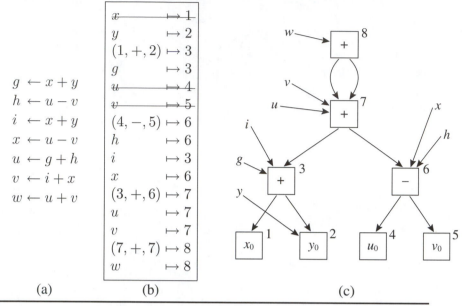

$$
\begin{aligned}
g &\leftarrow x + y \\
h &\leftarrow u - v \\
i &\leftarrow x + y \\
x &\leftarrow u - v \\
u &\leftarrow g + h \\
v &\leftarrow i + x \\
w &\leftarrow u + v
\end{aligned}
$$

(a)

$$
\begin{aligned}
x &\mapsto 1 \\
y &\mapsto 2 \\
(1,+,2) &\mapsto 3 \\
g &\mapsto 3 \\
u &\mapsto 4 \\
v &\mapsto 5 \\
(4,-,5) &\mapsto 6 \\
h &\mapsto 6 \\
i &\mapsto 3 \\
x &\mapsto 6 \\
(3,+,6) &\mapsto 7 \\
u &\mapsto 7 \\
v &\mapsto 7 \\
(7,+,7) &\mapsto 8 \\
w &\mapsto 8
\end{aligned}
$$

(b)

(c)

FIGURE 16.8. An illustration of value numbering. (a) A basic block; (b) the table created by the value-numbering algorithm, with hidden bindings shown crossed out; (c) a view of the table as a DAG.

incremental) work-list algorithm for liveness does: it makes the live-sets bigger. Thus, our proof (Exercise 10.2) that the algorithm finds a least fixed point of the liveness equations also applies to the propagation of additional liveness caused by the deletion of the definition of a. Even the proof that the liveness analysis terminates was based on the idea that any change makes things bigger, and there was an a priori limit to how big the sets could get.

But change (2) makes live-sets smaller, not bigger, so naively running our original algorithm starting from the previously computed *in* and *out* sets may find a fixed point that is not a least fixed point. For example, suppose we have the following program

$$
\begin{array}{rll}
0 & & d \leftarrow 4 \\
1 & & a \leftarrow 0 \\
2 & L_1: & b \leftarrow a + 1 \\
3 & & c \leftarrow c + b \\
3a & & a \leftarrow d \\
4 & & a \leftarrow b \cdot 2 \\
5 & & \text{if } a < N \text{ goto } L_1 \\
6 & & \text{return } c
\end{array}
$$

Liveness analysis shows that d is *live-in* at statements 1,2,3,3a,4,5. But a is not *live-out* of statement 3a, so this statement is dead code, and we can delete it. If we then start with the previously computed dataflow information and use Algorithm 10.4 (page 210) until it reaches a fixed point, we will end up with the column Y of Table 10.7, which is not the best possible approximation of the actual liveness information.

A more refined liveness analysis. Therefore, we must use a better algorithm. The solution is that at each point where a variable d is defined, we must keep track of exactly what uses it might have. Our liveness calculation will be very much like Algorithm 10.4, but it will operate on sets of *uses* instead of sets of *variables*. In fact, it is just like the reaching definitions algorithm in reverse. Let $uses(v)$ be the set of all uses of variable v in the program. Given a statement $s : a \leftarrow b \oplus c$, the set

$$live\text{-}out[s] \cap uses(a)$$

contains all the uses of a that could possibly be reached by this definition.

Now, when we delete a quadruple that uses some variable b, we can delete that use of b from all the *live-in* and *live-out* sets. This gives the least fixed point, as we desire.

Cascades of dead code After deleting statement 3a from the program above, the incremental liveness analysis will find that statement 0 is dead code and can be deleted. Thus, incremental liveness analysis cooperates well with dead-code elimination. Other kinds of dataflow analysis can similarly be made incremental; sometimes, as in the case of liveness analysis, we must first refine the analysis.

16.5   ALIAS ANALYSIS

The analyses we have described in this chapter consider only the values of Tree-language temporaries. Variables that *escape* are represented (by the front end of the compiler) in memory locations with explicit fetches and stores, and we have not tried to analyze the definitions, uses, and liveness of these variables. The problem is that a variable or memory location may have several different names, or *aliases*, so that it is hard to tell which statements affect which variables.

Variables that can be aliases include:

- variables passed as call-by-reference parameters (in Pascal, C++, Fortran);
- variables whose address is taken (in C, C++);
- *l*-value expressions that dereference pointers, such as p.x in Tiger or *p in C;
- *l*-value expressions that explicitly subscript arrays, such as a[i];
- and variables used in inner-nested procedures (in Pascal, Tiger, ML).

A good optimizer should optimize these variables. For example, in the program fragment

```
p.x := 5; q.x := 7; a := p.x
```

we might want our *reaching definitions* analysis to show that only one definition of p.x (namely, 5) reaches the definition of a. But the problem is that we cannot tell if one name is an alias for another. Could q point to the same record as p? If so, there are two definitions (5 and 7) that could reach a.

Similarly, with call-by-reference parameters, in the program

```
function f( ref i: int,  ref j: int) =
    (i := 5; j := 7; return i)
```

a naive computation of reaching definitions would miss the fact that i might be the same variable as j, if f is called with f(x,x).

The may-alias relation We use *alias analysis*, a kind of dataflow analysis, to learn about different names that may point to the same memory locations. The result of alias analysis is a *may-alias* relation: p may-alias q if, in some run of the program, p and q might point to the same data. As with most dataflow analyses, static (compile-time) information cannot be completely accurate, so the may-alias relation is conservative: we say that p may-alias q if we cannot prove that p is never an alias for q.

ALIAS ANALYSIS BASED ON TYPES

For languages with *strong typing* (such as Pascal, Java, ML, Tiger) where if two variables have incompatible types they cannot possibly be names for the same memory location, we can use the type information to provide a useful may-alias relation. Also in these languages the programmer cannot explicitly make a pointer point to a local variable, and we will use that fact as well.

We divide all the memory locations used by the program into disjoint sets, called *alias classes*. For Tiger, here are the classes we will use:

```
type list = {head: int,              {int *p, *q;
             tail: list}              int h,i;
var p : list := nil;                  p = &h;
var q : list := nil                   q = &i;
q := list{head=0, tail=nil};          *p = 0;
p := list{head=0, tail=q};            *q = 5;
q.head := 5;                          a = *p;
a := p.head                          }
```

(a) Tiger program   (b) C program

PROGRAM 16.9. p and q are not aliases.

- For every frame location created by `Frame.allocLocal(true)`, we have a new class;
- For every record field of every record type, a new class;
- For every array type a, a new class.

The semantic analysis phase of the compiler must compute these classes, as they involve the concept of *type*, of which the later phases are ignorant. Each class can be represented by a different integer.

The `Translate` functions must label every fetch and store (that is, every MEM node in the `Tree` language) with its class. We will need to modify the `Tree` data structure, putting an `aliasClass` field into the MEM node.

Given two MEM nodes $M_i[x]$ and $M_j[y]$, where i and j are the alias classes of the MEM nodes, we can say that $M_i[x]$ may-alias $M_j[y]$ if $i = j$.

This works for Tiger and Java. But it fails in the presence of call-by-reference or type casting.

ALIAS ANALYSIS BASED ON FLOW

Instead of, or in addition to, alias classes based on types, we can also make alias classes based on *point of creation*.

In Program 16.9a, even though p and q are the same type, we know they point to different records. Therefore we know that a must be assigned 0; the definition `q.head:=5` cannot affect a. Similarly, in Program 16.9b we know p and q cannot be aliases, so a must be 0.

To catch these distinctions automatically, we will make an alias class for each point of creation. That is, for every different statement where a record is allocated (that is, for each call to `malloc` in C or `new` in Pascal or Java) we make a new alias class. Also, each different local or global variable whose

Statement s		$trans_s(A)$
$t \leftarrow b$		$(A - \Sigma_t) \cup \{(t, d, k)\mid (b, d, k) \in A\}$
$t \leftarrow b + k$	(k is a constant)	$(A - \Sigma_t) \cup \{(t, d, i)\mid (b, d, i - k) \in A\}$
$t \leftarrow b \oplus c$		$(A - \Sigma_t) \cup \{(t, d, i)\mid (b, d, j) \in A \vee (c, d, k) \in A\}$
$t \leftarrow M[b]$		$A \cup \Sigma_t$
$M[a] \leftarrow b$		A
if $a > b$ goto L_1 else L_2		A
goto L		A
$L :$		A
$f(a_1, \ldots, a_n)$		A
$d : t \leftarrow \texttt{allocRecord}(a)$		$(A - \Sigma_t) \cup \{(t, d, 0)\}$
$t \leftarrow f(a_1, \ldots, a_n)$		$A \cup \Sigma_t$

TABLE 16.10.   Transfer function for alias flow analysis.

address is taken is an alias class.

A pointer (or call-by-reference parameter) can point to variables of more than one alias class. In the program

```
1   p := list {head=0, tail=nil};
2   q := list {head=6, tail=p};
3   if a=0
4        then p:=q;
5   p.head := 4;
```

at line 5, q can point only to alias class 2, but p might point to alias class 1 or 2, depending on the value of a.

So we must associate with each MEM node a set of alias classes, not just a single class. After line 2 we have the information $p \mapsto \{1\}, q \mapsto \{2\}$; out of line 4 we have $p \mapsto \{2\}, q \mapsto \{2\}$. But when two branches of control flow merge (in the example, we have the control edges $3 \rightarrow 5$ and $4 \rightarrow 5$) we must merge the alias class information; at line 5 we have $p \mapsto \{1, 2\}, q \mapsto \{2\}$.

Algorithm. The dataflow algorithm manipulates sets of tuples of the form (t, d, k) where t is a variable and d, k is the alias class of all instances of the kth field of a record allocated at location d. The set $in[s]$ contains (t, d, k) if $t - k$ might point to a record of alias class d at the beginning of statement s. This is an example of a dataflow problem where bit vectors will not work as well as a tree or hash table representation better suited to sparse problems.

Instead of using *gen* and *kill* sets, we use a transfer function: we say that if A is the alias information (set of tuples) on entry to a statement s, then $trans_s(A)$ is the alias information on exit. The transfer function is defined by Table 16.10 for the different kinds of quadruples.

The initial set A_0 includes the binding (FP, *frame*,0) where *frame* is the special alias class of all frame-allocated variables of the current function.

We use the abbreviation Σ_t to mean the set of all tuples (t, d, k), where d, k is the alias class of any record field whose type is compatible with variable t. Cooperation from the front end in providing a "small" Σ_t for each t makes the analysis more accurate. Of course, in a typeless language, or one with type-casts, Σ_t might have to be the set of all alias classes.

The set equations for alias flow analysis are:

$$in[s_0] = A_0 \quad \text{where } s_0 \text{ is the start node}$$
$$in[n] = \bigcup_{p \in pred[n]} out[p]$$
$$out[n] = trans_n(in[n])$$

and we can compute a solution by iteration in the usual way.

Producing may-alias information. Finally, we say that

p may-alias q at statement s

if there exists d, k such that $(p, d, k) \in in[s]$ and $(q, d, k) \in in[s]$.

USING MAY-ALIAS INFORMATION

Given the may-alias relation, we can treat each alias class as a "variable" in dataflow analyses such as reaching definitions and available expressions.

To take available expressions as an example, we modify one line of Table 16.2, the *gen* and *kill* sets:

Statement s	$gen[s]$	$kill[s]$
$a \leftarrow M[t]$	$\{M[t]\}$	$\{M[x] \mid x$ may alias t at $s\}$ $\cup$
		(the set of expressions containing a)

Now we can analyze the following program fragment, derived from the Tiger expression b:=a+a where a is a frame-resident variable:

$$
\begin{array}{lll}
1: & t & \leftarrow fp + 12 \\
2: & u & \leftarrow M[t] \\
3: & v & \leftarrow fp + 12 \\
4: & w & \leftarrow M[v] \\
5: & b & \leftarrow u + w
\end{array}
$$

First we discover that $fp + 12$ is available at line 3, so common-subexpression elimination rewrites the program as

$$
\begin{aligned}
1: \quad & t \leftarrow fp + 12 \\
2: \quad & u \leftarrow M[t] \\
4: \quad & w \leftarrow M[t] \\
5: \quad & b \leftarrow u + w
\end{aligned}
$$

Then we discover that $M[t]$ is available at line 4, so common-subexpression elimination rewrites it as

$$
\begin{aligned}
1: \quad & t \leftarrow fp + 12 \\
2: \quad & u \leftarrow M[t] \\
5: \quad & b \leftarrow u + u
\end{aligned}
$$

which is optimal.

What we have shown here is intraprocedural alias analysis. But an interprocedural analysis would help to analyze the effect of CALL instructions. For example, in the program

$$
\begin{aligned}
1: \quad & t \leftarrow fp + 12 \\
2: \quad & u \leftarrow M[t] \\
3: \quad & f(t) \\
4: \quad & w \leftarrow M[t] \\
5: \quad & b \leftarrow u + w
\end{aligned}
$$

does the function f modify $M[t]$? If so, then $M[t]$ is not available at line 4.

However, interprocedural alias analysis is beyond the scope of this book.

ALIAS ANALYSIS IN STRICT PURE-FUNCTIONAL LANGUAGES

Some languages have *immutable* variables that cannot change after their initialization. For example, **const** variables in the C language, most variables in the ML language, and all variables in PureFun-Tiger (see Chapter 15) are immutable.

Alias analysis is not needed for these variables. The purpose of alias analysis is to determine whether different statements in the program interfere, or whether one definition *kills* another. Though it is true that there could be many pointers to the same value, none of the pointers can cause the value to change, i.e. no immutable variable can be killed.

This is a good thing for the optimizer, and also for the the programmer. The optimizer can do constant propagation and loop-invariant detection (see

Chapter 17) without being bothered by aliases; and the programmer can understand what a segment of the program is doing also without the confusion and complexity introduced by stores through aliased pointers.

FURTHER READING

Gödel [1931] proved the *full employment theorem for mathematicians*. Turing [1937] proved that the halting problem is undecidable, and Rice [1953] proved the *full employment theorem for compiler writers*, even before there were any compiler writers.

Ershov [1958] developed value numbering. Allen [1969] codified many program optimizations; Allen [1970] and Cocke [1970] designed the first global dataflow analysis algorithms. Kildall [1973] first presented the fixed-point iteration method for dataflow analysis.

Landi and Ryder [1992] give an algorithm for interprocedural alias analysis.

EXERCISES

16.1 Show the dataflow equations for *reaching expressions* (page 340). Be specific about what happens in the case of quadruples such as $t \leftarrow t \oplus b$ or $t \leftarrow M[t]$ where the defined temporary also appears on the right-hand side. The elements of the *gen* and *kill* sets will be definition-IDs, as in *reaching definitions*. Hint: If the definition on page 340 is not clear enough to formulate a precise definition, be guided by the role that reaching expressions must play in common-subexpression elimination (page 341).

16.2 Write down the control-flow graph of basic blocks (not just statements) for Program 16.3, and show the *gen* and *kill* sets (for reaching definitions) of each block.

16.3 Show how to combine the *gen* and *kill* effects of two adjacent statements in the same basic block for each of:

a. Available expressions

b. Liveness analysis

*16.4 Modify the algorithm for computing *available expressions* to simultaneously compute *reaching expressions*. To make the algorithm more efficient, you may take advantage of the fact that if an expression does is not available at statement s then we do not need to know if it reaches s or not (for purposes of common-subexpression elimination). Hint: for each available expression $a + b$ that is propagated through statement s, also propagate a set representing all the statements that define $a + b$ and reach s.

16.5 Write down a work-list algorithm for liveness analysis, in a form similar to that of Algorithm 16.6.

16.6 Explain why a work-list algorithm such as Algorithm 16.6 will naturally visit the nodes of the graph in topologically sorted order. More specifically, if you make a list of the nodes in an acyclic graph, in the order that each node is *first* visited, the list is topologically sorted.

17

Loop Optimizations

loop: a series of instructions that is repeated until a terminating condition is reached

Webster's Dictionary

Loops are pervasive in computer programs, and a great proportion of the execution time of a typical program is spent in one loop or another. Hence it is worthwhile devising optimizations to make loops go faster. Intuitively, a loop is a sequence of instructions that ends by jumping back to the beginning. But to be able to optimize loops effectively we will use a more precise definition.

A *loop* in a control-flow graph is a set of nodes S including a *header* node h with the following properties:
- From any node in S there is a path of directed edges leading to h;
- There is a path of directed edges from h to any node in S;
- There is no edge from any node outside S, to any node in S other than h.

Thus, the dictionary definition (from *Webster's*) is not the same as the technical definition.

Figure 17.1 shows some loops. A *loop entry* node is one with some predecessor outside the loop; a *loop exit* node is one with a successor outside the loop. Figures 17.1c, 17.1d, and 17.1e illustrate that a loop may have multiple exits, but may have only one entry. Figures 17.1e and 17.1f contain nested loops.

REDUCIBLE FLOW GRAPHS

Figure 17.2a does not contain a loop; either node in the strongly connected component $(2, 3)$ can be reached without going through the other.

Figure 17.2c contains the same pattern of nodes 1, 2, 3; this becomes more clear if we repeatedly delete edges and collapse together pairs of nodes (x, y),

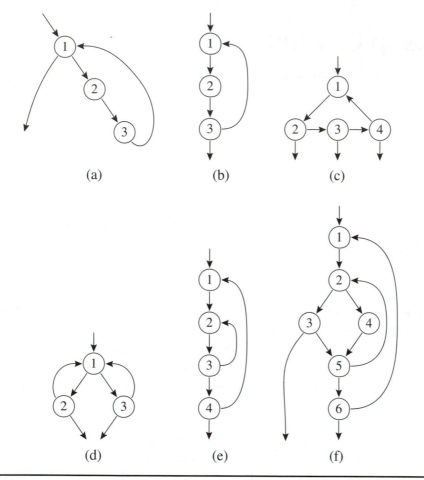

FIGURE 17.1. Some loops; in each case, 1 is the header node.

where x is the only predecessor of y. That is: delete $6 \rightarrow 9$, $5 \rightarrow 4$, collapse $(7, 9)$, $(3, 7)$, $(7, 8)$, $(5, 6)$, $(1, 5)$, $(1, 4)$; and we obtain Figure 17.2a.

A *reducible flow graph* is one that cannot be collapsed to contain any subgraph like Figure 17.2a. An *irreducible flow graph* is one that *can* be collapsed to contain such a subgraph.

Common control-flow constructs such as **if-then**, **if-then-else**, **while-do**, **repeat-until**, **for**, and **break** (even multilevel **break**) can only generate reducible flow graphs. Thus, the control-flow graph for a Tiger or Java function, or a C function without **goto**, will always be reducible.

The following program corresponds to flow graph 17.1e, assuming Tiger were augmented with **repeat-until** loops:

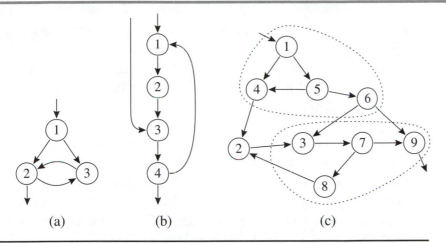

(a)   (b)   (c)

FIGURE 17.2.   None of these contains a loop. Dotted lines indicate reduction of graph (c) by deleting edges and collapsing nodes.

```
function isPrime(n: int) : int =
  (i := 2;
   repeat j := 2;
          repeat if i*j=n
                     then return 0
                     else j := j+1
          until j=n;
          i := i+1
   until i=n;
   return 1)
```

In a functional language, loops are generally expressed using tail-recursive function calls. The isPrime program might be written as:

```
   function isPrime(n: int) : int =
0       tryI(n,2)

   function tryI(n: int, i: int) : int =
1       tryJ(n,i,2)

   function tryJ(n: int, i: int, j: int) : int =
2       if i*j=n
3          then 0
4          else nextJ(n,i,j+1)

   function nextJ(n: int, i: int, j: int) : int =
5       if j=n
          then nextI(n,i+1)
          else tryJ(n,i,j)

   function nextI(n: int, i: int) : int =
6       if i=n
          then 1
          else tryI(n,i)
```

where the numbers 1–6 show the correspondence with the flow-graph nodes of Figure 17.1f.

Because the programmer can arrange these functions in arbitrary ways, flow graphs produced by the tail-call structure of functional programs are sometimes irreducible.

Advantages of reducible flow graphs. Many dataflow analyses (presented in Chapter 16) can be done very efficiently on reducible flow graphs. Instead of using fixed-point iteration ("keep executing assignments until there are no changes"), we can determine an order for computing the assignments, and calculate in advance how many assignments will be necessary – that is, there will never be a need to check to see if anything changed.

However, for the remainder of this chapter we will assume that our control-flow graphs may be reducible or irreducible.

17.1   DOMINATORS

Before we optimize the loops, we must find them in the flow graph. The notion of *dominators* is useful for that purpose.

Each control-flow graph must have a start node s_0 with no predecessors, where program (or procedure) execution is assumed to begin.

A node d *dominates* a node n if every path of directed edges from s_0 to n must go through d. Every node dominates itself.

ALGORITHM FOR FINDING DOMINATORS

Consider a node n with predecessors $p_1, \ldots, p_k$, and a node d (with $d \neq n$). If d dominates each one of the p_i, then it must dominate n, because every path from s_0 to n must go through one of the p_i, but every path from s_0 to a p_i must go through d. Conversely, if d dominates n, it must dominate all the p_i; otherwise there would be a path from s_0 to n going through the predecessor not dominated by d.

Let $D[n]$ be the set of nodes that dominate n. Then

$$D[n] = \{n\} \cup \left(\bigcap_{p \in \text{pred}[n]} D[p] \right)$$

The simultaneous equations can be solved, as usual, by iteration, treating each equation as an assignment statement. However, in this case each set

$D[n]$ must be initialized to hold all the nodes in the graph, because each assignment $D[n] \leftarrow \{n\} \cup \ldots$ makes $D[n]$ smaller (or unchanged), not larger.

This algorithm can be made more efficient by ordering the set assignments in quasi-topological order, that is, according to a depth-first search of the graph.

Technically, an unreachable node is dominated by every node in the graph; we will avoid the pathologies this can cause by deleting unreachable nodes from the graph before calculating dominators and doing loop optimizations. See also Exercise 17.2.

IMMEDIATE DOMINATORS

Theorem: In a connected graph, suppose d dominates n, and e dominates n. Then it must be that either d dominates e, or e dominates d.

Proof: (By contradiction.) Suppose neither d nor e dominates the other. Then there is some path from s_0 to e that does not go through d. Therefore any path from e to n must go through d; otherwise d would not dominate n.

Conversely, any path from d to n must go through e. But this means that to get from e to n the path must infinitely loop from d to e to $d \ldots$ and never get to n.

This theorem tells us that every node n has no more than one *immediate dominator*, $idom(n)$, such that

1. $idom(n)$ is not the same node as n,
2. $idom(n)$ dominates n, and
3. $idom(n)$ does not dominate any other dominator of n.

Every node except s_0 is dominated by at least one node other than itself (since s_0 dominates every node), so every node except s_0 has exactly one immediate dominator.

Dominator tree. Let us draw a graph containing every node of the flow graph, and for every node n an edge from $idom(n)$ to n. The resulting graph will be a tree, because each node has exactly one immediate dominator. This is called the *dominator tree*.

Figure 17.3 shows a flow graph and its dominator tree. Some edges in the dominator tree correspond single flow-graph edges (such as $4 \rightarrow 6$), but others do not (such as $4 \rightarrow 7$). That is, the immediate dominator of a node is not necessarily its predecessor in the flow graph.

A flow-graph edge from a node n to a node h that dominates n is called a *back edge*. For every back edge there is a corresponding subgraph of the flow

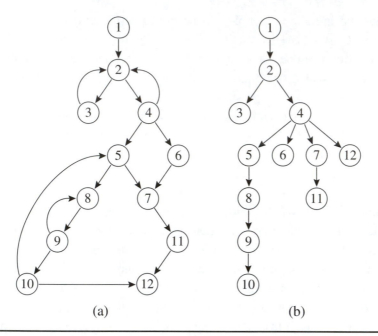

FIGURE 17.3.   (a) A flow graph; (b) its dominator tree.

graph that is a loop. The back edges in Figure 17.3a are $3 \rightarrow 2, 4 \rightarrow 2, 10 \rightarrow 5, 9 \rightarrow 8$.

LOOPS

The *natural loop* of a back edge $n \rightarrow h$, where h dominates n, is the set of nodes x such that h dominates x and there is a path from x to n not containing h. The *header* of this loop will be h.

The natural loop of the back edge $10 \rightarrow 5$ from Figure 17.3a includes nodes $5, 8, 9, 10$ and has the loop $8, 9$ nested within it.

A node h can be the header of more than one natural loop, if there is more than one back edge into h. In Figure 17.3a, the natural loop of $3 \rightarrow 2$ consists of the nodes $3, 2$ and the natural loop of $4 \rightarrow 2$ consists of $4, 2$.

The loop optimizations described in this chapter can cope with any loop, whether it is a natural loop or not, and whether or not that loop shares its header with some other loop. However, we usually want to optimize an *inner* loop first, because most of the program's execution time is expected to be in the inner loop. If two loops share a header, then it is hard to determine which should be considered the inner loop. A common way of solving this problem is to merge all the natural loops with the same header. The result will not necessarily be a natural loop.

If we merge all the loops with header 2 in Figure 17.3a, we obtain the loop $2, 3, 4$.

Nested loops If A and B are loops with headers a and b respectively, such that $a \neq b$ and a dominates b, then the nodes of B are a proper subset of the nodes of A. We say that loop B is nested within A, or that B is the *inner loop*.

We can construct a *loop-nest tree* of loops in a program. The procedure is, for a flow graph G:

1. Compute dominators of G;
2. construct the dominator tree;
3. find all the natural loops, and thus all the loop-header nodes;
4. for each loop header h, merge all the natural loops of h into a single loop, $loop[h]$;
5. construct the tree of loop headers (and implicitly loops), such that h_1 is above h_2 in the tree if h_1 dominates h_2.

The leaves of the loop-nest tree are the *innermost loops*.

Just to have a place to put nodes not in any loop, we could say that the entire procedure body is a pseudo-loop that sits at the root of the loop-nest tree. The loop-nest tree of Figure 17.3 is shown in Figure 17.4.

LOOP PREHEADER

Many loop optimizations will insert statements immediately before the loop executes. For example, *loop-invariant hoisting* moves a statement from inside the loop to immediately before the loop. Where should such statements be put? Figure 17.5a illustrates a problem: if we want to insert statement s into a basic block immediately before the loop, we need to put s at the end of blocks 2 and 3. In order to have one place to put such statements, we insert a new, initially empty, *preheader* node p outside the loop, with an edge $p \rightarrow h$. All edges $x \rightarrow h$ from nodes x inside the loop are left unchanged, but all existing edges $y \rightarrow h$ from nodes y outside the loop are redirected to point to p.

17.2   LOOP-INVARIANT COMPUTATIONS

If a loop contains a statement $t \leftarrow a \oplus b$ such that a has the same value each time around the loop, and b has the same value each time, then t will also have

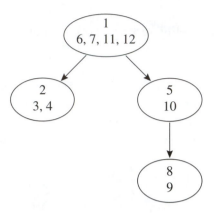

FIGURE 17.4. The loop-nest tree for Figure 17.3a. Each loop header is shown in the top half of each circle or oval (nodes 1,2,5,8); a loop comprises a header node (e.g., node 5), all the other nodes shown in the same circle or oval (e.g., node 10), and all the nodes shown in subtrees of the loop-nest-tree node (e.g., 8,9).

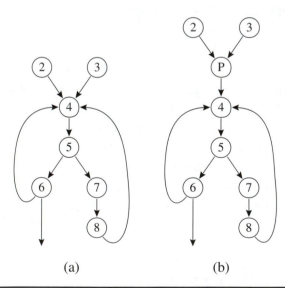

(a)   (b)

FIGURE 17.5. (a) A loop; (b) the same loop with a preheader.

the same value each time. We would like to *hoist* the computation out of the loop, so it is computed just once instead of every time.

We cannot always tell if a will have the same value every time, so as usual we will conservatively approximate. The definition $d : t \leftarrow a_1 \oplus a_2$ is loop-invariant within loop L if, for each operand a_i

1. a_i is a constant
2. *or* all the definitions of a_i that reach d are outside the loop,
3. *or* only one definition of a_i reaches d, and that definition is loop-invariant.

This leads naturally to an iterative algorithm for finding loop-invariant definitions: first find all the definitions whose operands are constant or from outside the loop, then repeatedly find definitions whose operands are loop-invariant.

HOISTING

Suppose $t \leftarrow a \oplus b$ is loop-invariant. Can we hoist it out of the loop? In Figure 17.6a, hoisting makes the program compute the same result faster. But in Figure 17.6b, hoisting makes the program faster but incorrect – the original program does not *always* execute $t \leftarrow a \oplus b$, but the transformed program does, producing an incorrect value for x if $a < b$. Hoisting in Figure 17.6c is also incorrect, because the original loop had more than one definition of t, and the transformed program interleaves the assignments to t in a different way. And hoisting in Figure 17.6d is wrong because there is a use of t before the loop-invariant definition, so after hoisting, this use will have the wrong value on the first iteration of the loop.

With these pitfalls in mind, we can set the criteria for hoisting $d : t \leftarrow a \oplus b$ to the end of the loop preheader:

1. d dominates all loop exits, *or* t is not *live-out* of any loop exit node;
2. *and* there is only one definition of t in the loop,
3. *and* t is not *live-out* of the loop preheader.

Implicit side effects. These rules need modification if $t \leftarrow a \oplus b$ could raise some sort of arithmetic exception or have other side effects; see Exercise 17.8.

Turning while loops into repeat-until loops. Condition (1) tends to prevent many computations from being hoisted from **while** loops; from Figure 17.7a it is clear that none of the statements in the loop body dominates the loop exit node (which is the same as the header node). To solve this problem, we can transform the **while** loop into a **repeat** loop preceded by an **if** statement. This requires duplication of the statements in the header node, as shown

L_0	L_0	L_0	L_0
$\quad t \quad\leftarrow 0$	$\quad t \quad\leftarrow 0$	$\quad t \quad\leftarrow 0$	$\quad t \quad\leftarrow 0$
L_1	L_1	L_1	L_1
$\quad i \quad\leftarrow i+1$	$\quad$ if $i \geq N$ goto L_2	$\quad i \quad\leftarrow i+1$	$\quad M[j]\leftarrow t$
$\quad t \quad\leftarrow a \oplus b$	$\quad i \quad\leftarrow i+1$	$\quad t \quad\leftarrow a \oplus b$	$\quad i \quad\leftarrow i+1$
$\quad M[i]\leftarrow t$	$\quad t \quad\leftarrow a \oplus b$	$\quad M[i]\leftarrow t$	$\quad t \quad\leftarrow a \oplus b$
$\quad$ if $i<N$ goto L_1	$\quad M[i]\leftarrow t$	$\quad t \quad\leftarrow 0$	$\quad M[i]\leftarrow t$
L_2	$\quad$ goto L_1	$\quad M[j]\leftarrow t$	$\quad$ if $i<N$ goto L_1
$\quad x \quad\leftarrow t$	L_2	$\quad$ if $i<N$ goto L_1	L_2
	$\quad x \quad\leftarrow t$	L_2	$\quad x \quad\leftarrow t$
(a) Hoist	(b) Don't	(c) Don't	(d) Don't

FIGURE 17.6. Some good and bad candidates for hoisting $t \leftarrow a \oplus b$.

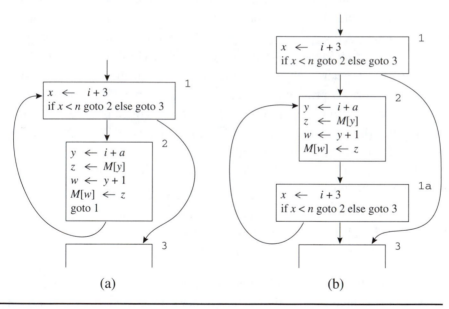

FIGURE 17.7. A **while** loop (a), transformed into a **repeat** loop (b).

in Figure 17.7b. Of course, all the statements in the body of a **repeat** loop dominate the loop exit (if there are no **break** or explicit loop-exit statements), so condition (1) will be satisfied.

$$s \leftarrow 0$$
$$i \leftarrow 0$$
$$L_1 : \text{if } i < n \text{ goto } L_2$$
$$\quad j \leftarrow i \cdot 4$$
$$\quad k \leftarrow j + a$$
$$\quad x \leftarrow M[k]$$
$$\quad s \leftarrow s + x$$
$$\quad i \leftarrow i + 1$$
$$\quad \text{goto } L_1$$
$$L_2$$

(a) Before

$$s \leftarrow 0$$
$$k' \leftarrow a$$
$$b \leftarrow n \cdot 4$$
$$c \leftarrow a + b$$
$$L_1 : \text{if } k' < c \text{ goto } L_2$$
$$\quad x \leftarrow M[k']$$
$$\quad s \leftarrow s + x$$
$$\quad k' \leftarrow k' + 4$$
$$\quad \text{goto } L_1$$
$$L_2$$

(b) After

PROGRAM 17.8. A loop before and after induction-variable optimizations.

17.3 INDUCTION VARIABLES

Some loops have a variable i that is incremented or decremented, and a variable j that is set (in the loop) to $i \cdot c + d$ where c and d are loop-invariant. Then we can calculate j's value without reference to i; whenever i is incremented by a we can increment j by $c \cdot a$.

Consider, for example, Program 17.8a, which sums the elements of an array. Using *induction-variable analysis* to find that i and j are related induction variables, *strength reduction* to replace a multiplication by 4 with an addition, then *induction-variable elimination* to replace $i < n$ by $k < 4n + a$, followed by miscellaneous copy propagation, we get Program 17.8b. The transformed loop has fewer quadruples; it might even run faster. Let us now take the series of transformations one step at a time.

We say that a variable such as i is a *basic induction variable*, and j and k are *derived induction variables in the family of* i. Right after j is defined (in the original loop), we have $j = a_j + i \cdot b_j$, where $a_j = 0$ and $b_j = 4$. We can completely characterize the value of j at its definition by (i, a, b), where i is a basic induction variable and a and b are loop-invariant expressions.

If there is another derived induction variable with definition $k \leftarrow j + c_k$ (where c_k is loop-invariant), then k is also in the family of i. We can characterize k by the triple (i, c_k, b_j), that is, $k = c_k + i \cdot b_j$.

We can characterize the basic induction variable i by a triple in the same way, that is $(i, 0, 1)$, meaning that $i = 0 + i \cdot 1$. Thus every induction variable

$$s \leftarrow 0$$
$$j' \leftarrow i \cdot 4$$
$$b' \leftarrow b \cdot 4$$
$$n' \leftarrow n \cdot 4$$

$s \leftarrow 0$ $L_1 : $ if $s > 0$ goto L_2

$L_1 : $ if $s > 0$ goto L_2

$s \leftarrow 0$	$s \leftarrow 0$
$L_1 : $ if $s > 0$ goto L_2	$j' \leftarrow i \cdot 4$
$i \leftarrow i + b$	$b' \leftarrow b \cdot 4$
$j \leftarrow i \cdot 4$	$n' \leftarrow n \cdot 4$
$x \leftarrow M[j]$	$L_1 : $ if $s > 0$ goto L_2
$s \leftarrow s - x$	$j' \leftarrow j' + b'$
goto L_1	$j \leftarrow j'$
$L_2 : i \leftarrow i + 1$	$x \leftarrow M[j]$
$s \leftarrow s + j$	$s \leftarrow s - x$
if $i < n$ goto L_1	goto L_1
	$L_2 : j' \leftarrow j' + 4$
	$s \leftarrow s + j$
	if $j' < n'$ goto L_1

(a) Before   (b) After

FIGURE 17.9.   The basic induction variable i is incremented by different amounts in different iterations; the derived induction variable j is not changed in every iteration.

can be characterized by such a triple.

An induction variable's value need not change by the same amount in every iteration of the loop. For example, the loop of Figure 17.9a the induction variable i is incremented by b in some iterations and by 1 in other iterations. Furthermore, in some iterations $j = i \cdot 4$ and in other iterations the derived induction variable j gets (temporarily) left behind as i is incremented.

DETECTION OF INDUCTION VARIABLES

Basic induction variables. The variable i is a basic induction variable in a loop L with header node h if the only definitions of i within L are of the form $i \leftarrow i + c$ or $i \leftarrow i - c$ where c is loop-invariant.

Derived induction variables. The variable k is a *derived induction variable* in loop L if:

1. There is only one definition of k within L, of the form $k \leftarrow j \cdot c$ or $k \leftarrow j + d$, where j is an induction variable and c, d are loop-invariant;
2. *and* if j is a derived induction variable in the family of i, then:
   (a) the only definition of j that reaches k is the one in the loop,

(b) *and* there is no definition of i on any path between the definition of j and the definition of k.

Assuming j is characterized by (i, a, b), then k is described by $(i, a, b \cdot c)$ or $(i, a + d, c)$, depending on whether k's definition was $j \cdot c$ or $j + d$.

Statements of the form $k \leftarrow j - c$ can be treated as $k \leftarrow j + (-c)$ for purposes of induction-variable analysis (unless $-c$ is not representable, which can sometimes happen with two's complement arithmetic).

Division. Statements of the form $k \leftarrow j/c$ can be rewritten as $k \leftarrow j \cdot (\frac{1}{c})$, so that k could be considered an induction variable. This fact is useful for floating-point calculations – though we must beware of introducing subtle numerical errors if $1/c$ cannot be represented exactly. If this is an integer division, we cannot represent $1/c$ at all.

STRENGTH REDUCTION

On many machines, multiplication is more expensive than addition. So we would like to take a derived induction variable whose definition is of the form $j \leftarrow i \cdot c$ and replace it with an addition.

For each derived induction variable j whose triple is (i, a, b), make a new variable j' (although different derived induction variables with the same triple can share the same j' variable). After each assignment $i \leftarrow i + c$, make an assignment $j' \leftarrow j' + c \cdot b$ where $c \cdot b$ is a loop-invariant expression that may be computed in the loop preheader. If c and b are both constant, then the multiplication may be done at compile-time. Replace the (unique) assigment to j with $j \leftarrow j'$. Finally, it is necessary to initialize j' at the end of the loop preheader, with $j' \leftarrow a + i \cdot b$.

We say two induction variables x, y in the family of i are *coordinated* if $(x - a_x)/b_x = (y - a_y)/b_y$ at every time during the execution of the loop, except during a sequence of statements $z_i \leftarrow z_i + c_i$, where c_i is loop-invariant. Clearly, all the new variables in the family of i introduced by strength reduction are coordinated with each other, and with i.

When the definition of an induction variable $j \leftarrow \cdots$ is replaced by $j \leftarrow j'$, we know that j' is coordinated but j might not be. However, the standard *copy propagation* algorithm can help here, replacing uses of j by uses of j' where there is no intervening definition of j'.

Thus, instead of using some sort of flow analysis to learn whether j is coordinated, we just use j' instead, where copy propagation says it is legal to do so.

After strength reduction there is still a multiplication, but it is outside the loop. If the loop executes more than one iteration, then the program should run faster with additions instead of multiplication, on many machines. The results of strength reduction may be disappointing on processors that can schedule multiplications to hide their latency.

Example. Let us perform strength reduction on Program 17.8a. We find that j is a derived induction variable with triple $(i, 0, 4)$, and k has triple $(i, a, 4)$. After strength reduction on both j and k, we have

$$
\begin{aligned}
& s \leftarrow 0 \\
& i \leftarrow 0 \\
& j' \leftarrow 0 \\
& k' \leftarrow a \\
L_1 : \ & \text{if } i < n \text{ goto } L_2 \\
& j \leftarrow j' \\
& k \leftarrow k' \\
& x \leftarrow M[k] \\
& s \leftarrow s + x \\
& i \leftarrow i + 1 \\
& j' \leftarrow j' + 4 \\
& k' \leftarrow k' + 4 \\
& \text{goto } L_1 \\
L_2
\end{aligned}
$$

We can perform *dead-code elimination* to remove the statement $j \leftarrow j'$. We would also like to remove all the definitions of the *useless variable* j', but technically it is not dead, since it is used in every iteration of the loop.

ELIMINATION

After strength reduction, some of the induction variables are not used at all in the loop, and others are used only in comparisons with loop-invariant variables. These induction variables can be deleted.

A variable is *useless* in a loop L if it is dead at all exits from L, and its only use is in a definition of itself. All definitions of a useless variable may be deleted.

In our example, after the removal of j, the variable j' is useless. We can delete $j' \leftarrow j' + 4$. This leaves a definition of j' in the preheader that can now be removed by dead-code elimination.

REWRITING COMPARISONS

A variable k is *almost useless* if it is used only in comparisons against loop-invariant values and there is some other induction variable in the same family that is not useless. An almost-useless variable may be made useless by modifying the comparison to use the related induction variable.

If we have $k < n$, where j and k are coordinated induction variables in the family of i, and n is loop-invariant; then we know that $(j - a_j)/b_j = (k - a_k)/b_k$, so therefore the comparison $j < n$ can be written as

$$a_k + \frac{b_k}{b_j}(j - a_j) \; < \; n$$

Now, we can subtract a_k from both sides and multiply both sides by b_j/b_k. If b_j/b_k is positive, the resulting comparison is:

$$j - a_j \; < \; \frac{b_j}{b_k}(n - a_k)$$

but if b_j/b_k is negative, then the comparison becomes

$$j - a_j \; > \; \frac{b_j}{b_k}(n - a_k)$$

instead. Finally, we add a_j to both sides (here we show the positive case):

$$j \; < \; \frac{b_j}{b_k}(n - a_k) + a_j$$

The entire right-hand side of this comparison is loop-invariant, so it can be computed just once in the loop preheader.

Restrictions:

1. If $b_j(n - a_k)$ is not evenly divisible by b_k, then this transformation cannot be used, because we cannot hold a fractional value in an integer variable.

2. If b_j or b_k is not constant, but is a loop-invariant value whose sign is not known, then the transformation cannot be used since we won't know which comparison (less-than or greater-than) to use.

Example. In our example, the comparison $i < n$ can be replaced by $k' < a + 4 \cdot n$. Of course, $a + 4 \cdot n$ is loop-invariant and should be hoisted. Then i will be useless and may be deleted. The transformed program is:

$$s \leftarrow 0$$
$$k' \leftarrow a$$
$$b \leftarrow n \cdot 4$$
$$c \leftarrow a + b$$
$$L_1 : \text{if } k' < c \text{ goto } L_2$$
$$k \leftarrow k'$$
$$x \leftarrow M[k]$$
$$s \leftarrow s + x$$
$$k' \leftarrow k' + 4$$
$$\text{goto } L_1$$
$$L_2$$

Finally, copy propagation can eliminate $k \leftarrow k'$, and we obtain Program 17.8b.

17.4 ARRAY BOUNDS CHECKS

Safe programming languages automatically insert array-bounds checks on every subscript operation (see the sermon on page 157). Of course, in well written programs all of these checks are redundant, since well written programs don't access arrays out of bounds. We would like safe languages to achieve the fast performance of unsafe languages. Instead of turning off the bounds checks (which would not be safe) we ask the compiler to remove any checks that it can prove are redundant.

We cannot hope to remove all the redundant bounds checks, because this problem is not computable (it is as hard as the halting problem). But many array subscripts are of the form $a[i]$, where i is an induction variable. These the compiler can often understand well enough to optimize.

The bounds for an array are generally of the form $0 \leq i \wedge i < N$. When N is nonnegative, as it always is for array sizes, this can be implemented as $i \leq_u N$, where $\leq_u$ is the unsigned comparison operator.

Conditions for eliminating array-bounds checking. Although it seems natural and intuitive that an induction variable must stay within a certain range, and we should be able to tell whether that range does not exceed the bounds of the array, the criteria for eliminating a bounds check from a loop L are actually quite complicated:

1. There is an induction variable j and a loop-invariant u used in a statement s_1, taking one of the following forms:

   if $j < u$ goto L_1 else goto L_2
   if $j \geq u$ goto L_2 else goto L_1
   if $u > j$ goto L_2 else goto L_1
   if $u \leq j$ goto L_1 else goto L_2

   where L_2 is out of the loop.

2. There is a statement s_2 of the form

   if $k <_u n$ goto L_3 else goto L_4

   where k is an induction variable coordinated with j, n is loop-invariant, and s_1 dominates s_2.

3. There is no loop nested within L containing a definition of k.

4. k increases when j does, that is, $b_j/b_k > 0$.

Often, n will be an array length. In a language with static arrays an array length n is a constant In many languages with dynamic arrays, array lengths are loop-invariant. In Tiger, Java, and ML the length of an array cannot be dynamically modified once the array has been allocated. The array-length n will typically be calculated by fetching the *length* field of some array-pointer v. For the sake of illustration, assume the length field is at offset 0 in the array object. To avoid the need for complicated alias analysis, the semantic analysis phase of the compiler should mark the expression $M[v]$ as *immutable*, meaning that no other store instruction can possibly update the contents of the *length* field of the array v. If v is loop-invariant, then n will also be loop-invariant. Even if n is not an array length but is some other loop invariant, we can still optimize the comparison $k <_u n$.

We want to put a test in the loop preheader that expresses the idea that in every iteration, $k \geq 0 \wedge k < n$. Let k_0 be the value of k at the end of the preheader, and let $\Delta k_1, \Delta k_2, \ldots, \Delta k_m$ be all the loop-invariant values that are added to k inside the loop. Then we can ensure $k \geq 0$ by testing

$$k \geq 0 \wedge k_1 \geq 0 \wedge \cdots \wedge k_m \geq 0$$

at the end of the preheader.

Let $\Delta k_1, \Delta k_2, \ldots, \Delta k_p$ be the set of loop-invariant values that are added to k on any path between s_1 and s_2 that does not go through s_1 (again). Then, to ensure $k < n$ at s_2, it is sufficient to ensure that $k < n - (\Delta k_1 + \cdots + \Delta k_p)$

at s_1. Since we know $(k - a_k)/b_k = (j - a_j)/b_j$, this test becomes

$$j < \frac{b_j}{b_k}(n - (\Delta k_1 + \cdots + \Delta k_p) - a_k) + a_j$$

This will always be true if

$$u < \frac{b_j}{b_k}(n - (\Delta k_1 + \cdots + \Delta k_p) - a_k) + a_j$$

since the test $j < u$ dominates the test $k < n$.

Since everything in this comparison is loop-invariant, we can move it to the preheader as follows. First, ensure that definitions of loop-invariants are hoisted out of the loop. Then, rewrite the loop L as follows: copy all the statements of L to make a new loop L' with header L'_h. Inside L', replace the statement

if $k < n$ goto L'_3 else goto L'_4

by **goto** L'_3. At the end of the preheader of L, put statements equivalent to

if $k \geq 0 \ \wedge \ k_1 \geq 0 \ \wedge \ \cdots \ \wedge \ k_m \geq 0$
$\quad \wedge \ u < \frac{b_j}{b_k}(n - (\Delta k_1 + \cdots + \Delta k_p) - a_k) + a_j$
$\quad$ goto L'_h
$\quad$ else goto L_h

The conditional **goto** tests whether k will always be between 0 and n.

Sometimes we will have enough information to evaluate this complicated condition at compile time. This will be true in at least two situations:

1. all the loop-invariants mentioned in it are constants, or
2. n and u are the same temporary variable, $a_k = a_j$, $b_k = b_j$, and there are no Δk's added to k between s_1 and s_2. In a language like Tiger or Java or ML, this could happen if the programmer writes,

```
let var u := length(A)
    var i := 0
 in while i<u
      do (sum := sum + A[i];
          i := i+1)
    end
```

The quadruples for `length(A)` will include $u \leftarrow M[A]$, assuming that the length of an array is fetched from offset zero from the array pointer; and the quadruples for `A[i]` will include $n \leftarrow M[A]$, to fetch n for doing the bounds check. Now the expressions defining u and n are common subexpressions, assuming the expression $M[A]$ is marked so that we know that no other STORE instruction is modifying the contents of memory location $M[A]$.

If we can evaluate the big comparison at compile time, then we can unconditionally use loop L or loop L', and delete the loop that we are not using.

Cleaning up. After this optimization, the program may have several loose ends. Statements after the label L'_4 may be unreachable; there may be several useless computations of n and k within L'. The former can be cleaned up by *unreachable code elimination*, and the latter by *dead-code elimination*.

Generalizations. To be practically useful, the algorithm needs to be generalized in several ways:

1. The loop-exit comparison might take one of the forms

   if $j \leq u'$ goto L_1 else goto L_2
   if $j > u'$ goto L_2 else goto L_1
   if $u' \geq j$ goto L_2 else goto L_1
   if $u' < j$ goto L_1 else goto L_2

   which compares $j \leq u'$ instead of $j < u$.

2. The loop-exit test might occur at the bottom of the loop body, instead of before the array-bounds test. We can describe this situation as follows: There is a test

   $s_2 :$ if $j < u$ goto L_1 else goto L_2

   where L_2 is out of the loop and s_2 dominates all the loop back edges. Then the Δk_i of interest are the ones between s_2 and any back edge, and between the loop header and s_1.

3. We should handle the case where $b_j/b_k < 0$.

4. We should handle the case where j counts downward instead of up, and the loop-exit test is something like $j \geq l$, for l a loop-invariant lower bound.

5. The induction-variable increments might be "undisciplined"; for example,

   ```
   while i<n-1
     do (if sum<0
           then (i:=i+1; sum:= sum+i; i:=i+1)
           else i := i+2;
         sum := sum + a[i])
   ```

Here there are three Δi, (of 1, 1, and 2 respectively). Our analysis will assume that any, all, or none of these increments may be applied; but clearly the effect is $i \leftarrow i + 2$ on either path. In such cases, an analysis that hoists (and merges) the increments above the **if** will be useful.

$$L_1 : x \leftarrow M[i]$$
$$s \leftarrow s + x$$
$$i \leftarrow i + 4$$
$$\text{if } i < n \text{ goto } L_1' \text{ else } L_2$$

$$L_1 : x \leftarrow M[i] \qquad\qquad L_1' : x \leftarrow M[i]$$
$$s \leftarrow s + x \qquad\qquad\qquad s \leftarrow s + x$$
$$i \leftarrow i + 4 \qquad\qquad\qquad i \leftarrow i + 4$$
$$\text{if } i < n \text{ goto } L_1 \text{ else } L_2 \qquad \text{if } i < n \text{ goto } L_1 \text{ else } L_2$$
$$L_2 \qquad\qquad\qquad\qquad\qquad L_2$$

(a) Before (b) After

PROGRAM 17.10. Useless loop unrolling.

17.5 LOOP UNROLLING

Some loops have such a small body that most of the time is spent incrementing the loop-counter variable and testing the loop-exit condition. We can make these loops more efficient by *unrolling* them, putting two or more copies of the loop body in a row.

Given a loop L with header node h and back edges $s_i \rightarrow h$, we can unroll the loop as follows:

1. Copy the nodes to make a loop L' with header h' and back edges $s_i' \rightarrow h'$.
2. Change all the back edges in L from $s_i \rightarrow h$ to $s_i \rightarrow h'$.
3. Change all the back edges in L' from $s_i' \rightarrow h'$ to $s_i' \rightarrow h$.

For example, Program 17.10a unrolls into Program 17.10b. But nothing useful has been accomplished; each "original" iteration still has an increment and a conditional branch.

By using information about induction variables, we can do better. We need an induction variable i such that every increment $i \leftarrow i + \Delta$ dominates every back edge of the loop. Then we know that each iteration increments i by exactly the sum of all the Δ, so we can agglomerate the increments and loop-exit tests to get Program 17.11a. But this unrolled loop works correctly only if the original loop iterated an even number of times. We execute "odd" iterations in an *epilogue*, as shown in Program 17.11b.

Here we have shown only the case of unrolling by a factor of two. When a loop is unrolled by a factor of K, then the epilogue is a loop (much like the original one) that iterates up to $K - 1$ times.

$$\text{if } i < n - 8 \text{ goto } L_1 \text{ else } L_2$$
$$L_1 : x \leftarrow M[i]$$
$$s \leftarrow s + x$$
$$x \leftarrow M[i + 4]$$
$$s \leftarrow s + x$$
$$i \leftarrow i + 8$$
$$\text{if } i < n - 8 \text{ goto } L_1 \text{ else } L_2$$
$$L_2 \quad x \leftarrow M[i]$$
$$s \leftarrow s + x$$
$$i \leftarrow i + 4$$
$$\text{if } i < n \text{ goto } L_2 \text{ else } L_3$$
$$L_3$$

$$L_1 : x \leftarrow M[i]$$
$$s \leftarrow s + x$$
$$x \leftarrow M[i + 4]$$
$$s \leftarrow s + x$$
$$i \leftarrow i + 8$$
$$\text{if } i < n \text{ goto } L_1 \text{ else } L_2$$
$$L_2$$

(a)

(b) After

PROGRAM 17.11. Useful loop unrolling; (a) works correctly only for an even number of iterations of the original loop; (b) works for any number of iterations of the original loop.

EXERCISES

17.1 Let G be a control-flow graph, h be a node in G, A be the set of nodes in a loop with header h, and B be the set of nodes in a different loop with header h. Prove that the subgraph whose nodes are $A \cup B$ is also a loop.

17.2 The immediate dominator theorem (page 363) is false for graphs that contain unreachable nodes. .

a. Show a graph with nodes d, e, and n such that d dominates n, e dominates n, but neither d dominates e nor e dominates d.

b. Identify which step of the proof is invalid for graphs containing unreachable nodes.

c. In approximately three words, name an algorithm useful in finding unreachable nodes.

17.3 Show that in a connected flow graph (one without unreachable nodes), a natural loop as defined on page 17.1 satisfies the definition of loop given on page 359.

17.4 Suppose any arithmetic overflow or divide-by-zero will raise an exception at run time. If we hoist $t \leftarrow a \oplus b$ out of a loop, and the loop might not have executed the statement at all, then the transformed program may raise the exception where the original program did not. Revise the criteria for *loop-*

invariant hoisting to take account of this. Instead of writing something informal like "might not execute the statement," use the terminology of dataflow analysis and dominators.

17.5 On page 367 the transformation of a **while** loop to a **repeat** loop is described. Show how a **while** loop may be characterized in the control-flow graph of basic blocks (using dominators) so that the optimizer can recognize it. The body of the loop may have explicit **break** statements that exit the loop.

*17.6 For bounds-check elimination, we required (on page 375) that the loop-exit test dominate the bounds-check comparison. If it is the other way around, then (effectively) we have one extra array subscript at the end of the loop, so the criterion

$$a_k + i \cdot b_k \geq 0 \ \wedge \ (n - a_k) \cdot b_j < (u - a_j) \cdot b_k$$

is "off by one." Rewrite this criterion for the case where the bounds-check comparison occurs before the loop-exit test.

*17.7 Write down the rules for unrolling a loop, such that the induction-variable increments are agglomerated and the unrolled loop has only one loop-exit test per iteration, as was shown informally for Program 17.10.

17.8 Some computations may cause arithmetic exceptions; for example, $a \leftarrow b/c$ can halt the program with a divide-by-zero exception. Show how the rules for hoisting loop-invariant computations (page 367) must be changed to take account of such exceptions.

APPENDIX

Tiger Language Reference Manual

The Tiger language is a small language with nested functions, record values with implicit pointers, arrays, integer and string variables, and a few simple structured control constructs.

LEXICAL ISSUES

Identifiers: An *identifier* is a sequence of letters, digits, and underscores, starting with a letter. Uppercase letters are distinguished from lowercase. In this appendix the symbol *id* stands for an identifier.

Comments: A comment may appear between any two tokens. Comments start with /* and end with */ and may be nested.

DECLARATIONS

A declaration-sequence is a sequence of type, value, and function declarations; no punctuation separates or terminates individual declarations.

$$decs \quad \rightarrow \quad \{dec\}$$

$$dec \rightarrow tydec$$
$$\rightarrow vardec$$
$$\rightarrow fundec$$

In the syntactic notation used here, ϵ stands for the empty string and $\{x\}$ stands for a possibly empty sequence of x's.

DATA TYPES

The syntax of types and type declarations in Tiger is

$$tydec \quad \rightarrow \quad \textbf{type } id \; = \; ty$$

$$ty \quad \rightarrow \quad id$$
$$\rightarrow \quad \{ \; tyfields \; \} \qquad \textit{(these braces stand for themselves)}$$
$$\rightarrow \quad \textbf{array of } id$$

$$tyfields \quad \rightarrow \quad \epsilon$$
$$\rightarrow \quad id : type\text{-}id \; \{, \; id : type\text{-}id\}$$

Built-in types: Two named types `int` and `string` are predefined. Additional named types may be defined or redefined (including the predefined ones) by type declarations.

Records: Record types are defined by a listing of their fields enclosed in braces, with each field described by *fieldname* : *type-id*, where *type-id* is an identifier defined by a type declaration.

Arrays: An array of any named type may be made by **array of** *type-id*. The length of the array is not specified as part of its type; each array of that type can have a different length, and the length will be decided upon array creation, at run time.

Record distinction: Each declaration of a record or array type creates a new type, incompatible with all other record or array types (even if all the fields are similar).

Mutually recursive types: A collection of types may be recursive or mutually recursive. Mutually recursive types are declared by a consecutive sequence of type declarations without intervening value or function declarations. Each recursion cycle must pass through a record or array type.

Thus, the type of lists of integers:

```
type intlist = {hd: int, tl: intlist}

type tree = {key: int, children: treelist}
type treelist = {hd: tree, tl: treelist}
```

But the following declaration sequence is illegal:

```
type b = c
type c = b
```

Field name reusability: Different record types may use the same field names (such as the `hd` field of `intlist` and `treelist` in the example above).

VARIABLES

$$vardec \quad \rightarrow \quad \textbf{var } id := exp$$
$$\rightarrow \quad \textbf{var } id : type\text{-}id := exp$$

In the short form of variable declaration, the name of the variable is given, followed by an expression representing the initial value of the variable. In this case, the type of the variable is determined from the type of the expression.

In the long form, the type of the variable is also given. The expression must have the same type.

If the initializing expression is **nil**, then the long form must be used.

Each variable declaration creates a new variable, which lasts as long as the scope of the declaration.

FUNCTIONS

$$fundec \quad \rightarrow \quad \textbf{function } id \ (\ tyfields) = exp$$
$$\rightarrow \quad \textbf{function } id \ (\ tyfields) : type\text{-}id = exp$$

The first of these is a procedure declaration; the second is a function declaration. Procedures do not return result values; functions do, and the type is specified after the colon. The *exp* is the body of the procedure or function, and the *tyfields* specify the names and type of the parameters. All parameters are passed by value.

Functions may be recursive. Mutually recursive functions and procedures are declared by a sequence of consecutive function declarations (with no intervening type or variable declarations):

```
function treeLeaves(t : tree) : int =
        if t=nil then 1
        else treelistLeaves(t.children)
function treelistLeaves(L : treelist) : int =
        if L=nil then 0
        else treeLeaves(L.hd) + treelistLeaves(L.tl)
```

SCOPE RULES

Local variables: In the expression **let** $\cdots$ *vardec* $\cdots$ **in** *exp* **end**, the scope of the declared variable starts just after its *vardec* and lasts until the **end**.

Parameters: In **function** id ($\cdots$ id_1: id_2 $\cdots$) = *exp* the scope of the parameter id_1 lasts throughout the function body *exp*.

Nested scopes: The scope of a variable or parameter includes the bodies of any function definitions in that scope. That is, access to variables in outer scopes is permitted, as in Pascal and Algol.

Types: In the expression **let** $\cdots$ *tydecs* $\cdots$ **in** *exp* **end** the scope of a type identifier starts at the beginning of the consecutive sequence of type declarations defining it and lasts until the **end**. This includes the headers and bodies of any functions within the scope.

Functions: In the expression **let** $\cdots$ *fundecs* $\cdots$ **in** *exp* **end** the scope of a function identifier starts at the beginning of the consecutive sequence of function declarations defining it and lasts until the **end**. This includes the headers and bodies of any functions within the scope.

Name spaces: There are two different name spaces: one for types, and one for functions and variables. A type a can be "in scope" at the same time as a variable a or a function a, but variables and functions of the same name cannot both be in scope simultaneously (one will hide the other).

Local redeclarations: A variable or function declaration may be hidden by the redeclaration of the same name (as a variable or function) in a smaller scope; for example, this function prints "6 7 6 8 6" when applied to 5:

```
function f(v: int) =
let var v := 6
 in print(v);
    let var v := 7 in print (v) end;
    print(v);
    let var v := 8 in print (v) end;
    print(v)
end
```

Functions hide variables of the same name, and vice versa. Similarly, a type declaration may be hidden by the redeclaration of the same name (as a type) in a smaller scope. However, no two functions in a sequence of mutually recursive functions may have the same name; and no two types in a sequence of mutually recursive types may have the same name.

A.3   VARIABLES AND EXPRESSIONS

L-VALUES

An *l-value* is a location whose value may be read or assigned. Local variables, procedure parameters, fields of records, and elements of arrays are all *l*-values.

$$
\begin{aligned}
lvalue \quad &\rightarrow \quad id \\
&\rightarrow \quad lvalue \; . \; id \\
&\rightarrow \quad lvalue \; [\; exp \;]
\end{aligned}
$$

Variable: The form *id* refers to a variable or parameter accessible by scope rules.

Record field: The dot notation allows the selection of the correspondingly named field of a record value.

Array subscript: The bracket notation allows the selection of the correspondingly numbered slot of an array. Arrays are indexed by consecutive integers starting at zero (up to the size of the array minus one).

EXPRESSIONS

l-**value:** An *l*-value, when used as an expression, evaluates to the contents of the corresponding location.

Valueless expressions: Certain expressions produce no value: procedure calls, assignment, if-then, while, break, and sometimes if-then-else. Therefore the expression (a:=b)+c is syntactically correct but fails to type-check.

Nil: The expression **nil** (a reserved word) denotes a value *nil* belonging to every record type. If a record variable v contains the value *nil*, it is a checked run-time error to select a field from v. **Nil** must be used in a context where its type can be determined, that is:

`var a : my_record := nil`	OK
`a := nil`	OK
`if a <> nil then ...`	OK
`if nil <> a then ...`	OK
`if a = nil then ...`	OK
`function f(p: my_record) = ... f(nil)`	OK
`var a := nil`	Illegal
`if nil = nil then ...`	Illegal

Sequencing: A sequence of two or more expressions, surrounded by parentheses and separated by semicolons (exp; exp; ... exp) evaluates all the expressions in order. The result of a sequence is the result (if any) yielded by the last of the expressions.

No value: An open parenthesis followed by a close parenthesis (two separate tokens) is an expression that yields no value. Similarly, a **let** expression with nothing between the **in** and **end** yields no value.

Integer literal: A sequence of decimal digits is an *integer constant* that denotes the corresponding integer value.

String literal: A string constant is a sequence, between quotes ("), of zero or more printable characters, spaces, or escape sequences. Each escape sequence is introduced by the escape character \, and stands for a character sequence. The allowed escape sequences are as follows (all other uses of \ being illegal):

\n	A single character interpreted by the system as end-of-line.
\t	Tab.
\^c	The control character c, for any appropriate c.
\ddd	The single character with ASCII code ddd (3 decimal digits).
\"	The double-quote character (").
\\	The backslash character (\).
\f___f\	This sequence is ignored, where f___f stands for a sequence of one or more formatting characters (a subset of the non-printable characters including at least space, tab, newline, formfeed). This allows one to write long strings on more than one line, by writing \ at the end of one line and at the start of the next.

Negation: An integer-valued expression may be prefixed by a minus sign.

Function call: A function application $id()$ or $id(exp\{, exp\})$ indicates the application of function id to a list of actual parameter values obtained by evaluating the expressions left to right. The actual parameters are bound to the corresponding formal parameters of the function definition and the function body is bound using conventional static scoping rules to obtain a result. If id actually stands for a procedure (a function returning no result), then the function body must produce no value, and the function application also produces no value.

Arithmetic: Expressions of the form $exp\ op\ exp$, where op is $+,-,*,/$, require integer arguments and produce an integer result.

Comparison: Expressions of the form $exp\ op\ exp$, where op is $=,<>,>,<,>=,<=$, compare their operands for equality or inequality and produce the integer 1 for true, 0 for false. All these operators can be applied to integer operands. The equals and not-equals operators can also be applied to two record or array operands of the same type, and compare for "reference" or "pointer" equality (they test whether two records are the same instance, not whether they have the same contents).

String comparison: The comparison operators may also be applied to strings. Two strings are equal if their contents are equal; there is no way to distinguish strings whose component characters are the same. Inequality is according to lexicographic order.

Boolean operators: Expressions of the form $exp\ op\ exp$, where op is & or |, are short-circuit boolean conjunctions and disjunctions: they do not evaluate the right-hand operand if the result is detemined by the left-hand one. Any nonzero integer value is considered true, and an integer value of zero is false.

Precedence of operators: Unary minus (negation) has the highest precedence. Then operators $*,/$ have the next highest (tightest binding) precedence, followed by $+,-$, then by $=,<>,>,<,>=,<=$, then by &, then by |.

Associativity of operators: The operators $*, /, +, -$ are all left-associative. The comparison operators *do not associate*, so a=b=c is not a legal expression, although a=(b=c) is legal.

Record creation: The expression *type-id* {*id*=*exp*{, *id*=*exp*}} creates a new record instance of type *type-id*. The field names and types of the record expression must match those of the named type, in the order given. The braces { } stand for themselves.

Array creation: The expression *type-id* [exp_1] **of** exp_2 evaluates exp_1 and exp_2 (in that order) to find n, the number of elements, and v the initial value. The type *type-id* must be declared as an array type. The result of the expression is a new array of type *type-id*, indexed from 0 to $n - 1$, in which each slot is initialized to the value v.

Array and record assignment: When an array or record variable a is assigned a value b, then a references the same array or record as b. Future updates of elements of a will affect b, and vice versa, until a is reassigned. Parameter passing of arrays and records is similarly *by reference*, not by copying.

Extent: Records and arrays have infinite extent: each record or array value lasts forever, even after control exits from the scope in which it was created.

Assignment: The assignment statement *lvalue* := *exp* evaluates the *lvalue*, then evaluates the *exp*, then sets the contents of the *lvalue* to the result of the expression. Syntactically, := binds weaker than the boolean operators & and |. The assignment expression produces no value, so that (a:=b)+c is illegal.

If-then-else: The if-expression **if** exp_1 **then** exp_2 **else** exp_3 evaluates the integer expression exp_1. If the result is nonzero it yields the result of evaluating exp_2; otherwise it yields the result of exp_3. The expressions exp_2 and exp_3 must have the same type, which is also the type of the entire if-expression (or both expressions must produce no value).

If-then: The if-expression **if** exp_1 **then** exp_2 evaluates the integer expression exp_1. If the result is nonzero, then exp_2 (which must produce no value) is evaluated. The entire if-expression produces no value.

While: The expression **while** exp_1 **do** exp_2 evaluates the integer expression exp_1. If the result is nonzero, then exp_2 (which must produce no value) is executed, and then the entire while-expression is reevaluated.

For: The expression **for** id := exp_1 **to** exp_2 **do** exp_3 iterates exp_3 over each integer value of *id* between exp_1 and exp_2. The variable *id* is a new variable implicitly declared by the **for** statement, whose scope covers only exp_3, and may not be assigned to. The body exp_3 must produce no value. The upper and lower bounds are evaluated only once, prior to entering the body of the loop. If the upper bound is less than the lower, the body is not executed.

Break: The **break** expression terminates evaluation of the nearest enclosing while-expression or for-expression. A **break** in procedure p cannot terminate a loop in procedure q, even if p is nested within q. A **break** that is not within a **while** or **for** is illegal.

Let: The expression **let** *decs* **in** *expseq* **end** evaluates the declarations *decs*, binding types, variables, and procedures whose scope then extends over the *expseq*. The *expseq* is a sequence of zero or more expressions, separated by semicolons. The result (if any) of the last *exp* in the sequence is then the result of the entire let-expression.

Parentheses: Parentheses around any expression enforce syntactic grouping, as in most programming languages.

PROGRAMS

Tiger programs do not have arguments: a program is just an expression *exp*.

A.4 STANDARD LIBRARY

Several functions are predefined:

```
function print(s : string)
```
Print s on standard output.
```
function flush()
```
Flush the standard output buffer.
```
function getchar() : string
```
Read a character from standard input; returns empty string on end of file.
```
function ord(s: string) : int
```
Give ASCII value of first character of s; yields -1 if s is empty string.
```
function chr(i: int) : string
```
Single character string from ASCII value i; halts program on out-of-range integer.
```
function size(s: string) : int
```
Number of characters in s.
```
function substring(s:string, first:int, n:int) : string
```
Substring of string s, starting with character "first," n characters long. Characters are numbered starting at 0.
```
function concat (s1: string, s2: string) : string
```
Concatenation of s1 and s2.
```
function not(i : integer) : integer
```
returns (i=0).
```
function exit(i: int)
```
Terminate execution with code i.

Bibliography

AHO, A. V., SETHI, R., AND ULLMAN, J. D. 1986. *Compilers: Principles, Techniques, and Tools*. Addison-Wesley, Reading, MA.

ALLEN, F. E. 1969. Program optimization. *Annual Review of Automatic Programming 5*, 239–307.

ALLEN, F. E. 1970. Control flow analysis. *SIGPLAN Notices 5,* 7, 1–19.

AMIEL, E., GRUBER, O., AND SIMON, E. 1994. Optimizing multi-method dispatch using compressed dispatch tables. *SIGPLAN Notices 29*, 10, 244–258. OOPSLA '94.

APPEL, A. W. 1992. *Compiling with Continuations*. Cambridge University Press, Cambridge, England.

APPEL, A. W., ELLIS, J. R., AND LI, K. 1988. Real-time concurrent collection on stock multiprocessors. *SIGPLAN Notices (Proc. SIGPLAN '88 Conf. on Prog. Lang. Design and Implementation) 23,* 7, 11–20.

APPEL, A. W. AND SHAO, Z. 1996. Empirical and analytic study of stack versus heap cost for languages with closures. *J. Functional Programming 6,* 1, 47–74.

BAKER, H. G. 1978. List processing in real time on a serial computer. *Commun. ACM 21,* 4, 280–294.

BAUER, F. L. AND EICKEL, J. 1975. *Compiler Construction: An Advanced Course*. Springer-Verlag, New York.

BIRTWISTLE, G. M., DAHL, O.-J., MYHRHAUG, B., AND NYGAARD, K. 1973. *Simula Begin*. Petrocelli/Charter, New York.

BOBROW, D. G., DeMICHIEL, L. G., GABRIEL, R. P., KEENE, S. E., KICZALES, G., AND MOON, D. A. 1989. Common Lisp Object System specification. *Lisp and Symbolic Computation 1,* 3, 245–293.

BOEHM, H.-J. 1993. Space efficient conservative garbage collection. In *Proc. ACM SIGPLAN '93 Conf. on Prog. Lang. Design and Implementation*. ACM Press, New York, 197–206.

BOEHM, H.-J. 1996. Simple garbage-collector-safety. In *Proc. ACM SIGPLAN '96 Conf. on Prog. Lang. Design and Implementation*. ACM Press, New York, 89–98.

BOEHM, H.-J., DEMERS, A. J., AND SHENKER, S. 1991. Mostly parallel garbage collection. In *Proc. ACM SIGPLAN '91 Conf. on Prog. Lang. Design and Implementation*. ACM Press, New York, 157–164.

BOEHM, H.-J. AND WEISER, M. 1988. Garbage collection in an uncooperative environment. *Software—Practice and Experience 18,* 9, 807–820.

BRANQUART, P. AND LEWI, J. 1971. A scheme for storage allocation and garbage collection in Algol-68. In *Algol 68 Implementation*, J. E. L. Peck, Ed. North-Holland, Amsterdam.

BRIGGS, P., COOPER, K. D., AND TORCZON, L. 1994. Improvements to graph coloring register allocation. *ACM Trans. on Programming Languages and Systems 16,* 3, 428–455.

BUMBULIS, P. AND COWAN, D. D. 1993. RE2C: A more versatile scanner generator. *ACM Letters on Programming Languages and Systems 2,* 1-4, 70–84.

CHAITIN, G. J. 1982. Register allocation and spilling via graph coloring. *SIGPLAN Notices 17(6)*, 98–105. Proceeding of the ACM SIGPLAN '82 Symposium on Compiler Construction.

CHAMBERS, C. AND LEAVENS, G. T. 1995. Typechecking and modules for multimethods. *ACM Trans. Program. Lang. Syst. 17,* 6, 805–843.

CHAMBERS, C., UNGAR, D., AND LEE, E. 1991. An efficient implementation of SELF, a dynamically-typed object-oriented language based on prototypes. *Lisp and Symbolic Computation 4,* 3, 243–281.

CHEN, W. AND TURAU, B. 1994. Efficient dynamic look-up strategy for multi-methods. In *European Conference on Object-Oriented Programming (ECOOP '94).*

CHENEY, C. J. 1970. A nonrecursive list compacting algorithm. *Commun. ACM 13,* 11, 677–678.

CHURCH, A. 1941. *The Calculi of Lambda Conversion.* Princeton University Press, Princeton, New Jersey.

COCKE, J. 1970. Global common subexpression elimination. *SIGPLAN Notices 5,* 7, 20–24.

COCKE, J. AND SCHWARTZ, J. T. 1970. Programming languages and their compilers: Preliminary notes. Tech. rep., Courant Institute, New York University.

COHEN, J. 1981. Garbage collection of linked data structures. *Computing Surveys 13,* 3, 341–367.

COHEN, N. H. 1991. Type-extension type tests can be performed in constant time. *ACM Trans. Program. Lang. Syst. 13,* 4, 626–629.

COLLINS, G. E. 1960. A method for overlapping and erasure of lists. *Commun. ACM 3,* 12, 655–657.

CONNOR, R. C. H., DEARLE, A., MORRISON, R., AND BROWN, A. L. 1989. An object addressing mechanism for statically typed languages with multiple inheritance. *SIGPLAN Notices 24,* 10, 279–285. OOPSLA '89.

COUSINEAU, G., CURIEN, P. L., AND MAUNY, M. 1985. The categorical abstract machine. In *Functional Programming Languages and Computer Architecture, LNCS Vol 201*, J. P. Jouannaud, Ed. Springer-Verlag, New York, 50–64.

DIJKSTRA, E. W., LAMPORT, L., MARTIN, A. J., SCHOLTEN, C. S., AND STEFFENS, E. F. M. 1978. On-the-fly garbage collection: An exercise in cooperation. *Commun. ACM 21,* 11, 966–975.

DIWAN, A., MOSS, E., AND HUDSON, R. 1992. Compiler support for garbage collection in a statically typed language. In *Proc. ACM SIGPLAN '92 Conf. on Prog. Lang. Design and Implementation*. ACM Press, New York, 273–282.

DIWAN, A., MOSS, J. E. B., AND MCKINLEY, K. S. 1996. Simple and effective analysis of statically typed object-oriented programs. *SIGPLAN Notices 31,* (to appear). OOPSLA '96.

DIXON, R., MCKEE, T., SCHWEIZER, P., AND VAUGHAN, M. 1989. A fast method dispatcher for compiled languages with multiple inheritance. *SIGPLAN Notices 24,* 10, 211–214. OOPSLA '89.

ERSHOV, A. P. 1958. On programming of arithmetic operations. *Commun. ACM 1,* 8, 3–6.

FENICHEL, R. R. AND YOCHELSON, J. C. 1969. A LISP garbage-collector for virtual-memory computer systems. *Commun. ACM 12,* 11, 611–612.

FRASER, C. W. AND HANSON, D. R. 1995. *A Retargetable C Compiler: Design and Implementation*. Benjamin Cummings, Redwood City, CA.

FRIEDMAN, D. P. AND WISE, D. S. 1976. Cons should not evaluate its arguments. In *Automata, Languages and Programming*, S. Michaelson and R. Milner, Eds. Edinburgh University Press, 257–284.

GEORGE, L. AND APPEL, A. W. 1996. Iterated register coalescing. *ACM Trans. on Programming Languages and Systems 18,* 3, 300–324.

GÖDEL, K. 1931. Über formal unentscheidbare Sätze der Principia Mathematica and verwandter Systeme I. *Monatshefte für Mathematik und Physik 38*, 173–198.

GOLDBERG, A., ROBSON, D., AND INGALLS, D. H. H. 1983. *Smalltalk-80: The Language and Its Implementation*. Addison-Wesley, Reading, MA.

GRAY, R. W. 1988. γ-GLA—a generator for lexical analyzers that programmers can use. In *USENIX Conference Proceedings*. USENIX Association, Berkeley, CA, 147–160.

HENDERSON, P. AND MORRIS, J. H. 1976. A lazy evaluator. In *Third ACM Symp. on Principles of Prog. Languages*. ACM Press, New York, 123–142.

HOPCROFT, J. E. AND ULLMAN, J. D. 1979. *Introduction to Automata Theory, Languages, and Computation*. Addison-Wesley, Reading, MA.

HUDAK, P., PEYTON JONES, S., AND WADLER, P. 1992. Report on the programming language Haskell, a non-strict, purely functional language, version 1.2. *SIGPLAN Notices 27,* 5.

HUGHES, J. 1989. Why functional programming matters. *Computer Journal 32,* 2, 98–107.

JONES, R. AND LINS, R. 1996. *Garbage Collection: Algorithms for Automatic Dynamic Memory Management*. John Wiley and Sons, Chichester, England.

KEMPE, A. B. 1879. On the geographical problem of the four colors. *American Journal of Mathematics 2*, 193–200.

KILDALL, G. A. 1973. A unified approach to global program optimization. In *Proc. ACM Symp. on Principles of Programming Languages*. ACM Press, New York, 194–206.

KNUTH, D. E. 1967. *The Art of Computer Programming, vol. I: Fundamental Algorithms*. Addison Wesley, Reading, MA.

KRANZ, D., KELSEY, R., REES, J., HUDAK, P., PHILBIN, J., AND ADAMS, N. 1986. ORBIT: An optimizing compiler for Scheme. *SIGPLAN Notices (Proc. Sigplan '86 Symp. on Compiler Construction) 21,* 7, 219–33.

LANDI, W. AND RYDER, B. G. 1992. A safe approximation algorithm for interprocedural pointer aliasing. In *Proc. ACM SIGPLAN '92 Conf. on Prog. Lang. Design and Implementation (SIGPLAN Notices 27, 7))*. ACM Press, New York, 235–248.

LANDIN, P. J. 1964. The mechanical evaluation of expressions. *Computer J. 6,* 4, 308–320.

LESK, M. E. 1975. Lex—a lexical analyzer generator. Tech. Rep. Computing Science Technical Report 39, Bell Laboratories, Murray Hill, NJ.

LIEBERMAN, H. AND HEWITT, C. 1983. A real-time garbage collector based on the lifetimes of objects. *Commun. ACM 26,* 6, 419–429.

MCCARTHY, J. 1960. Recursive functions of symbolic expressions and their computation by machine – I. *Commun. ACM 3,* 1, 184–195.

MCNAUGHTON, R. AND YAMADA, H. 1960. Regular expressions and state graphs for automata. *IEEE Trans. on Electronic Computers 9,* 1, 39–47.

MOON, D. A. 1984. Garbage collection in a large LISP system. In *ACM Symposium on LISP and Functional Programming*. ACM Press, New York, 235–246.

NAUR, P., BACKUS, J. W., BAUER, F. L., GREEN, J., KATZ, C., MCCARTHY, J., PERLIS, A. J., RUTISHAUSER, H., SAMELSON, K., VAUQUOIS, B., WEGSTEIN, J. H., VAN WIJNGAARDEN, A., AND WOODGER, M. 1963. Revised report on the algorithmic language ALGOL 60. *Comm. ACM 6,* 1, 1–17.

PAXSON, V. 1995. Flex—Fast lexical analyzer generator. Lawrence Berkeley Laboratory, Berkeley, California, ftp://ftp.ee.lbl.gov/flex-2.5.3.tar.gz.

PEYTON JONES, S. AND PARTAIN, W. 1993. Measuring the effectiveness of a simple strictness analyser. In *Functional Programming: Glasgow 1993*, K. Hammond and M. O'Donnell, Eds. Springer Workshops in Computer Science. Springer, New York, 201–220.

PEYTON JONES, S. L. 1987. *The Implementation of Functional Programming Languages*. Prentice-Hall, New York.

PEYTON JONES, S. L. 1992. Implementing lazy functional languages on stock hardware: the Spineless Tagless G-machine. *Journal of Functional Programming 2, 2*, 127–202.

RICE, H. G. 1953. Classes of recursively enumerable sets and their decision problems. *Transactions of the American Mathematical Society 89*, 25–59.

ROSE, J. R. 1988. Fast dispatch mechanisms for stock hardware. *SIGPLAN Notices 23,* 11, 27–35. OOPSLA '88.

SCHEIFLER, R. W. 1977. An analysis of inline substitution for a structured programming language. *Communications of the ACM 20,* 9, 647–654.

SEDGEWICK, R. 1988. *Algorithms*, Second ed. Addison Wesley, Reading, MA.

SETHI, R. AND ULLMAN, J. D. 1970. The generation of optimal code for arithmetic expressions. *J. Assoc. Computing Machinery 17,* 4, 715–28.

SHAO, Z. AND APPEL, A. W. 1994. Space-efficient closure representations. In *Proc. 1994 ACM Conf. on Lisp and Functional Programming*. ACM Press, New York, 150–161.

SHAW, R. A. 1988. Empirical analysis of a Lisp system. Ph.D. thesis, Stanford University, Palo Alto, CA.

SOBALVARRO, P. G. 1988. A lifetime-based garbage collector for LISP systems on general-purpose computers. Tech. Rep. 1417, MIT Artificial Intelligence Laboratory.

STEELE, G. L. 1975. Multiprocessing compactifying garbage collection. *Commun. ACM 18,* 9, 495–508.

STEELE, G. L. 1978. Rabbit: a compiler for Scheme. Tech. Rep. AI-TR-474, MIT, Cambridge, MA.

STRACHEY, C. AND WADSWORTH, C. 1974. Continuations: a mathematical semantics which can deal with full jumps. Technical Monograph PRG-11, Programming Research Group, Oxford University.

TURING, A. M. 1937. On computable numbers, with an application to the Entscheidungsproblem. *Proceedings of the London Mathematical Society 42*, 230–265.

UNGAR, D. M. 1986. *The Design and Evaluation of a High Performance Smalltalk System*. MIT Press, Cambridge, MA.

WADLER, P. 1990. Deforestation: Transforming programs to eliminate trees. *Theoretical Computer Science 73*, 231–248.

WADLER, P. 1995. How to declare an imperative. In *International Logic Programming Symposium*, J. Lloyd, Ed. MIT Press, Cambridge, MA.

WENTWORTH, E. P. 1990. Pitfalls of conservative collection. *Software—Practice and Experience 20,* 7, 719–727.

WILSON, P. R. 1997. Uniprocessor garbage collection techniques. *ACM Computing Surveys*, (to appear).

Index

abstract data type, 5
abstract syntax, *see* syntax, abstract
access link, *see* static link
activation record, 6, 120–129
addressing mode, 189, 193
ADT, *see* abstract data type
alias
    analysis, 340, 351–357, 375
    in coalescing register allocation, 235
`alloca`, 203
allocation
    of activation records, 120, 122, 165
    of arrays and records, 161
    of heap data, 275
    register, *see* register allocation
alphabet, 18
ambiguous grammar, *see* grammar
analysis
    dataflow, *see* dataflow analysis
    liveness, *see* liveness
approximation
    dataflow analysis, 213, 216, 335
    in garbage collection, 257
    of spill effect, 225
    of strictness, 328
argument, *see* parameter
array, 153, 155, 161
    bounds check, 157, 374–377
`Assem` module, 196
associativity, *see* right-associative, left-associative, nonassociative
attribute grammar, 12

Baker's algorithm, 274
basic block, 177, 178, 344, 348, 365
beta reduction, *see* inline expansion

binding, 99–106, *see also* precedence
    in FindEscape module, 135
    in type environment, 107
    in value environment, 109
blacklist, 281
block structure, *see* function, nested
buffered input, 36

C programming language
    linking to, 162
    writing compiler for, 18, 89, 120, 121, 126, 134, 147, 153–155, 160, 203, 249, 321, 352, 353, 356, 360
C++, 249, 292, 352
CALL, 169, 170, 175
call
    by name, 321
    by need, 322
    by reference, 128
    by-reference, 127
callee-save, *see* register, callee-save
caller-save, *see* register, caller-save
`Canon` module, 170
canonical tree, *see* intermediate representation, canonical
card marking, 270
CISC, 184, 193–195
class
    descriptor, 287–290, 293–298
classless language, 294
cloning, 294
closure
    conversion, 315–317, 319
    ϵ, 26, 28, 35
    function, 302, 304, 330
    Kleene, 19, 41